Promises and Agreements

Promises and Agreements

Philosophical Essays

EDITED BY

Hanoch Sheinman

OXFORD
UNIVERSITY PRESS

OXFORD
UNIVERSITY PRESS

Oxford University Press, Inc., publishes works that further
Oxford University's objective of excellence
in research, scholarship, and education.

Oxford New York
Auckland Cape Town Dar es Salaam Hong Kong Karachi
Kuala Lumpur Madrid Melbourne Mexico City Nairobi
New Delhi Shanghai Taipei Toronto

With offices in
Argentina Austria Brazil Chile Czech Republic France Greece
Guatemala Hungary Italy Japan Poland Portugal Singapore
South Korea Switzerland Thailand Turkey Ukraine Vietnam

Published by Oxford University Press, Inc.
198 Madison Avenue, New York, New York 10016

www.oup.com

Library of Congress Cataloging-in-Publication Data
Promises and agreements / edited by Hanoch Sheinman.
p. cm.
Includes index.
ISBN 978-0-19-537795-8
1. Promises. 2. Contracts. I. Sheinman, Hanoch, 1966–
BJ1500.P7P76 2010
170–dc22

1 3 5 7 9 8 6 4 2

Printed in the United States of America
on acid-free paper

Contents

Preface

This book comprises fifteen original free-standing contributions to the philosophical discussion of promises and agreements, and a context-providing introduction. No attempt has been made to cover all the important questions in this area. My initial attempt to divide the essays into *useful* groups ("the consequentialists," "the contractualists," etc.) proved unsuccessful. The essays in this collection are rather diverse. Some of the essays emphasize what's special or distinct about promises (e.g. Owens, Gilbert, and Markovits); others simply treat promises as a useful *example* of a general phenomenon they wish to illuminate (e.g. Smith, Hooker, and Norcross). Most of the essays focus on promises, but others discuss (or also discuss) contracts, conventions, and agreements (e.g. Markovits, Benbaji, and Sheinman). Most of the essays focus on promises to *another* (e.g. Darwall; Friedrich and Southwood), but one essay focuses on promises to oneself (Rosati). Several essays explore some broadly consequentialist perspective (Smith, Norcross, and Hooker); others do not. Most essays focus on perfectly *good* promises, but some essays focus on rather problematic promises (Chwang and Driver). Most of the essays are largely ahistorical, but others are historically informed (Owens and Phillips). And so it goes. The final section of the introduction (chapter 1) gives an overview of the collection.

Acknowledgments

This collection grew out of a conference that took place at Rice University in the fall of 2008. The conference was sponsored by the Rice University School of Humanities, James A. Baker III Institute for Public Policy, Humanities Research Center, and Philosophy Department. I would like to thank Gary Wihl, the Dean of Humanities, Allen Matusow, Associate Director for Academic Programs at Baker, Caroline Levander, Humanities Research Center Director, and Steven Crowell, Chair of Philosophy, for their generous support of this project. Many thanks to Stan Husi, the conference's Student Assistant, Whitney Smith, Event Coordinator, and Minranda Robinson-Davis, Philosophy Department Manager, for their professional support. Many thanks to Peter Ohlin, Oxford University Press Editor, for his unflinching support and seamless execution of this project. Finally, I would like to thank my colleague Casey O'Callaghan for his good advice and valuable suggestions.

Contributors

Yitzhak Benbaji (Bar-Ilan University and Shalom Hartman Institute). Benbaji teaches ethics, political philosophy, and philosophy of language. He is the author of "A Defense of the Traditional War-Convention" (*Ethics* 2008), "The War Convention and the Moral Division of Labour" (*Philosophical Quarterly* 2009), and "Parity, Intransitivity and a Context-sensitive Degree Analysis of Gradability" (*Australasian Journal of Philosophy* 2009).

Eric Chwang (University of Colorado at Boulder). Chwang's interests lie in the areas of applied ethics (especially medical ethics), normative ethics, political philosophy, rational choice, and the philosophies of science and language. He is currently preoccupied with the notion of consent. His publications include "Against the Inalienable Right to Withdraw from Research" (*Bioethics* 2008), "A Defence of Subsequent Consent" (*Journal of Social Philosophy* 2009), and "A Puzzle about Consent in Research and in Practice" (*Journal of Applied Philosophy* 2010).

Stephen Darwall (Yale University). Darwall writes about ethics from a broadly contractualist perspective. He is the author of *The Second-Person Standpoint* (Harvard 2006) and *Welfare and Rational Care* (Princeton 2002).

Julia Driver (Washington University, St. Louis). Driver's research is primarily in normative ethics and moral psychology. Driver has published on virtue ethics and consequentialism. She is the author of *Consequentialism* (forthcoming), *Uneasy Virtue* (Cambridge 2006), and *Ethics: The Fundamentals* (Blackwell 2001). Her other publications include "The Virtue of Ignorance" (*Journal of Philosophy* 1989) and "Modesty and Ignorance" (*Ethics* 1999).

Daniel Friedrich (Berlin School of Mind and Brain, Humboldt University, Berlin). Friedrich's research primarily focuses on the intersection between metaethics and philosophy of mind. In his Ph.D. thesis he defended an affective theory of desire. He is the coauthor (with Nicolas Southwood) of "Promises beyond Assurance" (*Philosophical Studies* 2009).

Margaret Gilbert (University of California at Irvine). Gilbert specializes in the philosophy of social phenomena and related fields in legal, moral, and political philosophy. Her publications include *A Theory of Political Obligation* (Oxford 2006), *Sociality and Responsibility* (Rowman and Littlefield 2000), and *On Social Facts* (Princeton 1989). Her contributions to the literature on agreements and promises include "Agreements, Coercion, and Obligation" (*Ethics* 1993) and "Is an Agreement an Exchange of Promises?" (*Journal of Philosophy* 1993).

Brad Hooker (University of Reading). Hooker champions a rule-consequentialist theory of morality. He publications include *Ideal Code, Real World* (Oxford 2000), "Rule-Consequentialism" (*Mind* 1990), and "Moral Particularism: Wrong and Bad" (in B. Hooker and M. Little, eds., *Moral Particularism*, Oxford 2003). Hooker has written on rule-consequentialism, contractualism, virtue ethics, intuitionism, practical reason, desert, and the meaning of life. He is now at work on a book on fairness.

Stan Husi (Rice University). Husi is writing a Ph.D. dissertation at Rice University. He works mainly in moral and political philosophy, with a focus on practical reasons and normativity. He is the author of "Why Reasons Skepticism is not Self-Defeating" (*European Journal of Philosophy* 2011).

Daniel Markovits (Yale University). Markovits works in the philosophical foundations of private law, moral and political philosophy, and behavioral economics. He is the author of *A Modern Legal Ethics: Adversary Advocacy in a Democratic Age* (Princeton 2008), and articles on the foundations of contract law, for example "Making and Keeping Contracts" (*Virginia Law Review* 2006) and "Contract and Collaboration" (*Yale Law Journal* 2004).

Alastair Norcross (University of Colorado). Norcross specializes in normative ethics and metaethics. He is the author of "Two Dogmas of Deontology: Aggregation, Rights, and the Separateness of Persons" (*Social Philosophy and Policy* 2008), "Reasons without Demands: Rethinking Rightness" (*Blackwell Contemporary Debates in Moral Theory* 2006), "Good and Bad Actions" (*Philosophical Review* 1997), "Comparing Harms: Headaches and Human Lives" (*Philosophy and Public Affairs* 1997), and is currently writing a book on "scalar utilitarianism."

David Owens (University of Reading). Owens works in moral philosophy and epistemology. He is the author of *Causes and Coincidences*

(Cambridge 1992), *Reason without Freedom* (Routledge 2000), and several contributions to the literature on promises, for example "A Simple Theory of Promises" (*Philosophical Review* 2006) and "Duress, Deception, and the Validity of a Promise" (*Mind* 2007).

David Phillips (University of Houston). Phillips specializes in metaethics and the history of ethics. His recent work includes "Mackie on Practical Reason" (*Ethical Theory and Moral Practice* 2007), "Hume on Practical Reason" (*Hume Studies* 2005), and "Thomson and the Semantic Argument against Consequentialism" (*Journal of Philosophy* 2003). He is at work on a book on Sidgwick's ethics.

Connie Rosati (University of Arizona). Rosati has published work exploring theories of welfare, internalism, moral motivation, normativity, and the objectivity of law. She is the author of articles such as "Objectivism and Relational Good" (*Social Philosophy and Policy* 2008), "Some Puzzles about the Objectivity of Law" (*Law and Philosophy* 2004), and "Agency and the Open Question Argument" (*Ethics* 2003). Rosati is currently writing a book on personal good.

Hanoch Sheinman (Rice University). Sheinman's areas of specialty are ethics and the philosophy of law. His publications include "The Social Diversity of Promises and Contracts" *Oxford Studies in the Philosophy of Law* 2011), "Promise as Practice Reason" (*Acta Analytica* 2008), "The Priority of Courts in the General Theory of Law" (*American Journal of Jurisprudence* 2007), and "The First Virtue of the Law Courts and the First Virtue of the Law" (*Legal Theory* 2007).

Michael Smith (Princeton University). Smith has published in the areas of metaethics, moral psychology, and metaethics. He has written extensively on the nature of belief and desire, the status of normative judgment, and the relevance of the views we take on both these topics to the accounts we give of our nature as free and responsible agents. He is the author of *The Moral Problem* (Blackwell 1994) and *Ethics and the A Priori* (Cambridge 2004).

Nicholas Southwood (Australian National University/University of Oxford). Southwood's recent research focuses mainly on foundational questions concerning practical reason and normativity. He is the author of *Contractualism and the Foundations of Morality* (Oxford 2010), and a number of articles, including "Vindicating the Normativity of Rationality" (*Ethics* 2008), "Epistemic Norms without Voluntary Control" (*Nous* 2009, coauthored with Philippe Chuard), and "Promises beyond Assurance" (*Philosophical Studies* 2009, coauthored with Daniel Friedrich).

Promises and Agreements

Chapter 1

Introduction: Promises and Agreements

Hanoch Sheinman

Abstract

> *Promises are routinely treated as a useful philosophical laboratory for testing moral, volitional, and social phenomena. Recently, they have also come to be treated as a philosophical topic in their own right. Promises are individual* acts *as well as social* practices. *To understand promises, then, is to understand individual acts of promising, practices of promising, and the relation between them. Philosophical accounts of promises are best regarded as packages of answers to several different questions (this essay will mention twelve). Closely–indeed, conceptually–related to promises are* agreements, *so a philosophical account of promises should explain the relation between promises and agreements. Also closely–and conceptually–related to promises are* contracts *(and treaties). Arguably, contracts just* are *legally binding agreements or interdependent promises. If this is right, then understanding promises and agreements is a precondition on understanding contracts (and treaties). This essay broaches some of the interesting issues in the growing philosophical literature on promises. It closes with an overview of the collection.*

Promises are currently enjoying something of a renaissance in philosophy. This collection comprises sixteen original essays that address some of the central issues in the philosophical study of promises and agreements (broadly conceived). The purpose of this introduction is to provide some context for the chapters that follow. I hope to do so by broaching some of the more interesting issues in the bourgeoning philosophical literature on promises. I close with an overview of the collection.

I. PROMISES IN PHILOSOPHY

Philosophers have always found promises interesting. Promises are routinely treated as paradigmatic examples of *moral* phenomena, for example moral obligations, rights, or powers (e.g. Scanlon, 1998: ch. 7; Shiffrin, 2008; Thomson, 1990: ch. 12; Watson, 2009); *volitional* phenomena, for example speech-acts (e.g. Searle, 1969: ch. 3, 2001: ch. 6, 2010; Robins, 1984; and Margaret Gilbert's contribution to this book); and *social* phenomena, for example social practices and rules (e.g. Hume, 2006: 110–117 [*Treatise*, bk. 3, pt. 2, sec. 5]; Kolodny & Wallace, 2003; Rawls, 1999a: ch. 2). (Of course, these characterizations do not have to be mutually exclusive; they might well bring out different aspects of the same multidimensional phenomenon.) Promises continue to generate useful problem cases for those working in the areas of ethics, philosophy of language (including speech-act theory), philosophy of action (including practical reasoning and joint agency theory), political philosophy, and the philosophy of law. Recently, however, promises have also come to be regarded as a topic of philosophical study in their own right. Of course, understanding promises will inevitably have the desirable byproduct of enhancing our understanding of related moral, volitional, and social phenomena. The intended consequence, however, remains understanding promises themselves. This approach is exemplified by the work of David Owens (e.g. 2006, 2007, and his contribution to this book). Compare also Vitek (1993).

The Duality of Promises

Promises lead a double life, as it were. There are individual *acts* of promising. And there are *practices* of promising. Philosophical accounts of promises seek to explain promising acts, practices, and their interrelation.

Promises as Commitment Relations

It is agreed on most hands that promising acts are three-place commitment relations: the promisor commits to the promisee to do what's promised. Practices of promising are practices of making, keeping, receiving, relying on, and otherwise engaging with individual promissory commitments.

Explaining promises requires identifying those elements that unify their different manifestations and demarcate them from related phenomena. Consider

(0) A's promise to B to do X.

It may be that (0) is made under some promising practice P. But clearly, (0) is distinct from

(i) P = the *practice* under which A promises B to do X.

It may also be that (0) involves A in communicating an *intention* to do X. Yet (0) is distinct from

(ii) A's communicated *intention* to B to do X.

Perhaps (0) also involves A in communicating a *prediction* that A will do X. Yet (0) is also distinct from

(iii) A's communicated *prediction* to B that A will do X.

Again, just as A can promise B to do X, A can *threaten* B to do X (i.e. that A will do X). Yet (0) is distinct from

(iv) A's *threat* (issued) to B to do X (i.e. that A will do X).[1]

To give one more example, there seems to be some affinity between (0) and

(v) A's *request* (addressed) to B to do X (i.e. that B will do X)

but (v) is clearly is distinct from (0).[2]

The differences between (0) and (i)–(v) are among the many putative facts that accounts of promises seek to explain.

But what makes promises interesting or important, philosophically speaking? Let me venture two complementary hypotheses.

The Problem of Promising

The first hypothesis is rather specific. Most people seem to think that, when you promise me to do X, you *thereby* give yourself a new reason, motive, or obligation to do X. At least in the central case, you give yourself a reason to do what's promised *simply by promising*. And this seems to give rise to the

Problem of Promising
How can one give oneself a reason (or motive, or obligation) to do X simply by promising to do X?

Many philosophers consider this a genuine puzzle, an interesting and important problem that requires at least some solution or *explanation*. See, for example, Hume (2006: 110–17 [*Treatise*, bk. 3, pt. 2, sec. 5]); Prichard (2002: ch. 12); Anscombe (1981: chs. 2 and 10); Watson (2009). See also David Owens's discussion in chapter 2.

It is worth saying a word about my choice to formulate the Problem of Promising in terms of *reasons* (or also in terms of reasons). After all, the more familiar formulation, which originates with Hume, refers to obligations.

The first thing to say here is that, like most philosophers currently writing about promises, I do not share Hume's skepticism about reasons for action in general. Like most contemporary philosophers, I am happy to acquiesce in the commonsense notion that, in the central case, promises give perfectly good reasons to do what's promised. Second, most philosophers think of obligations as reasons for action. (See e.g. Michael Smith's contribution to this book).[3] If this is right, then skepticism about practical reason leads directly to skepticism about obligation. More to the point, not everyone shares the view that promises give reasons *of the special kind that obligates.* We certainly need to know something about the way obligatory reasons differ from other reasons before we can discuss the view that promises give obligatory reasons.[4]

It is also worth saying a word about my choice to describe the Problem of Promising simply as a problem. On its more familiar version, the problem is a kind of paradox–or at least a mystery. (Cf. Stephen Darwall's remark, at the outset of chapter 11, that promises "appear shrouded in mystery".) This now classic way of framing the problem originates with Hume. The story begins with a description of our concept of promise as the concept of giving oneself a reason (or motive or obligation) to do what's promised simply by forming and communicating an *intention* to give oneself such a reason (or motive or obligation). The story continues by claiming that there is something mysterious–if not outright unintelligible–about this concept. Our concept of promise is then said to be mysterious (or even unintelligible). The story ends by explaining this concept away as a useful fiction. See Hume's claim that, in promising, "we *feign* a new act of the mind" (2006: 115). Here then is the

Classic Problem of Promising
(1) Our concept of promise is the concept of giving oneself a reason (or motive, or obligation) simply by forming and communicating an intention to give it, without doing anything else thereby.
(2) The concept in (1) is paradoxical or mysterious.

I find (2) considerably more plausible than (1). But what is the basis for (2)? Why should the concept in (1) be thought paradoxical? What is so mysterious about it? At least on the present formulation of the Classic Problem, the sense of paradox has nothing to do with skepticism about practical reason. It also has nothing special to do with doubts about the notion that promises give obligations or reasons of some special kind. What seems to me to generate the sense of paradox is the narrow understanding of our ordinary concept of promise in (1), namely its identification with the concept of giving oneself a reason *simply by forming and communicating an intention to give it, and without doing anything else thereby.* The sense of paradox seems to me to come of the assumption that there is simply nothing more to promising than a communicated intention to give oneself a reason to do what's promised.

Here is one way to bring out the sense of mystery in this narrow understanding of our concept of promise. The general problem concerns the gap between what we intend to do on the one hand and what we end up doing on the other. Unlike God, my intention to do X never guarantees (logically speaking) my doing X. (This is one lesson of the Road to Hell). And the point clearly extends to our *communicated* intentions. Suppose I tell you a joke with the intention of making you laugh. My action is not guaranteed to make you laugh. The world can come between my action and its intended outcome. Perhaps you do not find my joke funny. Perhaps your finding it funny fails to make you laugh.[5]

Now suppose I communicate to you my intention to do this: give myself a reason to do X. Why believe that I have thereby *given* myself a reason to do X?

If you are like me, you probably find the notion that I can give myself a reason in this self-fulfilling way very hard to believe. But maybe this sense of mystery depends on some common misconception or dogma. Maybe we should just realize that one *can* give oneself a reason simply by forming and communicating an intention to give it, without doing anything else in the process. See Margaret Gilbert's discussion of the second, "no willing dogma" in chapter 3. See also Searle (2001: ch. 6, 2010).[6] Be that as it may, if I am right to think that the same sense of mystery also depends on the narrow understanding of our concept of promise in (1), then the mystery will not arise unless we subscribe to (1). And I suspect that (1) is an overly narrow interpretation of our concept of promise.[7]

To be sure, it does seem plausible to say that, when we promise, we take ourselves to be giving ourselves a reason simply by *promising*. "Because I have promised to!" is an informative answer to "Why are you doing X?" What I see no special reason to believe is that, when we promise, we take ourselves to be giving ourselves a reason *simply by communicating some intention*. That the *only* thing we do in promising is the communication of some intention (however complex) does not seem to me to form part of our concept of promise.

But neither does our concept of promise explicitly identify what *else* we do in promising. A better way to understand the Problem of Promising, I suggest, begins with the assumption that our ordinary concept of promise is not so much mysterious as *inchoate*–incomplete or inexplicit. On this story, the Problem of Promising is the problem of completing, and/or making explicit, our concept of promise, and doing so in a way that explains how promising gives reasons. For those of us who share the assumption that promises are essentially reason- (or motive- or obligation-) giving acts, it is hard to see how promises can be explained *without* addressing the Problem of Promising. To borrow a phrase from Watson, "some kind of normative story is called for here" (2009).[8]

Promises and Self-understanding in Society

Interesting as it is, the Problem of Promising is but one among many problems that promises raise, none of which exhausts their philosophical significance. My second hypothesis is the more general one that we are interested in understanding promises because we are interested in understanding ourselves in society. We are all competent practitioners in the practice of promising, that is to say in some promising practice or another. We all make, receive, keep, and break—in short, engage with—promises on a daily basis. Understanding our engagement with promises, then, is a component of understanding ourselves in society.

II. TWELVE QUESTIONS FOR THE THEORY OF PROMISES

Begin with a couple of platitudes. We can think of theories of promises as sets of answers to related yet different questions about promises. In answering these questions, we seek to strike a balance between the theoretical demands of separation and integration. On the one hand, we do not want to run together genuinely different questions. One the other hand, since all these questions are, in one way or another, "about" promises, how we answer one question might well have implications for how we can answer another. In the last analysis, the best theory is the package of claims that makes most sense as a whole, compared with other packages.

***

Perhaps the first question that comes to mind is the

Question of Definition
(1) What are (individual) promises?

This is the question of how best to characterize the (speech-)act of promising. A good philosophical definition will bring out what is distinctive and illuminating about the promising action. Here I wish to make two methodological remarks.

Our Concept of Promise. To what extent should the philosophical definition of promises reflect our ordinary concept of *promise*? This depends on the kind of explanation we are after. Since Hume identified our concept of promise with that of giving oneself an obligation or motive simply by forming and communicating an intention to do so, and since he considered that concept unintelligible, his account of promising is debunking. It explains promises other than by explicating *our* concept of them, and treats that concept as a useful fiction.

Most philosophers working on promises are interested in nondebunking theories, however. From this perspective, the correct definition of promises has to comport with our concept of promise, and make sense of that concept. But in at least two ways, the definition also has to go *beyond* that concept. First, if I am right that our ordinary concept of promise is rather inchoate (incomplete or inexplicit), the correct definition should complete that concept and make it explicit. Suppose that we can only promise by employing some mechanism M, of which we are only vaguely aware. Presumably, the correct definition of promises will make explicit reference to M. But second, the correct definition of promises is also likely to deviate from our ordinary concept of promise. For example, philosophical accounts of promises that are particularly attuned to commonsense morality tend to reflect the common belief that promises give moral obligations and rights, and that breaking them is morally wrong, if not outright blameworthy. See, for example, Thomson (1990: 12), Scanlon (1998: ch. 7), and Shiffrin (2008). Others, however, define promises without reference to moral obligations or rights. See, for example, Searle (2001: 194); Gilbert (chapter 3). And some of these other philosophers, who take their cue from Hume, understand promissory commitments in broadly self-interested terms. See, for example, Baier (1985: ch. 10, 1994: 110–120); Sheinman (2008). (More about this Humean view shortly.) Some of these views might be thought to conflict with the common belief that promises are essentially moral commitments. (This is particularly true of the last-mentioned view, at least if we accept the common distinction between morality and prudence or self-interest.) To that extent, they are revisionary. Even so, none of these views can be plausibly described as debunking. They all retain the bulk of our most important beliefs about promises, and largely vindicate our ordinary concept of promise.

The Central Case Method. Turning to the more important methodological remark, I do not believe it is reasonable to expect even the most plausible theory of promising to provide an obvious, direct, or simple explanation of every single case of promising. Put positively, it seems to me eminently reasonable to expect that even the most plausible theory of promising would have to characterize at least some cases of promising as degenerate, defective, or otherwise noncentral. As long as the theory can explain these cases *indirectly*, namely by reference to the central cases of promising, this should not count against the theory. Two examples will suffice.

We have already mentioned the common view that promises are first and foremost moral obligations, rights, or powers. When we think about promises, on this view, we should direct our minds to the case of good moral agents, who are motivated to lead good moral lives. See, e.g., Scanlon (1998: ch. 7); Shiffrin (2008). A standard counterexample to this view is so-called *immoral* promises (a promise to kill for money, say). But at least in principle, the proponent of this view can reply that immoral promises are rather degenerate or *defective*. Such promises can be successfully made all right, but they make for very bad examples; they are examples but not *exemplars*. Of course, the claim is not the trivial one that immoral promises are morally defective; it is the nontrivial claim that the immorality of immoral promises renders them defective as promises. If this claim can be made out, the counterexample is neutralized.[9]

On another, broadly Humean theory (*disclosure*: I'm a subscriber), promises give self-interested reasons—in Hume's admittedly tendentious words, promise "is the sanction of the interested commerce of mankind"—which reasons are grounded in trust (in Hume's hyperbolic words, the promise-breaker "subjects himself to the penalty of never being trusted again in case of failure").[10] By doing what's promised, the promisor preserves the trust that the promisee and/or others have in her, thereby preserving her valuable power to promise them again. See Sheinman (2008), and compare Stan Husi's discussion of the Exhaustive Practice View in chapter 4. One apparent counterexample to this view is the proverbial deathbed promise (make it a *desert island* deathbed promise, if you like). But in principle, the proponent of this view can reply that deathbed promises are genuine yet somewhat defective promises. There are such promises, but they are not perfectly good ones—not promises par excellence. They should be explained by reference to promises to individuals who live to see the promises given to them being kept or broken.

These examples can be multiplied. The general point is that *every* theorist of promising is entitled, and can legitimately help herself to the opportunity, to explain some apparently embarrassing cases by arguing that the promises they feature are less than perfectly central or paradigmatic. And she can do so, moreover, without claiming that the acts in question are not promises at all.

Let me try to motivate the picture that underlies this *central case method*. The most general idea is that a philosophical explanation of some phenomenon does not end with analysis (necessary and sufficient conditions). The idea harks back to Aristotle's discussion of friendship in book 8 of the *Nicomachean Ethics*. Aristotle discusses two species of friendships: what we might call instrumental friendship (which includes two subspecies: "friendship for utility" and "friendship for pleasure") and intrinsic friendship (or "friendship for virtue"). According to Aristotle, both are genuine cases of friendship (the necessary and sufficient conditions are met).

Nevertheless, Aristotle takes pains to claim that intrinsic friendship is *the* central case of friendship ("complete friendship," "friendship without qualification," or "friendship most of all"). Instrumental friendship, he thought, is friendship all right, but it is somewhat defective *as a friendship*; it falls somewhat short of the central case ("coincidental friendship," "friendship by similarity," or "friendship to a lesser extent"). It is an example but not an exemplar.

Closer to home is a familiar distinction in speech-act theory. To explain speech-acts, it is not enough to identify their necessary conditions, for sometimes these conditions are met, but not in a perfectly good way. J. L. Austin made the point by distinguishing two kinds of "infelicities." When the speech-act does not "come off," or is not "achieved" at all, we have a case of "misfire"; when the act is achieved but not in a perfectly good way, we have a case of "abuse." The best—if not the only—way to explain this intuitive distinction is by providing examples. And Austin's example conveniently brings us back to promising. If I tell you that I promise you to do X, but intend not to do X, then I might successfully promise you to do X. Nevertheless, I abuse the procedure (Austin 1975: 16). Similarly, Searle regards the case of insincere promising as a genuine yet *defective* instance of promising (1969: ch. 3).

Why say that an insincere promise is a defective *promise*? Why not say that it is not a promise at all? See Raz (1982). Like Austin and Searle, I can find no knockdown argument, only a few considerations. First, it seems to me that both the speaker and the hearer treat the act as a genuine promise. The speaker intends to get the hearer to believe that she will perform the relevant act by promising him to perform it. And the hearer believes that he is being promised. Second, the act achieves all of its intended effects. Finally, and most important, the act achieves these effects precisely because it invokes (the rules of) some *promising* practice.

Why say that an insincere promise is a *defective* promise? Why not say that it is a perfectly good promise? (Cf. McNeily [1972], Owens [2006], and Chwang [chapter 6].) Because—to resort to a familiar metaphor—insincere promising would not be part of what the practice of promising were intelligently designed *for*; it would simply be foreseen as a side-effect. Insincere promises are parasitic on—explicable by reference to—sincere ones. This is borne out by a rough-and-ready test: Could you have the one without the other? You could have (a practice of) sincere promises only; it is not very hard at all to imagine a society in which everyone keeps all the promises she makes. But could you have (a practice of) insincere promises only? It is exceedingly hard to imagine a society in which everyone breaks every promise she makes!

In sum, I think we can plausibly maintain that promising has conditions of *success*, which must be met whenever a promise is made, and more stringent conditions of *perfection*, which must be met in perfectly good or paradigmatic cases of promising—cases of full-blooded promises, of promises par excellence. Again, I cannot overemphasize the imprecise nature of the distinction, and the lack of any clear-cut litmus test. Austin's admission that "these distinctions are not hard and fast" (1975: 16) is probably an understatement. Nevertheless, the distinction is intuitive enough. For an extensive discussion, and employment, of the central case method in the case of promising, see Kimel (2003: ch. 1).

It falls from the very concepts of promissory success and perfection that the more fundamental questions concern the latter. An account of promises is first and foremost an account of perfectly good promises, those that fall within the central case of promising.

***

One outstanding philosophical issue concerns what I earlier dubbed the *duality* of promises, namely the relation between individual promises, or promising *acts*, and promising *practices*. The issue is often framed as the debate between "the practice view" of promises and its opponents. This is misleading, as the relation between promises and practices gives rise to several different questions. I will mention five questions that concern promising practices: (2), (3), (7), (8), and (9). Questions (7) and (8) will be specifically *moral* questions. Question (9) is evolutionary. Questions (2) and (3) are neither. They both concern one issue that has preoccupied those writing on promises and practices. As we shall see, the two questions are *very* closely related. It might still be useful to state them separately, however. Begin with

> (2) Are promises—and so promissory reasons, motives, or obligations—essentially practice-based in that one cannot possibly promise—and so give oneself a promissory reason, motive, or obligation—other than by invoking some preexisting promising practice?

Hume (2006: 110–17 [*Treatise*, bk. 3, pt. 2, sec. 5]) and Rawls (1999a: ch. 2, 1999b: ch. 6) clearly answer in the affirmative. See also Mackie (1977: ch. 3, 1980: ch. 6), Kolodny & Wallace (2003), Tognazzini (2007), Deigh (2008: ch. 8), Sheinman (2008). See also Owens (chapter 2) and Husi (chapter 4). Others seem to believe that promises are practice-independent acts. On this view, promising practices fulfill a facilitating role in promising, but they are not quite of the essence. In principle, A should be able to promise B in a state of nature, understood as a state in which A and B share absolutely no promising practice (not even a local one). See, for example, Raz (1977: 214, 1982: 927), Scanlon (1998: ch. 7, esp. 296-98, 306).[11]

Some of those who answer (2) in the affirmative sometimes like to talk in terms of "the practice/institution/game of promising." See, for example,

Rawls (1999a: ch. 2), Hare (1964), Searle (1969), and Mackie (1977). On one natural interpretation, such talk refers to a single all-encompassing global promising practice everyone shares. I think this expression is better understood as shorthand for the many different promising practices agents can invoke. When you play baseball, you do not invoke the rules of some global practice of games; you invoke the rules of *baseball.* Similarly, when you promise, you typically invoke the rules of some particular promising practice. The practice can be rather local. (At the limit, you and I can have our own promising practice.) The question, then, is whether promising invokes *some* promising practice or other, necessarily.

***

Closely related to (2) is the

Question of Priority
(3) Does the practice under which any given promise is made enjoy explanatory priority over that very promise?

Arguably, an affirmative answer to question (2) entails an affirmative answer to question (3) (call it the *Priority of Practice* view). For if the act of promising cannot fail to invoke some promising practice, the practice invoked can be said to enjoy explanatory priority over the invoking promise. Not surprisingly, then, Hume and Rawls answer question (3) in the affirmative. Rawls (1999a: ch. 2) argues for this position by analogy. Before you had the game (practice) of baseball, complete with its three strikes rule to invoke, you could throw a hard ball at someone holding a stick, but you could not *strike him out*. Similarly, before you had the practice of promising, complete with its promise-making and -keeping rules to invoke, you could *say* "I promise" to someone, but you could not *promise* him. In both cases, then, "[t]he practice is logically prior to particular cases: unless there is the practice the terms referring to actions specified by it lack a sense" (37).

Many reject the baseball analogy. Some complain that the comparison fails to take promising seriously enough. Promising is more than just another game we play. For one thing, promising is pervasive, and does not seem to be *avoidable* in the way playing a game like baseball is. See, for example, Midgley (1974), Cavel (1979: ch. 11), and Vitek (1993: 36–48; 117–43). For another, promising seems to have a *moral* dimension games like baseball seem to lack. See, for example, Hanfling (1975) and Shiffrin (2008). On this view, even if we accept Rawls's claim that the practice of *baseball* enjoys explanatory priority over the individual acts made under it (e.g. striking out), we should reject the notion that a *promising* practice enjoys an explanatory priority over the individual acts made under *it* (e.g. making or keeping a promise).

The correct answers to questions (2) and (3) seem to depend on the possibility of a *practiceless* promise, by which I mean a promise that does not invoke any preexisting promising practice. But we can also approach these questions from the other direction, namely by entertaining the possibility of a *promiseless* practice, by which I mean a promising practice that presupposes no preexisting promise. Suppose that there can be no such practice, that every promising practice presupposes at least some preexisting promise. So the first promising practice came into existence after—and, in any event, no earlier than, the first promise. And this would seem to require a negative answer to questions (2) and (3).

Now some of the philosophers who reject the possibility of a promiseless promising practice go as far as to claim that promises are among the most basic building blocks of the entire social world. On this view, *all* social practices presuppose something very much like promises. Robins (1976 and 1984); compare Gilbert (2004: 85–6). This *Practice as Promise* claim is far-reaching. To see why, consider customary rules of etiquette, say, the rule that men are to bare their heads in church. Clearly, such a rule can evolve unintentionally over several years, without any man promising anyone to bare his head in church (or to uphold the said rule). On the face of it, the view that such purely customary practices are essentially promissory seems to miss the essentially *intentional* nature of promising. Promising is essentially intentional in the sense that, at least in the central case, the promisor intends to promise (or to give himself a reason by communicating an intention to give it). See Anscombe (1981: 13, 2000: sec. 47). But those who perform the many acts that eventually give rise to a customary practice (e.g. acts of taking one's hat off on entering a church) may well intend to perform these admittedly intentional acts without intending *to promise* (or give themselves reasons in the way promises do).

However, even those who reject Practice as Promise, and acknowledge the essentially intentional nature of promising, tend to reject the possibility of promiseless promising practices. Even if not all social practices presuppose promises, they maintain, *promising* practices must. Thus Thomson remarks that to have a practice of promises you have got to have some *eight* promises first; but you cannot have the eighth promise without a seventh. Eventually, you have got to have a first promise (1990: 303–4). More surprising is that Rawls, who clearly takes himself to endorse the Priority of Practice view—that is, who is answering question (3) in the affirmative—explicitly concedes the point. What you might be able to get without promises, according to Rawls, is *rules* of promising practices. However, until acted on, the rules of a practice remain a mere *blueprint* of that practice. So just as you would not confuse a blueprint of a house for the house itself, you should not confuse the yet un-acted-on rules of some promising practice for the practice itself.[12] To have a genuine practice of promising—as opposed to a mere blueprint of such a practice—you have got to have at least some individuals acting on the rules, that is to say, making and keeping individual promises (1999a: 37). Is Thomson right that you cannot have a practice of promises without eight or so promises? Is Rawls right that the rules of a promising practice are a mere blueprint of that practice?

So much for questions (2) and (3). Later I will raise very different questions about the relation between promises and practices (questions (7)-(9)). But there are three other questions I want to mention first.

***

Most philosophers believe that promises give *some* kind of obligation. For example, those who answer question (2) affirmatively believe that promises give *social* obligations, that is to say obligations imposed by rules of social practice or convention. As we have seen, many others think that promises give *moral* obligations. Still others think that promissory obligations are essentially *volitional*. These include Searle (2001: ch. 6), Robins (1984), and Gilbert (chapter 3). Finally, there are those who claim that promises give obligations (simpliciter). See, for example, Raz (1977) and Owens (2008). (On this view, moral promises give moral obligations, legal promises give legal obligations, etc.) Nevertheless, it is fair to say that much of the debate over promissory obligations concerns specifically moral obligations, obligations whose violation is morally wrong or even blameworthy. Indeed, the traditional debate over the obligation to keep a promise does not look like a debate over social or conventional obligations (say); it looks like a debate over moral obligations.

An analogy might help. Consider the debate over the obligation to obey the law. Trivially, I have a *legal* obligation—a kind of social or conventional obligation—to obey the law. So the debate over the obligation to obey the law does not seem to be about a social or conventional obligation. On the face of it, the debate is specifically moral—a debate in normative ethics. But then something similar might be said about the debate over the obligation to keep promises. That we all have a social or conventional obligation—an obligation of social practice—to keep the promises we make, within socially established limits, does not seem *particularly* controversial. (It should not be more controversial than the claim that we all have a legal obligation to perform the contracts we enter into, within legally established limits.) More to the point, you can certainly have such a social or conventional obligation *without* having a moral obligation, and vice versa. And for the most part, arguments over the obligation to keep promises are specifically moral.[13] Hence the

Questions of Right
(4) Is there a general moral obligation to keep one's promise?
(5) When, and in virtue of what, does one have a moral obligation to keep one's promise?

A full answer to question (5) will answer the yes-no question (4) as well, but not vice versa. To say that there is a general obligation to keep promises is to say that promises *as such* are morally binding. So if you answer (4) affirmatively, you think that, if A promises to do X, then A has at least some sort of moral obligation to do X. (Here as elsewhere the focus is on central cases of promising; you can answer (4) in the affirmative, and still countenance promises that give no moral obligation, provided only that you regard these promises as falling outside the central case.) But even those who deny the existence of a moral obligation to keep promises as such believe that many promises are morally binding. So they still need to answer question (5). To answer this question is to explain *why morally binding promises are morally binding.*

Many philosophers answer (4) affirmatively: in the central case, a promise gives a moral obligation to do what's promised. See Scanlon (1998); Shiffrin (2008); Kolodny and Wallace (2003); Tognazzini (2007); Watson (2009); and Rawls (1999b: 305). See also Prichard (2002); Hart (1958); and Hanfling (1975). Again, some of these philosophers think that certain kinds of promises are not morally binding at all. Some of them would probably subscribe to Eric Chwang's claim, in chapter 6, that coerced promises give no moral obligation, for example. But then these philosophers are committed to the view that promises of the relevant kind (say, coerced promises) fall outside the central case.

Many others deny that promises as such give moral obligations, that is to say, even in the central case. On this view, a perfectly good promise can fail to give a moral obligation. See, for example, the act-consequentialist account Alastair Norcross offers in chapter 9. Some of these philosophers think that certain kinds of promises—for example, so-called immoral promises, such as a promise to kill for money—are not morally binding in any way at all. These philosophers can still maintain that at least some promises of that kind (say, at least some immoral promises to kill for money) fall squarely inside the central case. They can consistently maintain that such promises are morally defective, but are not defective as promises; they are perfectly immoral yet perfectly *promissory* promises.

I earlier noted the current trend to treat promises as a topic of philosophical inquiry in their own right. The Questions of Right illustrate the limits of this approach. They look like substantive moral questions, whose answers presuppose choices between general theories of moral obligation. Surely even if there is a general moral obligation to keep promises as such, promissory moral obligations are hardly the only moral obligations there are. So understanding promissory moral obligations requires at least some understanding of moral obligations generally. The other side of the coin is that studying promissory moral obligations can contribute to our understanding of moral obligations quite generally. Promises can serve as a useful laboratory for testing claims and arguments of general moral interest. See, for example, the discussions by Smith (chapter 8), Norcross (chapter 9), Hooker (chapter 10), and Darwall (chapter 11).

Here is one general moral question facing anyone who seeks to answer questions (4) and (5): What do we mean by saying that A has a moral obligation to do X? See generally, Zimmerman (1996). As we have seen, it is often said that an obligation is a kind of reason for action, but surely not every old reason can be regarded as an *obligation*. Assuming that obligations are indeed reasons, they are surely reasons of a special kind. At a minimum, they must render contrary action *wrongful* in some way. And on the more common view, they also render the agent *blameworthy* for that action. (For some, moral blameworthiness is constitutive of the relevant kind of wrongness; see Darwall, 2006: ch. 5, esp. 93.) If I have an obligation to keep my promise to do X, my failure to do X is wrongful in some way. And if the obligation is moral, then the wrongfulness is moral, too; social or conventional (practice-internal) wrongfulness is neither necessarily nor sufficient.

You might think that the obvious answer to (4) is no. There are many cases in which it is perfectly okay to break a perfectly good promise. If you promise to meet me for lunch, but it turns out that the only way you can take your sick child to the hospital, or save a stranger, or avert significant harm is by skipping our appointment, then you should skip it. But this seems to have an obvious response, namely the

> Pro Tanto View of Promissory Obligation
> The obligations promises give are defeasible, pro tanto obligations. They are obligations that are liable to be defeated by countervailing reasons.

That you do not have an overall obligation to meet me for lunch all things considered might simply mean that your obligation to do so is defeated by the more important reason to go to the hospital, save the stranger, or avert harm. On the notion of a pro tanto (or prima facie) obligation, see Ross (2002), Raz (1999), Zimmerman (1996: ch. 5), and Searle (1980), as well as the discussion in Chwang (chapter 6), Driver (chapter 7), and Phillips (chapter 14).

The Pro Tanto View requires elaboration. As it stands, it tells us why a pro tanto obligation is *not* an all things considered obligation (it is defeasible); it does not tell us what a pro tanto obligation *is*. In particular, it does not tell us how a pro tanto obligation is supposed to differ from an ordinary reason. Presumably, a pro tanto obligation is still a genuine kind of obligation.[14] If so, then violating a pro tanto obligation is still a genuine kind of wrong—a pro tanto wrong, if you will. Unlike an overall wrong, a pro tanto wrong such as promise-breaking can be justified.[15] But a justified wrong, so goes the thought, is still wrong in some residual way. And arguably, acting against some ordinary reason is not necessarily wrong in any way at all. It is therefore fair to expect proponents of the Pro Tanto View to explain how the normative force of a promise differs from that of an ordinary reason (or give up on the notion that pro tanto obligations are a genuine kind of obligation).

To see the problem, suppose that I have exactly two conflicting ordinary moral reasons: an ordinary moral reason to keep my promise, and an even stronger ordinary moral reason to break it. In that case, I should think, there is simply nothing wrong with breaking my promise, morally speaking. Of course, I am acting against *some* moral reason. And this gives me something to regret, namely not being able to act on both moral reasons. But regretability does not entail moral wrongfulness. After all, life's full of regret. And by hypothesis, the reason in question is not an obligation—not even a pro tanto one. So what I regret cannot be morally wrongful.

It therefore seems to me that, subscribers to the Pro Tanto View need to do two things. They need to explain (i) how a pro tanto obligation to do X differs from an ordinary reason to do X. And they need to explain (ii) why a promise to do X gives a pro tanto obligation to do X rather than an ordinary reason to do X. (A failure to explain (i) is a failure to show that there can be *any* pro tanto obligations; a failure to explain (ii) is a failure to show that *promises* give pro tanto obligations.)

Several authors have emphasized the distinction between obligation (or wrong) simpliciter and obligation (or wrong) *to* someone in particular. Promissory moral obligations (or wrongs) are said to be a paradigmatic example of such directed or *relational* moral obligations (or wrongs). Of all the people in the world, they are directed at the promisee. See, for example, Kolodny & Wallace (2003); Darwall (chapter 11); Thompson (2004); Owens (2006, 2007). But see Connie Rosati's discussion of self-promising in chapter 5.

It is worth noting that appeal to the relational or directed nature of promissory obligations does not yet solve the difficulty with the Pro Tanto View. The problem of distinguishing pro tanto obligations from ordinary reasons for action rearises with respect to directed obligations. Presumably, directed pro tanto obligations are obligations all the same. Violating them is still wrong, albeit a directed one. If promise-breaking violates a pro tanto directed obligation, it still *wrongs* the promisee—that is to say, even if it is justified by countervailing considerations. See Owens (2007: 295–6). So we still need to explain how this directed pro tanto obligation, whose violation is (relationally) wrong, differs from an ordinary directed reason, whose violation—even harmful violation—is not necessarily wrongful (relationally or not). The question returns: What *are* (directed or nondirected) pro tanto obligations (or wrongs)?

On what is perhaps the most popular proposal, one has a pro tanto obligation to do X just when, *all else being equal*, one ought (has an obligation) to do X. So understood, a pro tanto obligation is a counterfactual property of acts:

> If A has a *pro tanto moral obligation* to do X, then, if A did not have any countervailing moral reason, it would be the case that X is what A ought morally to do all things considered.

The classic exposition of this view belongs to Ross (2002: ch. 2). See also Zimmerman (1996: ch. 5); Kagan (1998: 180–81) and Dancy (2004: ch. 1).

But isn't this true of at least some *ordinary* (i.e. nonobligatory) reasons? Suppose I have some positive yet nonobligatory moral reason to do X. Is it not true that, if I did not have *any* countervailing moral reason, X would be what I ought morally to do all things considered?[16] But if so, what exactly is the difference between a pro tanto moral obligation to do what's promised and an ordinary (nonobligatory) moral reason to do the same?[17]

Assume, however, that we had a coherent way to distinguish between pro tanto obligations and ordinary reasons for action. The Pro Tanto View of Promissory Obligation still faces a separate *epistemic* challenge. Suppose you promise to meet me for lunch, and that you thereby give yourself some moral reason to do so. But now it turns out that you can only take your sick child to the hospital, save a stranger, or avert significant harm by skipping our appointment. And this is clearly what you should do. How do we *know* whether your moral reason to meet me is a pro tanto (directed or nondirected) obligation (and so that acting against it is a pro tanto—directed or nondirected—wrong) or simply an ordinary (directed or nondirected) reason? (Eric Chwang and Julia Driver discuss the pro tanto nature of promissory obligation in the context of coerced promises and promises that are impossible to keep in chapters 6 and 7, respectively. In chapter 14, David Phillips defends Ross's version of the Pro Tanto View against Sidgwick's attack on commonsense morality.)[18]

***

Many philosophers think that promises are, or are typically, good or valuable. For simplicity, assume that promises are always good, and consider the

> Question of Good
> (6) What is the value of promising?

This is conveniently ambiguous between at least three questions. It can be a question about the value of promising *acts*, *powers*, or *practices*. I will limit my remarks to the value of promising acts (in the central case of promising). Consider the schema:

(1) Promising acts promote/realize V.
(2) V is a value: it is intrinsically good, something worth realizing for its own sake.
(3) Therefore, promising acts are valuable.
(4) Therefore, we have at least one reason to do them (i.e. to promise).

It is hardly surprising that *consequentialist* answers to the Question of Good fit this schema. Focus on the simplest form of consequentialism, namely act-consequentialism.[19] In particular, focus on an act-consequentialist who equates the good with welfare–an act-utilitarian. An act-utilitarian might plausibly argue that promising is good to the extent that it promotes interpersonal cooperation (broadly understood to include collaboration, coordination, and exchange). Cooperation, in turn, promotes overall welfare. In such cases, we have a perfectly good reason to promise. This act-utilitarian might argue as follows:

(1) Promising acts promote welfare (by promoting cooperation).
(2) Welfare is a value.
(3) Therefore, promising acts are valuable.
(4) Therefore, we have at least one reason to promise.

Compare the discussions by Michael Smith and Alastair Norcross in chapters 8 and 9.

Most answers to the Question of Good could not be plausibly described as consequentialist. Nevertheless, some of these views seem to fit the schema (1)–(4). Let me give, and briefly remark on, three examples.

Assurance. According to Tim Scanlon (1998: ch. 7), promissory obligations are grounded in the value of *assurance*. On what seems to be Scanlon's official view (302–4), assurance is not simply justified belief, or expectation, that something will happen; it is more like *true* justified belief, or knowledge, that it will happen. The focus here is on what Scanlon calls "potential promisees," namely all of us *as* promisees. We often have a reason to know that something will happen, in particular that A will do X. This knowledge includes our present justified belief at t that A will do X, as well as the fact that A does X at t + 1. Notice that this deviates from the ordinary usage of "assurance." It implies, for example, that broken promises do not assure, even when they lead the promisee to believe the promisor will do as promised. In addition, this nonstandard conception of assurance fails to generate a good argument under our schema. Here is what the argument looks like:

(1) Promising acts realize assurance.
(2) Assurance is a value.
(3) Therefore, promising acts are valuable.
(4) Therefore, we have at least one reason to promise.

But under Scanlon's nonstandard conception of assurance, the argument's first premise comes out false: in themselves, acts of promise-*making* realize no assurance at all; what realize assurance (under this nonstandard conception) are only the more complex acts of making promises and then *keeping* them. So we don't yet have a good argument for promising.

On the more common, and weaker, interpretation of Scanlon's view, A gives B assurance that A will do X when A leads B to believe—or believe reasonably—that A will do X. This conception renders the argument's first premise considerably more plausible.

Authority. According to David Owens, "promising is designed to serve our authority interest" (2006: 71, 75). "According to the authority-interest theory, promises exist because people have an interest in having the right to decide what they do" (74). The authority interest is an interest in having a certain moral power over human behavior—our own behavior and the behavior of others.[20] Each person has an interest in having the authority to act in accordance with her own judgment, and in having the authority that others act in accordance with her judgment. A promise grants the promisee authority (or right) over the promisor's action (2006: 69–75, 2007: 310–313).

The claim that a promise serves our authority interest is potentially misleading. Surely promising serves our interests *as promisees*. But we are also promisors. And a promise can only serve the promisee's authority's interest by disserving the promisor's authority interest. When A promises B to do X, A relinquishes her authority or right over her doing X, and grants it to B. Apparently, what promising serves is not our interest in authority itself but in its redistribution or *transfer* (from promisor to promisee).

We can define our authority interest more narrowly, as our interest in having authority over what *others* do. On this narrower definition, promising does seem to serve our authority interest.[21] But this does not change the fact that promises disserve our interest in having the authority to decide what *we* do. It's a zero-sum game: a promise can only serve the promisee's interest in having the authority to decide what the promisor does by disserving the promisor's interest in having authority to decide what the promisor does. The upshot is that promising serves one human interest in authority by disserving another.

This suggests an amendment to the authority interest theory. What promises serve is not so much our interest in authority as our interest in *transferring authority at will* (or by mutual consent). Promises are good (and we have reasons to make them) because they serve our interest in being able to *transfer* authority at will (or by mutual consent).[22] This *authority transfer* theory claims that A's promising B to do X is good because it serves A's and B's interest in transferring authority over A's doing X from A to B at A's will (or by A's and B's mutual consent).[23] Both you and I have an interest in its being the case that I can give you a bit of authority over my own behavior at will (or by mutual consent), and this explains what's good about my promise, and why I have a reason to give it.[24]

Autonomy. The transition from the authority interest theory to the authority transfer theory is, in effect, a transition to an *autonomy* theory. Indeed, several philosophers ground promising in the value of autonomy. See, for example, Raz (1977, 1982, 1986), Shiffrin (2008), Robins (1984), and Searle (2001). See also Rosati's contribution to this book. Joseph Raz, for example, claims that promissory obligations are ultimately grounded in the value of voluntary special bonds (1982: 928, 1986: 173–176). The shift from authority (or assurance) theories to autonomy theories marks a shift of focus from promisees to promisors. Thus, according to Seana Shiffrin, the power to promise is necessary for establishing and maintaining special voluntary relations between morally good agents:

> The idea that an agent can intentionally form an obligation through the exercise and expression of her will alone (and not by first transforming the state of affairs around her) comes part and parcel with any plausible conception of an autonomous agent. (2008: 500; see also Watson [2009: 165])

These last three views (assurance, authority, autonomy) explain promises in terms of values, but they could not be plausibly regarded as consequentialist, at least not without qualification. Why? Perhaps the first and preliminary point to make is that, even if these views could be described as consequentialist, they could not be described as *utilitarian*. This is because they all seem to assume that the value of promising—be it assurance, authority, or autonomy—is not simply a component of *welfare*; there is *more* to the value of promising than welfare (however broadly understood). Thus Scanlon, Owens, Raz, and Shiffrin would not wish to deny that assurance, authority, or autonomy promotes B's and/or A's welfare, say, by helping them cooperate on mutually beneficial terms. But their appeal to these values is largely unmediated by a theory of welfare or well-being. See, for example, Scanlon (1998: 303, ch. 3); Owens (2006: 52, 76); Raz (1986: ch. 14, esp. 390–395); Shiffrin (2008). See also Rosati (chapter 5).

So these views are not plausibly described as utilitarian, but why aren't they *consequentialist*? There are at least two points to make here. First, the simplest consequentialist theory of action is *act*-consequentialism, the view that an act is both right and obligatory just when and because it promotes the overall good.[25] This theory denies the existence of so-called *deontological constraints*: whether one has a moral obligation to perform some act is determined by the overall goodness of the outcome it produces (and goodness is understood impartially).[26] The notion that promising acts are valuable because they realize some value such as assurance, authority, and/or autonomy is perfectly consistent with the claim that promising acts impose deontological constraints. And indeed, assurance, authority, or autonomy theorists typically hold that, within limits, morality requires one to keep one's promise, regardless of whether one's doing so promotes the overall good.[27]

Second, consequentialism is sometimes understood as a view about the appropriate attitudes to take toward things. Such *attitudinal instrumentalism* tells us that actions, powers, and practices to be valued as instruments, for the sake of other things, and not also intrinsically, for their own sake. By contrast, under the three views in question (assurance, authority, autonomy), promising acts and powers to be valued intrinsically, for their own sake. (Owens and Shiffrin are particularly explicit on this point.)

It should be noted, however, that this claim is not obviously incompatible with our first, welfarist answer to the Question of Good. To be sure, an act-utilitarian thinks that promising is valuable for its contribution to human welfare, and that this contribution is the *only* reason why promising is valuable—the only value that makes a promise valuable. But arguably, he might also maintain that it is appropriate to value promises intrinsically in our daily lives. Arguably, the pervasive and obvious nature of their contribution to welfare makes it appropriate to value them for their own sake, rather than simply for the sake of welfare. If this is right, then a value monist needn't be an attitudinal instrumentalist. See Kagan (1988) and Frankfurt (1999: ch. 7).

Suppose we could show that acts of promising always realize some intrinsic value such as welfare, assurance, authority, and/or autonomy. Would this solve the Problem of Promising? Surely not. To show that promising realizes some value is to show that we have at least one reason to promise. If promising is reason-giving, this would show that we have at least one reason to give ourselves reasons. But it would not explain how we *can* give ourselves reasons simply by promising.

The same seems to be true of the value of promising *powers* (or practices). It is one thing to explain why being possessed of some power—say the power to walk on water—would be valuable, quite another to explain how one *can* be possessed of such power. Similarly, it is one thing to explain why the power to promise (or give oneself a reason thereby) would be (intrinsically) valuable, and so why we all have at least one reason to want to have that power. But explaining how we *can* actually have the power to promise (and give ourselves a reason thereby) is a different matter. The sheer fact that a power is valuable, or intrinsically valuable, does not yet explain how it can be had.

***

Earlier I noted that talk about "the practice view" of promises can mislead, because the relation between promises and practices gives rise to different questions. Questions (2) and (3) raised one set of closely related issues. I now want to mention two specifically *moral* questions about promising practices.

> (7) When one has a moral obligation to keep one's promise, does that obligation derive from the good- or right-making properties of some (actual or hypothetical) promising practice?

Like question (2), question (7) has preoccupied participants in the general debate over the relation between promises and practices. It is a *very* different question, however. Those who answer (7) affirmatively typically believe that the moral status of promise-keeping or -breaking acts is a matter of their conformity to justified rules or principles, which rules or principles are justified by *their* good- or right-making properties—or, more accurately, by the good- or right-making properties of their general acceptance as public standards of behavior. The justification of promise-keeping or -breaking acts proceeds in two stages. At the primary stage, we justify some practice rules directly as good or right; at the derivative stage, we justify acts indirectly by their conformity to these justified rules.

This two-stage approach has two versions. One version is associated with Hume and Rawls. It requires that the morally determinative rules be generally accepted in actual practice. (Cf. also Jules Coleman's pragmatic theory of corrective justice [2001: pt. 1, esp. lecture 1], and Yizhak Benbaji's conventionalist approach to just war theory in this book.) The more common version of the two-stage approach does not require the morally determinative rules to be generally accepted in actual practice; it is enough that the rules *would* have the relevant good- or right-making properties if they were generally accepted in actual practice. In a perfectly good sense, however, this is still *a* practice view of promissory obligations: it grounds every moral obligation to keep a promise in rules or principles that would have good- or right-making properties if they were the rules or principles of our practice.

Let me mention the two most influential versions of this two-stage view, as applied to promises. *Rule-consequentialism* claims that one has a moral obligation to keep a promise just when, and because, doing so conforms to the rules whose general acceptance as public standards of behavior would produce the best consequences. Brad Hooker's contribution to this book exemplifies this approach. When we, as a group, generally accept rules as public standards of behavior, we thereby make them part of our actual practice. In a perfectly good sense, then, rule-consequentialism is a practice view of promissory obligation: its explanation of the moral obligation to keep a promise makes essential reference to our practices. Rule-consequentialism is a practice view in virtue of its affirmative answer to question (7).

The second influential version of the two-stage view is *contractualism*. To be sure, the two-stage structure of this view goes missing from its label, which makes no mention of rules or principles. All the same, modern contractualists are all *principle contractualists*. They claim that one has a moral obligation to keep a promise just when, and because, doing so conforms to unrejectable *principles*, namely principles no one could reasonably reject as public standards of behavior.[28] See, for example, Scanlon (1998), Watson (1998), and Darwall (2006: ch. 12).

Modern contractualists often present their theory as an alternative to "the practice view" of promises. What often goes unnoticed is the perfectly good sense in which principle contractualism *is* a practice view of promissory obligation. When we generally accept principles as public standards of behavior, we make them principles of our actual practice. So principle contractualism explains promissory (and other) moral obligations in terms of our practices. It is a practice view in the sense that it answers question (7) affirmatively.[29]

To be sure, Hume and Rawls gave affirmative answers to questions (2) *and* (7), but I think these questions are better kept apart. It is possible to answer question (2) affirmatively, and insist that promises are essentially practice-based actions that cannot be performed other than by invoking an independent practice—thereby endorsing one practice view of promising—and still answer question (7) in the negative, and reject the notion that promissory moral obligations derive from the good- or right-making properties of actual or hypothetical practices—thereby rejecting another practice view.[30]

***

The other moral question concerning promising practices is this:

> (8) What rules or principles of promising do we, as a group, have reason to accept as public standards of behavior?

Compare questions (7) and (8). Question (7) refers to social practices, but is about the status of individual promissory acts. By contrast, (8) is a question we face together as *group* (which can be as large as a society and as small as a pair of individuals). It is a question about the reasons we have for choosing different sets of public rules to govern our making, keeping, breaking, and enforcing of promises. What principles should our society promulgate, teach, or enforce (for example)? And what principles should we make into law?[31] (See the discussion of the last question on this list.)

It is important in this context to remind ourselves that we never face the choice of a single all-purpose global practice and rules of promising, always the choice of some particular promising practice and rules. Hence question (7) should be understood as practice-specific: What should (the rules of) *this* promising practice look like?

Now the discussion of the rule-consequentialist and (principle) contractualist answers to the previous question raises an obvious possibility. If you are a contractualist, for example, you must think that the principles we have reason to accept as public standards of behavior are also the morally determinative principles, the principles that determine our moral obligations and the moral status of our particular acts. On this view, the answer to (7) already answers (8)! If you are *not* a contractualist, however, you are not committed to treating the unrejectable principles—those principles no one could reasonably reject as public standards of behavior—as morally determinative. You might plausibly maintain that the unrejectable principles occasionally require us to perform morally impermissible acts, and fail to require us to perform morally obligatory ones.[32]

***

There is yet another question about promising practices, which is not particularly moral at all: it is neither about the Right nor about the Good. It is nevertheless an important question, at least for those who explain promises in terms of practices. I have in mind the

Question of Origins
(9) Why do we have the promising practices that we have?

This is not the Question of Good, applied to promising practices. The question is not about what is valuable about promising practices; it is about how we actually came to have the valuable promising practices that we do. It is, we might say, a kind of evolutionary question. Part of the question is biological, but part of it is social or *cultural*. At present it is hard not to take promising for granted, but it is possible to imagine promiseless communities.[33] Hume plausibly assumed that, at some point in history, creatures with our psychology had no promising practices; such practices had evolved gradually over many years. He was not obviously right about this, but neither was he obviously wrong.

This research program faces an obvious methodological obstacle. Since promising practices are ubiquitous and ancient, we actually have no detailed record of promiseless communities. It is therefore practically impossible to trace the historical origins of promising. There is, however, an alternative way of understanding the question of origins. What we are after is not the historical origins of promising practices. Rather, we want to identify features of promising practices that made them *more likely to survive in culture*. To do this, we do not have to have detailed records of promiseless communities. We can take an indirect approach. We identify central features of promising practices. We then show that their presence in *other* practices has made those other practices more likely to survive in culture. This could provide indirect evidence for the claim that the same features have played some causal role in the cultural transmission of promising practices. This indirect strategy is employed in Nichols (2004), for example.[34]

One obvious feature of promising practices is their capacity to promote interpersonal *cooperation* (whatever its purpose); promising is an all-purpose cooperation device. It is reasonable to believe that conduciveness to cooperation is at least one attractor—one feature that makes social practices more likely to transmit in culture. At present, however, there is no consensus among scientists about how cooperation figures in human psychology. Some maintain that, unlike our primate ancestors, humans are born with a special capacity for shared cooperative activity, including an intrinsic motivation to cooperate with others (regardless of extrinsic incentives, such as reward or punishment). See, for example, Tomasello (2009: pt. 1). If this is right, then we might be able to explain the attraction of promising practices at the level of the individual actor: promising is attractive to you and me, as individuals. But others are circumspect. See, for example, the responses in Tomasello (2009: pt. 2).

Perhaps the cultural-evolutionary explanation of promising practices should focus on *groups*. By promoting interpersonal cooperation, promising practices helped galvanize groups, which are more likely to persist than promiseless communities.

***

Everyone believes that promises and agreements are closely—perhaps conceptually—related, but

(10) What is the relation between promises and agreements?

On one view, promises are agreements of sorts. A promise proceeds by way of offer and acceptance. To say "I promise you to do X" is not really to promise to do X, but merely to make some kind of offer. (Perhaps the offer is to *promise* to do X. Perhaps the offer is simply to *do* X.) The promise is complete only when the promisee *accepts* the offer. One typically accepts the promise by saying things like okay, but sometimes one can accept by silence. Either way, acceptance involves some intentional communication of consent; mere belief about the promisor's act or intention is not enough. See, for example, Thomson (1990), Owens (2006), Watson (2009: 156–7), and Gilbert (chapter 3).

(The motivation for this view seems to be the belief that (i) promises give directed obligations (or rights), together with the belief that (ii) a promise can give no such obligation (or right) without the promisee's consent.)

Whether or not you endorse the acceptance requirement—and choose to think of promises as agreements of sorts (i.e. accepted offers)—you can certainly try to think about agreements as promises of sorts. The most general idea is that A's and B's agreement that A is to do X and B is to do Y can be understood in terms of two simultaneous promises: one by A to B; the other by B to A. On the simplest proposal, A promises B to do X, and B promises A to do Y. But of course, not just any simultaneous promises will do. To add up to an agreement, the promises must be exchanged or *interdepend* in some way. What way? Arguably, they must interdepend in such a way that would warrant the judgment that the parties promise each other as one or *jointly*. On one proposal, agreement promises are mutually conditional *in content*. A does not promise to do X, but to do X *if* B does Y (or if B promises to do Y), for example. Another possibility is that the constitutive promises of an agreement interdepend in some *causal and/or motivational* way. Very roughly, each party promises *because* the other does. If some such account can be made to work, it can be claimed that an agreement is a promise of sorts, namely a *joint* promise.[35] I entertain this possibility in chapter 16; see also Bach (1995).

The idea that an agreement can be understood in terms of promises is controversial. Margaret Gilbert has argued that the obligations of two promises cannot possibility interdepend in the way the obligations of an agreement do. She claims that agreements are better understood as *joint decisions*. See Gilbert (1996: ch. 13, 2006: ch. 10, and chapter 3 of this book). Notice that the joint promise and joint decision accounts share the premise that agreements are instances of *joint intentional action* (and commitment). They bring shared agency theory to bear on the study of promises and agreements.

Another alternative to the notion that agreements consist of interdependent promises understands them as accepted offers. See Black (2007). Offers to do what, exactly? We probably do not want to explain agreements in terms of offers to enter into an agreement; this would simply presuppose an understanding of agreements. Perhaps the offer in question is not an offer *to*, but rather an offer *that*. Specifically, we can understand an agreement that (A is to do X and B is to do Y) as an offer that (A is to do X and B is to do Y), plus an acceptance. On the face of it, however, the notion of such a composite offer is no simpler than the notion of the agreement it seeks to explain. After all, it is precisely the essentially conjunctive nature of agreements that calls for an explanation.[36]

***

I close my list with two questions from the philosophy of law.

(11) What is the relation between contracts and promises?

I have just mentioned the view that agreements are joint promises. For the most part, contracts are legally binding agreements. On this view, then, contracts are legally binding joint promises. What distinguishes contractual from noncontractual agreements (or their constitutive promises) is the legal obligation to keep the former. Here, then, is a way of interpreting Charles Fried's "contract as promise" slogan (1981, 2007):

Contract as (Joint) Promise
A contract is a joint legally binding promise, namely interdependent legally binding promises.

The notion that contracts are promises of sorts seems to comport with law's self-understanding. The American Law Institute, for example, defines contracts as legally enforceable promises (Restatement (Second) of Contracts, sec. 1, 1981). But despite its initial plausibility, Contract as Promise has turned out to be controversial—or apparently controversial—in several different ways. ("Apparently" is important here; as we shall see, some claims that appear to deny the promissory nature of contracts in fact presuppose it.) Here I will confine myself to three bones of contention.

It has been claimed that promissory obligations are self-imposed or *voluntary*, but that contractual obligations are not really voluntary; they are superimposed by the legal system regardless of the will of the parties, or by one party regardless of the will of the other. See, for example, the literature on the so-called *death of contract* and the assimilation of contractual liability into tort liability, emanating from Gilmore (1974) and Atiyah (1981: ch. 7; 1990: ch. 2). See also the literature on so-called *contracts of adhesion*, emanating from Kessler (1943).[37]

A more subtle view relies on the central case method mentioned in my remarks on question (1). It treats contractual promises as genuine, successful promises, but insists that they are rather defective, nonparadigmatic, or otherwise *imperfect* promises; they fall outside the central case. Using a conveniently vague distinction (Macneil, 2001), perhaps we should say that promises are paradigmatically *relational*, implying that paradigmatic promises are embedded in some particularly close, personal, and ongoing context, but that contracts are paradigmatically *non*relational or *transactional*, implying that paradigmatic contracts are embedded in some particularly remote, impersonal, and discrete context. In this interesting story, perfectly good contracts turn out to be rather defective or at any rate *imperfect* promises. This idea is suggested by some remarks in Raz (1982), and developed in some detail in Kimel (2003, 2007). See also Bagchi (2007).[38]

Let me now turn to a recent controversy concerning the relation between contracts and promises. Seana Shiffrin has provided the organizing slogan: "the divergence of contract and promise." She holds that "contract and promise diverge in some significant ways" (2006: 720). Others have responded in kind, by insisting on "the convergence of contract and promise" (Fried, 2007) and "the correspondence of contract and promise" (Kraus, 2009). Shiffrin's claim is that contract and promise diverge too much, and that we should do something to decrease the divergence–and increase the convergence–of contract and promise. We can do so, she suggests, by enforcing contracts more vigorously than we actually do. Now Shiffrin's substantive normative-ethical claim here–that the law should enforce contracts more vigorously than it currently does (at least in America)–is controversial.[39] Here I will simply assume that Shiffrin's normative-ethical claim is correct, and meditate instead on the influential *image* of divergence/convergence she uses to make it.

The image of divergence or convergence suggests two independent spheres: the sphere of promise and the sphere of contract. (We can think of them as sets of promises or contracts, or as sets of promissory or contractual *norms*, namely norms governing promises or contracts.) At any given time, these two spheres completely converge, partly converge, or completely diverge as shown in Figure 1.1.

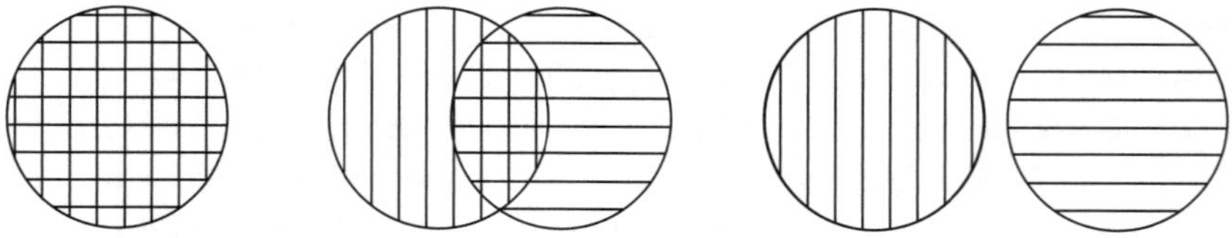

Figure 1.1 Convergence and Divergence

Focus on the middle image. By pulling the spheres of contract and promise away from each other, or pushing them closer together–and without changing the size of either sphere–we can increase or decrease the divergence of contracts and promises, making it the case that less or more contracts and promises converge. Suppose we thought that there is "too much divergence" between contracts (or contractual norms) and promises (or promissory norms). And suppose that, by changing the law–perhaps with a view to make the enforcement of contracts more vigorous–we could somehow push the sphere of contract closer to the sphere of promise. That would conveniently *decrease* the undesirable divergence of contract and promise.

This image of the relation between contracts and promises seems to fly in the face of Contract as Promise. For on *that* picture, contractual promises (or contractual norms) are a *subclass* of promises (or promissory norms). The sphere of contracts is *locked* inside the sphere of promises, as it were; wherever promises go, they take contracts with them. And contracts cannot extend beyond the sphere of promise. You just can't pull these spheres away from each other. Contact as Promise is illustrated in Figure 1.2.

Figure 1.2 Contract as Promise

Now of course, as the diagram clearly shows, we can still increase or decrease the divergence of promises and contracts by changing the relative *size* of the spheres. In particular, by changing the law of contracts, we can *contractualize* some noncontractual promises, thereby decreasing the divergence. At the limit, we can contractualize *all* promises, eradicating the divergence completely. (Alternatively, we can *decontractualize* some contractual promises, increasing the divergence. At the limit, we can decontractualize *all* promises, abolishing the law of contracts altogether.) The move from a contractless society (the leftmost shape) to a society in which all promises are contractual is illustrated in Figure 1.3.

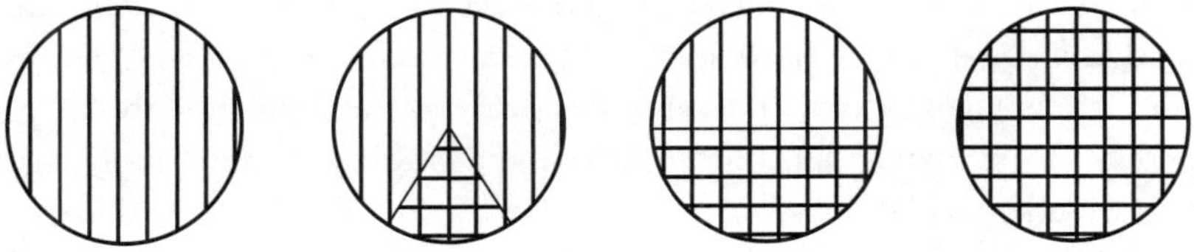

Figure 1.3 Contractualization

The crucial point is that contracts (or contractual norms) retain their promissory nature at all times. Again, a given act, or norm, cannot lose its promissory nature without losing its contractual nature.

Now Contract as Promise does not suggest that all contracts are perfectly good (full-blooded, paradigmatic, promissory) promises. Just as some noncontractual promises fall outside the central case of promises, so do some contractual promises. Recall, for example, the view that insincere promises are genuine yet not very good promises. An exactly similar claim can be made of contracts. As every student of contracts knows, insincere contracts can be perfectly valid, provided only that they are reasonably understood to be sincere. (Thanks to the famous objective test of contracts.)[40] But as the reference to sincerity in the objective test hints, insincere contracts presuppose sincere ones. And it is plausible to maintain that the former are parasitic on the latter. Contracts par excellence do not simply appear to be sincere; they also *are* sincere. If the doughnut hole represents the central case of promises (perfect promises), and the doughnut represents more or less imperfect promises, then the relation between contracts and promises is illustrated in Figure 1.4.

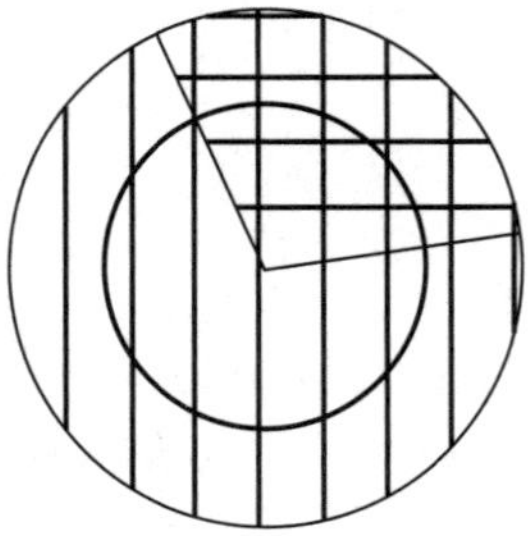

Figure 1.4 Contract as Promise

So there is an apparent tension between Contract as Promise and Shiffrin's image of the divergence of contract and promise and suggestion that we can decrease the divergence by enforcing contracts more vigorously. For all that, Shiffrin's substantive normative-ethical claim is perfectly compatible with Contract as Promise. If we *have* to put it in terms of divergence at all, we could say that there is too much divergence between contract law as we know it and as *it* should be. In particular, our actual contract law does not enforce contracts as vigorously as our morally ideal contract law. But this is just another way of saying that contract law should enforce contracts more vigorously than it actually does.[41]

Shiffrin claims that contract law does not enforce contracts vigorously enough. It is worth looking at the specific features of contract law that Shiffrin highlights (2006: pt. 2), and ask whether they can ground an argument for the divergence of contract and promise. Let me mention three examples:

(a) For the most part, the law does not offer the remedy of *punitive* damages for breach of contract; the standard remedy for breach is compensation.
(b) For the most part, the law does not offer the remedy of *specific performance* (injunction to *do* what the contract requires); the standard remedy for breach is *monetary* compensation.
(c) The law limits the amount of compensation for breach of contract in various ways. As a result, compensation fails to put the innocent

party in as good a position as the one in which she would be apart from the breach.

We can now imagine the following line of argument:

(1) There is an obligation to keep promises.
(2) Since the law includes doctrines such as (a), (b), and (c), there is no obligation to keep contracts, only to keep them or pay.
(3) Therefore, there is an obligation to keep promises, but no obligation to keep contracts.
(4) Therefore, contract diverges from promise: contracts are not a subclass of promises (individual and/or joint).

My imaginary argument equivocates on whether the obligation in question is moral or legal, so let us suppose, first, that the obligation in question is *legal*. In that case, premise (1) is trivially false (many promises are *not* legally binding). While this is sufficient to impugn the argument (under the first interpretation), it is still worth evaluating the more plausible and familiar premise (2). *Does the fact that the law does not enforce contracts nearly as vigorously as it can—as illustrated by facts (a), (b), and (c)—tend to show that there is no legal obligation to keep contracts, only not to break them without compensation?*

First, does the fact that the legal response to breach of contract is not *punitive* show that there is no legal obligation to keep contracts? Compare the law of torts. Here too the standard legal response to wrongdoing (a tort) is compensation. If I harm you through my negligence, and my act constitutes a tort, but not a criminal offense, then typically the law will not punish me. Does this tend to show that I had no legal obligation to refrain from harming you? Does the nonpunitive nature of the remedy tend to show that the law is indifferent between (i) one's not harming others and (ii) one's harming others and then compensating them after the fact? Is my legal obligation not to harm others through my negligent harm, or simply not to do so without compensation?

Second, let us acquiesce in the familiar Realist assumption that the unavailability of specific performance and/or punitive damages just means that the law never requires parties to perform the very action their contract specifies, only to perform that action or pay its value. Does this prove the claim that there is no obligation to keep contracts? Not necessarily. For why should we not take this assumption to prove, alternatively, that all contracts are *option* contracts to perform the acts they specify or pay their value? If so, there would still be a legal obligation to keep contracts, which one could discharge in two ways (i.e. by performing the acts they specify or paying their value).

Third, does the fact that the law does not enforce contracts as vigorously as it can—and, at the limit, not enforce them at all—show that it does not require the parties to perform the acts their contracts specify? It is easy to imagine a super-cooperative society, in which the sheer fact that contractors depend on each other for future cooperation, together with law's provision of *some* compensation for breach, is enough to make most contractors keep most of their contracts most of the time. Suppose the remedy for breach of contract in such a society were compensation in the symbolic amount of $1. Would this necessarily mean that there is no legal obligation to keep contracts?

Suppose now that the obligation in my imaginary argument is *moral.* Then premise (2) becomes implausible. Surely, the fact that the law fails to enforce contracts as vigorously as it can hardly means that there is no moral obligation to keep them.

Perhaps we should reconstruct (2) as a claim about law's moral message:

> (2′) Given the doctrines described in (a), (b), and/or (c), the law expresses the judgment (or sends the message) that there is no moral obligation to keep contracts, only to keep them or pay some compensation.[42]

Now this clearly presupposes the claim mentioned before, namely that the doctrines described in (a), (b), and (c) make it the case that there is no *legal* obligation to keep contracts, so let us simply grant this claim, for argument's sake. And (2') also seems to presuppose that, when the law fails to impose a legal obligation to keep contracts, it sends the message that there is no moral obligation to do so, either. So let us simply grant this claim too. Even so, substituting (2') for (2) requires us to reconstruct the rest of the argument as follows:

> (3′) Therefore, there is a moral obligation to keep promises, but the law expresses the message that there is no moral obligation to keep contracts.
> (4′) Therefore, the judgment the law expresses about our moral obligation to keep contracts can diverge from the truth about our moral obligation to keep promises. (And, if contracts are promises, from the truth about our moral obligation to keep contracts.)

But these conclusions clearly fail to discharge the notion that contracts diverge from promises; they are perfectly compatible with Contract as Promise.[43] Nevertheless (2') is an interesting claim in its own right: What moral judgment, if any, does the law express by the doctrines described in (a), (b), and (c)? And this raises a more general question: In what sense can the law be said to express judgments? And how do we ascertain what judgments the law expresses?[44]

***

The final question is also the most traditional question in this area. It is really a special case of question (8):

> (12) What rules or principles of contracting should we accept through our legal system?

We have already noted one of the questions that arise under (12): How, and how vigorously, should the law enforce contracts? Should the standard remedies for breach include punitive damages or specific performance? And what should be the *measure* of compensation? Should compensation aim at bringing the innocent party to the position in which he would be if the contract were performed (so-called *expectation* damages), or rather to the position in which he would be if the contract were not entered into in the first place (so-called *reliance* damages)?

Another traditional question concerns the kind of promises or agreements the law should or should not recognize and enforce. What promises or agreements should the law *contractualize* (or decontractualize)? For example, should the law contractualize so-called gratuitous or unbargained-for promises—promises that are not supported by consideration? (Should the Anglo-American doctrine of consideration be abolished?) And to what extent should the law contractualize contracts governing some highly *personal* relation such as marriage or cohabitation? And what about the contractualization—and commoditization—of organ sales, surrogacy, or adoption?

So like question (8), (12) is typically a question about *particular* rules of particular social practices (here: legal systems). And there is little that can be said about this question in general, except that it is a substantive, normative-ethical question, and will obviously depend on one's favorite moral theory, and the particular rule(s) in question. It is worth emphasizing that, like question (8), (12) is not a question about the morality of individual actions (e.g. making, keeping, or breaking contracts). It is a question about collective actions, about what rules we, as a society, have reason to accept as public standards for the regulation of behavior. Of course, in this case the public rules are legally binding, and this can make a big difference.

III. COLLECTION OVERVIEW

My twelve questions illustrate the kind of questions facing nondebunking theories of promises, and some of the central themes in the philosophical literature on promises and agreements. There are many other—and just as interesting—questions I have left out. Some of these questions are taken up in the essays that follow. Here is a brief overview.

Chapter 2: The Problem with Promising (David Owens)

Earlier I mentioned David Owens's claim that promising is valuable in virtue of serving our authority interest.[45] In chapter 2, he discusses the problem of explaining *bare wrongs*, defined as wrongs that affect no intelligible human interest (including welfare, fairness, and desert). As Hume recognized, the wrong of breaking a promise appears to be a bare wrong. This comes out in Hume's story about his promise to repay a debt. For one thing, the lender is an unsympathetic character (a "profligate debauchee," among other things), who neither needs nor deserves the money (and would misuse it). For another, Hume urgently needs the money for his own family. In short, no one stands to gain anything valuable from the repayment (Hume, 2006: 83–85). The problem is to explain why we take bare wrongs seriously as guides to action—why we treat them as genuine wrongs in the first place. According to Owens, Hume and some other practice theorists (e.g. Rawls) seek to solve the problem by denying that the wrong involved in promise-breaking is ever genuinely *bare*. While it does not harm anyone directly, it harms most everyone indirectly, by harming valuable *practices*. The human interest implicated is our interest in social *coordination*. Owens convincingly rejects this claim. It is just not true that promise-breaking always undermines the practice under which the promise is made. But Owens goes further to reject the more general *social coordination hypothesis*, the view that the function of promising is to enable us to coordinate our activities with other human beings, and that that is why it makes sense to make, accept, and keep promises. He offers two arguments against this thesis. First, we could have social coordination without a *practice* of promising. In principle, we could have an innate disposition to rely on promises, in which case we could make and keep promises without a practice (custom, habit) of making and keeping promises. And yet it seems that we do need such a practice. Second, we could have social coordination without a practice of *promising*. Hume thought that a practice of promising is *necessary* for coordination between strangers. But Owens claims that such cooperation could also be achieved thanks to the motive of *gratitude*, for example (Owens tells a story in which Hume's famous farmers reach the same crop-exchanging arrangement without promising each other).[46]

I find the social-coordination hypothesis plausible (although I'd frame it in terms of cooperation),[47] and Owens's objections inconclusive. Start with the second objection. Granted: promising is not the only way in which we reach interpersonal cooperation (and let us also grant, for argument's sake, that this is incompatible with Hume's claim that promising is "necessary"). How does this impugn the social coordination hypothesis? The thesis claims that we value promising for being an excellent coordination device; why does it have to be our *only* coordination device? (Compare: In cities with good public transportation, cars are unnecessary. But this does not impugn the claim that we value cars for the contribution they make to transportation. When we value cars, we value them as transportation devices.) What about Owens's first objection? Again, the social coordination hypothesis itself is agnostic on whether promises require practices; it is compatible with the claim that they don't. If it were true that we have an innate disposition to make and keep promises, then perhaps we *would* be able to achieve coordination by promising without promising practices. That would not impugn the notion that we value promising for its contribution to social coordination.[48] Now a proponent of the social coordination thesis does not *have* to accept that social coordination can be achieved in this way; he can insist that we *cannot* promise other than under some promising practice. That additional claim would require some argument. As Owens points out, the additional claim is hostage to empirical assumptions about human nature. In particular, it depends on the assumption that, given human nature—including the innate dispositions we have or do not have—promising could *not* function very well in the absence of promising practices. The general Humean idea is that promising practices are needed to mitigate our motivational limitations (which he generously summed up under "confined generosity"). That this is a partly empirical claim that might turn out to be false would probably strike Hume as one of its virtues.[49]

Chapter 3: Three Dogmas about Promising (Margaret Gilbert)

Earlier I mentioned Margaret Gilbert's joint decision account of agreements. In chapter 3, she describes and explains this account. She then extends it to promises, offering the

> *joint decision account* of promises: for one person to make a promise to another is for them jointly to commit themselves, by an appropriate, explicit process, to the decision that one of them ("the promisor") is to perform one or more specified actions. (p. 99)

For Gilbert, every joint action is a *joint commitment*, and every joint commitment comes with mutual obligations: "To every joint commitment corresponds a set of obligations. These are directed obligations with correlative rights. The parties are obligated to each other to conform to the commitment. In other terms, they owe each other their conformity." (p. 94) It follows that promises—joint decisions—generate obligations of joint commitment. "As long as the pertinent joint commitment has been created, and not rescinded, the promisor has an obligation of joint commitment to act as promised." (p. 100)

Gilbert's account is said to avoid the three dogmas in the essay's title, namely the assumptions that promissory obligations (i) morally require the promisor to do as promised, and derive from general moral principles; (ii) cannot simply be willed into being; and (iii) do not arise when the promised act is morally prohibited. Under the joint decision account, by contrast, promissory obligations (i) are not moral requirements to do as promised, and do not derive from any general moral principle; (ii) *are* willed directly into existence; and (iii) arise even when the promised act is morally prohibited.

I will raise two *structural* questions. First, Gilbert believes that every joint action is a joint commitment that gives mutual obligations. But joint commitment and obligations to do *what*, exactly? The most natural answer is: the joint commitment is to perform the joint action, and the obligations are to do one's part in *its* performance. Thus in the case of a joint walk, the walkers are jointly committed to walk, and each is obligated to do her part in the walking. It follows that, in the case of a joint decision, the joint commitment is to *decide*, and the obligation each party has is to do her part in the *deciding*. If an agreement or a promise is a joint decision, then it obligates each party to do her part in *deciding* to do as agreed upon or promised. But Gilbert claims that an agreement/promise obligates each party/the promisor to *do* what the agreement/promise requires her to do. There appears to be a mismatch between the content of the obligations generated by the joint decision on the one hand and the obligations generated by the agreement/promise it seeks to explain on the other.

My second structural comment grants Gilbert's joint decision account of agreements, but questions its extension to *promises*. A joint decision, like every joint commitment, is *symmetric*; it creates mutual obligations. Likewise, an agreement is symmetric: it creates mutual obligations. Specifically, each side is committed/obligated to the other to keep its part of the deal. It therefore makes good sense to describe their commitments/obligations as a joint commitment/obligation. Not so in the case of a single promise, which commits or obligates the promisor asymmetrically to the promisee, but not the other way around. The symmetric structure of agreements, which made the application of a joint decision or commitment account natural, appears to break down in the case of individual promises.

Chapter 4: Is Promising a Practice and Nothing More? (Stan Husi)

Several philosophers argue that the normative force of promises depends (in part) on promising practices. In chapter 4, Stan Husi argues for the stronger, *exhaustive practice* view: the normative force of promises (or "authority of promissory norms") rests *entirely* in promising practices. Promising practices themselves have no "practice-external authority." "Promising," as Husi puts it, "is a practice and nothing more, normatively speaking." (p. 110) Husi acknowledges that his view offers a revisionary interpretation of promising practices, but assures us that accepting it need not weaken our promissory commitments in any way. I personally find the claim that the normative force of individual promises is essentially practice-based—in the sense of depending on the existence of preexisting promising practices—eminently plausible. I also happen to share Husi's doubts about the notion that promises are essentially moral commitments. And yet I cannot see how appeal to practices can be the whole normative story. What I cannot see is how we can explain promissory commitments without appeal to the *intention* of the promisor. Promising, it seems to me, is not just a practice; it is the intentional invocation of practice. Husi might well be right that intention alone cannot do the trick. But it would be extremely surprising if we could explain the normative force of promises without appeal to intention.

Chapter 5: The Importance of Self-Promises (Connie Rosati)

Many philosophers think of promises as essentially relational or second-personal communicative acts, involving two persons. On this view, self-promises (e.g. my promise to myself to lose some weight by the holidays) are not really promises at all. Perhaps they are vows, or just ordinary decisions. Alternatively, they are promises, but rather imperfect ones, explicable by extension from relational or second-personal promises. In chapter 5, Connie Rosati turns the table on this view: "self-promising is, in a certain respect, normatively and practically basic." (p. 145) Rosati presents a preliminary, autonomy-based account of the function and importance of self-promises. On this account, self-promises are important to the extent that they serve our interest in autonomy, namely in having effective authority over ourselves. Her account is meant to have implications for the normative character of promises to others, and so for our efforts to arrive at a unified theory of promising.

Rosati acknowledges that any account that puts self-promises in its center needs to address two problems. First, how are such promises *possible*? After all, if you could promise yourself to lose weight by the holidays, you could always release yourself from that promise before the holidays! But if so, then in what sense did your promise bind you in the first place? And if it didn't, then how could it be a *promise*? The second problem, which she considers to be more serious, is to explain the *point* of promising yourself. You can always just *decide* to lose weight by the holidays. Why would you also want to promise yourself to do so? She explains why she thinks both problems can be handled.

Rosati's proposed account builds on Owens's authority interest theory, but she also departs from it in several ways. Most important, she rejects Owens's claim that our relevant interest is in having authority, or right, over what others shall do, that we care about securing this right just for its own sake. She thinks we have an interest "in real control—in *effective* authority." Rosati:

> But if this is correct, if our authority interest with regard to others is an interest in real control, then our authority interest, at its roots, is also not an interest in having a bare right that it be we, rather than others, who decide what we shall do; it is an interest, rather, in being *effective authorities over ourselves*. (p. 140)

Our key interest on this view is not in authority over others, but in control over *ourselves*—in other words, in our own *autonomy*.[50] It is this interest in autonomy that explains why we care about securing authority over other people's actions in the promise-to-other case. But it also explains why we care about securing authority over our own actions in the promise-to-self case. She writes:

> The authority interest theory has appeal, at least as I see it, because it taps into a deep truth about the connection between promising and agency, namely, that promising exists and has the normative significance it does because it serves to enlarge and enhance our autonomy. And this it can do, I want to suggest, not only through others making and keeping promises to us but also through our making and keeping promises to ourselves. (p. 140)

Chapter 6: On Coerced Promises (Eric Chwang)

Another supposedly "special case" is taken up by Eric Chwang in chapter 6. He argues that it is, in fact, irrational to rely on coerced promises. It is easy to see why I would want to coerce you to draw cash for me from this ATM at gunpoint right now; it is much harder to see why I would want to coerce you to *promise* me to do this later. Why would you perform these actions when my gun and I are no longer around? On the face of it, then, relying on a promise that was coerced is irrational in a way that relying on a coerced action or on an uncoerced promise is not. Chwang explains these twin facts by claiming, first, that coerced promises carry no *moral* force: they do not give the promisor reasons she does not already have for doing as promised, and second, that coerced promises carry no *predictive* force, either: they do not communicate reliable intentions to do as promised.

Chapter 7: Promising Too Much (Julia Driver)

In chapter 7, Julia Driver examines yet another "special case" of promising, namely the case of promises that are in some sense or another incompatible. You can make (or at least try to make) a promise that you cannot keep, even regardless of other promises you give. To take an extreme case, you can promise to be in two places at the same time. Or you can promise to meet someone, knowing full well that your only means of transportation is out of order. Or you can promise to meet someone, and shortly thereafter discover that your only means of transportation is out of order. Alternatively, you can make a promise that you can certainly keep, but not if you are to keep some *other* promise of yours. In both cases, you have promised more than you can keep; at least one promise would have to be broken. Driver discusses the implications of overpromising for the notion that "ought" implies "can." The problem arises if we assume that the promisor has an obligation to do as promised, and that obligation implies "ought." Thus if you promised to do X, you have an obligation to do X (and so you ought to do X). But if you cannot do X, then it is not the case that you ought to do X. It seems that we must either reject the claim that (i) you promised, or the claim that (ii) your promise obligates you to do X, or the principle that (iii) "ought" implies "can." And yet each of these claims seems plausible.[51]

Driver wants to preserve the claim that promising entails obligation, and she does not believe that this claim is compatible with the principle that "ought" implies "can." However, she thinks that we can do justice to the kernel of truth in this principle if we only acknowledge that promissory obligations are merely *pro tanto* obligations. If what I promise to do is, or becomes, impossible for me to do, I still have an obligation to do it, but this obligation is overridden by the impossibility. And so it is not what I ought to do, all things considered:

> The upshot of this view is that, in a way, one can have one's cake and eat it too. One has a pro tanto obligation to keep even impossible promises, though the obligation is overridden.... When we make the claim that promises entail obligations we are committed to two things: one, that when S promises A to *x*, S has taken on a pro tanto obligation to *x* that can be overridden for practical purposes by an inability, but the inability does not eliminate the obligation; so, when S promises A to *x*, S is obligated to *x* to A, even when there are good reasons not to *x*; and "ought" does not imply "can," because the "ought" exists even when the agent can't. Promises, even ones one cannot perform, carry with them a commitment. (p. 196)

Let me raise two quick questions. First, why think that the principle that "ought" implies "can" creates any problem at all in cases of *incompatible* promises? After all, the promisor here *can* keep each of his promises; he just can't keep them together. Second, if all-things-considered obligation implies "can," why doesn't pro tanto obligation imply "can"? Presumably (as we have seen in the discussion of the Questions of Right), a violation of a pro tanto obligation is still (pro tanto) wrongful, and perhaps even blameworthy. Why shouldn't the inability to perform an action be enough to remove the warrant to regard it as wrongful and blame the agent for it altogether?

Chapters 8–10 examine promissory obligations from a largely consequentialist perspective.

Chapter 8: The Value of Making and Keeping Promises (Michael Smith)

In chapter 8, Michael Smith tries to show how we can, in fact, have it both ways. We can have a consequentialist theory of promissory obligations–and not just any consequentialist theory; a full-fledged global or *act-consequentialist* one–and still explain the common view that we have an obligation to keep a promise regardless of whether so doing maximizes value *in the traditional sense of the expression* (in Smith's terms, this is the idea of maximizing neutral value)–or why it is "a distinctive feature of an agent's promissory obligations that they are targeted on the promises that he himself makes." (p. 210) If successful, this would combine the best of consequentialism and deontology. The argument focuses on the theory of value to be maximized, and has two important components. One is fairly common: we should be prepared to countenance values other than *welfare*. The bigger and bolder step is to claim that all values are *relative*. In principle, we can take any nonconsequentialist theory of promissory obligation, and explain it in terms of relative value for the agent.

For example, take Scanlon's plausible view that I have an obligation to keep my promise to you to do X because I intentionally lead you to expect me to do so. The best argument for this view, according to Smith, is to suppose that, given that it was *me* who created this expectation, meeting it has *nonwelfarist relative value for me*. And this gives me (and no one else) a normative reason to do what's promised. What Smith's argument suggests is that the very best arguments for nonconsequentialism will all turn out, on closer inspection, to be arguments for consequentialism, albeit versions of consequentialism that are grounded in relative values, which have hitherto escaped our attention.

Smith seems to me to demonstrate the *coherence* of his nonstandard consequentialist position: there is nothing conceptually fishy here. But as I see things, his account of promissory obligations faces two challenges, corresponding to its two major aspects. First, the deontological or *nonconsequentialist* theories whose reconstruction Smith recommends claim that promising typically gives us nonwelfarist *obligations* to do as promised. Showing that keeping a promise promotes *some* nonwelfarist relative value does not yet show that doing so *maximizes* relative value. Smith would not wish to deny that promise-keeping can promote or demote *other* relative values, including welfarist ones. Arguably, for example, both your welfare and mine have relative value for you (the promisor). Thus if keeping your promise harms you more than its breaking harms me, this might well give you a normative reason to *break* the promise. In the end, determining whether your promise-keeping maximizes relative value requires the same case-by-case balancing act that nonconsequentialists wish to rule out.

The second and deeper worry comes from the other, *consequentialist* direction. Smith claims that the plausible "core of consequentialism" is agnostic on whether value is neutral or relative. But part of the traditional attraction of consequentialism seems to me to lie precisely in the notion that value is neutral. Thus we must look at how your promise-keeping or promise-breaking affects everyone, yourself included. But in itself, the sheer fact that it is *you* who is performing the act is neither here nor there.[52]

Chapter 9: Act-utilitarianism and Promissory Obligation (Alastair Norcross)

Alastair Norcross defends the more traditional version of act-consequentialism in chapter 9. Traditional deontologists and rule-consequentialists claim that there is a prohibition on promise-breaking regardless of its consequences (at least within limits)—that there is a deontological constraint against promise-breaking. (In this sense, rule-consequentialism is a form of deontology.) Act-consequentialists deny this. There is no such thing as an obligation to keep promises as such, regardless of its consequences. Promising is an area where act-consequentialism seems to face particularly serious problems (the kind of problems that motivate Smith's move to relative value consequentialism). First, it is claimed that act-consequentialists cannot account for the self-evident fact that you should keep your promise even if this does not maximize (neutral) value. And second, it has been claimed that act-consequentialism is somehow *self-defeating*: it is not even clear that the institution of promising could exist in an act-utilitarian society. Norcross argues that act-consequentialism—indeed, act-utilitarianism—has the resources to explain the moral status of promissory behavior.

Chapter 10: Promises and Rule-Consequentialism (Brad Hooker)

It is the perceived problems with act-consequentialism that moved Rawls and others in the direction of rule-consequentialism.[53] In chapter 10, Brad Hooker presents a rule-consequentialist account of the moral obligation to keep promises. According to this account

> An act is wrong if it is forbidden by the code of rules whose internalization by the overwhelming majority of everyone everywhere in each new generation has maximum expected value in terms of well-being with some priority for the worst off. The calculation of a code's expected value includes all costs of getting the code internalized. If in terms of expected value two or more codes are better than the rest but equal to one another, the one closest to conventional morality determines what acts are wrong. (pp. 245–46)

Hooker identifies what he refers to as six "deontological aspects of promissory obligations":

> [P]romissory obligations (1) are not contingent on benefits to the promisee or others, (2) are self-imposed (autonomy), (3) are backward-looking in the sense that they depend on events in the past, (4) are agent-relative, (5) confer rights on particular others, and (6) give only some others (the promisees) the status of being wronged if the promise isn't kept. (p. 249)

Hooker's version of rule-consequentialism seeks to accommodate all six deontological features. His account of promissory obligations resembles Smith's in two respects. First, it is explicitly *nonwelfarist*: you can have an obligation to keep a promise even if this does not *benefit* people. (Like Rosati, he thinks the most relevant value at play is *autonomy*.) Second, promissory obligations are *agent-relative*. "*You* do not have a duty to keep *my* promises... And I have no duty to keep your promises." (p. 243). Hooker explains how these features fit within a rule-consequentialism framework.

As noted earlier, there is a sense in which rule-consequentialism is a practice theory of obligation; it tells us to perform those acts that conform to the rules whose general acceptance (or internalization) in practice would promote the good. Arguably, it is this aspect of rule-consequentialism that threatens to open it up to the famous rule worship objection.

Chapters 11–13 depart from the consequentialist framework. They discuss the relation between promising and the *personal*.

Chapter 11: Demystifying Promises (Stephen Darwall)

Stephen Darwall rejects *all* consequentialist accounts of promissory obligation, including rule-consequentialism. In chapter 11, he seeks to explain how one can place oneself under an obligation by expressing one's will to do so (this is one way of formulating what I earlier called the Problem of Promising). And he seeks to explain the sense in which the obligation created is *directed*—an obligation *to* the promisee. (Darwall claims that all consequentialist accounts fail to explain this directed, or relational, nature of promissory obligations; but note that Smith and Hooker at least *try* to explain it.) Darwall seeks to demystify promises by explaining them from the *second-personal* standpoint, a notion he develops in detail in a book (Darwall, 2006). Promising is a special case of a general (but still quite special) phenomenon of second-personal interactions, which also include consent, agreement, invitation, and request. In all these cases, the parties acquire new obligations to, and rights against, one another through interactions that presuppose their mutual accountability and their sharing a common basic second-personal authority.

Darwall's second-personal account of obligation raises several interesting questions. Here are two. First, what is the role of *practice* in this account? Darwall says the participants in the relevant interaction must *share* the second-personal authority. What does the sharing consist of? In particular, do we have to share this authority by virtue of accepting, or participating in, the same *practice*? In the case of promising, does the second-personal account presuppose a practice of promising whose rules authorize us to make promises and require us to keep them? (See Husi's distinction between practice-internal and practice-external normative authority.)

Second, just how *personal* is the second-personal account? Darwall's understanding of second-personal accountability is broadly Strawsonian. Your obligation to me to do X is understood in terms of the claim that your failure to do X wrongs me, which, in turn, is understood in terms of "personal reactive attitudes." Your failure to do X wrongs me if and only if I am entitled to blame you morally and personally for that failure. I am wary of both aspects of this characterization. First, the picture assumes that promising is a particularly *personal* affair, in which we must take the so-called participant stance toward one another. But can we not also make and receive perfectly good promises while taking the *objective* attitude? Does the reason-giving function of promising *depend* on getting personal? Second, is it not possible to make and receive promises without *moralizing*?

Chapters 12 and 13 bear directly on these questions, although in different ways.

Chapter 12: Promises and Trust (Daniel Friedrich and Nicholas Southwood)

There is no doubt an important connection between promises and trust, but what is the best way to characterize the relation? And what *kind* of trust is at play in promising? In chapter 12, Nicholas Southwood and Daniel Friedrich develop a view of promising that is as personal as Darwall's. According to the trust view Southwood and Friedrich offer, when A promises B to do X, A invites B to trust A to do X. When B accepts the invitation, A incurs an obligation to B not to betray that trust. Inviting B to trust A to do X involves signaling to B A's recognition of the importance that doing X has for B, and A's willingness to license B to have faith or optimism in A's character with regard to doing X. Notice that, on this view, the promisee trusts the promisor *at will*. But how is this possible? Even if the trusting agent's trust does not consist of his belief that the trusted agent will do as trusted, surely at least some belief of this sort must be present? See Hieronymi (2008). But belief is not a voluntary matter, and it surely depends on *evidence*. The worry is that, if I trust you simply by accepting your invitation, I am jumping to a conclusion in which I am not warranted. What could play the role of evidence in this trusting exercise?

My second question is exactly similar to the one raised earlier with respect to Darwall. For Southwood and Friedrich, the trust at play in promising is highly personal; it involves faith or optimism in the promisor's *character*. But is this really needed for promising? Think about Hume's farmers, who exchange mutually beneficial promises. Apparently, they have no special reason for optimism in each other's character, and yet they can trust each other to cooperate on the basis of largely self-interested considerations.

Chapter 13: Promise as an Arm's-length Relation (Daniel Markovits)

In chapter 13, Daniel Markovits seeks to depersonalize promises without demoralizing them. He rejects the view that promises are paradigmatically embedded in intimate relationships, which are animated by distinctly personal attitudes of trust and respect. (He associates this view with Shiffrin [2008]; another example can be found in Kimel [2003: ch. 1].) More to the point, Markovits also rejects the more modest, pluralist view in which perfectly good promises can be embedded in all manner of interpersonal relations, including intimate ones. (This is the view I favor.) Instead, he contends that "the immanent structure of the promise relation is in itself distancing, which is to say *opposed to intimacy*." (p. 295) On this view, promises are "arm's-length relations," where these are contrasted with intimate or love relations: "Although promising and love are both forms of recognition and respect, they are,...in important respects, opposed." (p. 303) The recognition of intimacy involves seeing the other as the particular person she is, in all her idiosyncratic glory; promising, on the other hand, requires seeing the other as a person, abstracting from the particular person she is:

> *the promise in itself is not a case of seeing the promisee...with the vividness that love requires.* Once true love has been achieved, promises between lovers wither away; and making new promises introduces a distance, a form of alienation even, into the love relation. Indeed, the genetic structure of promissory recognition is impersonal and in this sense *opposed* to intimacy. Promises prototypically do not promote intimacy, but rather an arm's-length relation. (p. 303)

Markovits concludes that "promise's highest form will be achieved not in personal promises—which are embedded in intimate relations whose own immanent structure...competes with promissory appreciation—but in promises among strangers, that is, among parties whose engagement arises entirely at arm's length." (pp. 313–14) In the central case, then, promises are embedded in the context of some relation that is animated by a distinctly impersonal

Kantian moral attitude of respect for person(hood), or recognition of humanity, which attitude is incompatible with genuine intimacy.

Markovits also claims that contractual promises are animated by the same kind of attitude, and so contractual promises can be perfectly good promises (arm's-length relations). In fact, he goes further still. He claims that contractual relations are *particularly* "arm's-length." He concludes that the legal practice of contracts "represents promise's highest and most complete expression." (p. 296)

I have taken up these claims in Sheinman (2011). As hinted earlier, I sympathize with Markovits's critique of the so-called relational view of promises, which takes close personal relations as *the* paradigm of promising. But it is less clear why the kind of respect involved in promising is *inherently* distancing. Intimate relationships depend on mundane coordination and cooperation in which promising can play a vital role. Consider the case in which my wife and I coordinate our respective chores. At least in my own self-understanding, when I tell her that I will pick up the kids today, I do not simply communicate to her my intention to do so (or prediction that I will do so); I also *promise* her to do so, thereby committing to her to pick up the kids today. To be sure, there is nothing particularly intimate about my promise. But nor can I detect anything particularly distancing about it, either.

I also sympathize with Markovits's rejection of the so-called relational view of contracts, in which paradigmatic contracts are embedded in some close, personal, or ongoing relationship. (This view is associated with Ian Macneil, for example. See Macneil, 2001.) But here, too, Markovits seems to me to go too far in the other direction. For it seems to me that at least some perfectly good contractual relations *are* in fact embedded in highly relational social contexts—including contexts of close or intimate personal relations. (If I were to buy my mother's house, the two of us would *have* to execute a contract, and I see no reason to think that it would be less than a perfectly good contract.)

Chapter 14: Sidgwick on Promises (David Phillips)

Henry Sidgwick is central to the development of the familiar contemporary theoretical contrast between utilitarianism and deontology; he aspires, as many utilitarians do, to argue for utilitarianism broadly on the grounds of its superior rationality. But if David Phillips's argument in chapter 14 is correct, then Sidgwick's own attempt to argue for it in this way is a failure. Commonsense morality includes the belief that there is a moral obligation to keep promises. Sidgwick's deontological predecessors, like William Whewell, and successors, like David Ross, argued that the principle requiring fidelity to promises is simply *self-evident*. Sidgwick denies this.

He proposes stringent criteria of self-evidence, whose clarity and precision condition requires a determinate verdict in every case, and argues that, unlike his own protoutilitarian axioms (e.g. "I ought to prefer the greater good of another to my own lesser good"), the principle of fidelity does not meet them. Sidgwick's basic claim here will strike students of contemporary particularism as familiar. On reflection, so goes the thought, a principle prohibiting promise-breaking is just a vague shorthand for a principle that prohibits promise-breaking *if* such and such conditions are met. But as soon as we consider the possible conditions, controversy arises:

> different conscientious persons would answer these and other questions in different ways: and though we could perhaps obtain a decided majority for some of these qualifications and against others, there would not in any case be a clear *consensus* either way... when the qualifications to which we referred are fairly considered, this confidence inevitably changes into hesitation and perplexity. (Sidgwick, 1981: 353–54)

Phillips agrees that the precepts of commonsense morality—including the principle of fidelity—fail to meet Sidgwick's stringent criteria of self-evidence, but claims that Sidgwick's own protoutilitarian principles *also* fail to meet them. Hence Sidgwick's official argument is unfair.

Phillips then considers an alternative, unofficial argument on behalf of Sidgwick, in which self-evidence does not require a determinate verdict in every case, and allows the axioms of commonsense morality to be relatively simple axioms like "I ought to keep my promises." Phillips notes that, once we move from the official to the unofficial argument, we introduce a new deontological opponent—Ross. Rossian deontological intuitionism does not try to meet Sidgwick's clarity and precision condition, interpreted as requiring complete determinacy. For Ross, famously, the only self-evident principles are principles of prima facie duty. When an action falls under more than one such principle, and these principles tend in opposite directions, its moral status can be determined only by a kind of balancing, whose results are never self-evident. Phillips contrasts Sidgwick and Ross on what kind of principles are self-evident, and concludes that the kind of story Sidgwick tells on behalf of the self-evidence of his proto-utilitarian principles can be told about the maxims of commonsense morality (understood as Rossian principles of prima facie duty). Phillips:

> Consider again the example of promising. The deontologist does seem to be able to say about promising something importantly parallel to what Sidgwick says about rightness and goodness. Just as a kind of universality is part of the concepts of objective rightness and goodness, so it is part of the concept of a promise that promises create obligations. Sincere employment of the concept of a promise therefore commits one to the existence of the obligations promises create. (p. 339)

Chapter 15: Contractarianism and Emergency (Yizhak Benbaji)

The traditional account of the ethics of war, epitomized by Michael Walzer's *Just and Unjust War* (1977), is understood as *natural* or preconventional. In chapter 15, Yizhak Benbaji offers a contractarian interpretation of the laws of war, in which the moral standing of the laws of war follows from their being terms in an actual agreement between states for the regulation of the conduct of combatants in the battlefield.

> On the contractarian interpretation, the equalities legislated by the war convention (i.e., the equality of soldiers vis-à-vis each other and the equality of civilians vis-à-vis each other) do not reflect preconventional moral equalities. Rather, the rules that command these equalities constitute a set of fair, mutually beneficial and hence, impartially justified rules. By accepting the rules, the parties *generate* the moral equalities between soldiers and civilians. Soldiers tacitly accept these rules, and since they are justified, their acceptance by soldiers allows for a redistribution of their preconventional rights and duties. (p. 351)

Benbaji illustrates this "actual contract" account by applying it to one of the most important laws of war, namely the basic prohibition on direct attack against civilians, and the exemption states have from that prohibition in cases of emergency—the so-called *supreme emergency exemption*. On the proposed contractarian account, the immunity of those civilians is conventional; in point of fact, states and soldiers *have* undertaken the duty to avoid attacking culpable civilians in order to immunize their own civilians from direct attack. However, the international agreement over this prohibition breaks down in some cases. And it is that area of breakdown that determines the scope of the emergency exemption. Roughly, what counts as "extreme circumstances" are those circumstances over the exempting effect of which states fail to agree. Thus it can be known ex ante that, in these circumstances, a rationally led state has no reason to prefer rule-governed war to total war. And according to Benbaji, the agreement breaks down as regards circumstances in which defeat in a rule-governed war would result in dehumanization, enslavement, or systematic murder.

Now one worry about an actual agreement account of the ethics of war is that it might end up allowing states (or at least powerful states) to exempt themselves from the basic prohibition. Even if the war convention does not require unanimity, it surely requires an agreement among the powerful states. By attacking civilians it regards as threatening, a powerful state can express its dissent from the view that the basic prohibition applies in this case, thereby exempting itself from it. Thus a powerful state can violate the basic prohibition and exempt itself from it at the same time.

In Benbaji's account, this problem is handled by claiming that the exemptions defined by the agreed-on rules "are of moral significance, only if the rules themselves are impartially justified." (p. 347) For him, a rule is impartially justified when it is fair and good for everyone. For good or for ill, this seems to me to bring Benbaji's contractarian account of the ethics of war very close to the kind of rule consequentialist account Brad Hooker advocates in chapter 10.

Chapter 16: Agreement as Joint Promise (Hanoch Sheinman)

In chapter 16, I propose a general account of agreements within a largely individualistic framework. According to this account, making an agreement is an essentially *joint action*, one the parties perform together as one. The action of agreement-making, which can only be performed jointly, can nevertheless be explained in terms of another action, which can also be performed individually, namely *promising*. Agreement-making on this view is a matter of joint promising. Two promises add up to an agreement—that is, joint promise—just when they are exchanged—or *interdepend*—in the right way. On the current proposal, the interdependence of agreement promises is *not* a matter of the promises being conditional in content; indeed, each party promises the other to do her part of the agreement, just like so. Instead, the interdependence of agreement promises is *causal-motivational*. Specifically, each party's belief that (she will promise later to do her part if and only if the other party promises later to do his) causes and motivates that very party to promise the other later; and each party is aware of this causal-motivational fact.

I would like to thank David Owens and David Enoch for their detailed written comments on an earlier draft of the introduction.

NOTES

1. Similarly, (0′) A's promise to B to do (X if B does not do Y) is distinct from (iv′) A's threat (issued) to B to do (X if B does not do Y).

2. For a discussion of requests, as one example of reason-giving speech-acts, see Enoch (2010).

3. But cf. e.g. Watson (2009) and Owens (2008), who deny that obligations are reasons.

4. Even if obligations turn out not to be reasons, we still need to know what they are before we can assess the claim that promises obligate. For convenience, I'm ignoring the minority view.

5. This gap seems to make trouble for the strongly cognitivist view of intention under which, necessarily, when I intend to do X, I cannot fail to *believe* that I'm doing (or will do) X. Cf. Paul (2009).

6. Cf. also Owens (2007: 303): 'Promisors exercise a form of normative power, they change the normative situation simply by communicating the intention to do so.'

7. Even J. L. Mackie rejects Hume's claim that promising involves the belief that we create an obligation by a special act of the mind (1980: 103).

8. Even this is not uncontroversial, however. Cf. e.g. Shiffrin (2008: 482), who has never felt the magnetism of the problem.

9. Cf. Margaret Gilbert's claim in chapter 3 that immoral promises give *nonmoral* obligations.

10. Both quotes are from Hume (2006: 114–15).

11. Many of those who answer question (2) in the affirmative (Hume and Rawls included), or at least do not answer it in the negative, characterize the social rules invoked in promising as *conventional*. Andrei Marmor has recently argued that the social rules of promising cannot be conventional (2009: 137–140).

12. Think about Prohibition. The rules were there, but where was the *practice*?

13. It is fair to ask what makes a reason or obligation moral, exactly. Here I am simply assuming that there is an intuitive distinction between moral and nonmoral reasons. Cf. e.g. Dancy (2004: 3).

14. Cf. Jonathan Dancy's claim that "there is no such thing as a *pro tanto* command" (2004: 17). Maybe there is also no such thing as a pro tanto obligation. Arguably, whatever a pro tanto obligation is, it isn't a genuine obligation, only a *relation* to an obligation—a potential or would-be obligation. But we should be open to the possibility that obligations proper include both overall and pro tanto obligations.

15. Cf. Owens (2007: 296): "the fact that one is justified in breaking the promise is perfectly consistent with the fact that one is wronging the promisee, that one is failing to discharge an obligation to him."

16. There is a natural sense in which the sheer fact that X is what one has most reason to do warrants the claim that one ought to do X all things considered.

17. Of course, proponents of the Pro Tanto View can always give up on the notion that pro tanto obligations are genuine obligations. They can simply say that promises give moral reasons and promise-breaking is action against moral reasons.

18. But cases in which a perfectly good promise seems to generate no moral obligation need not force one to choose between the Pro Tanto View and a negative answer to question (4). One familiar strategy is to say that the presence of certain circumstances or factors does not override or outweigh the general moral obligation to keep a promise, but rather *cancels* it altogether, functioning as a zero multiplier. Cf. e.g. Kagan (1988). On this *Canceling* view, the yes/no question (4) admits of no yes/no answer. On the one hand, some perfectly good promises give absolutely no moral obligation—not even pro tanto ones. At the same time, there is still a kind of general moral obligation to keep promises, namely one that applies in the absence of special canceling factors. Cf. Dancy (2004).

19. For a *rule-consequentialist* approach, see Hooker (chapter 10).

20. Owens distinguishes the authority interest: an interest in having a *right* to determine action, from the *control* interest: an interest in having physical control

(2007: 310). The authority interest "takes as its object the moral situation itself" (2006: 69); "it is an interest in having a certain moral power" (70).

21. Arguably, Owens's main thesis is confined to the interests of promisees. Thus he writes that promises "serve their recipient's authority interest by giving him the power to determine whether others wrong him if these others do, or fail to do, certain things" (2007: 312).

22. Owens thinks a promise involves acceptance by the promisee (2006: 72) and (2007: 306).

23. I think of this authority transfer theory as a friendly amendment, one that makes the authority interest theory as plausible as it can be. Owens claims that the authority interest is valuable intrinsically, for its own sake. The right to transfer authority at will may or may not be worth wanting for its own sake, but I am pretty sure the right to have *authority over someone else's action* is only worth wanting for the sake of something else. Why isn't a person who wants to have authority over someone else's action *for its own sake* an authority freak?

24. Cf. e.g. Melden (1977: ch. 2) and Robins (1984: ch. 5).

25. While all theories that define the right *in terms of* the good are consequentialist in a sense, it is not implausible to maintain that act-consequentialism is the only genuinely consequentialist theory of action. It has been claimed, with some plausibility, that rule-consequentialism is consequentialist only in the sense that rubber ducks are ducks. See Howard-Snyder (1993). But cf. Brad Hooker's contribution to this book.

26. But cf. Michael Smith's contribution to this book. Since for Smith all value is relative, he might well be able to accommodate deontological constraints within an act-consequentialist view. But is he right to claim that this view is still faithful to "the core" of consequentialism?

27. For the notion that promises erect limits on the promotion of the general good, see Rawls (1999a: ch. 2); Shiffrin (2008); Markovits (chapter 13).

28. Alternatively, the morally determinative principles need only be *acceptable*, namely principles everyone could reasonably accept as public standards of behavior. I'll stick with the more popular and demanding "unrejectability" version.

29. Derek Parfit's most recent view doubly exemplifies this kind of practice view: it combines rule-consequentialism with principle contractualism. He now holds that the supreme principle of morality is the *Formula of Universally Willable Principles*: "An act is wrong unless such acts are permitted by some principle whose universal acceptance everyone could rationally will" (2009: sec. 45).

30. This is the position I favor.

31. For an illuminating discussion of the relation between practices and principles in the legal context, see Coleman (2001).

32. Notice, however, that if this is your view, you should be prepared to reject the so-called publicity requirement.

33. It is, to be sure, virtually impossible to imagine promising away while holding everything else about our society fixed. To imagine promising away, you've got to imagine a society that is significantly different in other ways, too. Consider, for example, a society in which people do whatever they say they'll do. Either they don't say they'll do something, or they do it. Arguably, the need for promising would not arise in such a society.

34. Nichols does not discuss promising, however.

35. But there is no suggestion that a joint promise is a genuine promise; it is interdependent promises.

36. An analogous problem seems to me to haunt Michael Bratman's famous account of shared agency (1999: part 2; 2009). Bratman wants to explain essentially conjunctive phenomena, such as our shared intention that we *J*, in terms of my intention that we *J* and your intention that we *J*. But just how much simpler to understand is my essentially conjunctive intention that we *J*—that I am to do X (my part of the *J*-ing) *and* you are to do Y (your part of the *J*-ing)—than our shared intention to *J*?

37. Conversely, and more surprisingly, it has been argued that *contractual* obligations are voluntary (or self-imposed), but promissory commitments are not. See Pratt (2007).

38. I discuss this and other possibilities in Sheinman (2011).

39. Cf. e.g. the various responses to Shiffrin's article in the *Harvard Law Review* of 2007; cf. also Kraus (2009), and the articles by Dori Kimel, Richard Posner, and Steven Shavel in Ben-Shachar & Porat, 2010).

40. As illustrated by the famous case of *Lucy v. Zehmer*, 196 Va. 493 (1954).

41. Shiffrin: "By claiming that contract diverges from promise, I mean that although the legal doctrines of contract associate legal obligations with morally binding promises, the content of the legal obligations and the legal significance of their breach do not correspond to the moral obligations and the moral significance of their breach" (709). But *this* divergence does not seem to be between contracts (or contractual norms) and promises (or promissory norms). And indeed, Shiffrin sometimes describes the divergence of contract and promise as "the divergence between contract and morality" (710). Or (as I'd put it) between contract law and what *it* should be.

42. Cf. Shiffrin (2006: 724): The distinctive remedial regime of contracts "reflects an underlying view that promissory breach is not a wrong, or at least not a serious one." This claim seems significantly *stronger* than (2'); it seems to imply that law's remedial regime expresses a moral judgment about noncontractual promises (as well as about contracts). But even if we think that law's failure to enforce contracts as vigorously as it can expresses the view that it is morally okay to break a *contract*, why should we ever believe that such enforcement also expresses the view that it is morally okay to break promises in general?

43. We can also reconstruct (2') along the lines suggested in the previous note, as the claim that

(2″) Given the doctrines described in (a), (b), and/or (c), the law expresses the judgment that there is no moral obligation to keep promises.

This would force the following reconstruction of the rest of the argument:

(3″) Therefore, there is a moral obligation to keep promises, but the law expresses the judgment that there is no moral obligation to keep promises.

(4″) Therefore, the judgment the law expresses about our moral obligation to keep promises can diverge from the truth about it.

This, too, fails to discharge the divergence of contract and promise, and is perfectly compatible with Contract as Promise.

44. This question is faced by every *expressive* theory of law—every account that evaluates laws by what they express. Cf. e.g. Anderson & Pildes (2000) and Adler (2000).

45. For discussion, see Connie Rosati's contribution to this book.

46. Owens does not seek to solve the problem of the bare wrong, but he does say that the key to the solution is twofold: (i) accept that promise-breaking always affects some intelligible human interest (and so that it is not a bare wrong, after all) but (ii) deny that "the interest in question can be specified without using the notion of an obligation."

47. I find the focus on coordination too narrow. I'd recommend the broader *cooperation* hypothesis: we value promising for its contribution to interpersonal cooperation, broadly construed to include coordination as well as other forms of cooperation. No doubt Owens's twin objections would apply to that thesis, too.

48. And arguably, we could also value promising *intrinsically*—for its own sake—partly *because* they are instrumentally valuable.

49. A final remark about Hume's and Rawls's practice-based position as regards Owens's bare wrong problem. The view that Rawls advances in "Two Concepts of Rules"—and which he finds in Hume—does not seem to me to depend on the claim that promise-breaking always harms a valuable practice. On this two-level (rule- or practice-consequentialist) account, the wrong of promise-breaking lies instead in *nonconformity* to the rules of a practice that is justified (by its good consequences). Nonconformity is a *noncausal* relation; it cannot harm practices or otherwise *affect* human interests in any way at all. On this interpretation of Hume and Rawls, the wrong of promise-breaking is, in fact, a bare wrong, one affecting no intelligible human interest.

50. Rosati seems to assume that her move from authority to autonomy depends on her move from normative authority (or rights) to *effective* authority (or control). To me, the former move seems quite independent of the latter. As noted earlier (in the context of the Question of Good), promising gives the promisee authority over the promisor's action only by taking it from the promisor. So what's being served is not so much the parties' interest in authority as their interest in the voluntary transfer, or redistribution, of authority. And this looks like an interest in autonomy.

51. Suppose you promise at 1 to meet someone at 6, then go to the movies at 5, thereby making yourself incapable of keeping the promise. Do you still have an obligation to show up at 6? See Sinnott-Armstrong (1984: 252).

52. Remember Bernard Williams's famous example. The bandits force the following choice on Jimmy. He can kill one innocent person himself, thereby saving nineteen others, or he can let all twenty die at the hands of the bandits. Williams makes much of the fact that, in the first option, it is Jimmy who takes these innocent lives. Opting for the second option, Jimmy could reason: "What matters here is not to dirty my hands in this nasty business; it's *me* who has to decide, after all." To this, traditional consequentialists tend to respond: "What's so special about *your* hands here?" Can a proponent of a consequentialized moral theory avail herself of this response? Somewhat akin to Smith's approach is the consequentializing approach in Portmore (2007).

53. See most recently Parfit (2009).

REFERENCES

Adler, M. 2000. "Expressive Theories of Law: A Skeptical Overview," *University of Pennsylvania Law Review* 148: 1363-1501.

Anderson, E., & Pildes, R. 2000. "Expressive Theories of Law: A General Restatement." *University of Pennsylvania Law Review* 148: 1503–1575.

Anscombe, G. E. M. 1981. *Ethics, Religion and Politics.* Minneapolis: University of Minnesota Press.

———. 2000. Intention. Cambridge, MA: Harvard University Press.

Aristotle. 1999. *Nicomachean Ethics.* T. Irwin (trans.). Indianapolis: Hackett.

Atiyah, P. 1981. *Promises, Morals, and Law.* Oxford: Oxford University Press.

———. 1990. *Essays on Contract.* Oxford: Oxford University Press.

Austin, J. L. 1975. *How to Do Things with Words*. Cambridge, MA: Harvard University Press.

Bach, K. 1995. "Terms of Agreement." *Ethics* 105: 604–612.

Bagchi, A. 2007. "Contract vs. Promises." *Scholarship at Penn Law*, http://lsr.nellco.org/upenn_wps/176

Baier, A. 1985. *Postures of the Mind.* Minneapolis: University of Minnesota Press.

———. 1994. *Moral Prejudices.* Cambridge, MA: Harvard University Press.

Ben-Shachar, O., & Porat, A. 2010. *Fault in American Contract Law.* Cambridge: Cambridge University Press.

Black, O. 2007. "Two Theories of Agreement." *Legal Theory* 13: 1–22.

Bratman, M. 1999. *Faces of Intention.* Cambridge: Cambridge University Press.

———. 2009. "Modest Sociality and the Distinctiveness of Intention." *Philosophical Studies* 144: 149-165.

Cavel, S. 1979. *The Claim of Reason.* Oxford: Oxford University Press.

Coleman, J. 2001. *The Practice of Principle.* Oxford: Oxford University Press.

Dancy, J. 2004. *Ethics without Principles.* New York: Oxford University Press.

Darwall, S. 2006. *The Second-person Standpoint*. Cambridge, MA: Harvard University Press.

Deigh, J. 2008. *Emotions, Values, and the Law.* New York: Oxford University Press.

Enoch, D. 2010. "Giving Practical Reasons." *Philosophers' Imprint.*

Frankfurt, H. 1999. *Necessity, Volition, and Love.* Cambridge: Cambridge University Press.

Fried, C. 1981. *Contract as Promise.* Cambridge, MA: Harvard University Press.

———. 2007. "The Convergence of Contract and Promise." *Harvard Law Review* 120: 1–9.

Gilbert, M. 1996. *Living Together.* Lanham, MD: Rowman and Littlefield.

———. 2004. "Scanlon on Promissory Obligation," *Journal of Philosophy* CI: 83–109.

———. 2006. *A Theory of Political Obligation*. Oxford: Oxford University Press.

Gilmore, G. 1974. *The Death of Contract.* Columbus: Ohio University Press.

Hanfling, O. 1975. "Promises, Games and Institutions." *Proceedings of the Aristotelian Society* 75: 13–31.

Hare, R. M. 1964. "The Promising Game." *Revue International de Philosophie* 70: 398–412.

Hart, H. L. A. 1958. "Legal and Moral Obligation." In A. I. Melden (ed.), *Essays in Moral Philosophy.* Seattle: University of Washington Press, 82–107.

Hieronymi, P. 2008. "The Reasons of Trust." *Australian Journal of Philosophy* 86: 213–236.

Hooker, B. 2000. *Ideal Code, Real World.* New York: Oxford University Press.
Howard-Snyder, F. 1993. "Rule-consequentialism Is a Rubber Duck." *American Philosophical Quarterly* 30: 271-278.
Hume, D. 2006. *Moral Writings.* Indianapolis: Hackett.
Kagan, S. 1988. "The Additive Fallacy." *Ethics* 99: 5-31.
———. 1998. *Normative Ethics.* Boulder, CO: Westview Press.
Kessler, F. 1943. "Contracts of Adhesion." *Columbia* Law *Review* 43: 629-642.
Kimel, D. 2003. *From Promise to Contract.* Oxford: Hart.
———. 2007. "The Choice of Paradigm for Theory of Contract: Reflections on the Relational Model," *Oxford Journal of Legal Studies* 27: 233-255.
Kolodny, N., & Wallace, J. 2003. "Promises and Practices Revisited." *Philosophy and Public Affairs*, 31: 119-154.
Kraus, J. 2009. "The Correspondence of Contract and Promise." *Columbia Law Review* 109: 1603-1649.
Mackie, J. L. 1977. *Ethics: Inventing Right and Wrong.* London: Penguin Books.
Mackie, J. L. 1980. *Hume's Moral Theory.* New York: Routledge.
Macneil, I. 2001. *The Relational Theory of Contract: Selected Works of Ian Macneil.* London: Sweet and Maxwell.
Marmor, A. 2009. *Social Conventions.* Princeton: Princeton University Press.
McNeily, F. S. 1972. "Promises De-Moralized." *Philosophical Review* 81: 63-81.
Midgley, M. 1974. "The Game Game." *Philosophy* 49: 231-253.
Nichols, S. 2004. *Sentimental Rules.* Oxford: Oxford University Press.
Owens, D. 2006. "A Simple Theory of Promises." *Philosophical Review* 115: 51-77.
———. 2007. "Duress, Deception, and the Validity of a Promise." *Mind* 116: 293-315.
———. 2008. "Rationalism about Obligation." *European Journal* of *Philosophy* 16: 403-431.
Parfit, D. 2009. On What Matters. Draft.
Paul, S. 2009. "How We Know What We're Doing." *Philosophers' Imprint* 9: 1-24.
Portmore, D. 2007. "Consequentializing Moral Theories." *Pacific Philosophical Quarterly* 88: 39-73.
Pratt, M. 2007. "Promises, Contracts and Promissory Obligations." Law *and Philosophy* 26: 531-574.
Prichard, H. A. 2002. *Moral Writings.* New York: Oxford University Press.
Rawls, J. 1999a. *Collected Papers.* Cambridge, MA: Harvard University Press.
———. 1999b. *A Theory of Justice.* Cambridge, MA: Harvard University Press.
Raz, J. 1977. "Promises and Obligations." In P. Hacker and J. Raz (eds.), *Law, Morality, and Society*. Oxford: Oxford University Press, 210-228.
———. 1982. "Promises in Morality and Law." *Harvard Law Review* 95: 916-938.
———. 1986. *The Morality of Freedom.* Oxford: Oxford University Press.
———. 1999. *Practical Reason and Norms.* Oxford: Oxford University Press.
Restatement (Second) of Contracts. 1981. American Law Institute.
Robins, M. 1976. "The Primacy of Promising." *Mind* 85: 321-340.
———. 1984. *Promising, Intending, and Moral Autonomy.* New York: Cambridge University Press.
Ross, A. 2002. *The Right and the Good.* Oxford: Oxford University Press.
Scanlon, T. M. 1998. *What We Owe to Each Other.* Cambridge, MA: Harvard University Press.

Searle, J. 1969. *Speech Acts.* Cambridge: Cambridge University Press.
———. 1980. "Prima-facie Obligations." In Z. Vanstraaten (ed.), Philosophical Subjects. Oxford: Oxford University Press, 238–259.
———. 2001. *Rationality in Action.* Cambridge, MA: MIT Press.
———. 2010. *Making the Social World.* Oxford: Oxford University Press.
Sheinman, H. 2008. "Promise as Practice Reason." *Acta Analytica*, 23: 287–318.
Sheinman, H. 2011. "The Social Diversity of Promises and Contracts." *Oxford Studies in the Philosophy of Law.*
Shiffrin, S. 2006. "The Divergence of Contract and Promise." *Harvard Law Review* 120: 708–753.
———. 2008. "Promising, Intimate Relationships, and Conventionalism." *Philosophical Review* 117: 481–524.
Sidgwick, H. 1981. *The Methods of Ethics.* 7th ed. Indianapolis: Hackett.
Sinnott-Armstrog, W. 1984. "'Ought' Conversationally Implies 'Can.'" *Philosophical Review* 93: 249–261.
Tognazzini, N. 2007. "The Hybrid Nature of Promissory Obligation." *Philosophy and Public Affairs* 35: 203–232.
Thomson, J. 1990. *The Realm of Rights.* Cambridge, MA: Harvard University Press.
Thompson, M. 2004. "What Is It to Wrong Someone? A Puzzle about Justice." in R. J. Wallace, P. Pettit, S. Scheffler, and M. Smith (eds.), *Reason and Value* Oxford: Oxford University Press, 333–384.
Tomasello, M. 2009. *Why We Cooperate.* Cambridge, MA: MIT Press.
Vitek, W. 1993. *Promising.* Philadelphia: Temple University Press.
Walzer, M. 1977. *Just and Unjust Wars.* New York: Basic Books.
Watson, G. 1998. "Some Considerations in Favor of Contractualism." In J. Coleman and C. Morris (eds.), *Rational Commitment and Social Justice.* Cambridge: Cambridge University Press.
———. 2009. "Promises, Reasons, and Normative Powers." In D. Sobel and S. Wall (eds.), *Reasons for Action.* Cambridge: Cambridge University Press.
Zimmeman, M. 1996. *The Concept of Moral Obligation.* Cambridge University Press.

Chapter 2

The Problem with Promising

David Owens

Abstract

Why have philosophers since Hume regarded promising as problematic? Owens distinguishes two problems raised by Hume. The problem of the bare wrong *is the problem of how it can make sense to avoid a wrong when the wrong does not affect any intelligible human interest. The problem of* normative power *is the problem of how something can be a wrong simply because it has been declared to be a wrong. Owens argues that the problem of the bare wrong is more basic. Owens then examines the attempts of practice theorists like Hume and Rawls to overcome the problem of the bare wrong by arguing that, whenever breach of promise seems like a bare wrong, in fact human interests are adversely affected, because a socially valuable practice is damaged. Owens argues that the explanations of the practice theorists cannot cover all the cases. He then formulates an assumption that is shared by all practice theorists (and others), namely the assumption that we take promises seriously because they serve our interest in social coordination. Owens argues that, if this* social coordination hypothesis *were true, then there need be no practice of promise-keeping for promises to bind. Furthermore, were this hypothesis true, promising would be a social tool that we could largely do without. And so long as the intelligibility of promising is in doubt (because of the problem of the bare wrong), an adherent of the social co-ordination hypothesis should assume that we largely do without promising. So, Owens concludes, anyone who gives promising a key role in human social life must reject the social co-ordination hypothesis.*

Hume regarded a part of ordinary morality as deeply problematic in that it is hard to see how it would make any sense for people to conform to its rules, except when extraneous considerations were in play. I'll focus particularly on what Hume says about promising, but he sees property rights, the power of consent and political authority as raising essentially the same issues. What makes Hume's discussion so compelling is that it is driven by two widely held assumptions—one about human action, the other about obligation—assumptions that appear to conflict.

The widely held assumption about action is that sensible people can be moved to do something only if they can see some point in doing it, and that they can see some point in doing it only if doing it strikes them as good or desirable in some respect (whether or not it is either good or desirable on the whole). In Hume's hands, this becomes the psychological claim that "the Will exerts itself when either the good or the absence of the evil may be attained by any action of the mind or body" Hume (1978: 439).[1] Other philosophers may prefer the normative claim that a *reasonable* agent must see some good in what he does. In one form or another, this assumption is shared by philosophers who differ dramatically both about what makes it the case that something is good and about precisely how facts about what is good enter into our thinking about what to do.

The widely held assumption about obligation comes out in a question Hume puts to himself "may not the sense of morality or duty produce an action, without any other motive?" Hume (1978: 479). We often keep a promise, or respect someone's property rights, out of a sense of obligation, and without regard to any good this might do. Nor do we think this irrational. Breach of such an obligation is something most people would seek to avoid even though it appears to constitute what I shall call a *bare wrong*. The tension between our two assumptions generates the problem of the bare wrong.

I. THE PROBLEM OF THE BARE WRONG

Let's begin with property:

> Here are two persons who dispute for an estate; of whom one is rich, a fool and a bachelor; the other poor, a man of sense and has a numerous family. The first is my enemy; the second my friend. Whether I be actuated in this affair by a view to public or private interest, by friendship or enmity, I must be induced to do my utmost to procure the estate to the latter. Nor would any consideration of the right and property of the person be able to restrain me, were I actuated only by natural motives. (Hume, 1978: 532)

Once we eliminate all the extraneous reasons for respecting someone's right to inherit, the admitted fact that it is still *theirs* seems a negligible consideration, one which shouldn't weigh with us *at all*. Now promise:

> I suppose a person to have lent me a sum of money, on condition that it be restored in a few days; and also suppose that after the expiration of the term agreed on, he demands the sum: *I ask, what reason or motive have I to restore the money?* (479)

> For what if he be my enemy, and has given me just cause to hate him? What if he be a vicious man, and deserves the hatred of all mankind? What if he be a miser, and can make no use of what I would deprive him of? What if he be a profligate debauchee, and would rather receive harm than benefit from large possessions? What if I be in necessity, and have urgent motives to acquire something to my family? In all these cases, the original motive to justice would fail; and consequently the justice itself, and along with it all property, right and obligation. (482)

Hume concludes:

> From all this it follows, that we have naturally no real or universal motive for observing the laws of equity, but the very equity and merit of that observance; and as no action can be equitable or meritorious where it cannot arise from some separate motive, there is here an evident sophistry and reasoning in a circle. (483)

Now Hume finds neither obligation nor the idea of acting on an obligation intrinsically problematic.[2] For example, Hume says that "A rich man lies under a moral obligation to communicate to those in necessity a share of his superfluities" Hume (482). Here it would make perfect sense for the rich man to discharge this obligation, for he would thereby serve an obvious human interest. So why do the obligations generated by promising, property, and so on, and the wrongs associated with them, seem any more problematic to him?

To see why we should reformulate the first of Hume's assumptions as follows:

> (1) It makes sense to do something because you are obliged to do it only if the discharge of this obligation would serve some interest.[3]

A human interest in x makes it sensible to want, or at least to value x, by ensuring that x is good for us in some respect. Here I shall confine myself to the interest human beings have in the fulfillment of a promise.

Things are worth wanting or valuing for many different reasons. Hume implies that these considerations all, in the end, concern human welfare.[4] The "natural" obligations he recognizes (to care for one's children, or help the needy, or even return favours rendered—Hume, 1978: 478–479) involve a desire to benefit people, or to avoid harming them. Exactly whom one desires to benefit will depend on other factors—who your children are, who will benefit the most, who has been good to you—but the promotion of someone's welfare is the aim in all cases. Now in the examples Hume describes, nobody will be harmed should he violate his obligations, not Hume, nor the beneficiary, nor the public, and some will be much better off; hence the problem of bare wrong.

Is Hume taking too narrow a view of what constitutes a harm or a benefit? Perhaps human beings have an interest in knowing what is going to happen, even if no further interest would be served by this knowledge. One important method of securing such knowledge is by making wills and accepting promises. And if this epistemic interest is what moves people to extract promises and make wills and if it is always damaged whenever a promise is broken or the terms of a will are ignored, perhaps Hume's two characters (the person who borrowed money from Hume and the profligate debauchee) are harmed after all.

It is doubtful whether being given a false belief, even a false belief about matter that interests you, is in itself a harm. The Russian anthropologist Maklay promised not to photograph a Malayan servant who feared the loss of his soul and so refrained from doing so even while the servant was asleep (Foot, 2001: 47–50). Can Maklay have supposed that he would be harming the servant by taking the photograph simply because he would be falsifying one of the servant's beliefs about what would happen to him? Even if there is a harm here, this proposal fastens on something inessential to a breach of promise. Hume's debauchee might be so debauched that he neither knows nor cares whether his affairs are being managed honestly, or whether promises made to him are being kept. Still he can be wronged in either fashion. A more sober character might forget the promise or have little faith that the promisor will perform without thereby invalidating the promise.

Can we avoid Hume's problem by instead abandoning the assumption that human beings are concerned only with the promotion of human welfare? Human beings naturally take an interest in people's getting a fair share, in issues of distributive justice.[5] Suppose what would constitute someone's fair share can be determined without knowing either what they own or the promises that have been made to them. Then our concern with fairness could motivate compliance with an obligation without presupposing a prior concern with what we are obliged to do.

We do distinguish between whether someone *deserves* to have something (given their talents, efforts, what they have already got, what use they will make of it, and so forth), and whether they are actually entitled to it (Feinberg, 1970: 85–87). We are able to consider whether it is appropriate or fitting for them to have it apart from whether they have a right to it (e.g. because they own it).[6] It is a moot point whether satisfaction of this interest in fairness makes our lives go better. Perhaps our interactions with others tend to lose their savor unless they are informed by fair principles of cooperation (cf. Scanlon, 1998: 161–164). If so, this concern with fairness is an interest in the sense in which that term is used in (1). On the other hand, fairness may simply be something in which we reasonably *take* an interest even though its frustration would make our lives no worse. I shall leave these questions open, since I doubt that an interest in a fair or reasonable distribution can explain why we take bare wrongs seriously, however that interest is to be understood.

In the cases Hume considers, neither of the characters entitled to the money deserve to have it: they have too much already. Other people deserve it more, and things would be fairer if they got it. Still these others are not entitled to it, and many (Hume included) would think that the money ought to go to those who are entitled to have it. So the problem remains even once we allow that human beings are moved by their fellows' deserts as well as by concern for their wellbeing. A bare wrong does no one any harm. Nor is it wrong because it deprives someone of an item they deserve, or gives someone an item they don't deserve. A bare wrong has no *wrong-base*. How, Hume asks, can we take such bare wrongness seriously as a guide to action?

II. THE PROBLEM OF NORMATIVE POWER

As well as property-based and promissory obligations, Hume discusses at some length the obligations generated by the commands of our rulers. What all these obligations have in common is that they are created (or remitted) by the exercise of normative powers. Let me explain what I mean by this.

Many obligations are the product of our choices. I am obliged not to drink only because I chose to drive my car. And you are obliged to wait for me to pass (and not run out in front of me) only because I chose to drive along the road. In this case, the changes I make in the normative situation may not be intended or even foreseen by me. But even if the imposition of such an obligation is both foreseen and intended, and in that sense chosen, it is a product another choice: the decision to drive a car.

Now some obligations are a product of choice in a stronger sense than this. Some obligations exist because someone has communicated the intention of imposing such obligations (on themselves or on someone else) by communicating this very intention.[7] For example, the promisor is obliged to perform because he has communicated the intention of putting himself under an obligation to perform by communicating this very intention.[8] Of course, the promisor will need to do things in order to communicate this intention, and, where he succeeds, his obligation will be a product of this (intended) activity (speech or whatever). But, unlike the decision to drive a car, what makes this activity generate an obligation is the fact that it communicates the choice of this obligation. This is an obligation you *undertake* rather than *incur*.[9] Even if your driving communicates such a choice (and is so intended), that is not why it imposes the relevant obligations either on yourself or on others.

It is not just promissory obligations that are chosen in this stronger sense. When I order you to do something, I impose an obligation on you by communicating the intention to do exactly that. When I give you my car, I impose on myself and on others an obligation not to use it (without your consent) precisely by communicating the intention of creating such obligations. These examples all involve the exercise of *a normative power*, of a power to change what people are obliged to do by communicating the intention of so doing. People often exercise normative powers by employing a conventional form of words: "I promise" (give, consent, marry, order etc.) and philosophers have used the notion of a *performative* to pick out this class of verbs. But one can communicate the intention to undertake an obligation without using a dedicated form of speech.

Hume expresses doubts about the intelligibility of this sort of speech-act: how can the mere fact that someone has promised, given, ordered, and so on—make sense of our behaving differently from the way we would have behaved before? Speaking of promising in the *Treatise*, he says:

> 'tis one of the most mysterious and incomprehensible operations that can possibly be imagined, and may even be compared to *transubstantiation* or *holy orders*, where a certain form of words, along with a certain intention, changes entirely the nature of an external object, and even of a human creature. (Hume, 1978: 524)

How does Hume's puzzlement about normative power relate to the problem of the bare wrong? I suggest that they are two sides of the same coin. What makes breach of promise a wrong is that someone has communicated the intention that it constitute a wrong. Now something can be declared to be wrongful whether or not it is harmful, or constitutes unjust enrichment, or bears on human interests in any other way. So such wrongfulness raises the problem of the bare wrong: What sense is there in refraining from doing something simply because it has been *declared* to be wrongful? Yet how could bare wrongs, wrongs which have no adverse effect on anything that matters to us come into being unless we did indeed have the power to create them by declaration?

Nevertheless, it might be suggested that the problem of normative power has a life of its own. That would be an interesting result for the following reason. The problem of the bare wrong arises only if we impose some substantive constraints on what kinds of consideration can make sense of an action along the lines suggested by (1). And constraints that are at all restrictive are also likely to be controversial. Now suppose that there were an independent problem with the idea that promising and other performatives can make something a wrong. That further problem might be one we can't get around simply by expanding our list of the sorts of considerations that can motivate sensible action. But what could this further problem amount to?[10]

It can't be maintained that the communication of an obligation-creating intention makes literally no difference to the situation. After all, this communication is a real event and so why shouldn't its occurrence be enough to make sense of our tendency to behave differently in the light of it? Perhaps the utterance of something like "I promise" can make the right sort of difference only if "I promise" means something that it can't possibly mean. For example, Anscombe asks rhetorically

> how on earth can it be the meaning of a sign that by giving it one purports to create a necessity of doing something–a necessity whose source in the sign itself, and whose nature depends on the sign? (1981: 100)

But precisely what prevents one creating a motive, a motive that can explain why something is done, by communicating one's intention so to do to another human being? Any answer must invoke a substantive doctrine about the range of motives capable of making sense of human action. And such a doctrine will render promising problematic only in so far as it makes breach of promise look like a bare wrong.

Most breaches of promise are not bare wrongs, because most promises encourage some sort of reliance on (or at least expectation of) their fulfillment. Nevertheless, if my discussion is along the right lines, the atypical promise whose breach does no harm is, in a way, the central case of promising. Most frequently the wrong of breach of promise, the wrong made possible by declaration, is embedded in various other wrongs. Because promisors generally think that it is wrong to breach a promise, their promises tend to generate expectations of performance, and this fact tends to make breach of promise wrong in other ways. To appreciate what worried Hume about promising, we must pare off these other wrongs. We must focus our attention instead on *pure* cases of breach of promise, where breach of the promissory obligation is the only wrong done.

I'll assume that Hume's puzzlement about promise derives from his commitment to something like (1). That is what generates the problem of the bare wrong, and so the problem of normative power. Can these problems be solved without abandoning (1)?

III. PRACTICE THEORIES: HUME AND RAWLS

Hume thinks he can locate a human interest that makes sense of our inclination to keep our promises, respect property rights, and so forth, namely our interest in social coordination, in our knowing what each of us is going to do so that we can coordinate our activities. Few would deny that we have such an interest, and that it makes sense to act on it. How is this interest threatened in Hume's examples?

The problem of the bare wrong is posed by cases in which nobody will benefit from an individual promise's being kept, for example, from a debt's being paid. The people who need the money lose it, and those who acquire it don't benefit from having it, and so on. But, Hume will say, we are in danger of focusing too closely on the individual case. We all have an interest in being able to rely on the promises others make to us and in being able to make promises to them on which they can rely. This interest is served by everyone's firm adherence to a policy of keeping promises. It is not well served if we all retain the option of breaking our promises should we judge that the interests of the individuals involved would be furthered by breach of a particular promise. To give others the assurance they need if we are to cooperate, our promise must be more than an expression of our present view of what future action would be best.

If Hume is correct, the wrongs he considers are not so bare after all. When I refuse to repay my debt as promised on the grounds that everyone is better off if I keep the money, I undermine a valuable social practice, and thereby harm everyone who has an interest in the maintenance of that practice. How exactly is the practice undermined? Considering a case in which there is no apparent good in adhering to a rule of justice, Hume comments:

> Taking any single act, my justice may be pernicious in every respect; and 'tis only upon the supposition, that others are to imitate my example, that I can be induced to embrace that virtue. (Hume, 1978: 493)

By breaching my promise, I cause others not to keep promises where they judge it would be best not to keep these promises and so we are all led not to rely on promises. This reflection alone can get me to keep my promise even where there is no good in it.

Hume's is often called a *practice* theory of promissory obligation, in that he thinks that the wrong involved in breach of promise can be understood only by reference to the existence of a social practice of making and keeping promises. I agree with Hume and other practice theorists that promises don't bind unless people actually treat them as binding, but I reject their other claims. I contend that the function of a promise can't be to serve our interest in social coordination, and I suspect that, to identify the true function of a promise, we must reject the constraint (1) places on compliance with an obligation. But before broaching those more general concerns, I want to examine the two leading practice theories of promissory obligation—those of Hume and Rawls—in detail, and note some of the problems which they encounter, and which a better version of the theory must avoid.

The practice theory in all its guises faces what we might call *Prichard's Problem* (Prichard 1968: 169–172). Let us allow that, once the practice of making and adhering to promises somehow gets going, we all have an interest in maintaining and preserving it. Still, that does not explain how the practice could possibly arise amongst normal human agents, how it could ever make sense for us to keep our promises. The practice of promising is a practice of giving point to a future act of promise-keeping by communicating the intention of giving it that point. If such a procedure makes no sense, the fact that it would be greatly to everyone's advantage if it did make sense is of little consequence.

In addressing this problem, Hume and Rawls distinguish two stages in the evolution of the practice. At the first stage, people are motivated to keep their promises by something other than a sense of obligation. Once this practice is firmly established, we reflect on its role in our lives, and, realizing how we all benefit from this arrangement, we feel obliged to maintain it. At this second stage, we may keep our promises out of a sense of obligation. Let's see how this idea is implemented first in Hume and then by Rawls.[11]

Hume

According to Hume,

> interest is the *first* obligation to the performance of promises. Afterwards, a sentiment of morals concurs with interest, and becomes a new obligation upon mankind. (Hume, 1978: 523)

"Interest" here is our interest in having a reputation for reliability:

> When a man says *he promises anything*, he in effect expresses a *resolution* of performing it; and along with that by making use of this *form of words*, subjects himself to the penalty of never being trusted again in the case of failure. (522)

Should it become known that my promises are not to be trusted, I will no longer be able to get people to do things for me by promising to do things for them. To use Hume's own example, I won't be able to get my neighbour to help me take in my harvest by promising to help him take in his (Hume 1978: 520–521). And this incapacity would be a serious blow to my interests.[12]

Once the practice of promising is up and running, powered by the motivational fuel of self-interest, what role remains for the "sentiment of morals," the sentiment that concurs with, or endorses, the motive of self-interest when we reflect on the social benefits of everyone keeping their promises? Hume notes that while "a present interest" may blind us to the deleterious but remote consequences of our own actions, "it takes not place with regard to those of others; nor hinders them from appearing in their true colours, as highly prejudicial to the public interest, and to our own in particular" (Hume 1978: 545). The sentiment of morals leads us to condemn other people's breaches of promise, decrying the promisor's failure to recognize that his breach of promise harms everybody's interest, including his own. And that reinforces the motive of self-interest, by putting potential violators in fear of being condemned by third parties in addition to being excluded from their mutually beneficial arrangements. This is how the sentiment of morals backs up self-interest, and ensures that we keep our word.

But aren't we inclined to fidelity by our own sense of what is right, and not just by fear of other people's? The practice of promising, as we usually think of it, covers many cases in which it is pretty clearly not in the promisor's interests to keep their promise. If keeping the promise would be costly, and I'm reasonably sure that I will never have to deal with the promisee (or anyone who knows of the breach) again, the canny thing to do might well be to breach. (Think of a promise to purchase or sell a house.) Perhaps I won't even be subject to condemnation by third parties. True, I'm rarely completely sure that my reputation won't suffer. Nevertheless, it is often unlikely that it will, and yet abundantly clear that I am bound to perform. The motive of obligation must outrun that of self-interest, so how can our sense of obligation be no more than our endorsement of a practice based on the motive of self-interest?

Thus far I have been giving Hume's text the orthodox reading, a reading that fits much of his discussion. There is another interpretation. Toward the end of his treatment of promising, and *after* having described how the practice serves both private and public interest, Hume says:

> We cannot readily conceive how the making use of a form of words should be able to cause any material difference. Here, therefore, we *feign* a new act of mind, which we call the willing an obligation; and on this we suppose the morality to depend. (Hume, 1978: 523)[13]

Apparently, all of the above notwithstanding, Hume takes himself to have made no sense of the idea that we can give ourselves a motive for doing something by communicating the intention so to do. In the course of his discussion, we have gone from the superstition that we can do it, to the disillusioned pretence that we actually are doing it, but the act of promising itself remains unintelligible.

One can reconstruct Hume's two-stage genealogy of promises around this passage as follows. At the first stage, we are all mired in confusion. We imagine that it is possible to give an action a point by communicating the intention to give that action a point. And provided you don't reflect on what you are doing, you can act on that confused thought. Given how generally beneficial this confusion is, it would be no surprise if it occurred to us naturally and, with regular reinforcement, became a custom or a habit. The psychological mechanisms that generate and entrench this confusion—instinct, imagination, custom or habit—appear regularly in Hume's philosophy. Furthermore, reflection will not undo the work of imagination, for, as well as the nonsensical character of promising, reflection reveals its great social usefulness. Reflection actually reinforces our confused motive for participating in the practice.

This reading of Hume will not please philosophers uncomfortable with Hume's irrationalism, but it does enable Hume to avoid the problem raised earlier, for at no stage does the practice run on the fuel of self-interest alone. Perhaps we *make* promises only when we expect to gain by so doing. But where keeping the promises turns out not to be in our interests after all, we may still *imagine* ourselves (in our confusion) as bound to keep the promise even before we reflect on the social benefits of the practice. And, once we do come to reflect how beneficial this confusion is, we will continue to honor a wider range of promises than those recommended by mere prudence.

By allowing Hume to bite Prichard's bullet, we secure him the first stage of his genealogy of promising, but the second stage remains problematic, for we are still unable to endorse our tendency to keep all of the promises usually thought binding. Where a breach of promise will remain completely undetected, there is no fear that the practice of promising will be damaged:

> if we suppose, that the loan was secret, and that it is necessary for the interest of the person, that the money be restored in the same manner (and when the lender would conceal his riches), in that case the example ceases, and the public is no longer interested in the actions of the borrower; though I suppose there is no moralist, who will affirm, that the duty and obligation ceases. (Hume, 1978: 480)

Potential promisors won't be any the less likely to keep their promises because of a breach they know nothing about, and so, provided the promisee's interests are not damaged in any other way, even the most altruistic promisor would have no intelligible motive for keeping the promise. Confusion of thought might get him to keep the promise anyway, but a moment's reflection will reveal that (in this case at least) the confusion serves no purpose, that his sense of obligation, though real enough, is absurd.

Rawls

Like Hume, Rawls responds to Prichard's Problem with a two-stage account (1999: 301–308). At the first stage, we have a practice of keeping promises, a practice which serves both public and private interest by facilitating social coordination without invoking the notion of obligation. At the second, those who already conform to the rules of this practice come both to appreciate its benefits and to realize that they are obliged to conform to its rules.

Rawls does not tell us how people begin to make and keep promises, what gets them to participate in the practice to start with. Rawls just assumes that the practice has certain constitutive rules that people tend to obey. Now it is widely held that obedience to a rule involves a tendency to conform that one has because one thinks that one *ought* to conform. On this view, those who participate in the promising practice treat its rules as guides to what they ought to do. Yet this ought cannot be the ought of obligation, otherwise Prichard's problem will return. Nor can it be the ought of prudence, otherwise the scope of the practice will be curtailed. Rawls might avoid this difficulty by maintaining that conformity to the constitutive rules of a practice is a mere custom or habit. Rawls says that his account of why we are obliged to uphold the promising practice once it exists is meant to apply to the practice "however it may have come to be established" (1999: 307). But since Rawls implicitly endorses the assumption that agents must see some good in what they are doing,[14] it looks as if such a practice could not be established amongst rational agents.

Rawls's real advance over Hume comes at the second stage, when we come to assess the practice. Here Hume relies on the thought that the practice will be damaged should we breach, and thus the public interest in social coordination will be harmed. Rawls agrees that we are obliged not to undermine a just and socially useful practice, but he thinks that those who have "voluntarily accepted the benefits of the practice" have a further obligation. According to Rawls's *Principle of Fairness*, they "are obliged to do their part as specified by the rules of the institution" (1999: 301).[15]

For example, it is unfair to exploit the practice by promising your neighbour that you will help him with his harvest if he first helps you with yours unless you mean to perform. This is exploitation, because you would be trying to secure the benefits of the practice (i.e. present aid) without being willing to bear the costs of it (i.e. future performance). Note the problem here is not that you would be damaging the practice by failing to perform. Should your breach somehow go undiscovered, there may be no damage. Rather the point is that, whether found out or not, you would be getting something that you did not deserve in view of your unwillingness to reciprocate.

Here Rawls expands the wrong base, the list of considerations that give breach of promise its wrongful character. No longer is it just harm. The violator may do no harm, either to the promisee or the practice of promising. Still, he is taking something that he does not deserve. Anyone tempted to behave like this might intelligibly refrain for this very reason, even where their breach would go undiscovered. The idea that this item would be undeserved does not depend on some prior obligation not to take it. Rather (we are supposing), desert can provide a ground for a judgement of wrongness.

Rawls may now respond to our earlier worries about how stage one of his account is meant to work by biting Prichard's bullet. Suppose the practice of promising did indeed originate in a widespread confusion of thought. Nonetheless once the practice has got going, even the clearheaded among us may feel obliged to keep our promises, since the practice is a socially useful one. And those of us who voluntarily accept the benefits of the practice will have an even weightier (and perfectly rational) obligation so to do.[16]

Imagine that, by expanding the wrong base in the way Rawls suggests, we could bring all wrongful breaches of promise, including the seemingly bare wrongs, within the scope of the practice theory. Still, extensional adequacy is not the only test such a theory must pass. The wrong the practice theorist detects in a breach of a promise must be a wrong of the right sort (cf. Scanlon, 1998: 316). A breach of promise is primarily a wrong against the promisee, since the promisee is the person to whom the performance is owed. Third parties (including potential beneficiaries) may also be wronged by the breach, and perhaps these other wrongs are, in the end, more serious. Nevertheless, they presuppose that the promisee has himself been wronged. Can Rawls accommodate this structural fact?

Consider a case in which the promisee is not harmed by the breach. Rawls argues that the promisor has not played fair, and so his breach is still a wrong. But who is wronged by this breach? Rawls would reply that the promisor is dealing unfairly with all of those who uphold and maintain the practice; we are *all* wronged whenever the practice of promising is exploited in this way, regardless of whether the promisee (or anyone else) is actually harmed. Even so, there is surely a distinct wrong of breach of promise, a wrong directed specifically at the promisee. And where is *this* wrong to be found when the promisee is unharmed by (and perhaps even ignorant of) the breach?

Rawls might respond that, though the violator is being unfair to all of us who uphold the promising practice, he is being especially unfair to the promisee, whose individual propensity to rely on promises he is exploiting. Even when the promisee is not harmed, he is exploited in a way that others are not, and it is *via* the exploitation of him that the practice as a whole is exploited. This sounds plausible enough when we are dealing with a promisee who conscientiously keeps his own promises. But suppose Hume's debauchee is happy to accept my promises, even though he doesn't take his own promises very seriously. I would still wrong him by failing to pay my debt as promised (whether or not he is harmed).[17] Yet it could hardly be said that *he* deserves this sort of consideration, that I would be exploiting the practice of promising by exploiting *his* devotion to it in particular. He is no more willing to play fair than I.

In this section, I have raised doubts about the two most detailed and influential practice theories of promissory obligation. Implicit in both is a certain view about the function of a promise, namely that promises are here to facilitate social coordination. In the final section, I shall ignore the detail of these theories and focus on that shared assumption.

IV. SOCIAL COORDINATION

Promises bind because people actually treat them as binding. That is the truth in the practice theory. The leading practice theorists have also maintained that promising's function is to enable us to coordinate our activities with other human beings. In their view, that is why it makes sense to make, accept and keep promises. Call this the *social coordination hypothesis*. In this section, I shall argue that the latter hypothesis cannot sustain the former insight. First, we could have social coordination without a *practice* of promising, and, second we could have social coordination without a practice of *promising*.

As to the first point, it might seem obvious that, if promise is to be of any use as a tool of social coordination, people must be in the habit of fulfilling their promises. Given that we take promises seriously because they enable social coordination, it follows that promises would lose their binding force unless people were in the habit of keeping them. Yet at least one of Hume's contemporaries maintained that there need be no practice of promising for promises to serve our interest in social coordination. Writing in response to Hume's Treatise, Thomas Reid wondered why the obligation of a promise should depend on the existence of a prior practice of promise keeping. Reid did not doubt that promises would be "useless" unless people were (a) disposed to trust them and (b) disposed to keep them (1969: 443). But why, he asked, can't these dispositions be "an effect of their constitution" (444)? Perhaps people are innately disposed to both trust and respect promises, and have innate common knowledge of this fact about one another.[18] Call this the innateness hypothesis.

Reid argues at some length that the innateness hypothesis is true, but our concern is not with its truth. Rather I am interested in Reid's further claim that, were his hypothesis true, that alone would ensure that promises were binding. The practice theorist can't agree, so long as he maintains that promises do not bind unless human beings are in the habit of making and keeping promises. You can't be in the habit of doing something that you have never done. There is no such thing as an innate habit. Yet, given the innate dispositions and common knowledge Reid outlines, surely promises would serve the function of coordinating our activities regardless of whether there was any custom of so using them. Human history might, in principle, contain only a single promise, a promise that was entered into because it served at least one party's interest in coordination, and that was binding because breach of it would harm that interest. By adopting the social coordination hypothesis, the practice theorist breaks the connection between the existence of a practice and the normative force of a promise.

I take it Hume would regard the innateness hypothesis as psychologically implausible. He makes fun of the idea that our respect for property might be the product of an "original instinct." The rules governing the acquisition and transfer of property are too complex and variable for this to be at all plausible (Hume, 1975: 201–203). Doubtless he would say the same of the rules governing promissory obligation. We need not assess Hume's argumentation here, since latter-day practice theorists are unlikely to take the same tack. Their claim is the normative one that taking promises seriously makes sense only when there is a practice of promising. Reid's hypothesis constitutes a conclusive objection to this claim, at least so long as it is underwritten by the social coordination hypothesis. Let's now assess the merits of this hypothesis.

All of the most considerable practice theorists maintain not just that promising serves our interest in coordinating our activities with other human beings over time, but that this key interest can be served only by something like a promise.[19] They appear to endorse Hume's view that the "invention" of promising is "absolutely necessary" (1978: 484), because, at least when dealing with strangers, we can't generate the sort of cooperation required to get the harvest in unless human beings are in the habit of making and keeping promises.[20]

For Hume, promising is made necessary by the "confined generosity" (1978: 495) of human beings. Hume is no egoist. He allows that human beings care for family and friends as well as for themselves. Indeed he maintains that they have a greater affection for those close to them, taken together, than for themselves (487). What he denies is that we have any considerable interest in the welfare of strangers (at least so long as the brute instinct that leads us to empathise with the physical suffering of another creature, human or animal, is not in play—481). Given this, human beings cannot rely on the altruism of strangers to facilitate cooperative relations with them. As Hume says when discussing respect for property rights, "benevolence to strangers is too weak for this purpose" (492).

Hume's doubts about generalized benevolence seem well grounded, but there is another potential source of motivational support for cooperative activity. Among the virtues that are "common in human nature," Hume mentions gratitude (e.g. 1978: 479).[21] If someone does me a favour, I'll be inclined to do him a favor. Conversely, if someone harms me, I'll be much less inclined to help him out in the future. Since this fact is widely known, why can't it be exploited to set up the very cooperative arrangements among strangers that supposedly require a promise?[22]

Cooperation could arise as follows. I offer to help my neighbor bring in his harvest while making it clear that I am doing so because I expect my neighbor to be moved to reciprocate, and specifically to help me bring in my harvest next week. Since help next week is my expectation, other help given at other times would not constitute adequate reciprocation. Furthermore, since I am relying on this help, any failure to follow through would likely harm and thus wrong me. I might also make it clear that if he allows me to help without reciprocating, there will be a price to pay in that I will not depend on his gratitude again.[23]

The mechanism is formally similar to a promise, as Hume presents it. There too I indicate that I expect reciprocation because I expect a certain motive to come into play, namely conscientious adherence to the promise. And I also indicate that if there is no performance, there will be a price to pay in that I will no longer depend on his conscientiousness. But the motive of gratitude lacks the feature of promising that so mystified Hume. What brings that motive into play is not just the communicated intention of bringing it into play, but the bestowal of a benefit.[24] And a failure to reciprocate constitutes a harm, where reliance is involved, or unfair dealing, where it isn't. Such harm or unfairness could form part of a wrong base that conformed to (1).

Considering this very possibility in his discussion of the two farmers, Hume says the following:

> Men being naturally selfish, or endow'd only with a confin'd generosity, they are not easily induc'd to perform any action for the interest of strangers, except with a view to some reciprocal advantage, which they had no hope of obtaining but by such a performance. Now as it frequently happens, that these mutual performances cannot be finish'd at the same instant, 'tis' necessary, that one party be contented to remain in uncertainty, and depend upon the gratitude of the other for a return of kindness. But so much corruption is there among men, that, generally speaking, this becomes but a slender security; and as the benefactor is here suppos'd to bestow his favours with a view to self-interest, this both takes off from the obligation, and sets an example to selfishness, which is the true mother of ingratitude. (Hume, 1978: 519–520)

Let's allow that pure self-interest would provide a surer foundation for the sort of cooperative activity underwritten by a promise than the motive of gratitude.[25] Since Hume has failed to show that self-interest can be harnessed in this way, the comparison is irrelevant. What we should be asking is whether the procedure of invoking gratitude described above could provide a non-promissory foundation for cooperative activity. For this purpose, the motive of gratitude need only be as strong and ubiquitous as the motive (whatever it is) that actually underwrites the keeping of promises. Hume gives us no reason to doubt this. If human "corruption" really were sufficient to render gratitude useless for purposes of social coordination, the chances of coordination by any other means look slim.

Is the distinction between promissory obligations and obligations of reciprocity as clear-cut as I have been supposing? In a particular case, it may be impossible to tell whether two people are bound by an obligation of reciprocation or by a promissory obligation. Say that my neighbor and I babysit for one another. No *explicit* agreement was ever reached, but I have got into the habit of babysitting on Friday night in the expectation of having a child-free Saturday night. One weekend the arrangement breaks down for no good reason, and I find myself having to cancel Saturday night's entertainment. Here my expectations are disappointed, and I feel wronged, but what was the basis of my expectation? Did my neighbor tacitly promise to babysit for me this Saturday? Or is it rather that my neighbor is just not playing fair in helping me enjoy my night out as I helped him enjoy his night out? Such questions may have no clear answer, but that does not mean an obligation of reciprocation is no different from a promissory obligation. Rather what we have here are obligations of two quite different kinds that may serve the same purpose. Where social coordination is what matters, neither party will worry too much about exactly how it is being achieved. They will tolerate unclarity about precisely which social tool they are employing, and what the basis for their obligation is.

I have been assuming that obligations of reciprocation have a quite different normative basis from promissory obligations, but this may be doubted. When Rawls states his Principle of Fairness, he requires that the benefits of a social practice be "voluntarily" accepted, with the implication that one who has had the benefits imposed on him, or who cannot easily avoid receiving them, is not obliged to play his part. Something like this is, in many cases, a plausible restriction on obligations of reciprocation. What exactly does the notion of acceptance involve?

On one construal, someone who "voluntarily accepts" a gift *consents* to the imposition of an obligation of reciprocation. The consent here looks very like a promise to reciprocate, and seems to raise all the theoretical issues generated by such exercises of normative power (Hume 1975: 208). But this construal reads too much into the notion of acceptance. Someone can voluntarily accept a benefit simply by going out of their way to take advantage of it, without agreeing to take on an obligation to reciprocate, and indeed without even being aware that there is such an obligation (Simmons, 2001:

16–18). If I bring my children out each day at just the right moment for them to join the supervised crocodile that takes the children to school, I should expect to have to contribute to this arrangement at some point, if asked to do so. But the fact that I should expect this does not mean that I do expect it, let alone that I expressed such an expectation to anyone. The whole neighborhood may know how obtuse I am.

In this section, I have argued that our interest in social coordination can be adequately served without either a *practice* of promising or a practice of *promising*. Hume and his many followers are wrong to maintain that a practice of promising is indispensable, at least for that reason, to the social life of human beings. Hume is better placed than his followers, in that he makes a number of assumptions about human psychology whose truth might render such a practice indispensable. But later practice theorists show no inclination to adopt these assumptions, nor should they.

I'll conclude the paper by considering a final worry that prompts us to reconsider the overall direction of the argument. Hume and his fellow practice theorists are wrong to maintain that, without promissory obligation, social cooperation would become difficult, or even impossible, and human society could not exist in its present form. But can't an advocate of the social coordination hypothesis make do with the much weaker claim that promising is *one* perfectly good way of securing the needed cooperation, and that promises exist, and are taken seriously for just this reason? True, we have other tools of social coordination at our disposal, and so there may be some overlap in function, but the redundancy here is hardly complete. There are situations in which the motive of conscientiousness is available, but the motive of gratitude is not. Perhaps you have lost confidence in your neighbour's gratitude but not in their fidelity. Perhaps you have nothing to offer in return, but still hope that pity will lead them to promise without return. Why isn't this enough to explain why we have evolved more than one way of getting it together?

Were promissory obligation as firmly rooted in human interests as obligations of reciprocation, the practice theorist could be satisfied by this weaker claim. But, of course, our starting point was that (unlike the mechanism of reciprocation) promising appeared to generate bare wrongs whose connection to familiar human interests was obscure. Therefore, the very intelligibility of promissory obligation is in question. Since the attempts of Hume and others to allay these doubts failed, a picture of human life that minimized the role of promissory obligation, or even dispensed with it altogether, would be much more satisfying than one that had promissory obligation operating in tandem with other methods of coordination.

Recall Hume's farmers once more. We observe them conversing. The first farmer helps harvest the second's field today, and the second farmer helps harvest the first's soon after. We then ask the second farmer why he helped the first farmer out, and he replies by citing an obligation. What is the most plausible account of why he thought himself obliged to do this? Were Hume right to maintain that the *only* available answer here involves a promise, we might have to swallow it, even if this involved placing a deeply confused thought at the foundation of our social life. Where confusion is completely unavoidable, it may also be a stable source of motivation, but where there is an alternative mode of cooperative motivation, both intelligible and widely available, the case is quite different. Since human beings wish to make sense to themselves, dispensable confusion will be dispensed with and intelligible motives will be adopted. The anthropologist should conclude that the mechanism of reciprocation does the work of social coordination anywhere it can.

Far from giving promising pride of place in our social lives, the social coordination hypothesis renders it peripheral. That is exactly the conclusion several opponents of the practice theory have drawn. These writers contend that behind the façade of the exercise of normative power lies the reality of principles of reciprocity, adverse reliance, and due care for induced expectations.[26] For them, bare wrongs are an illusion. This conclusion can be avoided only by rejecting the social coordination hypothesis and amending the theory of rational agency implicit in (1).

The writing of this essay was made possible by the award of a Leverhulme Major Research Fellowship.

NOTES

1. I shall not go into the vexed question of whether Hume is a psychological hedonist. Certainly one could endorse this assumption without being a hedonist.

2. Though he does have a peculiar idea of what an obligation is. For Hume, one is obliged to do something when (a) the desire not to perform it would displease us, and (b) this sentiment is one we would endorse on reflection (Hume 1978: 517).

3. On some views, whether we should perform an action depends on whether that action would manifest dispositions, motives or traits of character that we ought to have: the value of an action depends on the value of the motives, and so forth, it manifests. Indeed Hume himself seems to hold this (Hume 1978: 477–8). (1) might appear inconsistent with such a view since it suggests that whether we should fulfill an obligation is a matter not of whether we should be motivated or disposed to fulfill it but rather of whether we should perform a specific action: the action of discharging it. As many authors have pointed out, these questions may have different answers (a generally valuable motive might be counterproductive in a particular instance, or might have beneficial effects on things other than the agent's actions). But (1) is consistent with the view that we ought to assess actions by first assessing the motives etc. which give rise to them. What (1) does is to place a certain restriction on motives for action, namely that an agent must see some good in what he is doing: motives on

which he acts must be to that extent directed at the good. This is a constraint that Hume, for one, clearly accepts. I thank Brad Hooker for pressing me on this point.

4. This welfarist assumption should not be confused with utilitarianism or consequentialism. A strict deontologist might object to coercion or deception on the grounds that they involve unjustified harm.

5. Hume includes "equity" on his list of "natural virtues" (1978: 578).

6. Something like this notion of what is fair or reasonable plays a foundational role in various accounts of moral obligation. See, for example, the notion of reasonable rejection in Scanlon (1998: 191–197).

7. They may communicate this complex intention without actually having it, so while the communication must be intentional, the imposition of the consequent obligation need not be. (Owens 2008: 739–741).

8. This communication is not sufficient for the imposition of the obligation. In fact, various procedural conditions must be satisfied (Owens 2007), and there may also be substantive constraints on the content of a valid promise. Nevertheless, the satisfaction of these various conditions need not ensure that breach of the promise threatens any human interest.

9. See Darwall's "Demystifying Promises," in this book.

10. I'm grateful to Shelly Kagan for pressing this question on me.

11. For a helpful discussion of both theories, see Kolodny and Wallace (2003: 120–125).

12. Hobbes takes a similar like in his reply to The Fool (1994: 90–92).

13. Mackie (1980: 100–104) gives us the orthodox reading, and dismisses this passage as a mistake on Hume's part.

14. For example, his remark that "the doctrine of the purely conscientious act is irrational" (Rawls (1999: 418).

15. Fried (1981: 14–16) offers a structurally similar theory of promise, appealing to the wrong of abusing a socially useful practice. Rawls speaks of accepting the benefits of a practice here, but perhaps the more neutral notion of accepting its products will serve just as well.

16. Thanks to Daniel Markovits for discussion of this point.

17. It would be a bit rich of him to complain of (or even resent) the breach, but it would be equally rich of a kidnapper to complain were his own children held to ransom. Both are still wronged, whether or not they are entitled to object.

18. Reid also argues that human beings can communicate the intentions involved in exercising various normative powers without employing conventional languages by instead using the natural language of voice and gesture (1969: 439–442). The practice theorist need not disagree with this, but will maintain that the normative significance of these communications depends on whether there is a practice of taking them seriously.

19. For example, Anscombe (1981: 18), Rawls (1999: 304–306), Foot (2001: 45), Prichard (1968: 174–175), Hart (1994: 193–200).

20. Hume also says that the rules of property are "not only useful but even absolutely necessary to human society" (1978: 501).

21. To bring the issue into focus here we must ignore some distracting connotations of the word "gratitude." There are *feelings* of gratitude, and gifts are often valued more as an expression of such feelings than anything else. Now such feelings

cannot be *demanded* and so, one might think, the whole idea of an obligation of gratitude is rather odd (Rousseau 1987: 73). What is needed to facilitate coordination between Hume's farmers is not gratitude so understood, but rather *reciprocation* in the form of hard labor, reciprocation which can be demanded. I owe thanks to Daniel Markovits for discussion here.

22. We could put the same question to Hobbes as follows: Why doesn't your fourth law of nature (recommending reciprocation) facilitate defensive arrangements just as well as your third law of nature (recommending the keeping of covenants made)? (1994: 89–95).

23. It has been suggested that empathy and reciprocal altruism are the twin foundations of social organization among animals (DeWaal 2006: 42–49). Only animals like ourselves who know about obligation can make any use of promising.

24. As with Rawls's principle of fairness, we should perhaps leave it open whether a benefit must be involved here. Perhaps the thing bestowed only needs to be accepted for a return to be required.

25. In fact, the motive of gratitude may have a wider scope than that of self-interest. It might lead you to reciprocate with the expected benefit even if, for some reason, no one would know whether you had reciprocated.

26. See Atiyah (1981: 184–215) and Scanlon (1998: ch. 7). Atiyah openly admits that significant parts of our promissory practice make little sense on his model. Scanlon is more hopeful of accommodating and explaining our practices without resort to normative powers. I have criticized various aspects of Scanlon's account, and proposed an alternative, in Owens (2006, 2007, 2008).

REFERENCES

Altham, J. 1985. "Wicked Promises." In I. Hacking (ed.), *Exercises in Analysis*. Cambridge: Cambridge University Press pp. 1–21.

Anscombe, E. 1981. *Ethics, Religion and Politics*. Minneapolis: Minnesota University Press.

Atiyah, M. 1981. *Promises, Morals and Law*. Oxford: Oxford University Press.

DeWaal, F. 2006. *Primates and Philosophers*. Princeton: Princeton University Press.

Feinberg, J. 1970. *Doing and Deserving*. Princeton: Princeton University Press.

Foot, P. 2001. *Natural Goodness*. Oxford: Oxford University Press.

Fried, C. 1981. *Contract as Promise*. Cambridge, MA: Harvard University Press.

Hart, H. 1994. *The Concept of Law* Oxford: Oxford University Press.

Hume, D. 1978. *Treatise on Human Nature*. Oxford: Oxford University Press.

———. 1975. *Enquiry Concerning the Principles of Morals*. Oxford: Oxford University Press.

Hobbes, T. 1994. *Leviathan*. Indianapolis: Hackett.

Kolodny, N., and Wallace, J. 2003. "Promises and Practices Revisited." *Philosophy and Public Affairs* 31: 119–154.

Mackie, J. 1980. *Hume's Moral Theory*. London: Routledge.

Owens, D. 2006. "A Simple Theory of Promising." *Philosophical Review* 115: 51–77.

———. 2007. "Duress, Deception and the Validity of a Promise." *Mind* 116: 293–315.

———. 2008. "Promising without Intending." *Journal of Philosophy* 105: 737–755.

Prichard, H. 1968. "The Obligation to Keep a Promise." In H. Prichard, *Moral Obligation* Oxford: Oxford University Press. *pp. 169-179.*

Rawls, J. 1999. *A Theory of Justice: Revised Edition.* Cambridge, MA: Harvard University Press.

Reid, T. 1969. *Essays on the Active Powers of the Human Mind.* Cambridge, MA: MIT Press).

Rousseau J. J. 1987. *Discourse on the Origin of Inequality.* Indianapolis: Hackett.

Scanlon, T. 1998. *What We Owe to Each Other.* Cambridge, MA: Harvard University Press.

Searle, J. 1969. *Speech Acts.* Cambridge: Cambridge University Press.

Simmons, J. 2001. *Justification and Legitimacy.* Cambridge: Cambridge University Press.

Chapter 3

Three Dogmas about Promising

Margaret Gilbert

Abstract

Philosophers who discuss everyday promises (as opposed to legal contracts) generally make the following three assumptions: when one who makes a promise is thereby obligated to do what was promised, that obligation is a matter of his (or her) being morally required to act as promised, this requirement deriving from a general moral principle or principles; the obligation of a promise cannot simply be willed into being; promises whose content is such that one is morally required not to act as promised are not obligating. I argue that these three assumptions are problematic, given two intuitive points: every promise obligates the promisor; the obligation in question is directed *in a sense I elaborate. I sketch an account of promising that respects these intuitive points, among others, and which does not support any of the three assumptions. According to this account, roughly, promisor and promisee together create—by virtue of mutual expressions of the will to do so—a* joint commitment *which obligates the promisor to act as promised, irrespective of the content of the promise. The kind of obligation in question is not a matter of moral requirement derived from a general moral principle but is a function of the existence of any joint commitment as such.*

The topic of promising connects with several broader issues. Among these is the question of how human beings can constrain or bind themselves with respect to their future actions. By promising, one binds oneself in a particularly intractable way: one who promises another that he (or she) will do something cannot unilaterally unbind himself but awaits release from the person to whom he has promised, his "promisee."[1]

There is a vast and expanding philosophical literature on promising. My main negative aim here is to highlight and question the three interrelated dogmas of the title, dogmas—more politely, assumptions—that prevail in that literature. I question them in light of two points that many (myself included) take to be intuitive.

My main positive aim is to demonstrate that there is a plausible theory of promising that respects the two intuitive points that render the three dogmas suspect and allows one to replace those dogmas with more intuitively plausible counterparts. According to the theory of promising I shall delineate, one who promises creates together with the person to whom the promise is made a *joint commitment* with a particular type of content.

Some Preliminary Points

I start with some preliminary points. First, in speaking of a *promise*, I do not mean to limit myself to situations in which someone utters the words "I promise," or an equivalent in a language other than English. A few words in support of this point may be useful, though it is not an uncommon one.[2]

Suppose that Jeremy says to Julia, "I'll phone you tonight," and Julia responds, "Okay." If Jeremy then fails to call, Julia may remonstrate with him: "You said you'd call." In other words, she may treat Jeremy's "I'll phone you" much as she would have treated his "I'll phone you—I promise," and she may be right to do so.

Supposing that she is, it would not be appropriate for Jeremy to respond that his "I'll phone you..." was a mere expression of intention or decision, or, as if it were, that "I changed my mind."[3] Nor could he appropriately respond "Well, I guess I was wrong, since I didn't call!" as if his "I'll call you" was a mere prediction. Nor would it be appropriate for him to say: "Well, I didn't *promise* to call!" and back this up with the observation: "I didn't say 'I promise'!" For the fact that he did not use the words "I promise" would not be enough to get him off the hook.

Perhaps Julia is less likely to say "But you promised!" in the case imagined. If so, that could be because Jeremy did not, indeed, say "I promise..." Otherwise, the two situations appear to be on a par.

This is not to deny that there are interesting things to say about the utterance "I promise." One of these is that it is a "performative" utterance in the sense of Austin (1962). Roughly, with a performative utterance one does what one says one is doing by saying that one is doing it. Thus one can also say "I hereby promise..."

No such thing can be said of Jeremy's "I'll phone you tonight." Yet, as said, what transpires between him and Julia when he says this and she says "Okay" may be much the same as it would have been had he said "I'll phone you tonight—I promise." In speaking of "promises," I mean to speak of what is common between these cases.

The second preliminary point is this: promises and *agreements* are "close cousins." I return to this point later in the essay.

The third preliminary point is that the focus of my discussion, like that of most philosophers who work on promises, is on everyday promises of the kind that Jeremy made to Julia in my opening example, as opposed to the smaller class of promises that fall into some category—in particular, contract—with which the law concerns itself. Those who make everyday promises may have no intention to create legal relations and may not create such relations in fact.

The law has its own reasons for allowing one or another transaction to establish a legal relation. Good as these reasons may be from the point of view of the law, the resulting judgments may or may not be helpful to those seeking to understand the nature and implications of what goes on outside the legal arena. Thus, though legal judgments may bear on whether or not a particular point is indeed an intuitive one, they cannot determine that question.

The fourth and final preliminary point has to do with the way in which a promise binds the one who makes it—the "promisor." It is generally assumed that there is at least one central intuitive sense in which a promisor is *obligated*, by virtue of having promised, to act as he has promised, at least if all else is equal. I shall not dispute this assumption.

Theorists often speak of a promisor's "promissory obligation," in the singular. This suggests that, when a promisor is obligated by virtue of having promised, obligation in just one sense of the term is at issue. Indeed, as I shall explain, different theorists of promising tend to focus on one and the same sense of "obligation."

In what follows I shall use the phrase "promissory obligation" on account of its familiarity. In using that phrase, however, I mean to allow that a promisor may be obligated, by virtue of his promise, in more than one sense.

I shall in due course distinguish two radically different senses of "obligation." I shall argue, in effect, that one must distinguish between the two senses in question if one is to understand the ways in which a promisor may be bound by his promise.[4]

One can put *the problem of promissory obligation* thus: in what sense or senses, if any, does one who promises thereby obligate himself to do the promised act—at least all else being equal?[5] The discussion in this essay bears closely on this issue.

I. THREE DOGMAS ABOUT PROMISING

The three dogmas I discuss are points that contemporary philosophers of promising tend to accept—either explicitly or implicitly.[6] To call them dogmas is not to say that philosophers have no reason to accept them. It is rather to say that they tend not to be examined with a critical eye. Their acceptance is consequential: they have helped to shape most contemporary theories of promising. All three dogmas concern promissory obligation. Taking each one in turn, I summarize it, then amplify the summary somewhat.

The Moral Requirement Dogma

The Moral Requirement dogma may be summarized thus: promissory obligation is a matter of moral requirement. More fully, it runs as follows: the obligation that a promisor incurs by virtue of his promise, when he does indeed so incur an obligation, is a moral requirement deriving from a general moral principle or several such principles. Thus, almost in so many words, Thomas Scanlon:

> When promises give rise to clear obligations, these can be accounted for on the basis of general moral principles. (1998: 315)[7]

It is understood that promisors may not be the only class of persons covered by the general moral principle or principles in question.[8]

Different theorists have different accounts of what a specifically moral requirement amounts to. They would generally agree that a moral requirement is to be distinguished from a legal requirement, and from a prudential requirement, among others. They would also generally agree that such requirements do not depend on contingent human agreements or other arrangements. More positively, it is common to argue for the existence of a moral principle or requirement by reference to significant values or interests that are, it is claimed, promoted by one's conformity to it.[9]

Both the "social practice" theories that he opposes, and Scanlon's own theory, among others, appeal to moral principles in their explanations of promissory obligation.[10] Scanlon's complex "Principle F" takes certain carefully specified empirical conditions to be the crucial aspects of promising, and says that, when those conditions are satisfied then, morally speaking, and subject to a further condition, the promisor must act as promised in the absence of special justification for not doing so.

In one of its formulations Principle F runs as follows:

If (1) A voluntarily and intentionally leads B to expect that A will do X (unless B consents to A's not doing so);
(2) A knows that B wants to be assured of this;
(3) A acts with the aim of providing this assurance, and has good reason to believe that he or she has done so;
(4) B knows that A has the beliefs and intentions just described;
(5) A intends for B to know this, and knows that B does know it; and

(6) B knows that A has this knowledge and intent; then, in the absence of special justification, A must do X unless B consents to X's not being done. (Scanlon, 1998: 304)

I take it that Scanlon might equally well have written "is morally required to" instead of "must," as far as his intentions went.

The No Willing Dogma

I turn now to the second dogma. Its first proponent, to my knowledge, was David Hume. In a famous passage in the *Treatise* (2000: 322), Hume notes that, according to "our common ways of thinking and expressing ourselves...the obligation [of a promise] arises from our mere will and pleasure." He proceeds to argue, skeptically, that the obligation of a promise is not and cannot simply be willed into being. In his words, more generally: "'Tis impossible that we cou'd ever will a new obligation". (2000: 332, n. 2).

Hume's skeptical conclusion about promises is the second dogma. I will refer to it as the *No Willing* dogma.[11] I think it fair to say that it has been a large part of the inspiration for contemporary theories of promissory obligation.[12]

Given that one accepts the Moral Requirement dogma, one is likely to accept the No Willing dogma for something like the following reason: the obligation of a promise is a moral requirement. As such, it is not the kind of thing that can be brought into being by a mere act of will—justified or not.[13]

The Immoral Promises Dogma

I now turn to the third dogma: in and of itself, one who makes an immoral promise is not thereby obligated to act as promised. I label this the *Immoral Promises* dogma.

An example of an immoral promise is Diana's promise to Sue that she will kill Clarence. The mere fact that Diana made this promise does not, surely, make it morally permissible for her to kill Clarence. On the contrary, if there are no other considerations bearing on the case, it is morally impermissible for her to do what she promised in this situation. Hence—in the sense of "immoral promise" at issue—her promise is an immoral one. According to the third dogma, Diana is not obligated to act as promised—all else being equal.[14]

The Immoral Promises dogma on my characterization of it is intended to be agnostic on the question of what kinds of obligation there are. Hence it is not intended to be implied by that characterization that obligation is therein understood to be a matter of moral requirement. Still, it is worth pointing out that one who holds the Moral Requirement dogma may be led by it to the Immoral Promises dogma.

According to the Moral Requirement dogma, the obligation of a promise, when it arises, is a moral requirement to keep the promise. Given its content, meanwhile, an immoral promise is such that one is not morally required to keep it, all else being equal. Rather, one is morally required not to keep it. Given the Moral Requirement dogma, then, an immoral promise, in and of itself, does not obligate the promisor.

This assumes something I take to be correct: if at this point in time, given current circumstances, I am morally required *not* to perform some action, A, then at this point in time, given the same circumstances, there is no moral requirement on me to *perform* A. Perhaps there would be such a moral requirement on me, if some of the current circumstances were not present; but that is a different matter.[15]

It is worth pointing out that given this assumption certain situations that have been described as involving conflicting *obligations* cannot be construed as involving conflicting *moral requirements*. Interestingly enough, such situations often involve conflicting promises. An example would be Jane's having promised Phyllis that she will attend Phyllis's wedding, and her also having promised Bob that she will drive his mother to an important appointment with the doctor—when it turns out, regrettably, that the doctor's appointment is at the very time of Phyllis's wedding. Evidently, the nature of these particular situations will be clearest when we have a satisfactory theory of promissory obligation.

II. TWO INTUITIVE POINTS ABOUT PROMISING

I now introduce two intuitive points about promissory obligation that might be thought firm in advance of one's acquaintance with the three dogmas. The problem for the dogmas is that these points undercut them.

At this moment in time, of course, the three dogmas may seem as firm as any other points. They may also seem to be irreplaceable. With respect to the first dogma, for instance: if promissory obligation is not a matter of moral requirement, what is it? If one can give an account of promissory obligation that is otherwise plausible and respects the two intuitive points, while failing to support the three dogmas, those dogmas should seem less compelling.

In saying that these points are "intuitive" I mean roughly this: given only one's understanding of them, it is hard to doubt their truth. Indeed, they may appear to be knowable a priori, or (more specifically) to be true by virtue of the meanings of the terms involved, or true by definition. Such judgments, being judgments, are open to pressure from arguments to the contrary. Such arguments are necessary, however, if they are to be discredited.

Prichard's Point

What, then, are these two points? The first is suggested by the Oxford philosopher H. A. Prichard when he writes: "Once call some act a promise, and all question of whether there is an obligation to do it seems to have vanished" (1968: 198).

I shall myself phrase the point I have in mind with more certitude, as I believe is appropriate, and in the material as opposed to the linguistic mode. I believe that it is intuitive *for at least one central sense of the term "obligation."* The point is this: if someone has promised to do something, then he is obligated to do it, by virtue of his promise. For the sake of a label, I shall call this: "Prichard's point."

Several philosophers have made statements that suggest it.[16] Some say that the statement that a promise obligates the promisor to perform the promised act is true by definition, or that it is analytic.[17] In either case Prichard's point as I have characterized it would be correct—and knowable a priori.[18]

Prichard's point seems to present a problem for the Immoral Promises dogma. According to that dogma, an immoral promise, in and of itself, *does not obligate the promisor*.[19] According to Prichard's point every promise obligates the promisor.

Perhaps the conflict between Prichard's point and the Immoral Promises dogma is only apparent. One pertinent issue here is this. On the face of it, an immoral promise is *possible*. Is that correct?

Though there is not a great deal of discussion of immoral promises in the literature, there is some, and it is generally agreed that immoral promises are indeed possible. One argument for this goes as follows: if what seems to be an immoral promise has not been kept, it can intelligibly be invoked by the promisee as a basis for complaint against the promisor. If it had not been made, it could not be invoked.[20] Having granted the possibility of an immoral promise, authors generally say that such promises do not obligate the promisor. In other words, they endorse the Immoral Promises dogma.

Let us grant, with the consensus, that immoral promises are possible. Whether or not there is indeed a conflict between the Immoral Promises dogma and Prichard's point depends, further, on precisely how that point is understood.[21]

Consider what I shall call the *weak reading* of Prichard's point, which runs roughly thus: it is a truth knowable a priori that, if one has promised to do something, then by virtue of his promise, as such, he is obligated to act as promised, *in the absence of sufficiently powerful countervailing considerations.* Given sufficiently powerful countervailing considerations, which are possible, he is not obligated to act as promised. On the weak reading, then, Prichard's point allows that a given promisor may *not* be obligated to fulfill his promise. In particular it allows that *the obligation of a promise may depend in part at least on the content of that promise.*

On the weak reading of Prichard's point it does not in itself constitute a challenge to the Immoral Promises dogma. It remains to ask whether Prichard's point should be given the weak reading. This I take not to be a question about Prichard's own intent, but about what is intuitive.

I propose that what is intuitive is this: promising is a source of obligation such that if one has made a promise one is in some sense obligated to do what one has promised, *all things considered.* In particular, a promise obligates *irrespective of its content.* I shall call this the *strong reading* of Prichard's point.

I make this proposal without attempting to specify the sense of "obligation" in question, while taking it to be a central, standard sense. I do take it that obligation in the sense of moral requirement is not at issue, if only because one who makes a promise is *not* morally required to act as promised irrespective of its content.

Recall now Prichard's own way of putting things: "Once call some act a promise, and all question of whether there is an obligation to do it seems to have vanished." On the face of it, he is not talking about an obligation "to do it, depending on what it is." Admittedly, given Prichard's use of the word "seems," his statement is somewhat tentative. This could be because he finds the point puzzling. He makes it clear that he does find it puzzling as he proceeds through the essay from which the quotation is taken. In short, I conjecture that Prichard's own tentativeness stems from his finding an apparently a priori truth hard to square with other things he believes. As I understand him, one of these is the Moral Requirement dogma. Another is the No Willing dogma.[22]

Be that as it may, in what follows I focus on the strong reading of Prichard's point: if one knows that someone has promised to do something, one knows that he is in some central, standard sense obligated to do it, *all things, including its content, considered.*

According to the Immoral Promises dogma, an immoral promise, in and of itself, does not obligate the promisor to act as promised. According to Prichard's point, one's promise obligates one to act as promised irrespective of its content. Thus an immoral promise obligates the promisor to act as promised irrespective of its immorality. It seems, then, that we must give up the Immoral Promises dogma if we accept Prichard's point.

Since the Immoral Promises dogma follows from the Moral Requirement dogma, we shall have to give both up, if we stick with Prichard's point. And then one clear basis for the No Willing dogma crumbles.

Promissory Obligations Are Directed

I now turn to a second intuitive point that creates a problem for the three dogmas. Though personally I find Prichard's point to be compelling, I take the second point to be the firmer of the two. It is in any case an important supplement to Prichard's point. In a brief statement to be amplified shortly: promissory obligation is relational or *directed* obligation.

If Olive has a *directed obligation*, there are one or more persons toward whom that obligation is directed. Her obligation is an obligation to Roger, say. It will be an obligation to Roger to do such-and-such.

It is generally understood that, correlative to any directed obligation is a right. This is a right of a particular kind, sometimes referred to in the literature as a claim-right. Thus, if Olive has a directed obligation *to Roger* to go to Chicago tomorrow, Roger has (in a common phrase) a *right against* Olive to her going to Chicago tomorrow.

If a promisor's obligation is directed to the promisee, then, a promisee will have a right against his promisor to the fulfillment of the promise. Intuitively, indeed, promisees have such rights.[23] Notably, these are "special" rights: the promise endows the promisee alone with a right to the promised action as such.[24]

Now philosophers frequently refer to "obligations to" and "rights against" without going further. And once one goes further, what one says may not correspond to what everyone who uses these phrases has in mind. There is, however, a well-known connection that has been made and that is pertinent to the case of promising. This is the connection between directed obligation and *owing*. Such a connection was assumed by H. L. A. Hart and Joel Feinberg among others. In terms of the previous example: If Olive has a directed obligation to Roger to go to Chicago tomorrow, then (equivalently) Olive owes Roger her going to Chicago tomorrow.

What, though, is owing? There is no doubt that this term is ambiguous. In the present context I believe it should be amplified at least to this extent: Olive owes Roger her going to Chicago tomorrow, if and only if, in an as yet unspecified intuitive sense, Roger can appropriately regard Olive's act of going to Chicago tomorrow *as his*.[25]

On reflection this may sound strange, if not impossible. In what sense can an action that is one person's to perform be another's? If there is more than one such sense, which sense is at issue here? I return to these questions later.

For now, I note that the construal of owing that I am adopting here suggests a particular amplification of a further intuitive point about promising. This is the judgment that by virtue of one's status as a promisee one is in a position to *demand* the promised act from the pertinent promisor if, say, he expresses an intention not to perform it in advance of the time for performance.

Evidently, in the sense of "demand" at issue here—and in what follows—it is not the case that everyone is in a position to demand any action of any another. Anyone can of course *purport* to be in a position to demand a given future action of another, in this sense of "demand," without actually being in a position to do so. And "demand" is doubtless sometimes used in a weaker sense, such that everyone *is* in a position to demand any action of another.[26]

Given my construal of owing, the suggested amplification of the intuitive point about promising just noted involves understanding demanding as follows: I am in a position to demand a certain action of someone if and only if that action is mine—in the sense at issue in the case of owing.

Independently of my construal of owing, I find it intuitive that a promisee is in a position to demand the promised act as in some sense his. Given that construal, it is plausible to assume that the sense of "his" involved in each case is the same.

Intuitively, also, a promisee is in a position to *rebuke* the promisor for non-performance of the promise after the time for performance has passed. Such rebukes can be seen as after-the-fact counterparts of demands in the sense at issue here.

These considerations throw doubt on the Moral Requirement dogma. Some pertinent concerns are as follows.[27]

Suppose that the obligation a promisor accrues is a matter of moral requirement deriving from a suitable moral principle. That is, he is now morally required to keep his promise. Now suppose that a promisor, Joe, appears to be about to break his promise to Mary. Does Mary have the standing to demand of Joe that he keep his promise on the grounds, simply, that *a moral principle is about to be violated*? Perhaps so. What needs to be shown, though, is that she has a *special* standing to demand of Joe that he keep his promise, given her position as Joe's promisee.

It is plausible to suppose that if anyone has the standing to demand conformity to a moral principle on the grounds, simply, that a moral principle is about to be violated, then everybody does—or at least everybody capable of making a demand in the first place. Suppose, then, that everybody has the standing to demand compliance whenever a moral principle is violated—several philosophers believe that something like this is the case. This does not help us understand how Mary comes to have a special standing to demand of Joe that he do what he promised to do. Suppose, alternatively, that the violation of a moral principle is not in and of itself enough to ground in anyone the standing to demand compliance—as I am myself inclined to think. Then again, obviously, we have not explained Mary's special standing to demand of Joe that he keep his promise. We can, then, set aside the matter of the standing that all—or none—have to demand compliance with any moral principle by virtue of its status as a moral principle.

What if the moral requirement in question is grounded in the interests of a particular person? Does that give the person in question a special standing to demand that the moral principle be conformed to?

Suppose that Jill, a healthy young student, is morally required to give up her seat on the subway to Jack, a frail professor, for the sake of saving him from unnecessary strain. It is by no means obvious—to me at least—that by virtue of this fact Jack, has the standing to *demand* of Jill that she give up her seat to him. It may be reasonable for Jack, to purport to be in this position—that may be a good way to get Jill to do the right thing, but that is another matter.

At this point the Moral Requirement dogma may seem to be in trouble: Intuitively, promissory obligation is a matter of owing, such that the promisee, as such, has the standing to demand the promised act from the promisor. How, then, can promissory obligation be a matter of moral requirement—or of moral requirement only?[28]

Here is one way, someone might think. Consider something like the consent clause in Scanlon's moral Principle F, and the moral requirements on particular people that derive from it. According to Principle F, if A fulfills its conditions with respect to B, he is morally required to do X "unless B consents to X's not being done." Is it the case that a person, A, owes a person, B, in particular, his doing X, if A is morally required to do X *unless B consents to X's not being done?*

Normally we would take it that for the promisee to "consent" to nonfulfillment of the promise is, in effect, for him to waive the right to fulfillment that he has as promisee. For present purposes, however, we cannot interpret the consent clause in terms of a notion of consent that presupposes B's right to fulfillment of the promise. The pertinent question is, in effect, whether invocation of a moral requirement conditional on a type of consent *that does not presuppose such a right in B* suffices to make it the case that B *has* the pertinent right. For present purposes, then, this question must take "unless B consents to X's not being done" to mean something like: "unless B says it is fine with him that X is not done."

In devising his consent clause Scanlon may both have interpreted it in terms of B's "saying it is fine with him that X is not done" and thought that given its presence B would have a right against A to A's doing X. Whether or not he thought this, it seems not to be true. More precisely, it seems not to be true given the construal of B's right such that it is correlated with A's owing B his (A's) doing X, in the sense of "owing" at issue here.[29]

Apparently, the two intuitive points about promissory obligation that I have noted pose problems for the Moral Requirement dogma. If that dogma is false, the other two dogmas require support from elsewhere, if they are to be supported. Insofar as they draw all their force from the Moral Requirement dogma, they are problematic.

I should emphasize that the falsity of the Moral Requirement dogma would not imply that a promisor is never morally required—and in that sense obligated—to fulfill a given promise. Nor would it imply that one is not morally required to keep each of one's promises, all else being equal. The falsity of the Moral Requirement dogma would imply, rather, that *the full story of promissory obligation cannot be told in terms of one or more moral requirements.* In fact the arguments I have deployed so far tend to the stronger conclusion that the *primary* story of promissory obligation cannot be a moral requirement story. They suggest, that is, that whatever moral requirements most firmly accrue to a promisor are founded on an obligation that is not a moral requirement.

Suppose that the Moral Requirement dogma is indeed false. We are then left with a problematic gap. What could go in place of the moral requirement approach to promissory obligation? Is there an alternative approach that respects both Prichard's point, and the point that a promisor incurs an obligation directed to the promisee? Assuming that both of these points relate to a single obligation, is there a plausible account of promissory obligation that respects the point that every promisor incurs a directed obligation to his promisee?

Before arguing for a positive answer, I note that the directedness of promissory obligation rules out an approach that construes such obligation as engendered by no more than a personal decision to act in a certain way.

One might be led to this approach by virtue of an important aspect of personal decisions, something that will be relevant later in this essay. One who decides to do something has, by virtue of his decision, sufficient reason to do that thing. By this I mean that rationality requires him to do it, all else being equal, where rationality is a matter of appropriately responding to relevant considerations. All else being equal, then, he ought to do it, in an appropriately broad sense of "ought."[30]

Given that this is so, there may be a sense of "obligated" in which he is obligated to do what he decides to do—though that use of "obligated" is not, I think, a central one. Be that as it may, it seems impossible to argue that someone's decision to act in a certain way, as such, makes it the case that he *owes anyone else* the action in question.

There are other arguments against a personal decision account of promissory obligation. One of these was alluded to at the outset of this essay:

one who binds himself by a promise cannot then unbind himself, but must wait for release from his promisee. This is not the case for one who binds himself through a personal decision. He is in a position unilaterally to rescind the decision or, in the vernacular, to change his mind.

A promisor can, of course, decide not to keep his promise, and sometimes he may have good grounds for so deciding. What he cannot do unilaterally is rescind the promise, and hence destroy its obligation.

III. JOINT COMMITMENT

I now sketch what I take to be a plausible alternative approach to promising. As I shall explain, this respects the two intuitive points I have brought into this discussion: Prichard's point, and the directedness of promissory obligation. It also speaks against each of the three dogmas. At the same time, it gives what I take to be reasonable results with respect to immoral promises.

According to this alternative approach, promising is a matter of what I call a *joint commitment*. I have written about joint commitment extensively elsewhere, and continue to develop my understanding of it. My aim in this section is to introduce it in sufficient detail for present purposes.[31]

I start with some discussion of the type of commitment I have in mind. Consider again the decisions of an individual human being, or *personal* decisions, as I shall put it. I take it that just by deciding to do something, there is a sense in which one *commits* oneself to doing that thing. To say that one is committed in the sense in question is not to say that one is morally required to do something; nor is it to say that one owes another some action. Rather, to commit oneself is to make it the case that one has sufficient reason to do a certain thing, in the sense explained earlier.

Commitments of the kind one incurs by making a personal decision may be referred to as "commitments of the will," insofar as they come into being simply by virtue of an exercise of will in some intuitive sense. In the case of a personal decision, all the person has to do is decide, and he is committed.

A personal decision creates what I call a *personal commitment*. Such commitments are unilaterally rescindable by the human being who makes them. They can, of course, be made in private without the knowledge of any other party.

There is reason to suppose that commitments of the will come in two versions: personal and joint. A *joint* commitment is not a composite of two or more personal commitments. It is a commitment *of* two or more persons *by* two or more persons.

I focus here on the basic case of a joint commitment.[32] Further, I focus on cases that involve parties who know and are in direct communication with each other.[33]

In order to *create* a new joint commitment each of the would-be parties must openly express to the others his readiness together with the others to commit them all in the pertinent way. Once these expressions are common knowledge between the parties, the joint commitment is in place—as they understand.[34] Each is therefore now committed to do what he can to promote satisfaction of the joint commitment in conjunction with the actions of the rest. For the sake of brevity I shall say that each is now committed to "conform" to the commitment.

Absent special background understandings, a single party cannot *rescind* a joint commitment unilaterally; the concurrence of all of the parties is needed. Thus he cannot unilaterally remove his own dependent commitment.

Any joint commitment can be described in a statement of the following form:

> A, B and so on (or those with property P) are jointly committed to do X as a body.

This formulation can be more fully articulated roughly as follows:

> A, B, and so on (or those with property P) are jointly committed as far as is possible (by virtue of their several actions) to emulate a single doer of X.

"Does X" is understood here in a broad sense so as to include "believes that p," for instance.

These formulations are intended to make it clear that the individual parties are not committed, through the joint commitment, *personally* to do X. Thus a joint commitment to believe that p as a body, for instance, does not require that each personally believe that p. If you like, the aim of this joint commitment is *to create a certain situation at the collective as opposed to the individual level: a situation that as far as possible approximates a single case of belief*. The same goes, with appropriate changes, for joint commitments with other contents.[35]

I take joint commitment to be a fundamental everyday concept that is an integral part of many central everyday concepts. These include those concepts expressible in nondistributive readings of such sentences as "We intend to go shopping," "We believe democracy is the best political form," and other ascriptions of psychological states whose grammatical subject is the first person plural. This has long been my position independently of any consideration of agreements or promises.[36]

The concept of joint commitment is a holistic or nonindividualistic one in the sense that it goes beyond the conceptual scheme of an individual human being's thoughts, beliefs, desires, and personal commitments.[37] It is not clearly holistic in any other sense.[38]

IV. JOINT COMMITMENT AND OBLIGATION

To every joint commitment corresponds a set of obligations. These are directed obligations with correlative rights. The parties are obligated to each other to conform to the commitment. In other terms, they owe each other their conformity. In this section I argue for the truth of this proposition.

Recall the sense of "owe" elaborated earlier. As initially put forward, the elaboration ran as follows: Olive owes Roger her going to Chicago tomorrow if and only if in an as yet unspecified sense Roger can appropriately regard Olive's act of going to Chicago as *his*. Subsequent discussion added, in effect, the following: Roger is in a position to demand of Olive that she go to Chicago if and only if he can appropriately regard Olive's act of going to Chicago as his–in the same sense.

It is easy enough to argue on this basis that those who are parties to a given joint commitment owe each other actions that conform to the commitment. Intuitively, the parties to a joint commitment are severally in a position to demand conforming actions from the other parties, by virtue precisely of the joint commitment itself. The actions in question, then, are owed to them by the other parties.

One can take this argument further. My initial elaboration of owing raised questions to which I said I would return. *In what sense* can another person's future action currently be mine? If there is more than one such sense, what sense is at issue in the case of owing?

We now have a basis for an answer to the last question, and hence at least a partial answer to the first. Apparently, there is a sense in which the parties to a joint commitment are severally justified in regarding actions that conform to the commitment as *theirs*.[39] What, then, is that sense?

If such a sense can indeed be found it will help to firm up the intuitive judgment that the parties to a joint commitment are in a position to demand conformity from one another, and so on. In order to find it, we need to examine what the joint commitment achieves and how it does this.

By jointly committing the two of us, and by that alone, you and I make it the case that each of us has sufficient reason to perform actions that conform to the commitment. Thus, all else being equal, each is rationally required to conform to the commitment. In at least this way, then, *we have together bound each one of us* to perform the actions in question. This binding was, indeed, the immediate consequence of the expression of the will of each in conditions of common knowledge.

I propose that, given these facts, there is an intuitive sense in which any one party to the joint commitment can appropriately say of the other's conforming actions: "They are mine–in my capacity as cocreator of the commitment." I shall not try to say what that sense is in other terms. Rather, I propose that the sense in question is clearly–indeed paradigmatically–exemplified in the circumstances just described.

If this is right, we have tracked down the intuitive sense in which one who is owed an action by another, where that correlates with his standing to demand that action, can appropriately regard the action as his.[40]

One final point about the obligations of joint commitment is in order here. I take it that the directed obligations and the correlative rights of joint commitment are content- and context-independent in the following way: as long as there is a joint commitment, there are corresponding directed obligations. That is not to say that in all cases one ought to fulfill these obligations all things considered. It is to say that when a joint commitment comes to be these obligations come with it and remain irrespective of their content and changes in the circumstances of the parties–unless and until the joint commitment is rescinded or fulfilled.[41]

V. PROMISES AS JOINT COMMITMENT PHENOMENA

On the Kinship of Promises and Agreements

Recall now the second preliminary point with which this essay began: promises and agreements are close cousins. In this section, I begin by saying something about the kinship of agreements and promises. I go on to propose a particular understanding of agreements, and a related account of promises.

It will be useful to have a sample agreement in view. I shall focus on the following case. After some discussion with Belle, Anne says "How about my doing the laundry after dinner, and your going to the store for groceries?" Belle responds "Okay." They have now made an agreement in which one future action is specified for each of the parties.

Each of them is now obligated to perform the action specified for her in the agreement. Anne is obligated to do the laundry; Belle is obligated to go to the grocery store. I shall call these obligations the parties' *performance obligations*.[42] A promisor may also be said to have a performance obligation or obligations the details of which are specified in the promise. In other terms, what I have been referring to, following custom, as his "promissory" obligations are performance obligations in the sense now in question.

I take it that an analogue of Prichard's point about promises holds for agreements–a point that appears to be knowable a priori: if one has agreed with another person that one will do something, then one is obligated to do it. Here, too, the obligation is content-independent: it derives from the fact that one is party to an agreement, and holds irrespective of the content of that agreement. Again, just as the performance obligations of a promisor are directed obligations, so are the performance obligations of the parties to an agreement. Thus in my example Anne is obligated to Belle to do the laundry. In other words, Anne owes Belle her, Anne's, doing the laundry. Belle, in turn, owes Anne her, Belle's, going to the grocery store.

Here, then, are some striking aspects of the cousinhood of promises and agreements. Both give rise to directed performance obligations that are content-independent, and this is knowable a priori.

Agreements

Theorists have tended to see promises as logically prior to agreements. I say this in light of the common proposal that a two-party agreement by virtue of which each party accrues a performance obligation is constituted by a pair of promises, one from each party to the other.[43] It is often said that these promises are "mutual," or that they have been "exchanged," without further elaboration of what such mutuality or exchange is taken to involve.[44]

One might reasonably object to this proposal by saying that the example agreement, for one, does not *look* like a pair of promises, mutual, exchanged, or whatever.[45] This objection may not be conclusive, but it does show that the pair of promises view has a case to answer.

It is not clear why philosophers have almost universally adopted the assumption that a pair of promises is involved in agreements in which both parties take on one or more performance obligations. They tend not to present any argument for it.

Possibly the thought is that if—and only if—we can build agreements out of promises, we may be able to give an account of both in terms of the personal beliefs, intentions, and commitments of individuals, an account of a type that may seem to be the only feasible kind. I do not mean to imply that one can give such an account of *promises*, but it may be thought that one can, in view of the fact that "I" promise whereas "we" make an agreement. Be that as it may, one can argue against "pair of promises" views roughly as follows.[46]

Intuitively, my sample agreement, like many others, has the following three features. First, the parties' performance obligations are *unconditional* in form: Anne is obligated to do the laundry tonight; Belle is obligated to go to the grocery store. There can of course be agreements such that one or more of the parties accrue *conditional* obligations through them. An example is Polly's agreement with Sue that each will go to the tennis court at five if and only if it not raining. The point is that in the sample agreement (and many others) the obligations are not conditional. Second, the performance obligations of the parties are *accrued simultaneously*—at the time the parties would be said to have agreed. Finally, these obligations are *interdependent* in a sense I now briefly explain.

Suppose that after Belle and Anne have had dinner, Belle tells Anne that she has decided not to fulfill her obligation under the agreement, in order to do something that accords better with her current inclinations. All else being equal, it seems that Anne is now in a position unilaterally to rescind the agreement. In particular, she does not need to petition Belle for her concurrence in such rescission. Thus she is in a position unilaterally to do away with her own obligation under the agreement. This is a matter of what an agreement is. It needs no grounding in "external" considerations such as fairness. Anne might reflect these points by responding, decisively "So much for our agreement!"

It is not clear that any promise pair has all of these three features. Discussion of the following pair of simple promises may serve here to illustrate the problem.[47] Suppose Cath has promised Dee that she will do the laundry that night. Dee has subsequently promised Cath that she will go to the store. True, Cath now has an unconditional obligation to do the laundry that night and Dee has an unconditional obligation to go to the store. However, these obligations are not accrued simultaneously. Cath accrues her obligation first. Further, the obligations in question are not interdependent in the pertinent sense, as I now argue.

Suppose that at this point Cath announces that she will not be acting as promised, since she wants to do something else. How, if at all, does this affect Dee's situation? Dee may of course decide not to *keep* her promise. After all, Cath will not be keeping hers. But she cannot unilaterally *rescind* her own promise and so bring it about that she has no obligation through it. That is—still—not up to her. She is not going to say "So much for my promise!" in parallel with Anne's imagined "So much for our agreement!" In sum, the performance obligations of these two promisors are not interdependent in the sense in which the performance obligations of the parties to the sample agreement are.

An account of agreements in terms of joint commitment allows one to account for the three features of the example agreement just noted and is otherwise plausible. To see this, consider again my sample agreement: Anne says "How about my doing the laundry after dinner, and your going to the store for groceries?" Belle responds "Okay."

It is easy to interpret what transpires through this dialogue roughly as follows: in conditions of common knowledge, Anne expresses to Belle her personal readiness to be jointly committed to endorse as a body the decision that she do the laundry that night and Belle go to the grocery store, and Belle does likewise. "Decision" in this formulation is used as roughly equivalent to "plan of action."

This is sufficient to jointly commit Anne and Belle in the way in question. Articulating that way along the lines detailed earlier: by virtue of their several actions they are to emulate as far as possible a single endorser of the decision in question. Anne thereby accrues an obligation to do the laundry, and Belle thereby accrues an obligation to go to the store; these unconditional obligations are accrued simultaneously, when the joint commitment is established.

Now suppose that after this happens Belle makes it clear that she has decided not to go to the store in order that she might better fulfill her personal inclinations of the moment. Anne can reasonably take her thereby to have expressed her personal readiness to join with Anne in rescinding the joint commitment. Anne's position in relation to her own obligation, then, has changed: she is now in a position to do away with it, by unilaterally completing the rescission of the joint commitment that grounds it.

In legal parlance my sample agreement is a *bilateral executory* agreement: each party has at least one performance obligation. What if Julia asks "Will you phone me tonight?" and Jeremy responds "Sure"? This is not a *bilateral* executory agreement, since only one person has a performance obligation. Yet one could quite naturally say that, in this case, Julia and Jeremy *agreed* that he would phone her that night. And their transaction can plausibly be construed along the lines proposed for the example of Anne and Belle. In this new case, the parties jointly commit themselves to endorse as a body the decision that Jeremy is to phone Julia that night.

I propose that, quite generally, and somewhat roughly: for two or more people to enter an agreement is for them jointly to commit themselves, by an appropriate, explicit process, to endorse as a body a certain decision with respect to what is to be done by one or more of the parties. I shall not attempt here to specify the nature of the explicit process in question. In practice it is easy enough to say, given an example, whether or not it is of the right kind clearly to constitute an agreement between the parties. The most important feature of the proposal, for present purposes, is the joint commitment that lies at its core.

For the sake of a label, I refer to the proposal just detailed as the *joint decision* account of agreements. In what follows I shall assume its correctness.[48]

Promises

The example just given of Jeremy and Julia's agreement concerning what he will do is very close to the example of a promise considered at the outset of this essay. There Jeremy tells Julia "I'll phone you tonight," and Julia responds

"Okay." In the example just given Julia asks "Will you phone me tonight?" and Jeremy responds "Sure."

This closeness suggests the following rough *joint decision account* of promises: for one person to make a promise to another is for them jointly to commit themselves, by an appropriate, explicit process, to the decision that one of them ("the promisor") is to perform one or more specified actions. As in the case of the joint decision account of an agreement, I shall not attempt here to specify the nature of the appropriate explicit process in question.

One point in favor of the joint decision account of promises is that, in the paradigm case, one person makes a promise to another, and *both are active in the process of constructing the promise*. More precisely, the promisee must do something of an accepting rather than a rejecting nature. Thus, in the example, without Julia's "Okay" or some such response, possibly nonverbal, Jeremy would not have promised anything to Julia.

Acceptance, one might add, is to be distinguished from simple acknowledgement. If Jeremy were to make a prediction, such as "I think I'll be calling you tonight, it's going to be hard being home alone," Julie might respond with "I hear you." This would be a case of acknowledgement without acceptance in the sense at issue.

Another point in favor of the joint decision account of promises is that even the promisee appears to take on some obligations, though not performance obligations. That is, these obligations are not specified in the promise. They, like the performance obligations of the promisor, are directed obligations. In this case they are directed to the promisor. Thus, in the example, given Jeremy's promise to Julia, if she takes her phone off the hook that night he may well rebuke her as follows: "I said I'd call you tonight—what were you doing taking the phone off the hook?" This suggests that he understands that she was obligated to him not to make his calling her that night impossible.

Someone might now voice the following concern: surely the promisee has the power of unilateral rescission of the promise? And surely that would not be true if promissory obligation was founded on a joint commitment—as in the joint decision account?[49]

In response, one might question whether the promisee does have the power unilaterally to rescind the promise. In many cases this may appear to be so because of the circumstances of the promise. For instance, the promise is solicited by the promisee because of the promisee's desires or needs, the promisor having no personal desire to perform the promise. The promisee having stated that there is no need for the promisor to act as promised, thus implying his readiness to rescind the promise with the promisor's concurrence, the promisor promptly concurs and the promise is canceled.

In some cases, however, the promisor might resist. Thus suppose Joe promises to return Jane's book on Tuesday. Jane calls him to say that it is not that important for her to have the book, so he may keep it. He might then say "No, I promised to return the book on Tuesday and that's what I'll do." It is at best not clear that Jane is a position to say "But the promise is over, I just said so."[50]

Sometimes people write of the promisee's "power of release." I think this is sometimes considered to be a power unilaterally to rescind the promise. In that case, its general existence can be doubted for the reasons given above.

There is, however, a clear sense in which the promisee does have the power of release with respect to the promisor—something that in no way runs counter to the joint decision account. Should the promisor wish the promise to be rescinded, he has only to ask the promisee.

In this case, the promisor's own concurrence in its rescission has been manifested, and all that is necessary is for the promisee to concur also. This state of affairs accords perfectly with a joint decision account. The same goes for the point, implied above, that the promisee's release is indeed *required* for the promise to be rescinded. The promisor is not empowered unilaterally to cancel the promise.

One who continues to insist that the promisee has the power of unilateral rescission or something very like it is not precluded from accepting a version of the joint decision account of promising. Thus he may feel able to accept something like the following account: a promise is a joint decision that one party, "the promisor," is to do something—a joint decision entered into by an appropriate explicit process—with which is associated the understanding that it stands at the pleasure of the other party—"the promisee".

As I now briefly explain, an account of promises as joint decisions does well when brought up against the two intuitive points that present problems for the three dogmas. This is another reason for taking the account seriously.

Consider first Prichard's point: if someone has promised to do something then he is obligated to do it by virtue of his promise. A joint decision account accords with this and, indeed, offers an explanation as to how it can be true—without exception—and knowable a priori. As long as the pertinent joint commitment has been created, and not rescinded, the promisor has an obligation of joint commitment to act as promised. There may be reasons not to fulfill this obligation in its particular circumstances or given its particular content. Its existence is not affected, however, even by the existence of factors such that all things considered one ought not to fulfill it.

Given the joint decision account of promising, what we may think of as the *primary* obligation associated with a promise is an obligation of joint commitment. This obligation is in a clear sense *intrinsic* to the existence of a promise as such. That said, it is possible that given an obligation of joint commitment, one is morally required to fulfill it all else being equal. Then, on the proposed account of promising, the promisor will have an obligation of joint commitment to act as promised *and* be morally required to so act, all else being equal. If that is so, it may help to explain the pull both of Prichard's point and of the moral requirement dogma. I return to the latter in the next section.

What of the second intuitive point: promissory obligation is directed obligation? That was amplified in terms of a particular understanding of owing—an understanding such that, as I have argued, the parties to a joint commitment owe each other conformity to that commitment.

Given the joint decision account of promising, then, the promisor owes it to the promisee to act as promised. In other terms, he is obligated to keep his promise; his obligation is directed to the promisee, and the promisee has the correlative right. Thus the primary, intrinsic obligation of a promisor is directed.

In this essay I have focused on what I take to be the paradigm case of promising: one person makes a promise to another, both being active in the process of constructing that promise. Promises may be spoken of in contexts that diverge from this paradigm in various ways. Thus someone may report that he "promised himself" to do something or that in his mind he made a certain "promise" or that he "promised" something to someone who turned a deaf ear to him, or who listened but offered neither an accepting nor a rejecting response.

An adequate account of the paradigm case of a promise may well be able to shed light on how such less than central cases come to be talked of as promises, as it may be able to shed light on why they are less than central. What is crucial, however, for any account of promising is that it illuminate the nature of paradigmatic promises and the obligation, or obligations, to which they give rise. I take the joint decision account of promising to have much merit in this connection. More generally, there is much merit in the idea of an account of promising in terms of joint commitment, however precisely the details are spelled out.

In my technical terminology all and only those who are jointly committed in some way constitute a "plural subject."[51] Some label is useful in the context of the wide variety of joint commitment phenomena. In this section, then, I have sketched a *plural subject account* of promising and explained some of the merits of some such account.

VI. RECONSIDERING THE DOGMAS

Acceptance of a plural subject account of promising allows us to jettison the three dogmas outlined earlier. Let me go through each, briefly, in turn.

The Moral Requirement Dogma. According to the first dogma, promissory obligation is a matter of moral requirement, where this, in turn, is a matter of the application of one or more general moral principles of conduct such as Scanlon's "Principle F," or a principle relating to conformity with a just and useful social practice. A plural subject account does not appeal to any such principle to explain the obligation of a promisor to perform the promise.

As said above, a plural subject account allows for the possibility that every promisor is morally required to do what he promised, all else being equal. This account allows therefore for the possibility that a given promisor has two distinct kinds of obligation as a result of his promise: he has an obligation of joint commitment to fulfill the promise, and he is morally required to fulfill it given its content and circumstances. Only the first of these kinds, of course, is such that every promisor has an obligation of that kind, irrespective of the content and circumstances of the promise.

Further, the possibilities just stated do not tend to justify the Moral Requirement dogma (though, as said earlier, they may help to explain it). That dogma would be false even given that they are more than possibilities. The dogma countenances only one kind of obligation as associated with promises—moral requirement. But, if the correct account of promising is a plural subject account, there are two kinds of obligation so associated—and the primary kind is not the kind on which the dogma fixes.

The No Willing Dogma. According to the second dogma, the obligation of a given promisor is not, and cannot, be directly willed into being. If the obligation in question is an obligation of joint commitment, however, it is in an important sense directly willed into being.

It is not willed into being by the will of the promisor alone, or by his promisee's will alone, but by the conjunction of their wills: each expresses that condition of his will that is preparedness to enter into the relevant joint commitment. Given only common knowledge of these expressions, the joint commitment and its inherent obligations are set.

The Immoral Promises Dogma. The third dogma is that immoral promises do not obligate. A plural subject account of promising will reject this.

By my definition of "immoral promise," one is not morally required to fulfill such a promise. A plural subject account can, of course, allow that this is so. Yet it entails that one who makes an immoral promise has an obligation to fulfill it. This is an obligation of joint commitment. The account thus neatly resolves the apparent conflict between Prichard's point in its most intuitive construal and the third dogma: all promises obligate, but one is not morally required—or obligated in *that* sense—to fulfill an immoral promise, all else being equal.

Briefly to summarize the argument of this essay: The three dogmas of the title are hard to reconcile with two intuitive points I detailed. There is a type of account of promises that both accommodates these intuitive points and implies the falsity of each of the dogmas. That is an account in terms of joint commitment—a plural subject account.

The first version of this essay was presented as an invited symposium talk at the Pacific meetings of the American Philosophical Association in March 27, 2005, where the commentator was Niko Kolodny. Subsequent versions have been presented at the University of California, Irvine, as the Zeno Lecture at the University of Utrecht, and at the University of Austin, Texas, in 2006, at the Graduate Center, CUNY, and the University of Southern California, in 2007, at the promises and agreements conference at Rice University, at California State University at Northridge, and to the students in my *Promises and Agreements* seminar at the University of California, Irvine, in 2008. I thank all of the discussants on those occasions, and Jonathan Adler, Hanoch Sheinman, Frank Stewart, Julie Tannenbaum, and Gary Watson for their comments on written material.

NOTES

1. Here and elsewhere in this essay I focus on the case of one person promising to another. Typically, this other is a single human individual. One can also promise something to a group of people, as when someone promises his parents, collectively, to take good care of himself. I shall focus on the case of a single individual promisee in this essay. I take this to be the paradigm or clearest type of case. For some remarks on other types of case see the text below.

2. Anscombe (1978) berates Hume for not realizing that you can promise without saying "I promise" or, indeed, using the word "promise." Among others who say that one can promise without using the word "promise" is Raz (1977).

3. Had Julia initially understood Jeremy to be informing her of his intention, and herself as acknowledging receipt of this information, she might have responded to his saying he had changed his mind, in explanation of not calling, in some such way as this: "*You should have let me know* that you had changed your mind." Should she take him to have promised, she would be discountenanced in a particular way by the information that he had changed his mind. Indeed, were he to tell her that is what he'd done, she might well say "What do you mean 'I changed my mind'?" implying that *he was not in a position* to do such a thing.

4. I don't say that there are *only* two prevalent senses of "obligation." That is probably not the case. I have written of "senses of obligation," rather than "kinds of obligation," because I have found it hard to discern the genus of which these two senses might pick out two species, and speaking of "kinds of obligation" may suggest that I think there is such a genus. Cf. Gilbert (2006: ch. 2).

5. There is a parallel with one version of the classic problem of political obligation, both in terms of the question, and in terms of the answer I am inclined to give. See Gilbert (2006).

6. Dissenting voices with respect to one or more of the dogmas include Raz (1977: 225) and Searle (2001: 194). In spite of such discussions, the dogmas are still generally entrenched.

7. Though Scanlon mentions "principles" here, and discusses several pertinent principles in the course of his discussion, he focuses on his principle F (see the text below) in his explanation of promissory obligation. His initial discussion of promising is Scanlon (1990).

8. Cf. Scanlon (1998).

9. In connection with promissory obligation, Scanlon (1998) appeals to the value that "assurance" has to human beings; and, among those who have most recently critiqued him, Owens (2006) appeals to an "authority interest" (as opposed to an "information interest"), and Shiffrin (2008) to the "values of trust."

10. The most prominent contemporary practice theorist is John Rawls. More recent proponents of this approach include Kolodny and Wallace (2003); Scanlon cites Joseph Raz, Neil MacCormick, and Judith Thomson as taking nonpractice positions similar to his own.

11. Note that my specification of what the No Willing dogma rejects, and Hume's specification of our common way of thinking, does not obviously limit the workings of the human will specifically to *the promisor's willing an obligation for himself*, the main option Hume considers. I shall later argue that there is another option that allows us to reject the No Willing dogma as stated here, and to justify the "common ways of thinking" to which Hume alludes. This invokes a sense of "obligation" that differs from that with which Hume was operating—he had his own version of the Moral Requirement dogma. See the next paragraph in the text, and the next note.

12. Theorists often suppose that what a promisor does, crucially, is express *an intention to obligate himself*. Precisely what further factors allow an obligation to accrue to the promisor is then seen as the issue, given that, as Hume argued, one's intention to obligate himself does not in and of itself do the trick. Other theorists attempt to show how promises can obligate without appealing to the promisor's intention to obligate himself—an intention Hume has after all discredited as the sole basis of promissory obligation. See Raz (1977) on the "intention conception" versus the "obligation conception," which Raz prefers.

13. Hume presents a specifically Humean version of the Moral Requirement dogma.

14. Altham (1985) offers a focused discussion of immoral promises. He invokes Anscombe (1978). Raz (1977: 212) suggests the prevalence of the immoral promises dogma.

15. Cf. Gilbert (1993a): moral requirements, qua *requirements*, are "context-sensitive"; given the original basis for a given requirement, it may disappear when something is added to that basis. This is not the same as its "remaining" though "overridden." See also Gilbert (2006: ch. 7).

16. Concurring authors include Searle (1964: 45 and Beran (1987: 6). Feinberg (1966: 138) speaks of the promisee's rights in such terms. (On promisees' rights see the second intuitive point, below.)

17. Raz (1977: 221) allows that explanations of an action taken or intended "in terms such as 'But I promised I'll do it' do sound complete. To add 'therefore it was

my duty to do it' is, we feel, to unpack what is already contained in the first statement, not to add to it."

18. That it is indeed an intuitive point is suggested by this reference to it in Anscombe (1978: 319): regarding the idea that all promises obligate the promisor. "We might indeed argue that it was not so.... *Showing this might however leave someone puzzled*;..." (emphasis mine).

19. Recall that the Immoral Promises dogma as represented in this essay is couched simply in terms of "obligation," not in terms of moral requirement. Those who hold it may well believe that the only obligation that could be at issue is obligation in the sense of moral requirement, but that is a separate issue.

20. Anscombe (1978), cited approvingly by Altham (1985).

21. I am indebted to Julie Tannenbaum for pressing this point, and for related discussion (personal correspondence, November 2008). The issue here was noted by Anscombe: in her terms, it is the possibility that the obligation of a promise is defeasible.

22. Prichard does not cite Hume, but his discussion resonates closely with Hume's skepticism about the willing of an obligation.

23. Raz (1977) discusses two conceptions of promising, according to each of which the promisee has a right to performance of the promised action. The larger part of the literature focused on promising has not, in fact, emphasized the existence of rights in the promisee. The focus has almost exclusively been on the obligations of the promisor, whose intuitively "directed" nature is often ignored. Robins (1984) is another exception.

24. See, for instance, Hart (1955: 183).

25. Cf. Feinberg (1970: 251): "If Smith owes Jones five dollars, only Jones can claim the five dollars as his own." Here Feinberg is at least ostensibly talking about owing money rather than owing an action. That said, the suggestion is that there is a close connection between what is *owed* and what is *one's own*. In some recent discussions I have written of the right-holder as in some sense *owning* the action to which he has a right. This way of putting things has provoked some resistance, and may be unnecessarily strong, insofar as it goes beyond talk of the action being in some sense *one's own*. Here I stick to what may be the weaker of the two locutions, thus following Feinberg more closely.

26. Cf. the discussion of commanding and other authority-presupposing terms in Gilbert (2006: ch. 1).

27. For a more detailed treatment see Gilbert (2004). My discussion there and in what follows resonates with some of the material in Thomson (2004).

28. In saying "moral requirement only" I mean to allow that more than one kind of obligation may accrue or tend to accrue to promisors.

29. Cf. Gilbert (2004: 94). The sense of "owe," and so on, that are at issue in Scanlon (1998) may well be a different sense from that with which I am working here.

30. I do not say that by deciding one gives oneself *a reason* for doing the thing decided on. For further discussion see Gilbert (2006: ch. 2). See also Robins (1984); Verbeek (2008).

31. For more detailed treatments see Gilbert (2003, 2006: ch. 7).

32. Roughly, a nonbasic joint commitment is created for the members of a population by some party or parties who have been authorized to do so by means of a basic joint commitment of those members. See Gilbert (2006: 140–1).

33. For more general discussion see e.g. Gilbert (2006: ch. 7).

34. On "common knowledge" see Gilbert (1989), also references therein.

35. For more on collective belief see e.g. Gilbert (1989: ch. 5) and Gilbert (1996). When speaking without such a qualifier as "Personally" as in "Personally, I don't think that p" a party to a collective belief that p must say things consistent with a belief that p, in order to conform to the constitutive joint commitment.

36. Gilbert (1989) can be seen as a long argument to the effect that joint commitments are a fundamental feature of everyday life. See Gilbert (1996).

37. In Gilbert (1989) I referred to this conceptual scheme as "singularist."

38. See Gilbert (1989: ch. 7) for discussion.

39. I say this on the basis of the intuitive standing of each one to demand such conformity of each one, and the assumption I am making that one has such standing if and only if there is a sense in which the conformity is one's own, the sense also implied by the statement that one is owed conformity.

40. Though I have been assuming the contrary, as is plausible, I suppose that in principle there could be more than one such intuitive sense. Should this be the case, the argument to this point has shown, at a minimum, that *one* of the pertinent senses has been tracked down.

41. For further discussion see Gilbert (2006: ch. 11).

42. These are the most salient obligations associated with an agreement and can reasonably be regarded as the primary obligations of the parties. That said, I mean to allow that other obligations may ensue from the agreement–I have in mind in particular obligations not to prevent the other's fulfillment of his performance obligations.

43. The idea of a pair of promises can presumably be extended to a triad of promises and so on, given more and more parties to the agreement, though there are some decisions to be made as to how this would go.

44. See Gilbert (1993b) for a number of references.

45. Ashley Dressel emphasized it in my Promises and Agreements graduate seminar, University of California, Irvine, November 2008.

46. For an extended treatment see Gilbert (1993b). See also Gilbert (2006: ch. 10). In a thoughtful response, Kent Bach (1995) has argued that an "exchange of promises" approach will work given a particular, rich notion of "exchange." I am not confident that this is so.

47. Gilbert (1993b) considers a wide range of possible promise-pairs in relation to the combination of features noted, and finds none of these pairs accounts for all three features. The promises in the example here are "simple" in the sense of "unconditional."

48. When there is a joint commitment to endorse as a body a certain decision (i.e. plan) that was not arrived at with the kind of explicit process requisite for an agreement the parties are aptly referred to as having formed a "joint intention" or, to use a more standard phrase (though this phrase has received other stipulative meanings) a "shared intention". For discussion of some of the literature on joint or shared intention see e.g. Gilbert (2009).

49. This concern was voiced in discussion by Maggie Little when I presented related material some years ago at a meeting of the British Society for Ethical Theory.

50. For concurring discussion see Vitek (1993).

51. See Gilbert (1989) and elsewhere. I do not intend to connote by the use of this phrase that some special kind of "subjectivity"—distinct from that possessed by individual human beings—arises in the context of a joint commitment. Rather, use by the parties of the first person plural pronoun as the subject term in certain sentences that refer to all of them is made appropriate in that context.

REFERENCES

Altham, J. 1985. "Wicked Promises." In I. Hacking (ed.). *Exercises in Analysis*. Cambridge: Cambridge University Press.

Anscombe, G. E. M. 1978. "Rights, Rules, and Promises." *Midwest Studies in Philosophy* 3: 318-323.

Austin, J. L. 1962. *How to do things with words*, Cambridge, MA: Harvard University Press.

Bach, K. 1995. "Terms of Agreement." *Ethics* 105: 604-612.

Beran, H. 1987. *The Consent Theory of Political Obligation*. London: Croom Helm.

Feinberg, J. 1966. *Rights, Justice, and the Bounds of Liberty*. Princeton: Princeton University Press.

———. 1970. "The Nature and Value of Rights." *Journal of Value Inquiry* 4: 243-257.

Gilbert, M. 1989. *On Social Facts*. London: Routledge.

———. 1993a. "Agreements, Coercion, and Obligation." *Ethics* 103: 679-706.

———. 1993b. "Is an Agreement an Exchange of Promises?" *Journal of Philosophy* 90: 627-649.

———. 1996. "Two Standpoints—The Personal and the Collective." In *Living Together*. Lanham, MD: Rowman and Littlefield. 1-20.

———. 2003. "The Structure of the Social Atom." In F. Schmitt (ed.), *Socializing Metaphysics*. Lanham, MD: Rowman and Littlefield. 39-64.

———. 2004. "Scanlon on Promissory Obligation: the Problem of Promisees' Rights." *Journal of Philosophy* CI: 83-109.

———. 2006. *A Theory of Political Obligation*. Oxford: Oxford University Press.

———. 2009. "Shared Intention and Personal Intentions". *Philosophical Studies* 144: 167-187.

Hart, H. L. A. 1955. "Are There Any Natural Rights?" Philosophical Review 64: 175-191.

Hume, D. 2000. *A Treatise on Human Nature*. Oxford: Oxford University Press.

Kolodny, N. and Wallace, J. 2003. "Promises and Practices Revisited." *Philosophy and Public Affairs* 31: 119-154.

Owens, D. 2006. *A Simple Theory of Promising, Philosophical Review* 115: 51-77.

Prichard, H. A. 1968. *Moral Obligation and Duty and Interest*. Oxford: Oxford University Press.

Raz, J. 1977. "Promises and Obligations." In P. M. S. Hacker and J. Raz (eds.), *Law, Morality, and Society: Essays in Honour of H. L. A. Hart*. Oxford: Oxford University Press, 210-226.

Rawls, J. 1955. "Two Concepts of Rules." *Philosophical Review* 64: 3–32.

———. 1971. *A Theory of Justice*. Cambridge, MA: Harvard University Press.

Robins, M. 1984. *Promising, Intending, and Moral Autonomy*. New York: Cambridge University Press.

Scanlon, T. 1990. "Promises and Practices." *Philosophy and Public Affairs* 19: 199–226.

———. 1998. *What We Owe to Each Other*. Cambridge, MA: Harvard University Press.

Searle, J. 1964. "How to Derive 'Ought' from 'Is.'" *Philosophical Review* 73: 43–58.

———. 2001. *Rationality in Action*. Cambridge: MIT Press.

Shiffrin, S. 2008. "Promising, Conventionalism and Intimate Relationships." *Philosophical Review* 117: 481–524.

Thomson, M. 2004. "What Is It to Wrong Someone? A Puzzle about Justice." In J. Wallace et al. (eds)., *Reason and Value* Oxford: Oxford University Press, 333–384.

Verbeek, B. 2008. "Rational Self-Commitment." In H. B. Schmid and Fabienne Peter (eds)., *Rationality and Commitment*. New York: Oxford University Press, 2008. 150–174.

Vitek, W. 1993. *Promising*. Philadelphia: Temple University Press.

Chapter 4

Is Promising a Practice and Nothing More?

Stan Husi

Abstract

Promising is a norm-guided affair. The question is wherein rests the authority of promissory standards? I argue that it entirely rests in promissory practices, a position I call the exhaustive practice position *(EPP). EPP claims that promising is a practice and nothing more, normatively speaking, and denies that the relevant standards embodied by promissory practices have any practice-external authority. I discuss what implications EPP would have for our promissory commitments. I address the worry that accepting EPP would make it harder for us to remain loyal to those commitments–that if we cannot safely consider promissory standards to be sanctioned by a practice-external authority, we shall be unable to sustain those commitments. I argue in opposition that acceptance of EPP need not prompt practically engaged agents to think any lower of their own promissory commitments. We can first-personally and self-reflectively stand by our promissory commitments even if, normatively speaking, we came to see them as part of practices and nothing more. I also contrast EPP with two competitors. First, with regards to the view that promissory norms are grounded in morality, I argue that (1) this view encounters difficulties in accounting for the significance of promising in the right way, and that (2) often promissory and moral demands diverge. I raise structurally similar worries with regards to a second view that promissory norms are grounded in self-interested reasons. In the final part, I acknowledge that EPP offers a revisionary interpretation of promissory practices, but argue that this presents no problem.*

Promising is a norm-guided affair. I make a promise, and suddenly I am subjected to standards telling me what to do next. I promise *I'll pick you up*, and now my watching TV at home, instead of picking you up, counts as a normative failure. Transforming practical episodes from normatively innocent into normatively guilty is no minor feat that standards pull off. Yet wherein rests the authority of those standards? One answer is that the authority of those standards rests entirely in promissory practices. Call this answer *the exhaustive practice position* (EPP). This position claims that promising is a practice and nothing more, normatively speaking, and denies that the relevant standards embodied in promissory practices have any practice-external authority. No justification of promissory norms flows from some practice-independent order, or so claims EPP.

What would EPP mean for our promissory commitments? Would its truth make it harder for us to remain loyal to those commitments? Some have thought so. They have argued that, unless we can safely consider promissory standards to be sanctioned by a practice-external authority, we shall be unable to sustain those commitments. In this essay, I seek to dislodge this concern. I will argue that EPP offers a self-affirmative, rather than a self-defeating, interpretation of promissory practices. Acceptance of EPP need not prompt practically engaged agents to take any less seriously their own promissory commitments. We can first-personally and self-reflectively stand by our promissory commitments even if, normatively speaking, we came to see them as part of practices and nothing more.

I.

What is it, then, for promising to be a practice and nothing more, normatively speaking? The EPP contains two components: (1) Promising consists in a system of norms or standards that (2) have no practice-external authority or justification. Let me say a few words about each component. The first component acknowledges that the practice of promising bears a constitutive relationship to a complex system of norms and policies that is observed by enough participants. To understand what some practice involves, we must understand what the legitimate moves within that practice are. Most important, we must understand what the missteps are. Practices clearly contain possibilities for failure, ways for things to go wrong. Norms deliver such formal possibilities. They supply models for what should be, for what makes sense or what is permitted, favored, or required within some practice. Norms make it possible that instances fail to comply with their directives. Every promissory activity, then, bears this formal relationship to the norms underlying the practice of promising: the activity complies or does not comply.

Surely not any old standard or norm is capable of undergirding a social practice. In order to do so, standards must exhibit a sufficient degree of complexity, interrelatedness, and continuity. Social practices usually incorporate multiple and interrelated layers of norms. On one level, we may have standards for what to do in certain contexts; on another, for what to do with standards (e.g. when to excuse and suspend them); on yet another, we may have standards for what to do with people who violate standards (rules concerning accountability); and so forth. The interaction between those standards must form a coherent and internally sound unity. In addition, enough people must be willing to regulate their conduct in accordance with the relevant standards, as well as to enforce and defend them. All this becomes very complex very quickly. In this essay, I cannot go much beyond this rough sketch. For a detailed account, see Copp (1995); see also Hart (1994: 55–58, 82–88).

Let me turn to the second component of EPP, which denies that the relevant practice-constitutive norms have any practice-external justification. If the first component postulated practice-constitutive norms, the second component confines the normative significance of promising to those practice-norms. The second component of EPP claims that promissory reasons and obligations are nothing but the dictates of a practice. They have force only from a practice-internal vantage point. Whether or not to keep a promise, thus understood, is essentially and exclusively a question about how promissory norms come down in a particular case: whether the promise concerns matters of importance to the promisee; whether the expectations created and the requisite execution are reasonable; whether we encounter excusing or exempting circumstances, and so forth. In answering these questions, we bring to bear promissory norms to a particular case and draw the conclusion. The promise-internal answer will then be complete, and nothing remains to be said but "You promised!" See Rawls (1955).

The second component of EPP, together with its normative restriction, is where the action is. What EPP denies in its second component is that promissory norms have the metanormative property of *being justified by something external to promissory practices*. It is important, however, not to misread EPP's rejection of external justification as a substantive criticism of promissory norms. It is, in fact, the chief point of this essay to argue that promissory norms do just fine without such justification.

The EPP's denial of practice-external authority requires one important qualification, though. The EPP is not intended to rule out that promissory practices might be embedded in further and more general social practices. If so, promissory norms may very well receive support from those more general practices. This option, however, would simply push back the question EPP is meant to address. What we would have to ask now is what metanormative status those more general practices have. Are they justified by something external to them? And if not, as EPP would have to say at some point in the progression to ever more general practices, what would that mean for our commitments to those "ultimate" practices? The core feature of EPP is its restriction to practice-norms, and the question of this essay is what this means for our commitments. Since the recourse to more general practices only pushes back our question, I suggest we limit the focus to promissory practices and simply assume, perhaps somewhat artificially, that any further and more general practices in which promising is embedded are part of the overall promissory package. What EPP denies is that promissory practices, inclusively understood, are and need to be justified by something that is not itself just another social practice.

The EPP advances a metanormative position and mostly stays silent on what conditions must obtain for something to be a promise and on what content in particular promissory standards have. Let me point out, however, that in specifying and reconstructing the contents of promissory norms, advocates of EPP are free to use what many of their opponents have said about promissory obligations. This may even include principles such as Scanlon's principle F, which specifies conditions under which agents who cause others to form certain expectations must live up to those expectations (1998: 304)—with the restriction, of course, that principle F only figures as a practice-internal rule in EPP. Similarly, promissory practice-norms may specify who has authority to do what under what conditions. The EPP is not hostile to authority talk per se. It only construes such talk as a practice-internal way of handing out licenses for who may do what. To use an example of Stephen Darwall, school internal norms allow teachers to give their students quizzes but not vice versa (2006: 51). In a similar vein, promissory standards may restrict who can make what kind of promise to whom, or who has claims for what. There is no reason why principles such as Scanlon's principle F and authority-licensing rules could not be part of the relevant practice-constitutive norms.

With regard to conditions for promising, I am quite sympathetic to accounts that take promissory acts to presuppose certain social practices. But whether or not promising is inherently practice driven, this would hardly imply any substantive metanormative conclusions. I readily admit it is possible that promising could be inherently practice dependent and yet have other than practice-internal normative force. In addition, EPP is only directed at the normative significance of promising *as such*. The position does not deny that we usually have all sorts of reasons to keep our promises, many of which have nothing to do with promising at all: I'd better share my toys with my little sister as promised, because if not, Granny won't give me that delicious candy. But that reason, however substantial, is not of the relevant kind. This essay focuses entirely on promissory obligations and reasons as they genuinely pertain to promising.

The EPP's rendition of promissory reasons and obligations in practice-internal terms places promising in large company. Practice-internal reasons are ubiquitous. Soccer players have soccer-internal reasons to pass the ball low so as to make it harder for the opposing team to get it. Members of a choir have choir-internal reasons to breathe in at different times. Wedding guests have wedding-internal reasons to rise when the bride enters. Chess-players have chess-internal reasons to get out the queen early. How promising, in contrast, could have genuine practice-independent authority remains a task not fully carried out yet, to say the least. So why not try without such authority? To many, this seems not an option. There is a profound worry that practices alone just won't cut it. Unassisted practices supposedly cannot be entrusted to sustain our promissory commitments completely on their own.

The worry is this. Norms are easy to come by; their authority, their status as legitimate guidelines, however, must appear an altogether more consequential matter. Norms of etiquette serves to illustrate the distinction between norms' formal dictates and their authority. The rule that one must answer in the third person to third person invitations clearly states a demand, but what is its normative force (see Foot 1972: 308)? We find norms governing virtually all corners of life. For every norm we can wonder why to take seriously what it demands. The fundamental question, then, must concern the normative status, and not the mere existence of norms. This is most firmly held when it comes to moral norms. Most would think James Griffin left out something crucial when he wrote: "To say that something 'ought to be' is to say that it is what conforms to some standard, norm, or regularity.... 'Moral oughts' are no different. They claim merely that there is a norm in the background to which a certain action would conform" (1996: 81). Norms in the background, however, are quite easily secured. We can thus understand why many would want to insist that, in addition to having norms in the background, these norms had better be authoritative independently of our acceptance of practices that embody them. It is understandable why many take issue with a view that denies such independent authority to promising.

II.

Let me contrast EPP with two competitors that seek to push beyond practices when it comes to the normative significance of promising: morality and social or individual benefit. Consider first the proposal that promissory norms are morally justified, in robustly practice-independent ways. It is clear that many authors are driven in that direction precisely by the kind of worry this essay addresses. Stephen Darwall, in his discussion of Reid's criticism of Hume on promising, first carves out a position very much like EPP: "Again, it doesn't matter if we reserve "promise"...for distinctive conventionally defined methods of voluntarily undertaken second-personal obligations." He then continues with approval: "Reid's point is that such conventional obligations will be possible only if we can presuppose an authority to make claims of one another and undertake voluntary obligations at all that does not itself depend upon antecedent conventions" (2006: 198). Other philosophers concur. Scanlon, for example, writes that breaking promises is "*wrong*: not just forbidden by some social practice but morally wrong" (1998: 306). For him, promising is a special case to be subsumed under the broader obligation of fidelity that is firmly grounded in principles that no one can reasonably reject. For Ross, we have prima facie moral duties to keep our promises. For Rawls, we have promissory obligations through our general obligation to support just institutions (1971: 295, 302–306). For consequentialists, of the act or rule type, we must keep our promises when, and because, doing so brings about the most good, or accords with rules the general observation of which would bring about the most good. (See chapters 9 and 10 here.)

Now EPP has two cards to play against moralists. First, it is unclear whether just any moral account of promising can stay true to the normative significance of promising. This especially applies to accounts that rely on general moral principles. For sure, moral principles would explain why we must keep our promises. By bolstering promissory obligations, one may think moralists must be well disposed toward promising. But this impression may be deceptive. Relying on general moral principles potentially contains difficulties for establishing the normative significance of promising in the right way—in the promising way, as it were. If promise-breaking is a wrong to be explained in exactly the same manner as other wrongs, it is hard to detect much distinctive contribution promising makes to that wrong. Consider soccer, again. It would be wrong to intentionally kick the ball right into the face the goalkeeper from a short distance, but this fact owes little to soccer. By doing so, one would cause gratuitous harm to another player, something morality forbids. This wrong, however, does not constitute a particular soccer-way for things to go wrong. Norms for soccer are not legitimized by serving more general moral duties. The same may be true for promising.

Consider the consequentialist model, for instance. That a promise has been made certainly feeds into the complex causal network that provides the backdrop against which moral evaluations are made. It generates certain expectations; it opens up additional possibilities for setbacks; it affects matters of coordination with huge repercussions. But whatever the exact ramifications of a promise, it is doubtful that this way of feeding into the framework does justice to any genuine and internal significance of promising. Thus, even if promises must always be kept, morally speaking, this does not necessarily endow promising as such with genuine normative significance.

Whether promises must always be kept, morally speaking, is in fact questionable—bringing us to EPP's second card. Immoral promises do not automatically cease to be promises. The mobster who promised in good faith to murder the witness is not at liberty to carry out that promise, morally speaking, not even a little bit. And yet his promissory obligation does not just evaporate in the face of morality's decisive precedence. Some philosophers have argued that immoral promises are null and void. But this is not generally plausible. Immoral promises are certainly morally void, but that's rather trivial. The question is whether they automatically are "promissorily" void, and that one may doubt. If there are any paradigmatic promises considered with the kind of seriousness philosophers commonly associate with the promissory enterprise, those made to and by the Mafia godfather qualify. If promises within "the family" don't count, I'm not sure which do. It is natural, then, to interpret the mobster's situation as falling under two conflicting obligations: an unambiguous promissory duty to carry out the promise and an unambiguous moral duty to defect.

In general, promissory obligations can facilitate virtue, vice, or neither. Recall how regrettably seriously many German army officers took their oath to Hitler. It surely would have been morally better if they had joined Claus Schenk Graf von Stauffenberg's assassination attempt despite their promissory obligations. It is a tricky question whether in such cases promissory reasons might not retain some moral force that is only outweighed or defeated by decisive countervailing moral reasons. I can find little to morally recommend serving Hitler solely in virtue of a promise, but I am not in a position here to rule out the possibility that this is not due to tininess of reasons as opposed to nonexistence. If my initial suspicion is correct, however, then promissory and moral duties potentially do not match up. If so, one could hardly supply the normative foundation for the other.

Let me now turn to the second kind of competitor, this one drawing on prudential and social benefits rather than on morality. What I have in mind here are broadly Humean practice-based accounts of promises (see Hume 2000). Though close cousins, EPP and broadly Humean approaches are nonetheless distinct. The view I defend is not that the normative significance of promising rests in the social benefits that promissory practices afford. If promissory practices were justified in the service of some social good, this would qualify as a sort of practice-external justification in my sense. Now global versions of the Humean view are less plausible than more individual ones, to which I shall turn shortly. Such versions place too much emphasis on global social aspects, and thereby fail to adequately engage the crucial perspective of the deliberating agent, who wants to know why he should keep his promise here and now. For that reason, I doubt that the general usefulness of a practice can make much contribution. Only few practices that it would be useful to have automatically usher individual commitments in us. We do not feel called on, for instance, to clean up litter in our neighborhoods on Sunday mornings, despite the obvious social benefits this would confer. What is good for society often fails to translate into reasons for individuals. Agents can thus reasonably wonder whether they should comply with practices they acknowledge are socially beneficial. *It would certainly serve the collective*, they may think, *but now here am I and not the collective making the choice; and I am certainly no mere servant of the collective.* In addition, it takes little imagination to construct cases where the execution of some promissory obligation would weaken the practice of promising as such. Suppose, as an admittedly unrealistic thought experiment, I make a promise whose execution would be so shocking to watch that most who witnessed it would become completely discouraged from ever making promises again. Still, this destabilizing effect need not exempt me from my promissory obligations.

Hanoch Sheinman has recently advanced a broadly Humean position that focuses on the individual promising agent, which he calls the *practice reason* account of promise, or *promise as practice reason* (2008a, 2008b). This view avoids the problem I have identified with Humean accounts that focus on the benefit of promising practices to society in general. According to the practice reason account of promise, when we promise, we give ourselves distinctively promissory reasons that are both practice-based and self-interested. In promising, we sign up to practice rules in the knowledge that breaking these rules would involve significant prudential costs. In particular, breaking practice rules that require us to keep our promises tends to diminish the trust other agents have in us, and this, in turn, tends to diminish our power to exchange promises with these agents in the future. Since the power to engage in such exchanges is valuable to us, we have a self-interested reason to preserve it by conforming to the promise-keeping rules, namely by keeping our promises. Promissory reasons are practice based, since it is in virtue of an existing social practice only that our self-interest can be engaged in that particular manner.

The EPP agrees with Sheinman's position in many ways, but not completely. I clearly share his emphasis on social practices, and rejection of the notion that promises are essentially moral commitments. But I am weary of Sheinman's treatment of self-interested reasons as constitutive components of the normative significance of promising. I agree that self-interested reasons play a major role in fueling promissory practices. Promise-keeping inclinations are substantially tied up with self-interested concerns regarding one's ability to make credible promises. So the practice reason account of promise seems to me to give a plausible account of the motivation to keep promises. But I do not think it gives a convincing account of the normativity of promises. In particular, I am worried about the way Sheinman interjects prudential reasons into promising.

The worry I have in mind is a version of the famous wrong-kind-of-reasons worry. I doubt that prudential reasons are of the right kind such that distinctively promissory reasons could be identified with them. Consider a covariation test, checking for coextensionality of promissory and self-interested reasons. If we can vary the prudential situation in ways that do not track the distinctively promissory normative situation, Sheinman's position is in trouble. I believe we can.

Consider, first, a case in which I do not promise, but my audience mistakenly believes I do, perhaps due to some irresolvable misunderstanding. Now, being concerned with my future promissory powers, I might well have prudential reasons to do what my audience wrongly assumes I promised. I have no promissory reasons, though, since I plainly did not promise. Consider a second case, where I do promise, but my audience quickly forgets my promise. Now I do have a promissory reason, but not a prudential reason, since my promissory trustworthiness would not be adversely affected by breaking my promise. In these cases and others, what to do in promissory terms and what to do in prudential terms often appear not to coincide. Sheinman addresses similar worries (2008a, 2008b).

Let me briefly turn to a second worry about the practice reason account of promise. Prudential concerns are often engaged in a manner after the fact as it were. In many circumstances, prudential aspects are affected only because the promissory normative situation is clear, and is common knowledge. It is because I am to keep my word that not doing so would result in adverse prudential returns. If we had concluded, in contrast, that I did not have promissory reasons to keep my promise after all—because of exempting circumstance, say—my promissory trustworthiness need not have become tainted. It is often precisely because the promissory normative situation is believed to be settled that prudence can enter the scene in the way Sheinman envisions. If prudential reasons presuppose the normative significance of promising, they cannot be taken to explain it.

III.

Let me return to the worry with EPP. Notice first that the objection leveled against EPP on the grounds of its supposed inability to sustain promissory commitments is highly indirect. It would not strictly speaking refute the claim that promising has no practice-external authority even if the worry was warranted. Promising could very well be a practice and nothing more, even if our allegiance to it was based on the mistaken belief that it was more than that. The EPP first and foremost advances a position on what promising is, normatively speaking, and not necessarily a proposal on how to make it thrive. Many believe that a full understanding of religious practices would place a heavy burden on their rational continuation, without thinking that this would falsify their account. Moreover, even if fully grasping what the practice of promising involves would make it harder for us to stand by our promissory obligations, this only needs to give rise to pragmatic concerns if acquiring that grasp is a likely scenario. And it might not. The illusion could be stable, possibly even be sanctified by other considerations. The practice could carry on despite its resting on illusionary roots. This situation may resemble the ways some reinforce their daily workout habits by considering themselves under a duty to do so. They may be fully aware that such a self-imposed duty lacks any real authority at their more reflective moments and yet at their less reflective moments continue to think so, effectively employing the help useful fictions provide on occasion.

Nonetheless, this indirectness does not make the objection less serious. For starters, a nondebunking view of promising would certainly be preferable all things considered. If EPP was short of an affirmative interpretation for promissory practices that could survive reflection, it would be inferior to competitors in this respect. Accounts that enabled us to reflectively stand by our promissory commitments without fooling ourselves would be better motivated. But more important, EPP, as I introduced the view, has greater ambitions than to merely take a stand on normative metaphysics. It also aspires to offer a self-embracing interpretation of promissory practices. Advocates of practice-views generally like practices. The concern that EPP may not be able to sustain promissory practices has force even for EPP's own advocates. The preservation of the relevant commitments that carry promissory practices must be something they care about. Because the objection can be pressed from EPP's own grounds without relying on anything extra, it makes it particularly worthy of a good response.

What is the response, then? How could we stand by our promissory commitments if we came to see them as part of a practice and nothing more? What I have to say, in essence, aims to establish the absence of *a negative* more than the presence of a *positive*. My goal is to dispel the impression that this is a philosophically hard question. To begin with, the objection rests on a rather sterile picture of our involvement in practices. We are not usually drawn to certain practices on rational grounds so much as we are acculturated to them. We usually remain loyal thereafter unless we find our commitments to be in conflict with other fundamental commitments. If we cannot see anything wrong with them, we retain them. And what is wrong with our habit of taking promises seriously, especially given that we take on our promissory obligations completely voluntarily? What other commitments do we have that would challenge our allegiance to promissory practices? There certainly are important questions about the status of norms. But in practical life we take them seriously only if our allegiance has already encountered substantive problems. Otherwise these questions retain an artificial aura of sophistry. The need for justification arises only against a presumptive background of suspicion.

Our loyalty to practice-norms does not even require any beliefs about their external legitimacy. Most people who play soccer aspire to play it well, not because of something else, but simply because they want to play soccer well. They are responsive to soccer-internal guidelines without regarding them as authoritatively grounded in anything other than soccer. Granted, they may not maintain these aspirations unless they can find a home for them within their larger projects and identities. But the fact that our allegiance to certain norms negatively depends on finding a home for them within our larger identities does not mean that we need to regard those norms as externally sanctioned. It is simply not true that everyone who aspires to play soccer well does so for reasons not related to soccer, even if it was true that he would abandon that aspiration in the absence of those other reasons. What is fair for soccer seems fair for promising as well.

Norms frequently maintain their particularly important standings within agents' deliberative spheres simply by reflecting what those agents care about. Here is one case. We do not like wasting our time. In our estimation of what counts as wasting our time we are guided by norms that reflect what activities are important to us. Those norms structure how we organize our time where some ways of using it count as better than others. Yet we do not need to believe that these practices and the concerns they reflect have any external authority. To me, for instance, watching sports is a waste of time. But that is just me. I certainly do not believe that my attitude toward sports reflects any external normative pressure on myself. I am simply guided by norms I do not consider externally sanctioned.

So far, this response is rather individualistic. Is this a problem, given the fact that promising is a social and not just *individualist* practice? Promising certainly involves not one but many agents. Focusing on the individual is well motivated, however. The final call on whether to stay faithful to promissory practices is to be made by individual deliberating agents. There are also independent reasons that push in an individualistic direction, however. Promising is more individualized than is often acknowledged. Promising is not enforced by any central agency. Nor is it usually enforced by third parties. Most of us do not care that much, if we are taking notice of other people's broken promises at all. Promise-breaking often is considered inconsequential. Think of deadlines. All this tends to have fragmentizing and individualizing effects on the practice of promising. What we end up with are many and not just a single practice of promising. There possibly is one promising-schema whose details are to be filled in by the participants of more individualized practices. Different promissory practices emerge in different contexts. Promising in the context of family involves other standards than promising in the context of business. Promising in an honor-society is a different practice than in laissez-faire academia. It is my sense that promising is mostly a personal affair, and loses its grip once personal ties fade. Often it is simply between you and me. I find it hard to recover much point in promise-exchange between complete strangers, for instance. What confidence to take in someone returning a spear if I was to return his boomerang is beyond me.

Let me turn now to a second point. The EPP does not deny that people usually have all sorts of extra reasons to observe promissory norms. Many are purely prudential. I may want that candy. The EPP does not take issue with having lots of nonpromissory reasons in play in addition to promissory reasons. Case by case, different coalitions of reasons may prompt us to keep our word. If enough people manage to do so enough of the time, the practice will carry on. The EPP only contests that these additional reasons are a necessary component of the normative significance of promising as such. Soccer, once more, makes the point. One should pass the ball low, I said, so as to make it harder for the opposing team to get it. In addition, one may also have reasons to pass the ball low because this limits the risk that the ball will be kicked out of the gated premises. The second reason is certainly a good one. One may now feel even stronger about passing the ball low. But this merely brings a consideration that has nothing to do with soccer to bear on a particular case that happens to be soccer. The same happens in promising.

The most prominent case it this. We often keep our promises not primarily because we promised, but because the promised activity is important. Suppose a colleague of mine promises to pick up a good friend from the airport. Now as I see him heading off to the bar, I realize he must have forgotten. As he quickly becomes incapacitated to carry out the task, I have no choice but to take over. So I pick up my friend. What is important is that my friend is picked up, not primarily that a promise is kept. This is what my friend and I care about. We may not even take much offense in the absentmindedness of our colleague. What I will later say to my colleague is that he really should have kept his promise, not primarily because he promised, but because it was important to do what he said he would be doing. That in many cases there are strong nonpromissory reasons in play does not show that promissory reasons themselves are somewhat deficient or lacking.

IV.

Let me address one final concern. The EPP admittedly does not represent how most people see promising now. The normative significance of promising, in all likelihood, is widely thought firmly grounded in something other than practices. What I had to offer consequently was revisionary to some degree. Is this a problem? I doubt it. In fact, I believe the revisionary nature of my interpretation is no exception. If we can trust common surveys, and if we extrapolate from generally held convictions about the nature of morality to the special case of promising, most people would probably believe that the authority of promissory obligations rests ultimately in God. Most philosophical approaches would not concur, and so would be no less idiosyncratic, in a statistical sense, when contrasted with dominantly held conceptions of the populace at large.

What this suggests is that it is imperative to keep separate *promising as something we do* and *promising as an activity we interpret*. We engage in normative practices, and we interpret that engagement. A moral theist and a secularist can engage in the very same practice and yet differ substantially in how they conceive of what they are doing. The theist would believe, and the secularist would deny, that the successful execution of the practice of promising consists in getting God's commands right and responding appropriately. And yet that need not prevent either party to issue reliable promises to the other. Neither needs to find the other guilty of some sort of equivocation when offering a promise. Now, the interpretation I am opposing does resemble that of the moral theist in this respect. It construes practical thought about promissory obligations as being responsive to what we are called on to do by an authority transcending our practices. There supposedly is something that authoritatively structures whether we must keep our promises and that has its source outside the rules of some social practice.

Now, in light of the revisionary character of many philosophical approaches, we have reasons to be careful not to assume prematurely interpretations to be inalterable components of interpreted practices themselves. Once the distinction between *promising as something we do* and *as something we interpret* is acknowledged, it should become possible, at least in principle, to replace one interpretation for another while keeping the interpreted activity in place. The conviction I share with most opponents of the EPP is that many of our normative practices are indeed indispensable; the lesson I draw from this is different, however. What I wonder is how such central pieces of our lives could be held hostage to uncertain metaphysical truths concerning authority. Rather than joining into the defense of promising by defending practice-external authority, I plead no such defense is needed to begin with. My opponents serve that practice poorly by forcing on us an interpretation that renders the very point of that practice dependent on normative metaphysics. In contrast, I suggest conserving the practice by revising the interpretation.

At the heart of the worry lies our reflective ability to stay indifferent toward the dictates of social norms, and to ask what reasons we have to do what they say. Many think this is a problem that requires a robustly metanormative solution that transcends social practices: the solution of finding an objective authority that provides normative backup for social norms. I believe it does not require a solution of that kind. The solution could be purely practical. We may question whether social norms have any practice-external authority and then conform to them anyway. If norms make sense to us, why should their possession of any additional metanormative backup be of any concern to us? We do stay loyal to many practices in a purely practical manner without holding metanormative beliefs about them. Soccer, weddings, choirs, chess illustrate the point. What is important for practices to carry on is that people stay loyal; not that they have certain beliefs. In any case, even if people had those beliefs, even if they took utmost confidence in the practice-external authority of promising, this may still not answer the practical problem. As Foot puts it, "the question remains as to why we should do what we are required to do" (1972: 310). Practice-external authority would not automatically settle the practical question. We still have to decide whether to go along with norms we take to be authoritative in that robust metanormative sense. If we shall be able to shrug this off as easily as we supposedly can with practice-norms, as I think we can, then how much progress have we really made on the practical front by inventing practice-external authority?

REFERENCES

Copp, D. 1995. *Morality, Normativity, and Society*. New York: Oxford University Press.

Darwall, S. 2006. *The Second-person Standpoint*. Cambridge, MA: Harvard University Press.

Foot, P. 1972. "Morality as a System of Hypothetical Imperatives." *Philosophical Review* Vol. 81, No. 3. (Jul., 1972): 305–316.

Griffin, J. 1996. *Value Judgment*. New York: Oxford University Press.

Hart, H. L. A. 1955. "Are There Any Natural Rights?" *Philosophical Review* Vol. 64, No. 2 (Apr., 1955): 175-191.

———. 1994. *The Concept of Law*. Oxford: Clarendon Press.

Hume, D. 2000. *A Treatise on Human Nature*. Oxford: Oxford University Press.

Rawls, J. 1955. "Two Concepts of Rules." *Philosophical Review* Vol. 64, No. 1 (Jan., 1955): 3–32.

———. 1971. *A Theory of Justice*. Cambridge, MA: Harvard University Press.

Scanlon, T. 1998. *What We Owe to Each Other*, Cambridge, MA: Harvard University Press.

Sheinman, H. 2008a. "Promise as Practice Reason." *Acta Analytica* 23: 287-318.

———. 2008b. Promise, Practice, Agreements: An Essay in Social Philosophy. Manuscript.

Chapter 5

The Importance of Self-Promises

Connie Rosati

Abstract

Many philosophers have been skeptical about the existence of promises to self, and in fact, self-promises appear to face a dilemma. Critics have argued that promises to self are conceptually impossible. Since the agent is both promisor and promisee, she can release herself from a self-promise at will, and so she was never really bound. Self-promises, in short, cannot be genuine because unlike our promises to others, they cannot create obligations. Even if it could be shown that self-promises are not conceptually impossible, they seem to be of little importance or effect. It seems clear why we would need and want to make promises to others, but why would we ever need or want to make promises to ourselves? In this essay, I attempt to address this dilemma. I argue that the supposed possibility of "self-release" does not show that promises to self are impossible. Insofar as there is a real difficulty for the possibility of self-promises, it lies in making out a plausible distinction between release from a self-promise and breach of that promise. But this difficulty, I suggest, can be answered. I go on to offer a preliminary defense of the importance of self-promises, arguing that their importance lies in how they may function to serve our interest in autonomy—in having effective authority over ourselves.

We often make promises to ourselves—or so it seems. We promise ourselves that we will complete a project or commence one. We promise ourselves that we will lose weight, eat better, exercise more. We promise ourselves that we will plan better or be more spontaneous, that we will take more care or take more chances. We promise ourselves that we will endeavor to be better people, that we will work to be wiser or kinder, more respectful of others or more self-respecting.

As these examples illustrate, our (apparent) self-promises can concern the same broad array of matters as our promises to others.[1] They can concern our character or our conduct, our self-regarding or our other-regarding attitudes and actions. Our self-promises can also be made in the same general ways as our promises to others. They can be undertaken formally or informally, and even ritualistically—consider the tradition of annual New Year's resolutions.[2] The making of self-promises is less in plain view, of course, than the making of promises to others. Our self-promising may involve the sorts of speech-acts typically involved in assuming promissory obligations to others, though performed in a way that only we can hear or record.[3] We promise, swear, pledge, vow, commit, if only internally or perhaps sotto voce; we thereby register the promise just in memory or in our private journals or diaries. Promises to self—kept or broken—can prompt an array of reactive attitudes. They can be as much a source of self-esteem or self-reproach, for example, as promises to others. In these and no doubt other ways, our self-promising seems to be of a piece with our "other-promising."[4]

Of course, the fact that we appear to make promises to ourselves, and even the fact that we may mouth (perhaps internally) certain canonical formulas, does not show that apparent promises to oneself are the genuine article. And in fact, some have doubted just this, arguing that promises to oneself are conceptually impossible.[5] Self-promises are, after all, *intra*-agential—the promisor, or party "bound," and the promisee, or party to whom the promisor is bound, are one in the same. But then, so the argument goes, self-promises differ critically from our ordinary *inter*-agential promises. When an agent makes a promise to another, she can escape her obligation only if the promisee releases her, or she is otherwise excused. When an agent makes a promise to herself, in contrast, she just *is* the promisee, and so she can simply release herself at will; as a consequence, she was never really bound.

Even if we allow that promises to oneself are possible, they remain rather mysterious. There are many reasons why we would need and want to make promises to others, and philosophers have typically appealed to these reasons in constructing theories of promising.[6] Even if disagreement exists about the normative function of our other-promising, no one doubts that *some* such function exists; and this function presumably accounts for how, in having made a promise to another, a person is genuinely bound (absent release) to whatever degree that she is.[7] But why would we ever need or want to make promises to ourselves? Self-promises seem unnecessary and, in any case, of little effect. They seem unnecessary because the agent could presumably just decide firmly on a course of action and act straightaway or in due course. To be sure, an agent might suffer from weakness of will, but self-promising could not itself remedy that problem, at least not directly and immediately.[8] Self-promises seem of little effect because whether an individual fulfills a promise to herself or defects, she gets something that she wants; indeed, assuming that an agent always acts on her strongest desires, the individual who defects from a self-promise gets what she most strongly wants. For this reason, self-promises seem not to protect a person's own interests in quite the way that other-promises, when fulfilled, tend to protect the interests of others.

A dilemma thus appears to exist for self-promising: either self-promises are not possible, and so apparent self-promises are not genuine promises, or they are genuine but pointless promises, ones we have no compelling reason to make or to keep. I hope to show that this is a false dilemma.[9] I begin by addressing the "impossibility" horn, doing so in two stages. First, I summarize and respond to the basic case made by others for thinking that self-promises are not possible. I then go on to explain how critics have mischaracterized the problem, insofar as there might be one, offering and addressing a corrected understanding of the problem.[10] In the remainder of this essay, I consider the "pointlessness" horn of the dilemma, which I take to pose the more serious problem for self-promising. My aim will be to arrive at a preliminary account of the function and importance of self-promises. As I hope will be evident, this account bears not only on the normative character of promises to self but on the normative character of promises to others, and so on our efforts to arrive at a unified theory of promising.

My rough account of the importance of self-promises has an affinity with and builds on a number of attractive ideas about promises advanced by other philosophers. In particular, it develops a suggestion Thomas Hill has made about the connection between promises to self and self-respect.[11] And it provides what might be viewed as a natural modification and extension of the "authority-interest" theory of promising recently offered by David Owens.[12] I shall suggest that the importance of self-promises lies in how successful self-promising can help to serve the authority interest we have in ourselves, an interest importantly related to self-respect and one we necessarily have insofar as we are autonomous agents.

One consequence of my account of the importance of self-promises is that the relationship between promises to self and promises to others is rather different from what many prominent treatments of promising would lead us to think. Philosophical work on the nature of promises suggests two basic views about self-promises and their relationship to other-promises. According to the first view, despite possessing some of the features of genuine promises, self-promises are merely pale imitations of our real, *inter*-personal promises. According to the second view, self-promises are real but an aberrant or nonstandard case of promising, the bona fides of which must be defended.[13]

Although I reject the first view and agree with those who have supported the genuineness of self-promises, I suspect that defenders of self-promising have not fully appreciated the normative significance of promises to self, and that may be precisely because they implicitly treat promises to others as paradigmatic. My account of the importance of self-promises reverses the normative priority of promises to self and to others. Not only are promises to self genuine promises, but they are also, in one quite critical, if limited, sense, normatively basic.

I. THE POSSIBILITY OF SELF-PROMISES

According to one plausible account of promises, an agent promises to Φ when she engages in a speech-act by which she means to communicate an intention to be bound or under an obligation to Φ.[14] For purposes of the discussion that follows, I shall accept this rough account. But what does it mean for an agent to communicate an intention to be under an obligation? It cannot mean, at least in the case of ordinary promises, an intention to be held physically to the promise—to literally be obliged. To be sure, legally enforceable promises may involve intending to be obliged, or better, agreeing to be obliged, at least in some manner. But even contract law—the law of exchanged promises—disfavors specific performance as a remedy for breach of contract; it disfavors, that is, literally obliging a person to fulfill her promise. And this is commonly said to be because specific performance comes disturbingly close to a kind of servitude—a point which, as we will see, is tied to plausible ideas about the normative function of promises. Still, a person's being made to pay damages under threat of legal sanctions is surely a form of being obliged. Here, at least, contract and promise come apart, for it is no part of our understanding of ordinary promises that the promisor communicates an intention to be under an obligation even in this sense. Rather, the promisor communicates an intention to be under an obligation to perform in the first instance, but otherwise to make reasonable efforts to mitigate the ill effects of nonperformance and to make amends, at least in the absence of excusing conditions and where appropriate. She thereby acknowledges, in effect, that depending on the significance of the promise, she may appropriately be subject to censure of one sort or another—to expressions of annoyance or anger, to moral criticism, to shunning or other displays of distrust, and possibly to a severing or altering of relationships.

As these considerations make clear, promissory obligation involves something more complex than the bare creation of an obligation to perform the promised act. Rather, when the promisor makes a valid promise, she incurs a set of obligations to the promisee. First, she incurs an obligation, other things equal, to perform the promised act. Second, she incurs an obligation, other things equal, to make reasonable efforts to mitigate the effects of failure to perform the promised act. And finally, she incurs an obligation, regardless of whether failure to perform is excused or not, to make such amends as may be proper. If I promise you a ride to the airport and find myself unable to perform close to the time of departure, I owe you timely notification so that you can arrange for alternative transportation. Depending on the circumstances, I may owe you assistance with cab fare or may be obligated to try to find someone else to take you in my stead. At the very least, I owe you an apology for my failure to perform. The precise obligations in play will depend, of course, on a variety of factors, including the relationship between promisor and promisee, the importance of the promised act for the promisee, and the degree to which the promisee reasonably relied on the promise.

What underlies this complexity is the basic conceptual connection between promising and obligation: the concept of a promise is the concept of an act with normative import. Predictably, then, skepticism about the conceptual possibility of promises to self rests on considerations about the normativity of promises. The classic expression of the basic problem can be found in Hobbes's *Leviathan*, when Hobbes explains why the Sovereign of a commonwealth cannot be subject to the civil laws. As Hobbes explains it, "having power to make and repeale Lawes, he may when he pleaseth, free himselfe from that subjection, by repealing those Lawes that trouble him, and making of new; and consequently he was free before. For he is free, that can be free when he will: *Nor is it possible for any person to be bound to himself; because he that can bind, can release; and therefore he that is bound to himself onely, is not bound.*"[15] Hobbes's idea is that if a person can (as he thought the Sovereign could) release himself at will from an obligation, he was never bound and so was never really obligated at all. The "obligation" was merely apparent.

Following Hobbes, the basic problem that has been raised for self-promising might be expressed as follows. When an agent, A, makes a promise to someone to Φ, she incurs an obligation to Φ. But it is a necessary condition on A's having an obligation to Φ that she not be able to release herself at will. When A makes a promises to herself, however, she can release herself at will. As a consequence, when A makes a promise to herself to Φ, she not only does not but could not incur an obligation to Φ. Therefore, A's promise to herself cannot be normative, and so A's self-promise cannot be a genuine promise.

An important qualification to the argument must be made, because even in the case of promises to others, not just any act of promising gives rise to an obligation to perform the promised act.[16] Consider the gruesome case of Armin Meiwes, who defended his cannibalism of Bernd Brandes on the grounds that Brandes had agreed to be eaten.[17] Let's imagine that Meiwes, having advertised for his meal on the Internet, was contacted by Brandes, who promised to meet him at a prearranged time and place for the purpose of being consumed and who promised, furthermore, that he would make no effort to escape or back out of the deal. Now surely, Brandes's promises notwithstanding, he had no obligation to follow through, and that fact is not altered in the least by the consideration that fulfilling the promise would enable Meiwes to realize a lifelong dream. There are some things one cannot be obligated to do, beyond those one merely cannot do, and so some things one cannot promise to do.[18] Just for this reason, my earlier claims about the set of obligations correlative to a promise explicitly invoked the notion of a "valid promise." Without trying here to settle the precise normative parameters on the content of permissible promises, let's simply add to the skeptical argument presented above the qualification that a promise must be valid.[19] And so the argument for the conceptual impossibility of self-promises concerns valid promises, and its conclusion is that an agent cannot make valid promises to herself.

Sometimes skepticism about the possibility of self-promises has been presented as part of a broader skepticism about duties to self. Marcus Singer, for example, has argued that "it is actually impossible...for there to be any duties to oneself, in any literal sense, for, if taken literally, the idea involves a contradiction."[20] Singer's argument for the impossibility of duties to self seems to be a version of Hobbes's argument for why the Sovereign is not bound by the civil laws. Yet it merits separate attention because of the support it appears to provide for the critical claim that an agent can release herself "at will" from obligations to self, and so, as we will see, from promissory obligations to self.

As Singer explains it, his argument rests on three propositions: "(1) If A has a duty to B, then B has a right against A; (2) if B has a right against A, he can give it up and release A from the obligation; and (3) no one can release himself from an obligation."[21] A duty to oneself, he argues, "would be a duty from which one could release oneself at will, and this is self-contradictory. A 'duty' from which one could release oneself at will is not, in any literal sense, a duty at all."[22] Singer goes on to argue that talk about duties to oneself—what is owed to oneself—can be at best metaphorical. When I say that I owe it to myself to take a real vacation, for example, I merely express my determination to take a vacation or my belief that it would be prudent to take a vacation.[23]

I shall turn in a moment to the bearing of Singer's argument against duties to self on self-promises in particular. Before doing so, however, I want to consider briefly his broader case against duties to self, for certain difficulties with the broader case affect the narrower case against self-promises. Consider the second claim on which the argument rests. As a general matter, one might reasonably challenge whether when a person has a right against another, she is entitled to release him from his correlative duties. A person's normative power with respect to any of her rights, and so with respect to another's obligation to perform any corresponding duties, arguably depends on the nature of the right in question and what grounds it. Brandes had a right to life, I shall assume, but on some plausible views about the importance and normative basis of that right, he had no power simply to "give it up" or to release Meiwes from the duty not to kill him. Suppose, for example, that Brandes right was grounded in a value that inhered in him as a person, a value that he was not free to trade or disregard. Then arguably Brandes had no normative authority to surrender that right or to permit its infringement without especially weighty reasons. That would explain why the law shouldn't have accepted (as it did not) Meiwes's defense that Brandes had agreed to the arrangement. Brandes was evidently suffering from a psychiatric disorder. But even if testifying psychiatrists had confirmed his mental competence to form the agreement, that would and should have been of no aid to Meiwes, and not merely because legal recognition of a defense like his would have bad social consequences on balance. Rather, Meiwes violated Brandes's right, a right Brandes had no power simply to surrender, and so he failed to act on an obligation from which Brandes had no power to release him. A person can, of course, decline to exercise or to stand on her rights. But if whatever moral rights we have are grounded in something like the normative status or agent-neutral value of persons, then our rights and others' duties are not, as a general matter, optional in the way Singer's second premise would seem to suggest.[24]

Suppose that a rights-holder cannot generally release another from his correlative obligations just at her choosing. Then Singer's case for the impossibility of duties to self would seem to require that matters change when the rights-holder and the apparently duty-bound are one in the same person. When a person has a right, relevantly situated others have duties to behave and refrain from behaving in various ways. But "relevantly situated others" must exclude the person herself; or alternatively, the person must be able readily to release herself in a way that she cannot release others, so that duties to self are impossible.

Perhaps agents sometimes lack in relation to themselves the duties that they have in relation to others and that others have in relation to them. One might nevertheless doubt that on a plausible account of our rights and their grounding, the agent herself would, as a general matter, be exempt from the duties correlative to her rights.[25] Suppose, again, that our rights and corresponding duties have their source in the normative status or agent-neutral value of persons. Then an agent is no more free to disregard or discount her own value than she is free to disregard or discount the value of another.

If she is not free to disregard her own value indirectly by, for example, "releasing" others from their duties toward her, she is also not free to disregard it directly. To say that she has no duties to herself, however, would amount to saying that at least so far as she herself is concerned, she is free to disregard or discount her value as she will. But that is inconsistent with the nature of the value that (on this view) she has.

Kant strikingly held that "Far from ranking lowest in the scale of precedence our duties toward ourselves are of primary importance and should have pride of place."[26] According to Kant, the man who "dishonours his own person" cannot be trusted and loses his capacity to fulfill his duties toward others. Whereas the man who "fails in his duty toward others loses worth only relatively," the man who "fails in his duty to himself loses worth absolutely."[27] The person who performs his duties toward others poorly but fulfills them toward himself maintains at least "a certain" inner worth.

I confess that I find the broadly Kantian view of rights sketched above—and even Kant's own strong claims about the primacy of duties to self—appealing. But my reasons for rejecting Singer's general case against duties to self does not turn on the truth of any particular account of our moral rights and their normative basis. What a consideration of this view shows is that Singer's second proposition is question-begging against some important views about what grounds our rights. These views may be mistaken, of course, but any argument against the existence of duties to self would have to proceed directly against these views and so would have to provide support for (2) before it could rest on (2).

The case against self-promises need not, of course, rest on a more general case against duties to self. Perhaps one can allow that we have duties to ourselves, while insisting that promissory obligations are different. Singer's argument against self-promises rests not simply on his case against duties to self, as I understand him, but on a comparison of the self-promisor to the other-promisor. In brief, Singer's argument appears to be this. In an ordinary, two-party promise, the promisee can release the promisor at will. The promisee to a self-promise just *is* the promisor. Therefore, the promisor to a self-promise can release herself at will. It is essential to an obligation, he tells us, that "no one can release himself from an obligation by not wishing to perform it or by deciding not to perform it, or, indeed, in any other way whatsoever."[28] Since such "release at will" exists in the case of self-promises, they cannot create obligations.

Singer's argument has force. The promisor cannot release himself from an other-promise in quite the way that he can release himself from a self-promise; he is, after all, subject to the will of another. But matters may be more complicated than it appears, for the notion of "release at will" may not, without careful spelling out, accurately capture the normative power of the promisee in the case of either inter or intrapersonal promises. The promisee of an other-promise may *not* always be able to release the promisor at will. And to the extent that she can release him at will, the explanation of why that is so may lend no support to the claim that self-promises cannot obligate because the self-promisor can release herself at will.

Whether a promisee can release the promisor at will would seem to depend on the nature of the promise. As Singer depicts our promises to others, we promisors can break our promises, but only our promisees can release us, either explicitly or by declining to exercise their rights, and they can release us for good reason or for no reason at all; promising is, from the standpoint of the promisee, something like employment at will from the standpoint of the employer. But suppose Jones kidnaps Smith and his child, and Smith manages to extract from Jones a promise that he will not torture the child. Surely Smith cannot at will release Jones from his obligation. And arguably the case is no different if it is Smith himself who Jones has promised not to torture, even allowing that Smith could both rationally and permissibly submit to torture under certain circumstances. More precisely, we cannot simply assume that Smith can release Jones at will where his own treatment is the subject of the promise, whereas he cannot if his child's treatment is the subject of the promise, without, once again, begging the question of whether there are duties to self.

Now one might insist that even in cases like these, Smith can, at will, release Jones from his promise. It's just that the release has no normative effect; it does not free Jones to do what he promised not to do because he had promised not to do what he is not permitted to do anyway. Just as there are some things one cannot validly promise to do or refrain from doing, there are some things that a promissory release cannot free up a promisor to do or refrain from doing. Jones has a standing obligation that neither the promise nor release from it can alter. As I see it, acknowledging that Smith's release is without normative effect amounts to acknowledging that Smith really cannot release Jones with respect to the promised act. Or rather, he can release Jones only in a rather formal sense. The release amounts to relieving Jones of the obligation to Φ (refrain from torturing) *on the grounds that* or *for the reason that he promised to Φ*.

No doubt in some cases, like that of Smith and Jones, the promisee extracts a promise, not in order to create an obligation, but as a device for either putting the promisor in mind of obligations he already has or motivating the promisor to behave in accordance with those obligations. But even when the promise serves one of these other purposes and cannot alter the promisor's obligations to act or not, it does add *something* to his obligations, as I will explain momentarily.

In my view, cases like that of Smith and Jones reveal that the sense in which a promisee can release the promisor is more complex than is captured by easy talk about "releasing at will." For what we can and cannot validly promise to do and what we can and cannot release another from doing depends on how our promises relate to the complex structure of our duties. It depends, we might say, on what we already and always owe to one another.[29] Promises might be divided into two broad categories. The first comprises promises to do things that we have a preexisting obligation to do, such as pay our debts, and promises to refrain from doing things that we have a preexisting obligation not to do, such as inflict bodily injury. The second comprises promises to do things that we have no preexisting obligation to do but that may be the object of a valid promise; these promises create obligations that we did not have before.[30]

In the former cases, the act of promising, for example, A's promise to Φ, may seem to do no independent normative work, given that it is not needed to explain the existence of A's obligation to Φ. But here, too, matters are more complex than it may seem, for our promises may serve, if not to create the basic underlying obligation, then to impose further obligations concerning the time, place, and manner of fulfilling it; our promises may also serve to pick out who will benefit from the fulfillment of our basic obligations. A has a "perfect duty" to repay her debts. But if A owes money to B and promises to repay by money order and by a certain date, she incurs obligations in addition to her duty to repay, though obligations she wouldn't have but for that duty. A has an "imperfect duty" to give to charity. But if she promises a certain individual or organization her support, she incurs obligations in addition to her general duty, at least when the individual or organization acts in reasonable reliance on the promise. Even when promises do not add to our obligations by further specifying our duties or the beneficiaries of our dutiful acts, in making and breaking a promise to do what she has a preexisting obligation to do, the promisor does seem to be legitimately subject to two distinct criticisms: she failed to do what she ought in any case to have done *and* she failed to keep her word.[31] If Jones tortures Smith's child (or Smith himself) he is properly subject to criticism not only for the torturing but for the breach of promise, though the former wrong will no doubt entirely eclipse the latter.

One might, of course, take the view that the only *genuine* promises are promises of the second sort. Real promises create obligations that didn't exist already; promissory speech-acts involving extant duties, at least where they create no additional duties, have purposes entirely separate from the function or purpose of promising proper.[32] And so one might think that a problem for self-promises remains with respect to what I have described as the second category of promises. Yet a perhaps insufficiently appreciated fact is that even promises in this second category derive their normative force from preexisting obligations. Here, A promises to Φ but the preexisting obligation is not specifically *to* Φ. Rather, the promisor has more general standing obligations, obligations that have their source in the normative status of persons or in the moral principles that determine what is owed to persons. She has, for example, standing obligations to act in ways that respond appropriately to the value of persons—that respect them as autonomous agents and manifest a proper regard for their good.[33] But for those standing obligations, the fact of her having made a promise would be without normative significance; the promisor would, in breaking a promise, do no one any wrong.

The fact that even category two promises depend on preexisting obligations bears once again on the nature of release. For one can reasonably question whether the promisee can always release the promisor at will even with respect to these sorts of promises. Let's grant that the promisee to a two-party promise can release the promisor at will when the promise is particularly trivial. As promises become more significant, bearing importantly on the promisee's autonomy or her good, it becomes less clear that even the promisee to an other-promise can release the promisor at will.[34] At least some case can be made that the promisee can release the promisor only when she genuinely decides to do so for what she takes to be good reason. For example, she may determine that the promisor's fulfilling the promise no longer accords with her aims or interests, in which case keeping the promise may neither manifest respect for her autonomy nor a proper regard for her good. Or she may judge that the promisor's circumstances make fulfilling the promise a more serious burden than she cares to impose in light of what she takes to be the relative weight of her own interests. But consider the individual who is not appropriately self-respecting or concerned for her own welfare. She may be too quick to release the finagling promisor who seeks release for no good reason or who simply manifests a desire not to act as promised. In cases like these, the promisor arguably is not truly released regardless of what the promisee may say; at least, our negative attitudes toward the promisor suggests that we regard the release as suspect. So either the promisee cannot always release the promisor "at will" or the notion of "release at will" is more normatively loaded than is ordinarily recognized—it isn't merely a matter of the promisee saying, "Never mind." Insofar as the foregoing considerations hold true in the case of other-promises, they hold also in the case of self-promises.

Suppose one insists, however, to adopt what I still think too crude a formulation, that in a two-party promise, the promisee can simply release the promisor at will. We would not be tempted to say that because the promisee can release the promisor at will, the promisor is not really obligated. So long as the promisee has not released the promisor, she is indeed bound. But then we should say the same thing about self-promises: although an agent, as promisee, can release herself, as promisor, at will, *so long as she does not release herself, she is indeed bound.*[35]

This consideration suggests that the real "impossibility" problem for self-promises, insofar as there is one, is *not* that the promisor can release herself at will. Rather, the problem would seem to be this: whereas in the case of two-party promises, we can coherently distinguish between the promisor's being *released* from a promise and his *breaking* that promise, in the case of promises to self, we cannot. Given that a plausible distinction between release and breach cannot be drawn in the case of self-promises, they cannot be normative; they cannot create genuine obligations.[36]

Yet even on this corrected understanding of the problem, self-promises have not been shown to be impossible, for surely we do recognize a distinction between release and breach in the intrapersonal case. From an agent's perspective there is all the difference in the world between changing her mind and acting against her own reflective judgment. Indeed, she may well recognize *at the moment of action* that she is acting against a considered decision, or compromising her values, or behaving self-destructively. In these cases, she may well think, looking forward, "I'm going to regret this in the morning," or she may acknowledge looking back that she has let herself down. It is certainly true that in the face of temptation or contrary desires, a self-promise once made may not seem like such a good idea after all.[37] And sometimes it is not; sometimes we are right to change our minds. But an agent might change her mind, acting against an earlier self-promise, and come to regret doing so later, just as she may come to regret changing her mind about fulfilling an other-promise.

How might we characterize the distinction between release from and breach of a self-promise? We might characterize it, I would suggest, in the same way that we might characterize the distinction in the case of other-promises. A promisee releases a promisor when the promisee would recognize herself as having communicated to the promisor a genuine change of mind.[38] In the case of a self-promise, the change is communicated just in the process of having considered the matter. A change of mind need not be fully rational or well-advised all things considered to count as genuine. We can release others or ourselves from promises for reasons we later conclude weren't so compelling after all. It does require, however, that one has freely thought about the matter and now decides differently for what one takes to be good reason. A promisor breaches a promise when she fails to perform the promised act in the absence of being released by the promisee. The breach may or may not be justifiable or excused. I submit that in the intra-agential case, then, we well-recognize the difference between changing our minds and acting against our unchanged minds. Consider the smoker who promises herself that she will quit but succumbs to her desire to smoke. In lighting up, she acts deliberately, but she may do so while denying that she has changed her mind. She may, on the contrary, acknowledge that she has broken a promise that she made to herself. She may, indeed, acknowledge repeatedly breaking the promise, though she is likely to report finding it an especially hard promise to keep.

The foregoing characterization of the distinction between release and breach leaves open the question of when release has normative force. Without attempting to settle the question, we might say two things. First, the existence of a coherent distinction between release and breach, such as I have tried to offer, is a necessary condition for a promisee's release of a promisor to have normative force. But in addition, a promisee's release has normative force—can alter a promisor's obligations with respect to the promised act—only where it lies within the promisee's authority to effect such an alteration. And that, I have already suggested, depends on the circumstances, the content of the promise, and how the promise interacts with our duties.

II. THE FUNCTION OF SELF-PROMISES

Even if we allow, as I have been arguing, that we lack compelling grounds for the view that self-promises are impossible, a puzzle remains, for they might seem to be unnecessary or of little import. What function, then, might self-promises serve? I indicated at the outset that the account I shall propose has an affinity with and builds on David Owens's authority-interest theory, and so it will be helpful for expository purposes to have a sketch of that attractive theory before us.[39] As will become clear, I do not agree with Owens's theory in all of its details, at least as I understand it. But once the theory has been suitably modified, I believe that we have the resources for a more complete theory of promising, one that encompasses both promises to self and to others.[40]

Owens's aim in developing the authority-interest theory is to identify the function of a promise by identifying a common interest that would explain why promising exists and is taken so seriously by us.[41] The function of a promise—that is, the function of *promises*—should not be confused with the purpose served by individual promises. Owens does not claim that each promise serves, or is undertaken to serve, the interest he identifies. On the contrary, he recognizes that promises can serves many purposes, and ordinarily, we have more specific aims and interests in mind when we attempt to secure promises from one another. Owens seeks to explain not the function of particular promises, then, but of promises as such. My inquiry into the function of self-promises likewise seeks to identify not the function of individual promises to self, which may serve many purposes, but of self-promises as such.

According to Owens, our (other-) promising exists because it serves our "authority interest."[42] Owens has us consider a case in which he is asked by someone at the office for a lift home. He imagines this person to be a rather bossy sort, so that he might be willing to express an intention to give this person a ride home, while being resistant to making a promise to do so. As Owens explains it, he might be reluctant, say, to give the other this veto power over his acts, and what underlies this reluctance is his "interest in having the right to decide what he shall do."[43] This interest should not be confused with a person's interest in making decisions that advance her welfare or her aims. We have that interest, to be sure, but in addition, we have "an interest in having the right to decide what we shall do, in our judgment rather than someone else's of what is reasonable for us to do having the authority to determine what happens."[44] Owens insists that this authority interest is not an interest in self-control, that is, "in it being our choice that determines what we do."[45] Instead, it is an interest in having the moral power or freedom to act in accordance with our own judgments about what we ought to do, rather than in accordance with another person's judgments. We have an interest in having the right to decide what we shall do quite apart from whether we will, in a given case, actually exercise it.[46]

As described thus far, our authority interest is an interest in having a right to decide—in having our very own judgments prevail as to what we ought to do and shall do. But when it comes to other-promises, where we are the *promisee*, what is at issue is *our* judgment as to what *another* shall do, and so where we are the *promisor, another's* judgment as to what *we* shall do. On the face of it, then, promising, from a person's standpoint as prospective promisee, would seem to be irrelevant to her authority interest, and from her standpoint as prospective promisor, would seem to be at odds with it. As Owens observes, however, our decisions often depend for their effectiveness on the actions of others. Owens's coworker, for instance, can reasonably decide to wait for a lift home only if Owens (or someone else) agrees to provide one. Insofar as we are each motivated by our interest in having the right to decide for ourselves what we shall do, we will also be motivated, in those cases in which our decisions depend on another's actions, "to seek the right to require another to behave in a certain way."[47] And we may be willing, in return, to sacrifice some portion of our own freedom of action. "A promise effects such grants of authority."[48]

Because of the interdependence of our decisions, our authority interest in having the right to decide what we shall do encompasses an interest in being able to acquire authority over what another shall do. This is not, according to Owens, an interest in controlling another person's actions—an interest in "other-control"—anymore than our authority interest in our own actions is an interest in self-control. Whether it is our own actions that are at issue or those of another, we value for its own sake the authority to determine what shall be done, whether or not the action will occur.[49]

The function of promising, then, is to serve our authority interest.[50] In making a promise to another, we grant her the authority to require us to do the promised act. As Owens expresses it, "A promise grants the promisee the right to require performance from the promisor; to use Kant's metaphor, in accepting my promise you 'take possession of my choice.'"[51] But for the promisor to grant this authority, he cannot reserve the right to change his mind, provided, say, that he warns the promisee in advance or compensates the promisee. "The promisor's obligation is to let the promisee decide, and the promisor discharges this obligation by leaving it up to the promisee to determine whether this promise must be fulfilled."[52] Promissory obligations arise, according to Owens, only for those who deliberately communicate an intention of taking on an obligation, and this fact flows from the function of promises. Because the effect of a promise is to confer authority on the promisee, thereby restricting the promisor's authority over his own life (at least with respect to the promised action), the obligation can only be incurred by an exercise of the promising agent's own authority.[53]

I find the authority interest theory quite appealing, though subject to certain qualifications. First, I would want to stress a qualification that Owens himself makes and that was insisted on earlier, namely, that the promisor cannot grant the promisee an authority that it isn't his to grant.[54] He can only grant to another what already lies within the scope of his own authority. As Owens observes, a promise has no force where the promisor lacks authority to do the promised act.

Second, and here I would depart from Owens, the promisee's authority is likewise limited; she lacks the authority unreasonably to refuse release from a promise. She lacks this authority just as she lacks the authority to otherwise behave wrongfully. And so the promisor does not incur an obligation simply to let the promisee decide whether the promise must be fulfilled. I will not attempt to settle here whether we should count the promisor's refusal to do the promised act when the promisee unreasonably refuses to release her as self-release or justified breach. Let me simply observe that the fact that the promisee lacks authority to refuse release unreasonably suggests that there *may* be room to argue that self-release is possible even with respect to other promises.[55] And if self-release is possible, then it is not true that only the promisee can release the promisor from an other-promise; and so, again, self-promises do not differ from promises to others in quite the way some have thought.

Failure to notice the tripartite character of promissory obligations described earlier may explain a tendency to overlook this possibility; it may also explain why some have thought that any promise whatsoever creates some obligation to do the promised act.[56] Even if the promisor can either release herself from or justifiably breach an obligation to do the promised act, she may retain obligations to mitigate and to make amends. Some may assume that insofar as she is not obligation-free, that must be because she remains obligated to perform the promised act. Instead, I have suggested, the act of validly promising itself standardly creates multiple obligations. With respect to invalid promises, where the promisor can have no obligation to do the promised act because she has a preexisting obligation not to do it, she may still, in virtue of having made a promise, incur obligations to mitigate or to make amends. And here, again, one might mistakenly assume that she has the latter obligations because any act of promising must really create some obligation to do the promised act. Instead, she may not be obligation-free because even acts of promising to do what one may not do can trigger duties of respect for persons and a regard for their good. She may not be obligation-free, that is, because of the way the normativity of acts of promising rests on preexisting duties.

So far we have it that promising functions to serve a promisee's authority interest by securing for the promisee authority over the actions of another. If something like the authority-interest theory is correct, then what is the function of *self*-promising? Promising, we might say, is both possible and necessary only for finite agents who have the capacity for self-governance and so who have an authority interest at all. But if the function of our promises is the securing of authority over the actions of another, then the function of our self-promises would seem to be the securing of authority over our own actions—which is to say, over ourselves.

Return for a moment to Owens's claims about the nature of our authority interest. Recall that according to Owens, the promisee wants the authority to determine what another shall do for its own sake. Here I wish to offer a third qualification, which expresses perhaps a more basic point of disagreement. I am unpersuaded that our interest is in having authority over what another shall do just for its own sake and quite apart from whether the action will be performed, though perhaps this puts the point more strongly than Owens intended. It would hardly be rational for us to seek the right to decide what another shall do if the securing of that right, through the securing of a promise, had no tendency to increase the likelihood of performance, and to increase it *because* of that very promise. To be sure, promises hold appeal for the prospective promisee, in part, because the act of promising alone may manifest a certain respect for her authority, that is, for her "capacity to take decisions with respect to matters of importance" to her.[57] Indeed, the practice of promising, as we know it, can only arise from within what Stephen Darwall has called the "second-person standpoint," a standpoint in which we each acknowledge and respond to the authority of the other, engaging in person-to-person address.[58] But promises would be empty and mere illusory displays of respect if we did not, in the end, consider ourselves answerable to the authority of another and so obligated to guide our conduct accordingly,[59] *and what's more*, were we not more likely to guide our conduct by our promises on account of seeing ourselves as answerable to another's authority.

In the case of our dealings with others, then, our authority interest is not in having a bare right to decide; we have an interest in real control—in *effective* authority. Our interest in real control partly explains why we try to choose our promisors carefully. We seek promises not from those who we merely believe will make them sincerely, thereby acknowledging our authority; we seek them from those who we believe take our authority seriously and so can be trusted, other things equal, to do as they have promised. But if this is correct, if our authority interest with regard to others is an interest in real control, then our authority interest, at its roots, is also not an interest in having a bare right that it be we, rather than others, who decide what we shall do; it is an interest, rather, in being *effective authorities over ourselves*.[60] Owens says that our authority interest is not an interest in self-control, but it seems to me that it is, or more precisely, it is an interest *in our own autonomy*, and our being autonomous requires that we be effective authorities over ourselves.[61] The authority-interest theory has appeal, at least as I see it, because it taps into a deep truth about the connection between promising and agency, namely, that promising exists and has the normative significance it does because it serves to enlarge and enhance our autonomy.[62] And this it can do, I want to suggest, not only through others making and keeping promises to us but also through our making and keeping promises to ourselves.

My proposal is that self-promising exists because of our interest in our own autonomy—in being effective authorities over ourselves; one way we can enhance our autonomy and operate as effective authorities over ourselves is through acts of self-promising. I want to elaborate on this proposal by considering and responding to the two considerations offered at the outset for doubting the importance of self-promises.

Recall that self-promises, in contrast to other-promises, were alleged to be of little effect, because whether the self-promisor keeps or breaks her promise she gets something that she wants, and perhaps even what she most wants. It obviously does not follow, however, from the fact that she still gets something that she wants that she has secured her interests or acted on her values. Contrary to what skeptics about self-promising might suggest, self-promising can serve to protect or promote our own interests or values just as other-promising can serve to protect or promote the interests or values of another. The sad truth is that people all too often do rather badly at acting on their interests or in line with what they most value.[63] They may plan poorly, exercise deficient self-control, fail to attend to their interests, or simply fail to act as they rationally decide to act. Insofar as self-promising can enhance our autonomy, it is one device for helping to ensure that we act in ways that better serve our good or our values.[64]

A second reason for doubting the importance of self-promises is more serious. That reason, remember, is that a person seemingly can just decide or *resolve* and act when the time is ripe, and so there seems to be no reason to engage in self-promising. What lies behind this challenge, as I understand it, is the thought that we can already act autonomously, and enhance our autonomy, by resolving and acting on our resolutions. As a consequence, there seems to be no work for self-promises to do. Answering this challenge requires that we address two questions. First, what is the difference between resolving and promising? And second, insofar as resolving and promising may both serve our authority interest, as seems plausible, what is the difference in how they serve that interest that would explain why, in our efforts to exercise authority over ourselves, we sometimes resolve and sometimes promise?

An initial difficulty is that we often use the words "resolve" or "resolution" and "promise" interchangeably. That is to say, sometimes when we say that we resolve to Φ we just mean that we promise to Φ. In its more exacting sense, though, we might say that to resolve to Φ is just to form a firm intention to Φ, an intention of the sort meant to withstand likely temptations.[65] But observing this points to a further difficulty, for promises themselves, at least sincere promises, are a species of (firm) intention. To promise sincerely is, likewise to intend firmly, and presumably one also promises, and self-promises, in order the better to withstand temptation.[66] What, then, might the difference be?

According to Richard Holton's recent account of resolution, the way strength of will is possible is via our possession of a faculty of will power, through the exercise of which we are able to stick by our resolutions, our firm intentions, in the face of the desires they were meant to overcome.[67] Action through the exercise of will power is unlike action through well developed habits—those unthinking patterns of action where will power is no longer needed in order for our intentions to prevail. For one thing, phenomenologically, the exercise of willpower involves a feeling of struggle that is absent with such automatic action. But in addition, it does not involve, as automatic action does, an absence of thought about the resolution. On the contrary, one is aware of one's resolution and may even be aware of the considerations on which it rests. That awareness, though, does not involve *suspension* of the resolution–bringing it into question; and it does not involve, and indeed, had better not involve, *reconsideration* of the resolution. One "rehearses" the resolution, without reconsidering it. And one exercises will-power precisely by refusing to reconsider it.

Suppose that some such account of what resolutions are and how we stick to them is correct. We can begin to see why a role for self-promises might remain. The basic difficulty we confront, as beings with the capacity for autonomy, is precisely that we often fail to do as we decide, and this failure notoriously fuels and shapes philosophical inquiry into the nature of autonomy. The chasm that may open between decision and action has more than one source, but as a general matter, it exists because we are not "unified selves." We find ourselves with many desires not all of which can be jointly satisfied. We are often drawn to differing ends and the differing selves we might be pursuing these ends. Part of the project of building a life and of building a good for ourselves lies in deciding among ends, choosing among our possible aims, and so among our possible lives and selves.[68] Even having chosen a life course, however, we may continue to experience conflicting desires and the tug of alternative paths. Managing these conflicts often involves commitment and concerted effort. Just as we cannot accomplish all that we might like without enlisting others to act in ways that further our ends, so we cannot accomplish all that we might like without enlisting our sometimes recalcitrant or divided selves to act in ways that further what we have determined, on reflection to be our good or our ends.

One way to address the problem and stick with what we decide is to develop habits so that action in line with our decisions becomes automatic. Another way is to develop the capacity for and exercise of will power, so that we can more or less successfully stick to our resolutions, refusing to reconsider them in the face of the desires they were meant to override or overcome. Yet most of us have limited capacity to develop habits, and most of us have limited willpower. As beings with the capacity for autonomy, we will need to avail ourselves of the entire array of tools that may be available to us for supporting action in accordance with our reflective decisions, desires, and values. Among those tools is self-promising.

As already noted, sincere promises, like resolutions, are a species of intention, and promising, like resolving, is forming a firm intention meant to withstand certain desires or motivational forces that would undermine the intention. The commonality between resolutions and sincere promises should be unsurprising, for both express a kind of commitment.[69] Still, promises differs from resolutions and work to support the intentions they express in a distinctive way, for promises have a conceptual connection to obligation which resolutions lack. Promising, unlike resolving, therefore carries a special sanction. If one fails to do as one has rationally resolved to do, where that failure does not reflect a rational reassessment, one is legitimately subject to *rational* criticism. If, in contrast, one fails to do as one has validly promised to do, where one is not excused or exempted from any duties incurred in promising, one is legitimately subject to *moral* criticism.[70]

In making a valid promise, to self or others, we open ourselves up to particular sorts of censure. If self-promises serve our authority interest in ourselves, then, opening ourselves up to these sorts of censure must in some way serve to enhance our autonomy. I suggest that it does so in the following way. Promising, by exposing us to the possibility of moral criticism, tends to exert a motivational pressure that merely deciding or resolving does not. Where a matter is sufficiently important to us, and where we know that we might be tempted not merely to act on the desires our intentions were meant to defeat but to *let ourselves down*, we may undertake, through self-promising, to add motivational weight to help tip the scale toward the course of action we favor.

But why might the possibility of the censure to which we expose ourselves in promising have the motivational impact I am suggesting? Why don't we just brush off the criticisms when, by breaking a promise, we get something that we want? In the case of promises to others, we are responsive to censure in no small part because we are social creatures and so tend to coordinate our responses to one another.[71] Moreover, considerations of self-interest prompt us to act in ways that maintain our social standing as reliable promisors; our ability to enlist others in the service of our ends generally depends on our reliability as someone they can enlist in the service of their ends. We may also simply have a natural desire to maintain the esteem of others.[72] But promising may also have a motivational hook that lies deeper, in the very thing about us that equips us to be promisors and promisees to begin with, namely, our capacity for autonomous agency.

Tom Hill comes close to this thought when he observes—correctly, I believe—that when we make a promise to ourselves we may stake our self-respect. Hill conjectures that in those cases in which self-promises do make a moral difference, the difference they make may depend not on the importance of the outcome, as in the case of promises to others, but on the way self-promising alters one's situation so as to put one's self-respect on the line.[73] I have some doubts about the suggested contrast between self- and other-promises. The outcomes of promises to self and to others may be equally trivial or equally consequential; self-promises are not per se less consequential than promises to others. And other-promises may equally put one's self-respect on the line.[74] So might resolving. Nevertheless, Hill's suggestion of a link between self-promises and self-respect points us in the right direction. The tools we employ to achieve or maintain our self-governance may all, in more and less significant ways, risk our self-respect, but promises and self-promises may put our self-respect at risk in a distinctive way. For they may put our self-respect on the line by putting our authority on the line in a way that invokes and stakes our second-person standing.

Given our interest in our own authority—an interest we necessarily have as autonomous agents—self-promising engages a standing motivation: the motive of being authorities over ourselves, of having an authority that enables and entitles us to choose and decide, to effectively determine what we shall do, and to command respect in virtue of that very authority. It is important to recognize that although self-promises are intrapersonal, they are nonetheless, like our interpersonal promises, *second-personal* in Darwall's sense. They involve person-to-person address, though here, of the agent to herself. The idea of an agent addressing herself may seem odd, at least initially, but common sense talk assumes that we do engage with ourselves second-personally. Much of this is done through an inner dialogue akin to our respectful engagement with another, engagement that acknowledges their standing and rests on our mutual standing. We reason with ourselves, negotiate, take ourselves in hand, or take ourselves to task. We also make promises to ourselves.

Self-promises add motivational force to the intention to do the promised act by enlisting the motive of being authorities over ourselves on the side of doing as we have promised to do. By promising ourselves, rather than simply deciding or even resolving, we up the ante. We make ourselves answerable to ourselves and to others, giving ourselves something to answer about; at the same time, we stake our authority over ourselves, and thereby, our self-respect and claim to second-person standing. An unexcused failure to do as we have promised ourselves—a failure to be moved in accordance with our interest in our own authority—is, after all, a failure to govern ourselves, and so it may put our authority in doubt. This explains why failing to keep promises to oneself, at least where they are sufficiently important, is not merely disappointing but humiliating—a source of shame.[75] This is why repeated failure to keep promises to oneself is corrosive of one's self-confidence and self-respect.

I have said that self-promises differ from resolutions in making a person susceptible to moral criticism. In virtue of promising—of engaging ourselves second-personally—we make ourselves answerable for our failures, and we may be held to account. But one might point out that we outsiders do not respond in identical ways to breach of promises to others and to self. When a promise to another is broken, at least an important one, we are inclined to resent and blame the promisor; we may even tell him that what he did was wrong, inconsiderate, inexcusable. The self-promisor might be inclined to blame and resent herself and to engage in self-castigation, but we are not so inclined to blame or resent or castigate the person who breaks a promise to herself.

While this is generally true, we should not overstate the point. For we sometimes do blame and resent people who break promises to themselves, and we do sometimes take them to task. In the first place, a promise to oneself need not be a promise *concerning* oneself; the content of a promise to oneself may instead involve actions that most directly affect other people. But even when the content of a self-promise does concern the promisor herself, we sometimes blame and resent her for failing to treat herself as she ought, and we may express to her our disapproval.

Any differences that exist between self- and other-promises when it comes to our reactive attitudes and our practices of moral criticism do not, in any case, furnish grounds for denying my rough account of the importance of self-promises. The self-promisor who breaks a self-regarding promise does indeed wrong herself, sometimes trivially but sometimes quite grievously. We often have good grounds even in the latter cases, however, for not responding to her failure by expressing, or even feeling, blame and resentment. After all, the person who commits the wrong is also the chief victim of the wrong; to express our judgment of her failure—to blame her—would seem to amount to inflicting a double punishment. Perhaps more important, the differences in how we may respond to breach of other-promises and self-promises manifests a certain wisdom not only about human psychology but about the underlying moral failing that may often exist in the intrapersonal case, as well as the remedy for that failing. Consider the abused wife who promises herself that she will no longer tolerate the abuse but who remains with her husband. As a matter of morality, her moral failing plausibly consists in an insufficient appreciation of and responsiveness to her own value. As a matter of psychology, she likely requires not a moral rebuke but a reminder of her own worth. Given the nature of the failing, what she has done is appropriately subject to moral criticism even if *she* isn't appropriately criticized.

III. THE PRIMACY OF SELF-PROMISES

Insofar as the foregoing observations are correct, they put us in a position to begin to appreciate the importance of self-promises and the sense in which they have a certain normative and practical primacy. I have suggested that it is partly through our acts of self-promising that we can exert authority over ourselves and enhance our autonomy. To be an effective self-promisor, insofar as we engage in self-promising, is to be effective authorities over ourselves. But insofar as all of our acts of promising depend on our being effective authorities over ourselves, self-promising is, in a certain respect, normatively and practically basic. More precisely, our self-promising is normatively and practically basic not just in itself but rather as *one among those other devices by which we support our self-governance.*

In seeking to extract a promise from another, you will not have succeeded in satisfying your authority interest if the other lacks effective authority over her own decisions and actions—if she lacks the autonomy necessary to be a successful promisor. But then a person's capacity as an other-promisor rests on her capacity as an autonomous agent, a capacity that can be supported by various devices, including self-promising. Put somewhat differently, for another to be an effective promisor to you she must be an effective authority over herself. If she is not, then she is not fit to engage in second-personal address and so not fit to be a promisor at all. It is in this critical albeit limited sense that self-promising has a certain normative and practical primacy.[76]

These observations suggest that in order to be fit for second-personal address, we must, among other things, have some disposition to treat ourselves as authoritative and to be effective authorities, and so to do as we decide. We are imperfectly so disposed, however, hence the need to move beyond bare decision to develop habits, form resolutions, make self-promises.

My claims about what is at stake in being a reliable self-promisor, and more fundamentally, an effective authority over oneself, find support in common moral thought. The less someone is true to her word, the less she can be counted on to act as she has promised to act, the less we are inclined to deal with her as someone with normative standing and the more we view her as something to work around rather than someone to work with. Our stance toward her becomes increasingly third-personal. Of course, a person's failure to fulfill promises to others can be wholly calculative, and so it not only need not manifest a lack of effective authority over herself but may manifest the very opposite. Still, her pattern of broken promises will sometimes be rooted in a failure of autonomy. This will almost certainly be the case when it comes to repeatedly broken self-promises. We may come to treat another third-personally, then, because she is not to be trusted but also because she is not an effective agent and so not a being in whom trust can be placed. Our distancing is arguably more acute—it is in any case distinctive—when an individual not only does not but cannot keep her commitments.

It is our interest in being effective authorities over ourselves—our interest in our own autonomy—that explains why we make promises to ourselves and treat them as seriously as we do. Of course, we don't treat all self-promises seriously; we don't treat all other promises seriously. Though in making promises to ourselves, we may stake our authority and our self-respect, the stakes are not *always* so high. But that is just a reminder that an account of the function and importance of self-promises such as I have offered is not intended as an account of the function and importance (or not) of specific self-promises.

ACKNOWLEDGMENTS

I want to thank all of the participants at the "Promises and Agreements" conference for helpful discussion of a preliminary version of this article, and Hanoch Sheinman for helpful suggestions following the conference. Thanks also to Mark Timmons for instructive comments on that same initial draft, as well as for an enlightening conversation about self-promises and duties to self. At the beginning stages of work on this essay, I had a wonderful opportunity to meet with Lauren Fleming and exchange ideas about promises and self-promises. I later received invaluable comments and questions about the penultimate draft from Fleming and from members of the Philosophy Department at the University of Warwick. Time constraints prevented me from addressing adequately a great many of their concerns, but I here wish to acknowledge with appreciation their thoughtful responses.

NOTES

1. In saying this, I do not mean to deny that there may be some things we can promise only to others or only to ourselves.

2. See Justin Wolfers, "Economics and New Year's Resolutions," *New York Times*, December 28, 2007, briefly summarizing seven theories about the nature of New Year's resolutions suggested by guests at his Christmas Eve supper. Some might want to distinguish promises from resolutions, vows, and the like. For present purposes, what interests me are those commitments, whatever we might call them, that have whatever normative force promises are widely thought to have. I shall mostly stick to the term "promise" to refer to this class of commitments, though I occasionally use such terms as "vow," "resolution," and "pledge." I turn later to a direct consideration of resolutions proper and how self-promises might differ from resolutions. For enlightening discussion of how resolutions work, as well as of why keeping resolutions can be rational, see Holton (2003, 2004).

3. Of course, not all utterances that use the terms "promise," "vow," and so on are instances of genuine promises, and genuine promises need not employ the standard terms. As Owens (2006: 53) observes, the use of such expressions as "I promise" and "Trust me..." may be sufficient to constitute a promise, but they are not necessary. This is as much true of promises to others as of promises to self.

4. For detailed comparison of promises to others and to self see Hill (1991).

5. For an early expression of doubt about whether there can be self-promises, which I consider briefly later, see Hobbes (1968, ch. 26, sec. 2, p. 313). For more recent discussion, see Von Wright (1983: 83). An extended argument against the idea of duties to self, including promissory obligations, can be found in Singer (1959,

1963). Hill (1991) critically examines and rebuts the claim that promises are conceptually impossible. See also Habib (2009).

6. Philosophers have suggested, for example, that we have reason to want to create expectations and to be able to rely on and have others act in reliance on the expectations thus created. Having created expectations through our promises, we incur obligations to fulfill our promises, perhaps as part of a broader obligation not to lie or mislead. See Scanlon (1998: ch. 7). Or, to take another example, we have an "authority interest"—an interest in having the authority to decide what another shall do—and so we have reason to engage in promising, along with an obligation to fulfill promises we have made. See Owens (2006).

7. For defenses of various theories of promising, including practice, expectation, pledging, and authority-interest theories, see, e.g., Hume (1896/1978: bk. 3, pt. 2, sec. 5), Rawls (1971: 344–350), Scanlon (1998: ch. 7), Downie (1985), and Owens (2006).

8. This would seem to be true even if self-promises, like other-promises, operate to strengthen our motivation to act, perhaps by making us liable to certain sorts of normative criticism as well as to negative reputational and practical consequences.

9. Throughout, I shall assume that insofar as self-promises are possible, they are also efficacious—at least as efficacious as other-promises. That is, I assume that having made a promise tends to lead us to do the promised act to roughly the same extent in the case of self-promises as in the case of other promises. I take no position as to whether self-promises are more or less effective than other devices that might serve essentially the same function.

10. Some others have offered compelling defenses of the possibility of self-promises. See Hill (1991) and Habib (2009). I find much to agree with in their excellent discussions, and at least some of what I say may simply express in a different way points they have each already made. But there are some significant differences and disagreements. For example, I am inclined to think that the normative power exercised in promising is more restricted than Habib evidently thinks it is. And I am inclined to disagree with Hill's contention that promises to others are generally binding in a way that promises to self are not, that self-promises do not generally create *moral* obligations as opposed to personal obligations. I hope to have added various points to the defense of the possibility of self-promises, including some useful, if controversial, suggestions about the obligations to which promises give rise and the relationship between promises and our broader duties. Most important, because I believe that the real "impossibility" problem, such as it is, is not quite the problem critics have pressed, my discussion identifies and begins to address a difficulty that has not yet been properly addressed, at least so far as I am aware.

11. Hill (1991: 153–154). Hill's remarks about the connection between self-promises and self-respect come in the concluding paragraphs of his essay following a long defense of the conceptual possibility of promises to self, and so he evidently means simply to leave us with an intriguing suggestion.

12. See Owens (2006).

13. For two very helpful defenses of the genuineness of self-promises that follow this pattern, see Hill (1991) and Habib (2009). Additional support for the genuineness of self-promises can be found, if perhaps only implicitly, in the work of philosophers who have defended the existence of duties to self. For a classic defense not only

of the existence of duties to self but of their priority, see Kant (1930, especially 116–126). See also Wick (1960, 1961) and see Kading (1960).

14. See Owens (2006: 54) and Altham (1985: 13, citing Finnis [1980: 298]). Some might disagree with inclusion of the specification that the promisor communicates an intention to be *under an obligation.* (Owens explains why he thinks (contra someone like Scanlon) that this specification must be added.) This is not, of course, to say that the promisor actually intends to Φ. For very different ideas as to what promising does or does not require, see, e.g., Von Wright (1983) and Fox and DeMarco (1996).

15. Hobbes (1968: ch. 26, sec. 2, p. 313, emphasis added). I was reminded of Hobbes's argument on reading Allen Habib's helpful reconstruction and discussion of it. See Habib (2009).

16. For helpful discussion, see Altham (1985). I reject the view that even "wicked promises" create obligations so that the promisor ought to perform, it is simply that the "ought" of the promise is overridden in such cases by contrary obligations. See Altham (1985: 4, discussing Searle [1969: 178]). In my view, a promise creates an obligation to perform that may come into conflict with, and be overridden by, a stronger obligation only when the promise is to do something that it would ordinarily be permissible to do. In such a case, fulfilling the promise would indeed be what the promisor ought to do in the absence of any overriding obligation.

17. See Luke Harding, "Victim of Cannibal Agreed to be Eaten," *Guardian*, December 4, 2003, www.guardian.co.uk/world/2003/dec/04/germany.lukeharding.

18. The claim that promises to do what is immoral or impermissible do not give rise to obligations should not be confused with the claim that it is never obligatory to keep an immoral promise, where that is a promise entered into immorally, rather than a promise the object of which is to do something immoral. Jones's promise to lie to Smith is a promise to do something immoral, whereas Jones's lying promise to Smith to repay a debt is an immoral promise. As Fox and DeMarco (1996: 201–202) argue, one might well have a moral obligation to keep an immoral promise. If Jones really can manage to repay his debt to Smith, he ought to do it, and to do it in part because he promised, the fact that it was a lying promise notwithstanding. An agent's obligation to keep her promise is not nullified, they argue, by its being a lying promise. Fox and DeMarco offer a rather different take on how moral considerations affect the validity of promises. They observe that "No promise, no matter how pristine, can by itself create any obligation" (207). But rather than claim that promises must be to do what it is permissible to do, they argue that the critical question concerns "what conditions must be met at the time of keeping a promise, in order for a promised act to be morally justified or obligatory." This question, they claim, can be answered "only by applying moral principles and rules to the promised act, as to any other act."

19. See Altham (1985: 7), for discussion of the idea of a society's practice of promising as having a "sphere of validity." As Altham observes, "If a given promise does fall within the sphere of validity, that is still not sufficient to establish that it creates an obligation to perform. For there is the further question whether it is acceptable that there should be a promising practice in which that promise, made in those circumstances, should be valid." When I talk about promises as valid or not, I mean to suggest, not a sphere of validity relative to a given society's practice of promising, but

bounds of validity set by morality itself, which may be partly dependent on facts about social practices. For other discussion of promises to do forbidden acts, see, e.g., Von Wright (1983: 94–96).

20. Singer (1959: 202). Singer's article prompted a flurry of critical responses. See Wick (1960 and 1961, responding to Mothersill), Mothersill (1961, responding to Wick's critique of Singer's article), Kading (1960), and Knight (1961), and see Singer (1963, replying to critics).

21. Singer (1959: 202).

22. Ibid., (202–203).

23. Ibid., 203.

24. I say "as a general matter" to allow that among the rights we may have are some we can waive or with respect to which we can release another from his duties.

25. Admittedly, it may *sound* odd to describe a person as having rights against herself, and so as having correlative duties to herself, and that fact is not irrelevant. But the metaphysical status of rights and correlative duties cannot turn simply on how certain ways of talking sound. For insightful discussion of rights against oneself, see Hill (1991: 148–149).

26. See Kant (1930: 117–118).

27. Ibid., 118.

28. Ibid., 202–203. The passage reads in full as follows: "no one can release himself from an obligation by not wishing to perform it or by deciding not to perform it, or, indeed, in any other way whatsoever. In other words, no one can release himself from an obligation, just as no one can release himself from a promise. To be sure one can *break* the promise or the obligation. One can refuse to perform it. But this is not to release oneself. One can, however, be *released* from a promise by the person to whom he had made it. For one can give up his right against someone, or decide not to exercise it, and by this means release someone else from an obligation. But a duty to oneself, then, would be a duty from which one could release oneself at will, and this is self-contradictory. A 'duty' from which one could release oneself at will is not, in any literal sense, a duty at all."

29. To borrow Tim Scanlon's expression. See Scanlon (1998).

30. As Baier (1985: 174–175) observes, promises are not peculiar in giving rise to obligations that didn't exist before: "It is the norm in human life that our actions change the moral state of play, as it were" (174).

31. Altham makes a somewhat different claim about the effect of promising to do what one is already obligated to do. "A promise in such circumstances can still have a point. It *adds* the obligation arising from it to the one that already exists. Since both are obligations to do the same thing, its effect is to make the obligation weightier. A kind of dishonour attaches to a breach of promise to pay that does not attach to a merely admitted debt" (Altham: 1985, 12–18). One, in effect, makes breach of the duty worse. The promise to do what one is already obligated to do might sometimes make the obligation weightier, but I doubt that this is invariably the case. Jones's obligation not to kill Smith is not made weightier if he promises Smith not to kill him. But Jones will be subject to additional kinds of moral censure, having displayed, through the making and violation of the promise, additional defects of moral character.

32. To make out this view, we would require a complete theory of promises that spells out what distinguishes "genuine promises" from promise-like acts that serve

normative purposes different from those of promises proper. Developing such a theory is obviously beyond the scope of this essay.

33. The suggestion I make here roughly follows Darwall's discussion (Darwall: 2002) of the two attitudes we take up toward others.

34. Downie (1985: 266) makes essentially the same point. Suppose, he says, that I promise to mow the lawn of the old lady next door. "If the old lady, seeing that I shall be put to some inconvenience by my commitment to cut her grass, tells me that I need not bother, I do not necessarily regard myself as excused, any more than I would if she behaved in some sort of indefensible way toward me. I both cases, I have incurred an obligation regardless of the attitudes of the other party." My example in the text follows Downie's but is expressed in a way intended to bring out what I take to be factors relevant to supporting the thought that something more is required for genuine release from a promise.

35. Habib (2009) makes the same basic point, though he comes at it from a different direction. His discussion is quite illuminating, though I am not persuaded by the examples that he uses to make the point.

36. Although, as indicated earlier (note 10), I do not believe this challenge has been sufficiently addressed, there is certainly much insightful discussion of release and breach in Hill (1991) and Habib (2009), and perhaps a more informative account of the distinction than I am about to offer could be extracted from their remarks.

37. A related problem arises in the case of resolutions with what Richard Holton has called the phenomenon of "judgment shift" (Holton 2004). As Holton describes it, an agent may rationally resolve to Φ, but temptation may take both desire and judgment with it, so that it is apparently no longer rational to stick with one's resolution. Holton argues that in fact it is sometimes rational to "stick to one's resolutions," adopting a strategy of "rational nonreconsideration" for preserving their rationality. So long as an agent does not reconsider her resolution, sticking by it is not akratic.

38. More will obviously need to be said beyond the brief remarks in this paragraph to explain what counts as a genuine change of mind and to mark out fully and precisely the distinction between release and breach. My chief point is simply that whatever way of marking the distinction suffices for the two-party case should also suffice for the one-party case.

39. My account may be compatible with other theories of promising as well, but it builds on and fits neatly with the authority-interest theory.

40. This is, of course, not to suggest that Owens would want anything to do with my proposal.

41. Owens (2006: 74).

42. Owens (2006: 69). I do not mean to suggest that Owens himself means for his account to be only of the function of promises to others. But his examples all concern what I have been calling other-promises, and so he apparently treats such promises as paradigmatic.

43. Ibid., 70.

44. Ibid.

45. Ibid.

46. Ibid.

47. Ibid.

48. Ibid.

49. Ibid., 72. This, at least, is how I understand Owens's insistence that we value the authority "for its own sake."

50. Ibid., 71.

51. Ibid.

52. Ibid., 72.

53. Ibid.

54. Ibid. Owens offers this qualification in footnote 28, observing, for example, that the promisor has no authority to promise to kill or maim.

55. Of course, a good deal will depend on what counts as "unreasonable" refusal, and I cannot undertake to settle that here. I assume, though, that refusal would certainly be unreasonable in those cases in which fulfilling the promise would be grossly unfair to or inflict serious physical damage on the promisor. More precisely, refusal would be unreasonable when keeping the promise would seriously impair the promisor's most basic interests where nothing of fairly comparable importance is at stake for the promisee.

56. See note 16.

57. Owens (2006: 72).

58. Darwall (2006).

59. This much Owens acknowledges when he observes that to satisfy our interest in having our authority respected, "promissory obligation must reach all the way to the act" (Owens: 2006, 72).

60. We find this idea, for example, in Harry Frankfurt's early suggestion that freedom of the will is the freedom to have the will we want, that is, to make certain second-order volitions *effective*. See Frankfurt (1971).

61. What is the distinction? For one suggestion, see Velleman (1989: 185–186), characterizing self-control as second-best to autonomy.

62. It has been suggested to me that our real interest is not in autonomy as such but in acting as the balance of reasons favors. When we act autonomously, we may in fact be poor detectors of what the balance of reasons favors, so that we would be better off were we not self-governing. I recognize, of course, that autonomous choosers may sometimes be poor choosers. But I believe the objection both underestimates the intrinsic benefit to us of our being in a condition in which we effectively govern ourselves and fails to consider the extent to which what reasons apply to us, and so what the balance of reasons may be, turns on facts about our own reflective preferences and evaluations. (It also overlooks the fact that we need to be self-governing even to be effective followers of those who may be better detectors of the balance of reasons.) The term "authority" gets used in various ways. In one sense, being an authority is being a kind of expert. In another, more basic sense, it is simply being the one who effectively decides. I take it that the authority we have and fundamentally value is authority in the latter sense. Our interest in our own authority is an interest in our standing as agents able and entitled to choose and decide, whose choices and decisions can be effective in determining what we do and what happens, and whose status as such agents calls for respect. It is not an interest in ourselves purely insofar as we may be accurate detectors of the balance of reasons. Consider that we value, among other things, being able to make our own mistakes.

63. Obviously, not everything that we value is something that benefits us or that we judge to be of benefit to us.

64. Of course, no such device is fool-proof.

65. See Holton (2003, 2004).

66. I mostly hereafter drop the qualifier "sincerely," but it should be understood that I mean to be talking about sincere promises as opposed to insincere or immoral promises. See note 18.

67. Holton (2003).

68. I explore some of these ideas in a bit more detail in Rosati (2007).

69. See Downie (1985: 267). On Downie's view, a promise is essentially a matter of pledging oneself: the "subset of intentions which is promises is demarcated by the circumstances in which intending becomes pledging." Once we consider that promising is a species of commitment, I think it should be surprising that so many have doubted the genuineness of self-promises.

70. The ideas in the paragraph, and in my discussion more generally, echo some observations Hill (1991: 141–143) makes about why we would engage in self-promising. As he observes, making ourselves subject to guilt and disapproval may increase the likelihood that we will act as we desire or decide to act, rather than give in to a competing impulse. Hill also stresses, in a way I have not, the fact that fulfilling a self-promise serves our interests. I herein attempt to fit considerations like these into a fuller account of the relationship between self-promising and autonomy and flesh out how self-promising might work differently from other tools we use to ensure that we act in line with our decisions.

71. Gibbard (1990).

72. Downie (1985: 269–270) makes this point.

73. Hill (1991: 153–154). Hill's discussion is far more subtle than my summary in the text captures. He introduces self-respect in the process of explaining the temptation—wrong, he thinks—to regard promises to oneself as morally binding. He explains it as due to concentrating on certain special cases in which it is difficult to deny that the self-promises are morally significant. In these cases, according to Hill, there is a morally significant reason to do the promised act quite apart from the promise, but the agent views the promise as morally significant, not because it makes obligatory what previously was not, but because it puts her "self-respect on the line, making failure more than ordinary weakness of will" (154). Hill suggests that promises in these cases "seem to transform the situation, making nonperformance worse, and limiting the range of reasons for which one can honorably decide to abandon the project." Hill goes on to suggest that the "ultimate ground" of such obligations to self as there may be is self-respect. My discussion attempts to generalize and develop some of what Hill says, though in ways he would likely not endorse. Because I evidently take a different view from Hill about the source of our obligations to self and perhaps regard those obligations as being broader than Hill does, I restrict my discussion in the text to his basic insight that an important connection exists between self-promising and self-respect.

74. For related discussion, see Downie (1985: 269–270): "in stating one's intentions by means of certain words, such as 'I promise', or with a certain emphasis or ritual...one is signaling that the circumstances are such that the intended projects have been made central and essential in one's total concerns. The self has been iden-

tified with the projects, and carrying them out has become not only a moral obligation of practical consistency but a strong moral obligation of honour or self-fidelity; one is not the man one was taken to be, not the man whose future projects were described in the stated intentions, not a man of one's word.... [W]henever there is a promise, whether involving others or not, the promiser has identified his will with the project. He has, as it were, pinned his self on the future as describe in his pledged actions. By making the keeping of the promise essential to the preservation of his personal integrity, he will be diminished as a person if he breaks his word. This strong sort of practical consistency of self-fidelity is not only present in all cases but is *morally central* to promissory-obligation." Although I am sympathetic to much of what Downie says, I do not think that promising always involves the kind of identification with a project or the making of it central to one's concerns that he describes.

75. Downie (1985: 267), makes essentially the same point in developing his pledge theory of promising. He observes that "we feel a certain shame or sense of unworthiness when we fail to adhere to a rule or plan we have adopted."

76. My claim is not, I should stress, about any sort of temporal priority of self-promising. No doubt we get into the business of promising, whether to self or to others, as a part of our development into full-blown autonomous agents.

REFERENCES

Altham, J. E. J. 1985. "Wicked Promises." In I. Hacking (ed.), *Exercises in Analysis*. Cambridge: Cambridge University Press, 1-21.

Baier, Annette. 1985. "Promises, Promises, Promises." In *Postures of the Mind: Essays on Mind and Morals*. Minneapolis: University of Minnesota Press, 174-204.

Darwall, Stephen. 2002. *Welfare and Rational Care*. Princeton: Princeton University Press.

———. 2006. *The Second-person Standpoint*. Cambridge, MA: Harvard University Press.

Downie, R. S. 1985. "Three Accounts of Promising." *Philosophical* Quarterly 35: 259-271.

Finnis, John. 1980. *Natural Law and Natural Rights*. Oxford: Clarendon Press.

Fox, Richard M., and DeMarco, Joseph P. 1996. "On Making and Keeping Promises." *Journal of Applied Philosophy* 13: 199-208.

Frankfurt, Harry. 1971. "Freedom of the Will and the Concept of a Person." *Journal of Philosophy* 68: 5-20.

Gibbard, Allan. 1990. *Wise Choices, Apt Feelings: A Theory of Normative Judgment*. Cambridge, MA: Harvard University Press.

Habib, Allen. 2009. "Promises to the Self." *Canadian Journal of Philosophy* 39: 537-588.

Hill, Thomas E., Jr. 1991. "Promises to Oneself." In *Autonomy and Self-Respect*. Cambridge: Cambridge University Press, 138-154.

Hobbes, Thomas. 1968. *Leviathan*. New York: Penguin.

Holton, Richard. 2003. "How Is Strength of Will Possible?" In S. Stroud and C. Tappolet (eds.), *Weakness of Will and Practical Irrationality*. Oxford: Clarendon Press, 39-67.

———. 2004. "Rational Resolve." *Philosophical Review* 113: 507-535.

Hume, David. 1896/1978. *A Treatise of Human Nature*. L. A. Selby-Bigge (ed.). Oxford: Oxford University Press.

Kading, Daniel. 1960. "Are There Really 'No Duties to Oneself'?" *Ethics* 70: 155–157.

Kant, Immanuel. 1930. *Lectures on Ethics*. Louis Infield (trans.). Indianapolis: Hackett.

Knight, Frank H. 1961. "I, Me, My Self, and My Duties." *Ethics* 71: 209–212.

Mothersill, Mary. 1961. "Professor Wick on Duties to Oneself." *Ethics* 71: 205–208.

Owens, David. 2006. "A Simple Theory of Promising." *Philosophical Review* 115: 51–77.

Rawls, John. 1971. *A Theory of Justice*. Cambridge, MA: Harvard University Press.

Rosati, Connie S. 2007. "Mortality, Agency, and Regret." In Sergio Tenenbaum(ed.), *Moral Psychology*, Poznan Studies in the Philosophy of the Sciences and the Humanities, vol. 94. Amsterdam: Rodopi.

Scanlon, Thomas. 1998. *What We Owe to Each Other*. Cambridge, MA: Harvard University Press.

Searle, John. 1969. *Speech Acts: An Essay in the Philosophy of Language*. London: Cambridge University Press.

Singer, Marcus G. 1959. "On Duties to Oneself." *Ethics* 69: 202–205.

———. 1963. "Duties and Duties to Oneself." *Ethics* 73: 133–142.

Velleman, J. David. 1989. *Practical Reflection*. Princeton: Princeton University Press.

Von Wright, Georg Hendrick. 1983. "On Promises." In *Practical Reason, Philosophical Essays*. Vol. 1. Ithaca, NY: Cornell University Press.

Wick, Warner. 1960. "More about Duties to Oneself." *Ethics* 70: 158–163.

———. 1961. "Still More about Duties to Oneself." *Ethics* 71: 213–217.

Chapter 6

On Coerced Promises

Eric Chwang

Abstract

It is less rational to rely on a coerced promise than it is to rely either on a coerced (non-promissory) action or on a non-coerced promise. In this paper I defend a two-part explanation for that intuitive judgment. First, coerced promises carry no moral force. That is, they do not generate additional moral reasons, above and beyond whatever reasons already exist, for the promiser to fulfill her promise. This undercuts the idea that the general moral obligation to keep one's promises can be used to defend the reliability of coerced promises—that general obligation does not apply to coerced promises. I argue for this thesis by, first, explaining why the importance we attach to the activity of promising cannot extend to coerced promises and, second, refuting four recent alleged counterexamples to the thesis. The second part of the explanation is that coerced promises carry no predictive force either. That is, they do not communicate reliable intentions to fulfill promise, even independently of moral motivations. This undercuts the idea that promissory intentions can be used to defend the reliability of coerced promises—the general connection between promising and intending does not apply to coerced promises. I defend this thesis by arguing that, while it is possible to coerce promissory intentions, rational agents may be unable to promise sincerely when threatened, and, further, coerced promises typically give no evidential support that the promiser intends to do as she says.

I. THE PROBLEM

Suppose a mugger jumps out of the bushes, points a gun at his mark, and insists, "Your money or your life!" The mark convinces him she has no money on her person, so the mail-in mugger says, "Promise me you'll mail me some money tomorrow; otherwise I'll kill you now." If the mark acquiesces then she makes a coerced promise. The mail-in mugger might think that he is quite clever, to have extracted a promise of money when he could not extract instantaneous money. However, coercing the promise of future money is in an important sense grasping at straws. After all, it is clearly not as profitable as coercing immediate money. A typical mugger who coerces his mark for $100 can expect more money than the mail-in mugger coercing a promise for the same amount via post. It is also more rational to rely on an uncoerced promise for money than on a coerced one. An Oxfam representative, for example, might accost me on the street and implore, "Please mail some money to Oxfam tomorrow!" If I acquiesce and thereby promise, the Oxfam representative can be more sure that I will keep my promise than the mail-in mugger can be that his mark will keep hers.

Why these differences? One potential explanation is that it is conceptually impossible to coerce a promise. This is wrong—Margaret Gilbert has argued decisively that it is possible to coerce a promise.[1] I will not pause to review Gilbert's argument or defend her conclusion here, due to space constraints. Instead, I will merely assume that it is possible to coerce a promise, and I will argue that two other facts explain the sense that attempting to coerce a promise is akin to grasping at straws. First, coerced promises carry no moral force. That is, they do not generate additional moral reasons, above and beyond whatever reasons already exist, for the promiser to fulfill her promise. However, this negative moral thesis is not the entire explanation. After all, even if coerced promises exert no moral force, it might still be rational to rely on them, because people use promissory language to communicate their intentions. Thus, I will also argue for a second thesis: that coerced promises typically carry no predictive force either. That is, they do not reliably create or indicate extra intentions to fulfill the promise, above and beyond whatever intentions the promiser already had to fulfill it.

Two crucial points are in order before continuing. First, I claim only that reliance on a coerced promise is irrational (or even more cautiously, that reliance on a coerced promise is less rational than reliance on a coerced act or on a noncoerced promise), not that the attempt to coerce it is irrational. It may well be rational for the mail-in mugger to attempt to coerce a promise, for example, even if I am right that the resulting promise has neither moral nor predictive force. That is because his unfortunate mark may be ignorant or skeptical of this essay's central thesis. If the attempt to coerce the promise costs little, then it may well be prudentially rational for the mail-in mugger to go ahead—the net expected pay-off of attempting it may be greater than that of not bothering. My goal is explain why, in spite of this, the attempt to coerce a promise is still a much less reliable means of ensuring performance of the promised act than either coercing the act directly or else eliciting the promise noncoercively. Attempting to coerce a promise is akin to grasping at straws in a way that neither attempting to coerce a nonpromissory act nor eliciting the promise without coercion are.

Second, coerced promises will typically be artificial in at least one respect. If, for example, the mail-in-mugger can credibly threaten his mark with harm after he was to have received her money, then he is arguably still coercing an action, rather than coercing a promise of future action. It is just a more protracted mugging for money that takes place over a span of several days, rather than a routine mugging that lasts at most a few minutes: "(Promise me you'll) mail me some money tomorrow; otherwise I'll find you and kill you next week." He may even continue to use the word "promise," as in the parenthetical addition in the previous sentence, but such use would be confused. To ensure that our examples of coerced promises are not confused in this very immediate way, we must build into them the assumption that the coercer cannot produce a credible threat after the promise has been given. For example, we might suppose that the mail-in mugger is abroad and is leaving for his native country tomorrow, never to return.

II. MORAL FORCE

Coerced promises exert no moral force, which means that they do not provide any additional moral reason to fulfill the promise. Of course, this is compatible with the claim that one ought to or perhaps even is obligated to perform the promised act in question. In this section I will explain why we ought to deny moral force to coerced promises. In the next section, I will examine four recently proposed alleged counterexamples to the thesis that coerced promises carry no moral force.[2]

The Value of Promises

Why do we value promises? By this I mean to ask not why an individual might value some particular token promise, but rather something like why we as a society of rational and communicative agents value the practice of making and keeping promises. The answer to this latter question strikes me as very obvious and straight-forward. The reason we value the ability to make a promise is that we want to give promisers the moral power to create and then assume obligations on their own. For example, if I promise to help you move, then I thereby, all by myself, create and then assume a moral obligation to help you move. Certainly, there are other ways I can acquire the obligation to help you move, without my promise, but the reason promising is important and useful is that it gives me a way to assume that obligation voluntarily, all by myself.[3] Now, if my promise is coerced, then in the relevant sense I am no longer acting alone and voluntarily in assuming the promissory obligation. Rather, it is more accurate to say that it is being foisted on me. Thus the essential moral kernel we want to capture in recognizing the importance of promising is incompatible with giving moral force to coerced promises. The point of granting moral power to promissory activity is to give the power to promisers to let them incur obligations when they choose, all by themselves. And that does not happen when one is coerced into promising. In the remainder of this section I will make six further points that help clarify this idea.

Against Counterbalancing

Consider a counterbalancing picture, according to which promises always carry moral force even when they are coerced, but this moral force is counterbalanced by the immorality of coercion. Sometimes the immorality of coercion suffices to outweigh the moral force of the coerced promise, and sometimes not, depending on various factors. Such a picture may seem attractive, but it is incorrect.

One reason it is incorrect is that it is part of the moral principle about promissory moral force that the promise in question cannot be coerced. In other words, the principle "promises have moral force" is really shorthand or elliptical for the more informative principle, "uncoerced promises have moral force." It is not as if promises are like Ross's prima facie duties, so that there are multiple principles at play, one telling us that promises always have moral force (without exception), and others restricting the range of that first principle, so that we end up with a downstream rule according to which coerced promises can have various force, depending on how weighty the various principles are in particular cases. Rather, the one principle about promises says that uncoerced promises have moral force. (And this principle is almost certainly elliptical or shorthand for some even more complex principle, for example one ruling out deceived promises.) That is because, again, the point of promissory activity is to allow people to create and then assume obligations all by themselves. That coerced promises carry no moral force is built into this idea.

I have just argued that the counterbalancing view is incorrect because it is inconsistent with the best explanation of the importance of promissory activity. Another reason it is incorrect, though, is that it generates counterintuitive results independently of my larger thesis. For it is not in general true that if my means of acquiring your promise involves a coercive element then your promise thereby loses moral force. I might, for example, employ coercion on a third party to acquire your promise, in which case it retains all its original moral force. For example, suppose Amber wants to offer an employment contract to Beatrice, but she is too lazy to bring it to Beatrice in person. Amber might coerce an innocent passerby, Carrie, to bring the contract over: "Carrie, bring this contract to Beatrice, or else I'll shoot you!" Carrie, under threat of death, acquiesces. Beatrice knows that the employment proposal is between her and Amber, and that Carrie was merely the coerced messenger, so the proposal itself is not coerced, though coercive means were used to make it. In this case, the mere fact that the promise (contract) was elicited immorally and via a coercive step does not thereby reduce its moral force. Beatrice is not allowed to renege on the resulting promise just because Carrie had to bring over the contract at gunpoint. (Imagine, to make this vivid, that Amber and Beatrice are white American landowners before the Civil War, and Carrie is Amber's slave.) Of course this is compatible with the thought that Beatrice should voice her indignation at Amber's wrongful coercion, but reneging on the resulting promise is not automatically the best or only way to do so.

Consent as Analogy

Consider the analogy between promising and consenting. We generally think that consent can change what would otherwise be an impermissible act into a permissible one. For example, if I do not consent to it, then you are not allowed to drill in my teeth, but if I do then you might be. I said "might be" because, of course, there are exceptions, such as if the consent was coerced. For example, if a parent coerces her child to consent to tonsillectomy, that consent thereby carries no moral force. This is compatible with the claim that the surgeon still ought to operate, and it is compatible with the claim that the child ought to have consented (without being coerced). But the coerced consent itself should have no bearing on the surgeon's deliberations about whether he ought to proceed. Indeed, in spite of a massive bioethics literature on consent, no strand of thought in that literature attempts to argue that coerced consent can be valid; coerced consent is uncontroversially recognized to be invalid, without exception. The reason for this is that the practice of recognizing consent allows people to create and then give, all by themselves, moral permissions to others. If I consent to your drilling in my teeth, then I create a moral permission to drill and give that permission to you. Of course, there are other ways in which you might acquire that permission, without my having a say in the matter, but the point of consent is to allow consenters to be able to create and give moral permissions voluntarily, all by themselves.

Coercion versus Inducement

Compare coerced promises with induced ones. I will discuss in more detail later the difference between coercion and inducement, but for now we can say that inducements are welcome but coercion is not. For example, I would rather not be confronted by a mugger waving a gun in my face and saying "Your money or your life." In contrast, I welcome a potential employer waving an unsigned contract in my face and saying "I'll pay you a hefty salary to come work for me."

Both coercion and inducement are forms of outside influence, of changing the payoffs of an agent's actions. However, only coerced promises are unduly influenced in the way that compromises promissory moral force. That is because a coercer is manipulating the situation surrounding the agent's choice in an unwelcome way, but an inducer does so in a welcome way. A coerced agent thus is precluded from going down the path she otherwise would have chosen (keeping both her money and her life), and she is thereby less responsible for her choice between the remaining alternatives. In contrast, an induced agent is also influenced, but in a way she welcomes. Thus, in the relevant sense the induced agent still made her choice voluntarily, without undue outside influence, so that it still appropriate to assign responsibility to the induced agent for making the choices she made. "I couldn't help it; he waved a gun in my face" is a legitimate excuse that absolves responsibility for one's actions—such as handing over one's wallet or taking a job—in a way that "I couldn't help it; he waved an unsigned contract in my face" is not.

Coercion versus Force

We should also distinguish coerced promises from what we might call forced promises.[4] A coerced promise, roughly, requires an intentional agent to coerce, whereas a forced promise is made on the basis of unfortunate circumstances in nature. For example, if you put a gun to my head and threaten to shoot unless I give you money, you are attempting to coerce me to give you money. However, if through no fault of anyone's I need sugar quickly (I am diabetic), and you are a nearby convenience store proprietor, then I may be forced to give you money in exchange for some orange juice. You are not attempting to coerce me, though circumstances may force me into give you money regardless.

Now of course this "coerced" versus "forced" terminology is arbitrary and stipulative, but the distinction it demarcates is morally significant. Coerced promises never have moral force, though forced promises often do. That is, if I am coerced into promising to mail you some money tomorrow (you have a gun to my head), then the resulting promise does not create an additional moral reason for me to carry out the exchange. In contrast, if my diabetic condition forces me to promise to mail you some money tomorrow for your orange juice today, then by promising I do thereby generate an additional moral reason to mail money to you.[5]

Three-party Coerced Promises

What about a three-party case? Suppose, for example, that Arnold coerces Bill into promising to help Charlie move, where Charlie is ignorant of the coercion. Does Bill's promise generate a moral reason for him to help Charlie move? No, because it was coerced. Of course, this is compatible with the thesis that Charlie is justified in relying on Bill's promise and justified in being indignant that Bill reneged. Yet here, as usual, coercion acts as an excusing condition: because Bill was coerced, he is excused from responsibility for reneging on the resulting promise. This is analogous to nonpromissory coercion. Alice coerces Barbara to break Connie's finger, where Connie is ignorant of the coercion. Connie is justified in relying on Barbara not to break her finger and justified in being indignant at her broken finger, but Barbara is not responsible for it.

Now, of course there is the important difference that in the promissory case what is coerced is the promise-making, not the promise-breaking. Thus one might suspect that an agent can be coerced into making a promise, for which she is thereby not responsible, and yet she might still be held responsible for breaking it. This is incorrect: if one is not responsible for making a promise then one is likewise not responsible for breaking it. We can preserve this intuitive principle by distinguishing between the moral force generated by promises and that generated by expectations.

A pair of contrasting examples will help explain this distinction. Suppose first that Jones has the justified yet false belief that Smith promised to help him move. Smith knows all this, and he knows that helping Jones move will be much less costly than reneging. Plausibly, Smith has a moral reason to help Jones move, in spite of not having promised, and that is because Jones's reliance generates a moral reason, even though Smith is not responsible for this reliance. Now consider a contrasting example, where Jane knows that Samantha promised to help her move, yet Samantha (faultlessly) does not remember doing so. If Samantha knows that Jane is relying on her to help, then that generates a moral reason for Samantha to help, the same reason as for Smith. However, if Samantha were then to discover the truth—that she did in fact promise—then she would realize she has an additional moral reason to help, not shared with Smith: the moral force of a genuine promise.[6]

This distinction also explains the intuition that Bill ought to help Charlie move, even if Arnold coerced Bill into promising to do so. Bill's coerced promise has no moral force, but this is compatible with Charlie's (faultless) reliance having moral force. After all, Bill's unfortunate situation is analogous to Smith's. Both, if they are sensitive moral agents, should feel an unease because someone is faultlessly relying on them for help. And those expectations are enough to generate moral reasons to help. Yet in both cases the reliance has been foisted on them, so they are not responsible for it. In Smith's case, that is because no promise has, in fact, been made; in Bill's case it is because his promise was coerced, and therefore without moral force.

e it gives promisers the power to create
ht object to this by wondering whether
promissory practice, reasons that can
. The short answer is that no other such
wer is that the burden of proof is now on
me up with one. After all, my explana-
power to incur obligations, all by them-
we find important in promissory activity,
d add nothing. Still, perhaps something
what seems the most promising alleged
victim's interest for coerced promises to
night do something even more horrible
mple, the mail-in mugger might kill his
re money. Thus, the inability to enforce
sequences for their victims.[7]
this objection. First, it concedes that
e refuse to enforce coerced promises.
mugger might just walk away on dis-
on hand. Further, even if the conse-
ld be better if we enforced coerced
be best off with an exception-less rule
s. This is because, once we admit that
omises, there will be an incentive for
in their interactions, so that they too
use. In other words, indirect conse-
quences via reputation effects matter too.[8]

A second worry is that this objection applies most naturally to contracts, not to promises. Mere promises are not enforceable in courts, regardless of whether they are coerced. Thus, the mail-in mugger might be disappointed to learn that he cannot appeal to the legal system to enforce his mark's coerced promise, but in just the same way my neighbor might be disappointed to learn that he cannot appeal to the legal system to enforce my uncoerced promise to help him move. My concern in this essay is the moral force of promises, not the legal validity of contracts.

A third problem also relies on the distinction between ethics and the law. Enforceability is at bottom a legal matter, whether the law should enforce various promises (or better, contracts). Moral force is of course a moral matter. Now, one way to justify a legal rule, say of enforcing certain coerced promises, is by appealing to the analogous moral rule, here that those coerced promises have moral force. But the absence of this kind of straightforward inference from moral to legal is compatible with another method of justifying the legal rule, via appeal to protecting potential victims. Thus, it is possible that the objector and I are both right: coerced promises have no moral force, and yet the law should sometimes enforce them anyway.

A final problem is that enforceable promises no longer generate the puzzle I want to address. That is because an enforceable coerced promise is in the relevant sense equivalent to a protracted coerced action. For example, if the mail-in mugger can appeal to the courts to ensure that he gets his money within a week, then he can produce a credible threat of harm—namely legal punishment—at the time when he is supposed to receive the money. Obviously, in that case he is perfectly sensible in attempting to coerce a promise, in which case the example is no longer interesting. I am interested in explaining why, for example, a promissory mugging is unreliable when the mugger cannot produce any credible threat at the time that the money changes hands, including even the threat of legal sanction. The phenomenon I want to explain would not arise in a world in which all promises are enforceable.

III. ALLEGED COUNTEREXAMPLES

In this section I consider four recently alleged examples of coerced promises with moral force. I argue that each suffers from the same two defects. First, they are most plausibly construed as coerced actions rather than as coerced promises, and once they are modified to be genuine cases of coerced promises they become too artificial to be applicable to the real-world concerns that might have motivated us to countenance moral force in coerced promises to begin with. Second, they blur the distinction between threats and offers, which while delicate is extremely important in the conceptual analysis of coercion. The examples are genuinely coercive only if they are made on the basis of threats, in which case the resulting promise carries no moral force, and they carry genuine moral force only if they are made on the basis of offers, in which case they are not coerced.

Surrender

I begin with wartime surrender.[9] My discussion of this example will be by far the lengthiest, because the same points I develop here apply straightforwardly to the other examples as well. Suppose Winning is winning a war against Losing, and that Winning makes the following proposal to Losing: "Promise to lay down arms and never pick them up again, and we will stop fighting; otherwise, we will annihilate you." Losing acquiesces. This may seem like a morally forceful coerced promise, but in fact it is not.

Surrender as Coerced Action versus Coerced Promise

First, typical cases of surrender are best interpreted as coerced action rather than as coerced promises. Recall the caveat I mentioned at the end of section 1: if Winning is able to produce credible threats against Losing after the time of surrender, that surrender is essentially a coerced action—here the action being the laying down of arms and refraining from picking them up again—rather than a coerced promise of future action. This is so even if promissory language is confusedly invoked.

This point is important because one might mistakenly think that the only way we can make sense of the significance and legitimacy of the actual practice of surrender in the real world is by countenancing the moral force of coerced promises. That is false; in actual cases of surrender the victor is never so foolish as to relinquish the ability to produce credible threats against the loser after surrender. In other words, the best explanation for the legitimacy of real-world surrender proposals need not invoke morally forceful coerced promises. In the real world, victorious nations do not relinquish the ability to make credible threats against their surrendering foes.

Threats and Offers

Of course, we can construct artificial cases where Winning is not able to produce a credible threat against Losing after the time of surrender. For example, we could just stipulate that Winning, perhaps foolishly, will melt down its weapons once the surrender is signed. However, now a second problem for the surrender example emerges, namely that the example straddles the distinction between threats and offers. If the surrender proposal is a threat, then while it is certainly coercive it also carries no moral force. On the other hand, if the surrender proposal is an offer, then while it carries moral force it is thereby no longer coercive.

The difference between threats and offers is roughly that if I propose to make you better off then my proposal is an offer, whereas if I propose to make you worse off then it is a threat. For example, proposing to shoot you if you do not hand over your money makes you worse off; proposing to exchange my goods for your money makes you better off (even if you reject the proposal, on the understanding that your rejection carries no penalty). If we add the innocuous principle that there is an essential, if rough, connection between proposals you welcome and proposals that make you better off, then we can connect this analysis of threats and offers with the earlier analysis of coercion and inducement: threats coerce, and offers induce.

Of course, questions regarding what makes you better or worse off are essentially comparative. Robert Nozick, in his seminal article on coercion, notes that two kinds of comparative baselines exist. Moral baselines ask whether you are worse or better off than you should be, and predictive baselines ask whether you are worse or better off than you would otherwise be.[10] Now, we do not have to settle the best way to think about baselines, because my conclusions follow regardless. That is fortunate, for the proper way to demarcate threats from offers is disputed.[11] The important point for my purposes is not that some one particular way of distinguishing is best, but only that we distinguish.

Surrender as Threat

Suppose first that Winning's surrender proposal is a threat. An easy way to do this is to use a moral baseline and assume that Winning does not have the moral right to annihilate Losing. After all, if we use a predictive baseline then real world surrender proposals seem always offers, because in the natural course of events that would otherwise transpire the victor would annihilate the loser. Suppose, then, that Winning has no right to annihilate Losing, yet Losing surrenders and then breaks its promise and begins to fight again. If Winning were to complain that Losing has broken its promise not to pick up arms again, how might Losing respond? Of course, one possibility is that Losing does not care about morality at all. But another option is open, one that is both within the bounds of morality and perfectly reasonable: their earlier promise was made on the threat of annihilation, and Winning did not have the right to make this threat. Therefore, the promise is morally bankrupt, because coerced promises have no moral force.

An example may help persuade. Let Winning be Nazi Germany, and Losing be France. Nazi Germany is not morally permitted to annihilate France, and it coerces France to surrender via the threat of annihilation otherwise. Now suppose French citizens are debating whether to start a resistance against the occupation. If one citizen were to say, "we should not start a resistance, because we promised that we would not when we surrendered," it would be perfectly natural for another to respond, "but that surrender carries no moral force, because we were (wrongfully) threatened with annihilation if we didn't."[12] The first citizen, if he is to continue this debate, must say more about why France ought to respect the surrender agreement even though it was coerced.

In other words, if we assume that Winning is not morally justified in continuing to fight to the point of annihilating Losing, then surrender is not a persuasive counterexample to the thesis that coercive promises have no moral force. The reason it is not persuasive is that it is perfectly reasonable to interpret the example in a way friendly to the thesis that it allegedly contradicts. A persuasive counterexample would have to be an uncontroversial case that is obviously a morally binding coerced promise. The example of surrender made on the basis of threat is too controversial to be persuasive.

I should stress this point about dialectic and the burden of proof. I have argued that there is a general presumption in favor of the thesis that coerced promises never carry moral force. Any counterexample to that thesis must be less controversial than the thesis it is being used to refute, if it is to be effective. For, in the face of any controversial counterexample, it is always open for the defender of my thesis to reject the counterexample. Here is an analogy. Suppose I want to argue that one can know something without knowing that one knows it. And suppose my candidate example is my knowledge that I am not a brain in a vat: I intend to prove that I do not know that I know that I am not a brain in a vat. Clearly, this is a bad argumentative strategy, because my assumption is shaky—it is contentious whether I even know that I am not a brain in a vat in the first place. Of course, contentiousness is compatible with truth: it might very well be true that I know that I am not a brain in a vat. But, dialectically, if I want to convince my interlocutors I should not begin by presupposing something so controversial, to wit that I know that I am not a brain in a vat.

The White Flag Objection Objection: What if Losing surrenders after it has displayed a conventionally understood symbolic gesture of surrender, such as waving a white flag or falling to its knees? The moral power of the white flag is uncontroversially accepted, after all.[13] So suppose Losing initiated the surrender proceedings by waving a white flag. Surely in this case if Losing were to pick up arms again it would be acting immorally; we would judge Losing to be dastardly and dishonorable if it waved the white flag and then turned around and attacked again after Winning let down its guard.

We must be careful when thinking about white flag scenarios. Recall that we are presupposing a coercive context in which Losing waves the white flag: Winning is not permitted to annihilate Losing yet is threatening to do so regardless. In such a scenario, it is perfectly reasonable to infer that if Losing waves the white flag it is coerced into doing so. After all, as Nozick has reminded us, a threatener can coerce without making an explicit proposal.[14] In particular, it can be clear from the circumstances that

Winning will not initiate its own surrender proposal but will instead continue to fight until one of two things happens: either Losing is annihilated or else it waves the white flag and then surrenders. In such a situation Losing is clearly coerced into waving the white flag, but then intuitively the resulting surrender agreement still carries no moral force. Suitably modifying the France and Nazi Germany example should make this point clear.

Granted, white flag intuitions are much stronger in cases where the winning country is permitted to annihilate the losing country. For example, if Losing started an unprovoked, unjustified war of aggression on Winning, but now is facing annihilation, then we think that Losing would be dastardly or dishonorable to renege on its surrender agreement if it initiates that agreement by waving the white flag. However, in this kind of case the surrender proposal that results is an offer rather than a threat, which brings us to the other horn of my initial dilemma.

Surrender as Offer

Suppose, then, that Winning's surrender proposal is an offer. One way this might be true is if the distinction between threats and offers is made on the basis of a predictive baseline. For we can stipulate that, as seems typically the case in the realworld, if Winning were not to make the surrender proposal it would just annihilate Losing instead. However, another way Winning's surrender proposal might be an offer is if we use moral baselines and then assume that Winning is morally permitted to annihilate Losing—an example might be (a suitably cleaned-up variant of) the Allies proposing surrender to Japan in World War II. Now, suppose Winning, perhaps in response to Losing waving the white flag, makes the following proposal: "Look, we are permitted to annihilate you, but we are going to offer you a deal: we will refrain from annihilating you—which, again, would be perfectly within our moral rights—but you have to promise never to pick up arms again." This proposal is not coercive, because it is an offer rather than a threat. It is an offer rather than a threat because it proposes a course of events that is better for Losing than the relevant baseline scenario, no matter whether that baseline is predictive or moral: surrender is better than annihilation. Therefore, even if Losing promises on the basis of an offer, and even if that promise carries moral force, the promise was induced rather than coerced.

Surrender as Coercive Offer Objection: my argument thus far assumes that only threats can coerce, whereas perhaps offers can coerce as well. Notably, David Zimmerman and Joel Feinberg have each independently argued that offers can coerce.[15] In this subsection, I will argue for two points. First, Zimmerman and Feinberg are wrong. Second, the conceptual possibility of coercive offers is irrelevant for my thesis as originally intended anyway, in which case this objection is just a request for unnecessary precision.

Zimmerman says that an offer is coercive if the offeree both prefers it to the preproposal situation and prefers to move from the actual preproposal situation to some alternative preproposal situation that is feasible, and that the offerer has actively prevented the offeree from obtaining.[16] A surrender offer is likely to count as coercive on Zimmerman's analysis because the loser might prefer surrender to continued fighting and yet might also prefer a return to something like the prehostility state of affairs to both. The prehostility state of affairs (or something approximating it) is feasible, and the winner's military campaign is actively blocking the losers from obtaining it. Thus, surrender offers are coercive.

Zimmerman's conceptual analysis is incorrect, however. Situations which Zimmerman would describe as Al making a coercive offer to Bob are better described merely as situations where both (i) Al (wrongfully) harms Bob by actively preventing Bob from obtaining something Bob wants and (ii) Al exploits Bob by proposing an offer that is not as good as it should have been. Bob has no additional grievance of coercion in Zimmerman-cases, and we do better to reserve coercion-talk for cases where Al threatens Bob. After all, suppose (i) and (ii) both hold in some offer situation, and then Al makes the further move of putting a gun to Bob's head and saying "Okay, it's no longer an offer; now it's a threat: do what I want, or I shoot you." Zimmerman has no more moral vocabulary to describe the moral worsening of the situation that has just occurred. He could, of course, invent a term to cover this more serious moral offense, but then the obvious reply is that by "coercion" we meant to be discussing the referent of this other term all along.

According to Feinberg, an offer is coercive if it proposes a choice between two evils, such that one of the two evils is greatly preferred to the other.[17] For example, if I am happily employed in Colorado, but then offered an even better job in New York, that offer is not coercive. In contrast, suppose my job in Colorado is miserable (evil), and I am offered another job in New York that is also miserable, though significantly better than my Colorado one. In that case the offer is coercive. Arguably, surrender offers are coercive on this account as well. The choice between surrender and annihilation is the choice between two absolute evils, yet surrender is greatly preferred to annihilation.

Feinberg's analysis is defective on two counts. First, it wrongly presupposes that there is a universal metric by which we can determine whether a state of affairs is absolutely good or evil, full stop. States of affairs can be better or worse than one another, but this is an essentially comparative judgment. The only sense we can make of absolute yet nonarbitrary judgments of the goodness or badness of states of affairs is by neglecting to articulate our implicit and perhaps most contextually salient comparison class. For example, when I say that my job in Colorado is wonderful, I am implicitly comparing it to many other worse and particularly salient jobs that I might have had instead. But it makes no sense to repudiate all implicit comparison classes and then to say that my job in Colorado is wonderful, full stop.

The other problem with Feinberg's analysis is that it robs coercion claims of their intended significance. One of the most important reasons we care about coercion is that it reduces responsibility: if I am coerced into doing something, then I am not morally responsible for having done it. However, Feinberg readily admits that one is still morally responsible for accepting a coercive offer.[18] For example, if you offer me a job in New York, then I retain full responsibility for my choice to take it, even if both the new job and my old one were evil on absolute terms. In contrast, if you put a gun to my head and threaten to kill me if I do not take it, then I am no longer responsible for having taken it. The most theoretically elegant way of expressing this difference is as the difference between inducement and coercion.

I do not have the space for a full discussion of the inadequacies of theories which countenance coercive offers. However, even if I am wrong, three further points can be made. First, even if I am wrong it is at least controversial whether coercive offers are possible. Besides Nozick, Alan Wertheimer is perhaps the most notable scholar on coercion, having produced the first and most influential book-length philosophical treatment of the subject, and he also rejects Zimmerman's and Feinberg's arguments, concluding that if we care about coercion for moral and legal purposes then we ought to rule out the possibility of coercive offers.[19] But, to repeat, dialectically persuasive counterexamples cannot rest on controversial assumptions.

Second, I am perfectly happy to restrict my thesis so that it is compatible with the existence of coercive offers. When I said that coerced promises have no moral force, what I really meant to say was that coerced promises *made on the basis of threats* have no moral force. The italicized clause is vacuous, but it will provide clarification for those who (mistakenly) think that offers can coerce. And the more cautious thesis, that coerced promises made on the basis of threats carry no moral force, is surely the kernel of truth in the repudiation of the moral force of coerced promises. Taking a cue from Feinberg, we can say that agents retain moral responsibility if they choose to accept a coercive offer. For example, Losing retains moral responsibility for accepting Winning's coercive surrender offer. After all, in the important and relevant sense, Losing was still able to make the promise all by itself, without undue outside influence. Even coercive offers are welcome, so Losing is still responsible for its choice.

Third, recall my original motivation: to explain why it is foolish to rely on a promise that was coerced. In light of the distinction between threats and offers, my motivation can be restated more precisely: to explain why it is foolish to rely on a promise that was coerced *on the basis of a threat*. As before, the italicized addition is vacuous, but it may be helpful for those who (mistakenly) think that offers can coerce. There is nothing especially problematic about relying on a promise that was coerced on the basis of an offer.

Contrasting two examples should make that last point clear. Let us suppose in both examples that my job in Colorado is an absolute evil. Now, in *Miserable New York*, a recruiter proposes to let me come work for him in New York, as long as I promise to mail him some money. (He will never see me again, but he left me a mailing address.) This job in New York, while significantly better than my very evil Colorado job, is still evil on absolute terms. Contrast that with *Wonderful California*, where a different recruiter makes a noncoercive offer: the California recruiter approaches me and offers an absolutely good job in California in exchange for the promise of future money. *Wonderful California* may raise interesting issues about, for example, how self-interested agents can guarantee reciprocity in exchange, but it does not have even a whiff of grasping at straws, which is my explanatory target. And, for all intents and purposes, *Miserable New York* is the same—it raises no further interesting issues. That is, neither the *Wonderful California* nor the *Miserable New York* recruiters would be irrational to rely on my promise in the way that the mail-in mugger would be. Recruiters can rationally expect most people to follow through on their offer-based promises, but muggers should not expect most (rational) people to follow through on their threat-based promises. Thus, even if the phenomenon I want to explain is not captured precisely by the simple language of coercion, it is still adequately captured by the slightly more complex language of threat-based coercion. And in the case of offer-based coercion, the irrationality phenomenon that I want to explain does not even arise.

Shotgun Wedding

A second alleged example of a coerced promise with moral force is the shotgun wedding.[20] Pa holds a shotgun to Ben's head and tells him that he needs to promise to marry to Emily, whom (it is common knowledge that) Ben has impregnated. As before, we need to make some artificial additions to the example in order for it to be plausible that Pa is coercing the promise of marriage rather than merely coercing the wedding (or marriage) itself. Otherwise the example is most naturally interpreted as one where promissory language is confusedly used to describe a protracted coerced action. That is important because, as before, we do not need to license moral force in coerced promises in order to explain the legitimacy of real-world shotgun weddings. In a real-world shotgun wedding, what is coerced—if anything is coerced at all—is not a promise, but rather a prolonged action.

But suppose, for the sake of furthering the argument, that (it is common knowledge that) Pa has a terminal disease and will die before the wedding day. Is this a morally forceful coerced promise? No. As with the surrender example, there is a dilemma depending on whether Pa is morally permitted to shoot Ben for having impregnated Emily. First suppose no. In this case the promise of marriage is indeed coerced, because it was made on the basis of a threat. However, it is perfectly natural to say that the coerced promise is therefore morally impotent. Of course, this is compatible with it being the case that Ben ought to marry Emily and indeed that Ben ought to promise to marry to Emily. The claim here is only that the coerced promise generates no moral force of its own, to add to previously extant considerations.

Perhaps an analogy will help. Suppose Johnny (intentionally and wrongfully) steps on some other child's sand castle. Of course, Johnny ought to apologize, but suppose Johnny's mother points a gun at Johnny's head and says "Promise to apologize, or I'll shoot you." (It is common knowledge that, tragically, Johnny's mother will be whisked away to a foreign country after the promise but before the apology, never to return or be in any contact with Johnny ever again.) Johnny acquiesces. Does Johnny's coerced promise exert any moral force? No. Yes, Johnny ought to apologize, and perhaps Johnny even ought to promise his mother that he will apologize without her having to resort to threats to acquire that promise. But if Johnny promises and then refuses to apologize, he has committed only one wrong (in addition to the wrong of stepping on the sand castle), namely the wrong of not apologizing. He has not also committed the further wrong of breaking a promise. And that is because his promise was coerced (not because coerced promises are impossible, which is false). As with the surrender case, we can account fully for our moral intuitions about this case without having to add an alleged extra wrong of a broken coerced promise.

Likewise in the shotgun wedding. On the assumption that Pa is not permitted to shoot Ben with the shotgun in retaliation for impregnating Emily, Ben's coerced promise of marriage carries no moral force. And this is compatible with the claims that Ben ought to marry Emily and even that Ben ought to promise Pa to marry Emily without Pa's having to threaten him first.

Now suppose that Pa is morally permitted to shoot Ben for having impregnated Emily.[21] In this case, the shotgun wedding proposal is an offer, not a threat. Pa says, "Look, I am allowed to shoot you with this shotgun in response to what you did to my daughter, but I propose instead that you marry her, which is better for you than being shot." Offers do not coerce, or, if they do, not in the way that is of interest here. Thus, the shotgun wedding promise either carries no moral force or else is not coercive.

Parental Discipline

David Owens suggests that a child's promise to behave, elicited via parental coercion, has moral force.[22] This is incorrect. Again, we must first eliminate the worry that parents typically are able to produce a credible threat after the time at which the child must carry out her promised action. Otherwise this case, like those that preceded it, is best interpreted as one where the parents confusedly use promissory language to describe a protracted coerced action. And, as before, the contortions necessary to eliminate this worry will render the resulting case artificial—because the parent will have to lose contact with her child after the time of the promise—and therefore irrelevant to real-world motivations for acknowledging morally forceful coerced promises.

But even after we waive that worry, the same dilemma that arose for surrender and shotgun weddings remains. Either the parent is morally permitted to carry out her proposed punishment, or not. If not, then her coerced promise has no moral force—Johnny and the threat of being shot in the head for trampling the sand castle illustrates this point.

If, on the other hand, the parent is morally permitted to carry out her proposed punishment, then the parent is making an offer, which is not coercive. Suppose, to modify the sand castle example, that the mother's punishment is ten minutes of quiet time (instead of being shot in the head), and suppose that the mother is morally permitted to wield this punishment in response to Johnny stepping on the sand castle. In that case, the mother's proposal, "Apologize, or else you get ten minutes of quiet time" is again an offer, because it proposes a course of action—the apology— that is expected to be preferable to the morally permitted and otherwise expected option of ten minutes of quiet time.

Judges and Criminals

The last alleged example of a coerced promise with moral force also comes from Owens; it is the custom of some judges to use the threat of punishment in order to get criminals to promise to reform.[23] It is not merely that the judge coerces reform via the threat of punishment. No, the practice in question is that the judge also coerces the promise of reform. Once elicited this coerced promise allegedly carries its own moral force, so that a criminal who fails to reform is then guilty of two wrongs (failing to reform and breaking a promise) rather than just one.

As before, we must take care to ensure that the examples are clear cases of coerced promises rather than of coerced actions. In particular, it is quite natural to interpret judges as confused if they insist not just that the criminal behave but also that the criminal promise to behave. Really, they are incorrectly using promissory language to coerce an action (good behavior). After all, the legal system will still be able to produce credible threats on the criminal after the time of his promise. We can of course construct fanciful yet coherent examples where the legal system cannot produce a credible threat after the criminal is set free, in which case this promissory language would not be confused. But, as before, such artificial examples bear too little resemblance to the real world to be able to conclude that common, everyday, real-world considerations commit us to the moral force of coerced promises.

And again, the same dilemma arises. Either the court is morally permitted to carry out its threat, or it is not. If it is not, then the proposal is coercive, because a threat, but it carries no moral force. For example, suppose the criminal shoplifted, and the threat is the death penalty. The proposal, "Promise not to shoplift, or else we'll execute you" is certainly coercive, but the promise that results is morally impotent. That is, even if the criminal ought to refrain from shoplifting, and even if he ought to promise to refrain (without being threatened first), the fact that the criminal's promise was coerced means the promise does not add any moral force to the moral demand that he refrain. If the shoplifter is coerced into the promise to refrain—via the threat of the death penalty—and then goes on to shoplift, he may be guilty of having shoplifted, but he is no more blameworthy for having also broken the coerced promise.

If, on the other hand, the court is morally permitted to carry out its threat, then the proposal is best construed as an offer, and is therefore not coercive. For example, if the legal system is morally permitted to incarcerate the criminal for a week, then the proposal "Promise to behave, or else we will incarcerate you for a week" is an offer, and therefore not coercive, even if the resulting promise has moral force.

IV. PRACTICAL FORCE

In this section, I will argue that coerced promises typically carry no practical force. That is, coerced promissory behavior is not good evidence of intention to fulfill the promise. In a typical case, if I say that I promise to do something, then you can conclude that I intend to do it. And in a typical case where it is common knowledge that I intend to do something, you can raise your epistemic credence that I will do it. Might this work for coerced promises? If, for example, the mark gives a coerced promise to mail some money, does this give the mail-in mugger a good reason to think that the mark will mail the money, independent of moral concerns?

We must disentangle some questions. First, we can ask about the connection between promising and intending. One way the mail-in mugger might be confused is in thinking that a genuine promise to do something automatically carries with it the genuine intention to do that thing. That is false, because insincere promises are still promises. Indeed, one can promise to do something without intending to undertake an obligation to do that thing as well, and insincere promises are again good examples.[24] At this point one might further conclude that, even if it is possible to coerce a promise, it is not possible to coerce promissory intentions (such as the intention to fulfill the promise or the intention to undertake the obligation to fulfill a promise). However, this further conclusion would be too hasty.

Possibility of Coerced Intentions

Is it possible to coerce intentions? One easy answer to this question appeals to an analogy to beliefs. Plausibly, it is not possible to choose to believe something when one has strong evidence to the contrary, in which case it is likewise impossible to coerce someone into believing it. Analogously, perhaps it is not possible to coerce intentions, in the same way that it is not possible to coerce beliefs. But this answer is too easy because, even if doxastic voluntarism is false, it is not clear that intentions are analogous to beliefs in the relevant respects. Yes they are both mental states, but that is insufficient to motivate the analogy between them.

Another easy answer to this question is that, yes, it is possible to coerce intentions because, in general, if I coerce you into X-ing, and X-ing requires intending to X, then I have also coerced you into intending to X. For example, if I coerce you into making a cucumber and avocado sandwich for me, and your making a cucumber and avocado sandwich for me entails your intending to make a cucumber and avocado sandwich for me, then I have also coerced you into intending to make a cucumber and avocado sandwich for me. This opposing answer is also too easy, for two reasons.

First, it may not even apply to the relevant promissory intentions. Promissory intentions can include the intention to fulfill the promise and also the intention to undertake the obligation to fulfill the promise. The easy answer now under consideration entails that I can coerce you to intend to make a cucumber and avocado sandwich by coercing you into making it—the intention comes along for free, so to speak. But it is less clear whether this move will work for the intention to undertake an obligation to make the cucumber and avocado sandwich. What action could I possibly coerce which would bring along that obligation-intention for free? If I put a gun to your head and say, "Undertake an obligation to make a cucumber and avocado sandwich for me, or else I'll shoot," you may mouth agreement just to get the gun out of your face, but it would be quite implausible to suppose that I can thereby generate obligations in that manner, let alone the intention to undertake obligations.[25]

Second, the most interesting cases of coerced promises are ones where the promise is coerced precisely because it is not possible to coerce the promised action. Recall that the mail-in mugger attempts to coerce the promise of future money precisely because the mark has no money on her person to give.

A more fruitful approach to our question than either of the two previous easy answers begins by noting that one can form intentions voluntarily in cases where it may be impossible to form analogous beliefs voluntarily. For example, I can choose whether to intend to eat a cucumber and avocado sandwich for lunch, though I cannot choose whether to believe that a cucumber and avocado sandwich is on my desk now. Given that I can voluntarily form intentions in a way that I cannot voluntarily form beliefs, the suggestion that intentions can be coerced even though beliefs cannot is more promising. For, if I can choose whether to do something (give you money, form an intention), then it seems I can be coerced into doing that thing (give you money, form an intention). After all, if I can choose to do something then I can choose on the basis of reasons, and attempts at coercion merely provide a certain type of reason—namely conditional threats—that are not special in any relevant way.

Now, even if it is granted that we can choose our intentions on the basis of reasons, including conditional threats, there seems to be something especially problematic about coerced promises. That is because in a typical case of coerced promises the promisee will have no good reason (moral, prudential, or otherwise) to follow through on her intention, once the time comes to fulfill the promise. For example, once the mark is no longer threatened by her mail-in mugger, she has no good reason to follow through on her promise by mailing him money. Then the question arises whether it is possible for her to form an intention to do something that she can foresee in advance she will have no good reason to do.

I have just described some essential features of Gregory Kavka's toxin puzzle.[26] A toxin will cause you to be in pain temporarily if you ingest it. A wealthy person proposes to give you a lot of money at midnight tonight if, at that time, you intend to ingest the toxin the following morning. All that is required for your receiving the money is that you intend tonight to ingest tomorrow, not that you actually ingest tomorrow. Indeed, the money will be transferred to you before you have to ingest. Is it possible to intend to ingest, when you know that ingesting will be bad for you, though not so bad that you would prefer abstaining to acquiring the money?

There is an extensive literature on the toxin puzzle, but thankfully our question here is simpler than the hardest questions one might ask about that puzzle. The most interesting questions about the toxin puzzle relate to what is possible for rational agents, but none of us are perfectly rational in the sense required for standard decision theory. Thus, we want to know whether it is conceptually possible to coerce an intention in a potentially irrational agent. In particular, even if it is impossible for a perfectly rational person to intend to do something she knows she will have no good reason to do, it still is at least conceptually possible that a mail-in mugger might coerce a less-than-perfectly rational mark into the relevant promissory intentions.

Futility of Coerced Intentions

Thus, it is at least conceptually possible to coerce intentions. Still, even if it is conceptually possible to be coerced into forming an intention, lingering questions remain. One question, as we saw at the end of the previous section, is whether it is possible to coerce a perfectly rational agent into intending to do something that she knows she has no good reason to do. Returning to the mail-in mugger, is it possible for a perfectly rational mark to intend to mail the money, if she foresees that she will have no good reason (moral, prudential, or otherwise) to do so when the time comes?

On the analogous toxin puzzle, Kavka thought that a rational agent will not ingest the toxin, and so cannot intend to. Others disagree, arguing that because it is in the agent's interest to intend, that gives her a (defeasible) reason to inculcate the disposition to ingest when that time comes, so that it can be rational to intend and indeed, come morning, even to ingest as well.[27]

As I said earlier, this dispute over the toxin puzzle is difficult, and I have nothing novel to say about it. I mention it because commitments on the toxin puzzle carry over to the analogous case of the mail-in mugger. I am content to conclude conditionally that if Kavka is right then it is impossible for a rational mark to form promissory intentions in the mail-in mugger case. In that case, it is futile to attempt to coerce a promise from a (known to be) rational mark.

More can be said, however, for there is another, less contentious, argument for futility. In particular, the potential mail-in mugger faces another practical problem: How will he ever know that his mark has formed the relevant promissory intentions? In other words, even if he can coerce a promise, how will he know that the mark's promise is sincere? The analogous question is glossed over in discussions of the toxin puzzle—where it is assumed that the player's intentions are transparent—for the sake of other more theoretical concerns. However, our interest here is practical, so the question poses a legitimate concern.

The worry is that observable promissory behavior is much less trustworthy if it is coerced. In a typical uncoerced case, if I say I promise to mail some money to Oxfam, that promissory performative counts as evidence that I have formed the relevant promissory intentions. However, such performative evidence is not nearly so strong in a coerced case. For a coerced performative indicating that I intend to do something is not (good) evidence that I so intend. In other words, if you coerce me into saying I promise to do something, then my saying that I promise is no longer good evidence that I intend to do it, and no longer good evidence that I intend to undertake the obligation to do it.

This also suggests that attempting to coerce promises will typically be futile. Not merely because rational people cannot intend to do what they know they will not have any good reason to do, which is disputed, but rather (or also) because an attempted coercer will typically be unable to acquire sufficient evidence that he has succeeded in coercing the relevant intention.

I say "typically" because this is not always the case. The victim may be horribly bad at bluffing, for example, so that if she were to say "I promise to mail some money to you" without the requisite intention, she would send an involuntary observable cue—a facial tic, perhaps—to the coercer that she lacks the requisite intention. Then the sophisticated coercer might try to coerce her victim into the promissory performative, not because that suffices for her to have promised and promises automatically generate moral or predictive force, but rather because he can watch her performance for clues as to her intentions. This is atypical. In a typical case, the coercer's access to his victim's intentions is mediated by the victim's voluntary behavior, and such behavior is no longer a reliable indicator of intentions when the victim has an external incentive to engage in promissory behavior.[28]

Note that, in principle, similar remarks apply to induced promises as to coerced promises. That is, while induced promises are conceptually possible, there is a worry about whether the promiser's performative is good evidence that she has the requisite intention. For example, supposing I know that you will give me $1,000 today if I merely promise to house-sit for you next month, I have an incentive to engage in a promissory performative, even when I do not intend to fulfill my promise.[29]

However, there are two important asymmetries between typical cases of coerced versus induced promises. First, considerations of reputation differ. That is, we are typically more concerned with maintaining a good reputation with people who try to induce us into promises than we are with people who try to coerce us into promises. For example, I am more concerned to develop a good reputation amongst potential house-sitting employers than I am to develop a good reputation amongst potential mail-in muggers. Second, induced promises do, but coerced promises do not, have moral force. Therefore, it is typically more wrong for someone to renege on an induced promise than on a coerced one.[30]

V. CONCLUSION

I started with the thought that it is irrational to rely on coerced promises, or more precisely that it is less rational to rely on coerced promises than it is to rely on uncoerced promises or on coerced actions. The explanation for this is two-fold. First, coerced promises have no moral force. Second, coerced promises typically have no practical force as well. In other words, a person attempting to coerce a promise has no good reason, whether based on what the promisee ought to do or on what she intends to do, to expect in typical cases that a (rational) coerced promisee will fulfill her promise. Of course, I do not expect this essay to convince the people who might actually try to coerce promises; my audience is philosophers, not would-be promise-coercers. Rather, exploration of this topic is intended to shed light on conceptual and moral issues that arise from the interrelated notions of promises, coercion, moral force, and intentions.

ACKNOWLEDGMENTS

Thanks to participants at two talks at the University of Colorado at Boulder's Center for Values and Social Policy and to participants at the Rice University conference Understanding Promises and Agreements for valuable feedback. Special thanks to David Boonin, Chris Heathwood, Hanoch Sheinman, and Alan Wertheimer for comments on earlier drafts. Thanks to Emma Kobil for some last-minute proofreading. And finally, thanks to Amber Arnold and Barrett Emerick, whose innocent questions about the possibility of self-promises exposed a loose thread in a much earlier draft, the persistent unraveling of which necessitated that this final version be very different, basically rewritten from scratch—thanks a lot, you two.

NOTES

1. See Gilbert (1993). Gilbert decisively rebuts two arguments. The Obligation Argument claims that promises by definition obligate, but coerced promises never do. This argument is flawed because promises do not always obligate. The Voluntariness Argument claims that promises are by definition voluntary but coerced promises are not. This argument is flawed because it equivocates on two senses of "voluntary." Strictly speaking, Gilbert's arguments concern the possibility of coerced agreements, and agreements are not the same as promises. (If the upshot of her essay is right, agreements are not even mere promise-pairs.) But her arguments about the possibility of coerced agreements apply straightforwardly to coerced promises too. See Gilbert (2006): 228.

2. See, most notably, Gilbert (1993), Deigh (2002), and Owens (2007).

3. What I say here is not intended to be novel; it is intended to be a statement of common sense. It is therefore similar to what many others have said about promises. For example, Owens (2007) argues that we care about promises not only because they give us predictive information about what the promiser is likely to do but also because promises generate rights of authority in the promisee. And Searle (2001) insists that promises are agent-created reasons. I merely combine these two insights.

4. See, for example, Kavka (1986): 396.

5. What about a case where the convenience store proprietor knows about my diabetic condition, and so jacks up the price of orange juice? He is not attempting to coerce me, though he is attempting to exploit me. Do exploitative promises carry moral force? For example, assuming commercial surrogacy contracts exploit, does a desperate commercial surrogate's promise to relinquish the baby have moral force? This issue is interesting, yet tangential to my concerns. The intuitive idea that promises give us the power to create and assume obligations all by ourselves does not dictate an answer to this question about exploitative promises. For, even if the desperate surrogate's exploited promise was made in the relevant sense voluntarily or all by herself, there may be legitimate reasons to curb or restrict the power to create and assume voluntary obligations.

6. A third contrasting kind of case will make the distinction even more clear: one can make a promise on which (it is common knowledge that) the promisee will not rely. In such cases, the promise can still generate moral reasons to fulfill even if there is no reliance on the fulfilling.

7. For a statement of an argument along these lines, see Bar-Gill and Ben-Shahar (2005).

8. This is just the sort of consideration that many find persuasive on the question of whether to negotiate in hostage situations. Even if the consequences of negotiation are sometimes favorable, it might be better to adopt an exceptionless rule against negotiation, to inculcate a hardline reputation which eliminates the incentive for future hostage-taking.

9. Deigh (2002) defends surrender as the only type of coerced promise that has moral force.

10. Nozick (1969): 447–449.

11. For some nice discussion and a full bibliography, see Anderson (2008).

12. At this point, assume that the surrender proposal is initiated by Nazi Germany, rather than by France. I will soon discuss the scenario where France initiates the surrender proceedings by, e.g., waving a white flag.

13. Deigh's discussion of the moral importance of conventional signs such as waving the white flag or falling to one's knees at Deigh (2002): 490 suggests this.

14. Nozick (1969), 444.

15. Zimmerman (1981); Feinberg (1986): ch. 24.

16. Zimmerman (1981): 132–133.

17. Feinberg (1986): 235.

18. Feinberg (1986): 248.

19. Wertheimer (1987): chapter 12. Wertheimer's discussion is more nuanced and complex than my simplified summary, but not in a way that is harmful to my overall point.

20. Gilbert uses this as an example of a binding coerced agreement in Gilbert (1993): 702 and following. It also works as a coerced promise, if we assume (it is common knowledge that) the marriage proposal will be accepted.

21. As with the surrender case, we might also suppose that we ought to use predictive baselines, and that had Pa not made the surrender proposal he very likely would have shot Ben. The argument using moral baselines is more vivid, so I will continue to make my points with that implicit assumption.

22. See Owens (2007): 298. Owens misdescribes the scenario as one of parental warning, but warnings are distinct from threats (and from offers), and warnings do not coerce. (And unlike my analogous insistence that offers do not coerce, the thesis that warnings do not coerce is undisputed.) See Nozick (1969): 453–458 for more on this distinction. This error is easy to remedy, though of course "parental coercion" sounds less like what a loving parent should do than does "parental warning."

23. Owens (2007): 298.

24. This latter question is relevant because an influential thesis about promising is that a promise to do something communicates, not the intention to do that thing, but rather the intention to undertake the obligation to do that thing. See, for example, Raz (1977).

25. Note that even if Raz is right to say that promises communicate the intention to undertake obligations, it does not follow that if I attempt to coerce you into undertaking obligations, I am thereby attempting to coerce you into promising.

26. Kavka (1983). Of course, the toxin puzzle is an offer, not a threat.

27. See, for example, Gauthier (1998) and Harman (1998).

28. More cautiously, the victim has that external incentive when dealing with a naïve coercer, one who wrongly thinks that a coerced performative is still good evidence of intentions. If it is common knowledge between victim and coercer that performatives in the context of attempted coercion are not good evidence of intentions, then the victim of course no longer has any reason to engage in such performatives. Perhaps in this second-stage common knowledge situation, engaging in performatives once again becomes good evidence of intentions, in which case the victim once again has a strong external incentive to engage in them. This leads us to a third-stage common knowledge situation, where the coercer and victim both know all the above. Then the victim once again no longer has any reason to engage in performatives.

But that leads to a fourth stage of common knowledge. And so on. As long as engaging in performatives incurs some cost, this game may lack a pure solution.

29. Considerations related to Kavka's toxin puzzle also apply to induced promises, as this example should make clear.

30. If the moral importance of promise-keeping reduces to reputation effects then I have just stated the same asymmetry twice.

REFERENCES

Anderson, Scott. (2008). "Coercion." In Edward N. Zalta, ed., *The Stanford Encyclopedia of Philosophy*, fall 2008 ed., <http://plato.stanford.edu/archives/fall2008/entries/coercion/>.

Bar-Gill, Oren. and Ben-Shahar, Omri. (2005). "Credible Coercion." *Texas Law Review* 83, no. 2 (February): 717–780.

Deigh, John. (2002). "Promises under Fire." *Ethics* 112, no. 3 (April 2002): 483–506.

Feinberg, Joel. (1986). *Harm to Self*, vol. 3 of *The Moral Limits of the Criminal Law*. New York: Oxford University Press.

Gauthier, David. (1998). "Rethinking the Toxin Puzzle." In Jules L. Coleman and Christopher W. Morris, eds., *Rational Commitment and Social Justice: Essays for Gregory Kavka*. Cambridge: Cambridge University Press, 47–58.

Gilbert, Margaret. (1993). "Agreements, Coercion, and Obligation." *Ethics* 103, no. 4 (July 1993): 679–706.

———. (2006). *A Theory of Political Obligation*. Oxford: Oxford University Press.

Harman, Gilbert. (1998). "The Toxin Puzzle." In Jules L. Coleman and Christopher W. Morris, eds., *Rational Commitment and Social Justice: Essays for Gregory Kavka*. Cambridge: Cambridge University Press, 84–89.

Kavka, Gregory. (1983). "The Toxin Puzzle." *Analysis* 43: 33–36.

———. (1986). *Hobbesian Moral and Political Theory*. Princeton: Princeton University Press,.

Owens, David. (2007). "Duress, Deception, and the Validity of a Promise." *Mind* 116 no. 462 (April): 293–315.

Nozick, Robert. (1969). "Coercion." in [31]Morgenbesser et al., eds., *Philosophy, Science, and Method: Essays in Honor of Ernest Nagel*. New York: St. Martin's Press, 440–472.

Raz, Joseph. (1977). "Promises and Obligations." In P. M. S. Hacker. ed., *Law, Morality and Society: Essays in Honour of H. L. A. Hart*. Oxford: Clarendon Press.

Searle, John. (2001). *Rationality in Action*. Cambridge, MA: MIT Press.

Wertheimer, Alan. (1987). *Coercion*. Princeton: Princeton University Press.

Zimmerman, David. (1981). "Coercive Wage Offers." *Philosophy and Public Affairs* 10, no. 2 (spring): 121–145.

Chapter 7

Promising Too Much

Julia Driver

Abstract

This paper begins with the idea that we can learn a good deal about promising by examining the conditions and norms that govern promise-breaking. Sometimes promises are broken as a deliberate plan, other times they are broken because they are simply incompatible with other, more significant moral norms, or because it becomes clear that they are impossible to keep. There are cases where people make promises that are actually incompatible with each other. Politicians, for example, often give such incompatible promises, either intentionally, or by making too many commitments, some of which turn out to be incompatible. In making such promises, agents guarantee that at least one promise be broken. Is the agent who makes incompatible promises under any obligation? If 'ought' implies 'can,' and promises entail obligations, then it seems that one cannot, in fact, make promises one cannot keep. This paper explores the problem by drawing analogies between incompatible promises and other promises that cannot be kept. It suggests that we can deny 'ought' implies 'can' strictly speaking, but recognize that there is a practical limit on what the agent can be called on to do. On this view, even promises to do the impossible commit the agent. Similarly, politicians who promise too much are still obligated to do as promised.

We can learn a good deal about promising by looking at the conditions and norms that govern the breaking of promises. It is generally accepted that promises give rise to *pro tanto* obligations. A great deal of weight is placed on "pro tanto." A *pro tanto* obligation still has weight, even when it is overridden in specific circumstances. It is to be contrasted with a *prima facie* obligation, which is an obligation that can be overridden and eliminated, so that it has no more force in the circumstances. Moral dilemma cases often involve *pro tanto* obligations: if Melissa has made two promises that are incompatible, one obligation does not cancel out the other. Each obligation still has force even though she can only fulfill one. On the other hand, *prima facie* obligations are obligations only at first blush; if one believes someone is being assaulted, one may feel a duty to help him, but this is eliminated once one finds out that he is being arrested by the police, and not in fact being assaulted.[1]

In the case of promises, again, when one promises the obligation one takes on is *pro tanto* and not eliminated in light of other circumstances. If one breaks a promise, the default position is that one has failed to live up to an obligation, and so breaking a promise is a moral failure. It is not simply a failure to live up to an announced prediction of what one will do. This may explain why, when someone seems to announce ahead of time the intention to break a promise, there is immediate moral blame attached to the announcement.

Arnold Schwarzenegger campaigned for Governor of California in part on a no tax platform. He promised not to raise taxes. Yet, he would later suggest that the budget deficit in California be closed in part by increasing taxes—for example, increasing the sales tax in California by 1 percent. Political commentators picked up on this right away. William Schneider, a CNN political correspondent, reported that in order for Schwarzenegger to break the budget deadlock in the California state legislature, he put raising taxes on the table, "thereby breaking his promise."[2] But did he?

This case—we will call it (A)—raises some interesting issues. What is it to break a promise? Are there some promises that cannot be kept? Is *proposing* to break a promise itself blameworthy? In examining these issues I have several goals in mind. One is to show how the consequentialist can defend proposals to break promises, and that this is a potential problem for Kantians, but not for the usual Kantian reasons. Proposing to break a promise is not breaking a promise. It is quite clear that Kantians would not go along with the permissibility of breaking a promise, but the question at hand here is different, concerning the proposal to break a promise. Further, I would like to examine what it is to break a promise, and whether or not there are some promises that cannot be kept, that are inevitably to be broken. Offhand, it seems obvious that, of course, some people make promises that can't be kept. But this is puzzling, if we also think that promises entail obligations, and we buy into the "ought" implies "can" principle.[3] My claim will be that "ought" does not imply "can," so there are some promises that cannot be kept.

I. PROMISE-BREAKING

The reaction to Schwarzenegger's proposal to consider raising taxes included accusations that he had broken his promise. This does not seem correct. I propose the following account of promise-breaking.

(PB) S has broken a promise to A to *x* when:
S has made a promise to A to x;
S fails to *x*[2]; [3]and
S has not been released from the promise (either actively or passively).

If the promisee actively releases the promisor from the promise, by saying things like, for example, "You don't have to do it," then the promisor has not broken the promise when he fails to fulfill the promise. It is also possible that there are passive forms of release. Some hold that when a promisee dies, the promisor is released, because one cannot be obligated to the dead since the dead no longer exist as persons.

If (PB) is correct then Schwarzenegger has not broken his promise yet, since he has just proposed raising taxes, he hasn't actually raised them.

But some might object that (PB) is false—not *any* failure to *x* would count as breaking the promise. Suppose that Alice says:

(1) I promise to go grocery shopping for my mom tonight.

She has taken on an obligation to shop for her mother. Suppose also that later in the day her young daughter becomes ill and she can't find a babysitter. So, she stays home, and fails to do the shopping for her mother. Some may have the intuition that this isn't breaking a promise because it is understood that if something really important comes up, then one "can't" go shopping. That is, it is understood that if living up to the content of the promise expression involves violating a more important norm (for example), then the promise is null and void. This treats (1) as really being:

(1') I promise to go grocery shopping for my mom tonight, if no more significant norm would be violated in my so doing.

This suggestion is that promises are conditional. So, when Alice fails to go shopping in those circumstances she hasn't broken a promise. But this observation does not undermine (PB) at all. That's because if we reinterpret the promise along the lines of (1') then the obligation that Alice assumes is to go shopping as long as nothing more important interferes, and she has not violated that obligation. But this worry raises an interesting issue of how we interpret promises—are they implicitly conditional, or not?

Of course, sometimes they will be. The context matters a great deal in whether or not it is reasonable to take the promise as conditional on something. But I don't think that it is a standard feature of promises that they are conditional. Here's another way to look at what is going on with (1). Again, it is standardly held that promises give rise to *pro tanto* obligations. These are obligations that can be overridden by competing norms, or other circumstantial features. On this view we needn't hold (1) to be conditional to justify Alice staying home. Instead, she is breaking her promise to not go shopping, which she was obliged to do, but that *pro tanto* obligation has been overridden by a more important moral consideration—the well-being of her daughter. What promising does is provide a *pro tanto* reason for doing what one has promised to do.

How do we decide between the two? One standard test for considering whether or not an obligation has been violated is to ask whether or not the failure should result in some kind of compensation to the promisee. If the answer is yes, then there was an obligation that was overridden, if the answer is no, then no obligation was actually violated. A more natural reading of (1) is that when Alice fails to go shopping she has violated the obligation, and that it is not in fact a conditional obligation. This is because she still owes *something* to her mother—perhaps an offer to shop some other time. If, rather than (1) she had uttered (1'), there would be no obligation to do anything.

This observation also cuts against the view that competing pro tanto obligations simply cancel at least one of the obligations in question. One might think that one has a pro tanto obligation to go grocery shopping when it is true that one *would* have an obligation (strictly) to go shopping if there were no opposing considerations. In the case of competing promises there are considerations that cancel one obligation or the other (or possibly even both). But again, this doesn't do justice to the phenomenology above—that the promise imposes an obligation to the agent even when the specific act promised cannot be performed. The picture I propose is that one still has an obligation, even when it cannot be fulfilled and this is cashed out in terms of a requirement to do something relevant that one *can* do, and to feel bad about not being able to fulfill the obligation that one still has. For purely practical purposes, of course, one will not be required to do the impossible.

Someone could also object to (PB) by holding that *intending* to not live up to the promise is actually what is involved in breaking a promise. Since Schwarzenegger intends to raise taxes, he has broken his promise. But this cannot be right. Suppose that he formulated the intention to raise taxes, but then received new information about unexpected sources of revenue for the state, and changed his mind. Simply in virtue of having the intention to break the promise he did not, in fact, break his promise—for the promise to be broken he has to actually raise taxes.

Perhaps, instead, *trying* to break the promise is sufficient for promise-breaking. This alternative suggests a bit more investment than intending. Perhaps Schwarzenegger's suggestion to raise taxes is an *attempt* to not live up to the promise. But again, this doesn't seem right in cases where there is an interceding change of mind. He tries to raise taxes, but then gets new information, changes his mind, and keeps his promise. Even though he did in the past try, he failed, so he ends up not breaking the promise.

But perhaps, even though the promises hasn't been broken, when someone intends to break a promise she has done the *moral equivalent* of breaking a promise. So, what is blameworthy in (A), if anything, is the intention to break the promise, or the trying to break the promise, not that the promise itself has been broken.

Clearly the Kantian condemns the attempt, and, likely even, the intention. Indeed, given the fact that a Kantian is an evaluational internalist this is really what is morally significant about promise-breaking itself.[4] If the agent exercises her will in a clear conflict with the Moral Law, she has acted wrongly. But the more interesting feature of the Kantian view (since most other theories would also condemn immoral intentions) is that it is the same wrong as the wrong involved in a successfully completed promise-breaking. So the Kantian seems to have an insight about this case. While, as a purely formal matter, Schwarzenegger may not have broken the promise, in any respect that matters morally he *has* done the equivalent of breaking his promise. This might be what Schneider is picking up on when he claimed that Schwarzenegger broke his promise. If the promise ends up fulfilled it will be due to *external* factors, that is, factors external to Schwarzenegger's agency—such as the state legislature deciding not to go along with the raising of taxes.

But this kind of response doesn't allow for sophisticated strategy in practical deliberation. Suppose that Schwarzenegger has formed the intention to break his promise *if necessary*. However, he predicts that the state legislature will not go along with the proposal. Indeed, that prediction is an important consideration for him in making the proposal. He is predicting that he will not have to break his promise. On the Kantian view this seems equally impermissible. But a consequentialist would hold that it is perfectly fine (given, of course, that raising taxes has negative utility in this context). On the consequentialist view what Schwarzenegger is doing may not be blameworthy—it *depends* on the other circumstances. This same point holds for *trying*.

The Kantian position is quite extreme. It would also condemn intending to break a promise even when no promise was actually made. Perhaps Schwarzenegger only dreamt he made a promise. Or, to use an example from the other Schwarzenegger career, he "promised" while enmeshed in a virtual reality that he thought was real, though it actually wasn't. The actuality of the promise in the sense of there being a promisee on the other end to satisfy any "uptake" conditions is irrelevant on the Kantian view. The agent simply needs to believe it.[5]

Again, for the consequentialist the immorality of this will depend on effects. There may well be good reasons to intend to break a promise. It may even be the case, in some instances, where intending to break the promise is the best strategy for making sure the promise is actually fulfilled. This is a real strength for the consequentialist position. In the case of the Kantian, promising *for real* drops out of the moral equation, whereas for the consequentialist it is still in the game, so to speak. It really is the *actual* promise-breaking that is important. Intending to break a promise may still be bad, of course, but whatever it is it is not he moral equivalent of actually breaking a promise.

II. INEVITABLY BROKEN PROMISES

There is an analogy to be drawn between (A) and seemingly paradoxical promising cases considered by ancient and medieval philosophers. Aristotle used an interesting promise-breaking case to present his "solution" to the Liar Paradox—the example of the man who promises to break his promise to go to Athens. The idea was that this is like telling the truth about being a liar. If we relativize the lies, he thought, the paradox dissolves. I'm not interested in the paradox, but I am interested in the case.[6] Later commentators thought the really interesting feature of this case was practical. What ought the man do? Should he keep his first order promise, and thereby break the metapromise, or should he keep the metapromise? Giles of Rome believed that the metapromise was sinful, so that's the one that should be broken. In any case, this is an example of a case in which breaking *a* promise is inevitable. It seems a counterexample to the absolutist prohibition against promise-breaking. The absolutist needs to modify the view that all first order promises must be kept but that some second order promises can be broken without blame, depending on the circumstances.

To pursue the analogy, it could be that the critics of Schwarzenegger are protesting that he is, in effect, promising to break his promise. Even if it turns out that he doesn't have to break his promise not to raise taxes, this kind of promise is still blameworthy, since he is promising to do something that is inherently bad. They would hold that the metapromise is sinful. It is like any other promise to do something bad—one may have undertaken an obligation to a particular individual to do something bad, but one is not obligated to do it—indeed, one is obligated to break one's promise under those circumstances. Promising to do the immoral, "wicked promises," are interesting because it isn't clear that they violate the claim that promises entail obligation, though they are often taken to show this. What these cases show at best is that there is no absolute obligation to do what was promised attached to making a promise.

There are two ways to frame the promise to break a promise. In (A) we have a case in which the agent promises to break a promise that he made in the past—we can call these *retrospective metapromises*. There are also cases in which the agent ahead of time promises to break a promise she will make in the future—we can call these *prospective metapromises*. The following is an example:

> (S) Samantha is the governor of a large state. She would like to be able to finance statewide health care for all the citizens in the state. She knows that if she promises, at the next meeting of the state legislature, to try to block such legislation, then her opponents will, reflexively, support heath care. Her advisors are appalled, so she promises them that she will break that future promise, should it become necessary.

(S) seems worse than (A). This is because not only does Samantha intend to break her promise, but she has a long-term plan to do so, whereas Schwarzenegger could just be rationally responding to new information. (A) strikes me as one of those situations that politicians frequently find themselves in, due to over promising. They need to assure voters in order to get elected, and then confront practical problems with living up to those assurances later. Maybe they shouldn't make so many promises. They should be far more cautious and double check that what they have promised on various occasions are things that are, *practically*, compatible with each other and not merely compatible in an ideal world.

However, agents also need to worry about being overly cautious. Someone who cuts back on promises, cuts back on the obligations he incurs. The extreme is the person who never promises because he's worried about whether he will be able to fulfill them all is not participating in an important facet of social morality. As Stephen Darwall notes, we can view promises as one type of transaction. Other transactions, which rely on mutual recognition of authority and status between members of the moral community, also bring about obligations. Other examples are things like ordinary agreements to go for a walk, or eat lunch.[7] While I disagree with Darwall on the source of the obligation, it is quite clear that these transactions are common. Trying to minimize them would involve cutting out interactions that enhance our lives. Of course, one needs to be responsible in taking on these obligations, but there also need to be norms governing transaction clashes. These norms hold that in dilemma situations—including fairly mild ones, such as arranging to go for a walk with two different people at the same time—the well intentioned person has some guidance in how to navigate the conflicting transactions. The common-sense norm, which I suggest here, is that when one promises to x one takes on a *pro tanto* obligation to x, and what this means specifically in the case of promises and other transactions is that one has taken on an obligation to x, and when one breaks a promise, even when one has to break a promise, there is a debt. Then there are norms in place to settle that debt—this specifies satisfying the next best practically feasible alternative. In the case of over promising, one then needs to consider which promise is the most important under the present circumstances. Of course, sometimes this might not be possible, particularly in institutional settings.

One possible example of over promising that illustrates this arises in the airline industry. It is the overbooking of flights. Essentially, when overbooking, an airline is promising a seat on a flight to too many people, more people than the airline has seats for. The airline cannot keep all the promises. The practice is defended because the airline can predict that a certain number of people will not show up for the flight. By overbooking the airline increases efficiency by making sure all seats are filled. This is good for the airline, and drives down flight costs. It also leads to less pollution, so there are environmental benefits. The usual defense is that the alternatives to overbooking have not proven successful (e.g. penalizing no-shows, etc.). Given that we care about increased airline efficiency, reducing pollution, and so on, and given we find the arguments that are supposed to show that alternatives have failed, can overbooking be justified? Yes. Again, the Kantian would likely disagree. Of course, in this particular case when the over promises are made the airline doesn't know which ones *in particular* that it will be breaking, if any. But that shouldn't make a morally relevant difference to the Kantian. Note also that the promises that can't be kept in the overbooking cases don't somehow become null and void, devoid of normative force. The airline owes compensation in those cases *because* of the promise. In these sorts of cases one honors as many as possible, and then compensates the others.

Samantha in the case described above has put herself into a situation where she may be forced to break a promise. She cannot both keep the promise to her advisors and keep the promise to the legislators. She has an obligation to block health care legislation and she has an obligation to break her promise to block health care legislation. She is not *able* to satisfy her overall obligation, since the discrete ones are incompatible. Does she still have an obligation to the people she disappoints? Yes. Indeed, in this case given her normative commitments she will opt to break the first order promise of blocking health legislation. Having let down some of her colleagues, she owes something to them. What, specifically, she owes doesn't much matter. Perhaps it's just an apology, or help with some other legislative initiatives, and so forth. But that something is owed indicates that the obligation doesn't just evaporate simply because the promise cannot be kept, given that the metapromise is kept. Thus, promises entail *pro tanto* obligations.

So, I'd like to suggest that "ought" does not imply "can." There are some promises that cannot be kept, that will inevitably be broken, and those promises still entail obligations. But this sounds drastic, I will argue, because promising provides a special, conventional, context. It is one in which we have enormous interests at stake in maintaining.

III. WHY WE THINK "OUGHT" STRICTLY IMPLIES "CAN"

The "ought" implies "can" claim (OIC) is the topic of much debate.

(OIC) S has an obligation to do *x* only if S can (is able to) do *x*.

The OIC claim places a constraint on when someone can be said to be under an obligation. If the putative obligation is not something the agent has the ability to fulfill, then there is, in fact, no obligation at all. Obligations are supposed to indicate what can be reasonably morally expected of someone and doing the impossible cannot be reasonably expected.

Some writers have claimed that, plausible though it seems, OIC is false. One argument used against the principle is offered by Walter Sinnott-Armstrong, and is very relevant to the promising cases. He points out that if OIC is true, then "an agent could escape having to do something simply by making himself unable to do it."[8] The example he uses is that of Adams who, at noon, promises to meet Brown at 6 p.m., but then goes to a movie at 5 p.m., which makes it the case that he cannot meet Brown at 6 (since the theater is too far away). Is it true at 5 p.m. that Adams has an obligation to meet Brown at 6 p.m.? Not if OIC is true. And, he argues, this is strongly counterintuitive—it would be quite reasonable for Brown to castigate Adams at 6 p.m. for not living up to his obligations. "He ought to be here now!" is reasonable and true, even if he can't be "here, now." Lots of similar cases can be provided. The general worry is that OIC gives people an obligation loophole. And one can see how this would be worrying when it comes to promises. Can I avoid an obligation by framing my promise in such a way as to include an impossibility? Sinnott-Armstrong's case trades on the agent taking advantage of running out of time. A promisor could simply promise something that can't be done—perhaps via a conjunction—and escape obligation. Again, this seems highly counterintuitive.

However, there's no denying that something like OIC seems incredibly plausible, so we need to try to isolate the kernel of truth in OIC. Sinnott-Armstrong and Michael Stocker have both suggested that we consider that something like "ought" conversationally implies "can" (OCIC). If OIC is interpreted as expressing simply a conversational implicature, then it can be true that I ought to do something even though I can't do it.[9] This would explain why

(2) I ought to help my mom tonight, but I can't do it because my car broke down

can be true rather than just incoherent or confused. One characteristic of conversational implication is that it can be cancelled. Example (2) illustrates that as well. The "but" cancels the implication that the promisor can help his mom tonight. How the conversational implication works is determined by pragmatics. That is, there are features of the context in which the ought-claim is uttered that determine how we interpret the implication. Sinnott-Armstrong lists, as examples, advising, blaming, and deliberating. Though the standard is that OCIC, there are cases where it doesn't. Promising to break promises, I hold, would be one of those cases. Also, Sinnott-Armstrong (1987) suggested this strategy as a way of getting out of the promising paradox mentioned at the beginning. If we deny OIC, then we can keep "promises entail obligation" and "people sometimes make promises they can't keep."[10]

Imagine that the speaker's sister says:

(3) You ought to help Mom tonight.

And the speaker responds:

(4) But I can't since my car broke down.

The truth of (4) does not show that (3) is false, on the OCIC view that Sinnott-Armstrong recommends. What (4) does is speak to the issue of what is normally conversationally implied by (3), that is, that one can do it. So, Sinnott-Armstrong claims that statements like (3) which are advising statements typically conversationally imply "can." But when a person is deliberating about what to do there is no such implication.

Statements like (2) seem perfectly natural. The following, however, is odd sounding:

(5) I promise to x, even if I can't.

If the implicature from "ought" to "can" is cancelable, and OCIC is true, then (5) is puzzling. Is this a problem, then, for OCIC? An alternative pragmatic explanation of the implicature is to claim that "ought" *conventionally*, rather than strictly or conversationally, implies "can." Some of the differences between conversational and conventional are that conventional implication cannot be canceled, and the conventional implication is not calculable from the Gricean rules of conversation. But (2) demonstrates that the implicature from "ought" to "can" (ability) is cancelable. Example (5), however, deals with the move from *promising* to *ability*. Given we want to keep "some people make promises they can't keep" then promising does not entail ability, nor does it semantically presuppose it. Since the implicature seems uncancelable, given the oddity of (5), it is not an example of a conversational implicature. But it does seem that here we can make use of *conventional* implication without being inconsistent. Unlike entailment, implicature (either conversational or conventional) has to do with *how* something is said. In the case of "ought" and "can" there is an implicature that is conversational, but in the case of promises and abilities the implicature is conventional. Whenever I say "I promise to *x*" for the promise to be felicitous I must believe that I can *x*. Both place the relation in the realm of pragmatics. The pragmatics of promising, one could argue, presuppose (in a way to be discussed further below) that one thinks one can, and that one thinks one's audience thinks one can.[11]

This analysis of the oddity of (5) is supported by the very commonly held view that promising is a conventional practice. One needn't commit oneself to an entirely practice based account to hold this modest view about promising. However, the practice based accounts offer insightful observations about the conventional nature of promising, even if one doesn't believe such accounts give an exhaustive explanation of their normativity. The classic example is Rawls's view that making a promise involves a background of rules of a kind of practice.[12] This can be given a utilitarian or nonutilitarian basis, but the basic idea is that when people engage in promises they are benefiting from the social practice and are bound by its rules. Failure can result in erosion of the practice, which in turn has a negative impact on the social good supported by the practice, or, as Rawls himself would maintain, is not fair since the promise-breakers benefit without taking on the costs. In the case of promises, this is keeping the promise that was made.

Or, against the social practices account, one could point to Scanlon's account, which holds that promises are a kind of action that give rise to expectations in others, and the wrong in breaking a promise has to do with disappointed expectations of the promisee, not harms to the social group as a whole.[13] These sorts of accounts all face difficulties in accounting for the source of normativity for the act of promise making. As others have pointed out, *even if* Scanlon is right that practice accounts don't account for the source of normativity, it is still quite true that promising depends on social practices.[14] The two need to be kept distinct. What I need to account for in the conventional implication with respect to promises and abilities is just the idea that social practices underlie promising regardless of the normativity issue. This points to something true about the pragmatics of our promises, independent from this particular issue of how they get their normative force. In the background, then, will be assumptions of the sort I mentioned here—that the promisor sincerely and with good reason believes she has the ability to keep the promise.

A lot of the case for abandoning OIC rests on our intuitions about what utterances sound natural to us. Defenders of OIC will of course claim that in ordinary language we employ a variety of different senses of "ought"—and, when it comes to OIC the only "oughts" for which OIC obtains are the "oughts" that mean "obligation" or something close to that, like "has most reason to do, all things considered." In the cases that Sinnott-Armstrong discusses to support his claim, the "oughts" are weaker—having to do with evaluating someone's action as a negative example for others (for example). So, it could be that when one utters (2) what one means in the first half of the utterance is that "It would be a good thing for me to help Mom tonight" rather than "I have an obligation to help Mom tonight."

So, switching to OCIC seems like a very good idea to me, and worth looking into further. Since conversational implication relies so much on pragmatics, one further way of understanding the relation between "ought" and "can" is that "can" is a pragmatic presupposition of many "ought" utterances—consider the first part of (2),

(2a) I ought to help my mom tonight.

If "can" is a pragmatic presupposition of "ought" then "I can help my mom tonight" is a pragmatic presupposition of (2a) that I negated by uttering the latter half of (2). It is in virtue of the pragmatic presupposition that we get the conversational implication.

To say that an utterance pragmatically presupposes something, let's say, F, is to say that whenever the utterance is used or made in a conversationally acceptable manner, the speaker both assumes F and takes his audience to assume F.[15]

So, if Alice says that she is obligated to go grocery shopping for her mother, then it is reasonable to assume that she believes she can do it and it is reasonable for the audience to assume she can. But it does not follow from this that it is true that she can. So, in ordinary conversational contexts "I am obligated to *x*" presupposes "I can do *x*." It is pragmatic rather than semantic because "can" is not part of the meaning of the term "ought." When we move to promises and what they imply, the conventions of promising are those of providing assurance. When one utters a promise one is assuring one's audience that one will do something, not simply predicting that one will do it. So, when one utters something of the form of (5) it looks pragmatically paradoxical, since one is assuring and then, in the same breath, taking away the assurance. Consider a slight variation:

(5a) I promise to *x*, but I might not be able to *x*.

This sounds odd, too, because the "might not be able to" detracts from the assurance function.

When I say "I promise…" given the appropriate uptake conditions I thereby have an obligation, but I don't thereby have an ability. When I claim to have an obligation to do something, the assumption is that I believe that I can do it, but can is not strictly implied and is not part of the truth conditions of "I ought." Now consider:

(5b) I promise to go shopping for my mom, *even if* I can't do it.

This sounds really strange. It sounds strange because it looks like the utterer has doubts about whether or not she can actually help her Mom. Or, to employ Gricean terminology, it actually sounds like she flouting a conversational maxim. Example (5b) doesn't look like part of a cooperative exchange—instead, it looks sarcastic. Given we assume that when people promise they at least believe they can keep the promise, and that is part of the normal context for promising, (5b) reads as a violation of the cooperative principle. And therein lies its oddness. Promises give rise to obligations, and they do so with the expectation that the agent uttering the promise believes she can fulfill the promise. To borrow terminology from Searle, and other speech-act theorists, we might then make this a condition of a *felicitous* promise. The promisor must believe that she can do what she promises to do.

(6) I have an obligation to go shopping for my mom, even if I can't do it.

This doesn't read as oddly as (5b). When one utters (6), unlike (5b), one is not taking an obligation on oneself. One is simply recognizing that an obligation exists.

If obligations entail the ability to fulfill the obligation, and if promises entail obligations (even *pro tanto* ones), then promises entail the ability to fulfill them, so that "I promise *x*" entails "I can do *x*" so that "I can do *x*" is part of the truth conditions for "I promise to do *x*," and this just seems wildly implausible.

One might try to deny this by arguing that it is not implausible at all, that instead we often think of "I promise to *x*" as being conditional on the ability to do *x*, so that it really ought to read "I promise to *x*, if I can *x*." This treats what I'm viewing as a pragmatic factor, or pragmatic presupposition as really being semantic, part of the meaning of the promise itself. But this doesn't seem right to me for the same reason that using other conditionals doesn't seem right to me. If Susan promises to solve a puzzle for her friend, and then it turns out the puzzle was an impossible one, it doesn't seem right to say there was no promise at all that went unfulfilled there. At least Susan should say she's sorry and offer to buy her friend a cup of coffee, or do something that is possible—that is, a practically feasible alternative. The reaction to the failure in the case of viewing it conditionally just doesn't seem right. Now, the claim "But I can't" does get one off the hook, but it gets one off the hook the same way that "But I had an emergency!" or "I couldn't get a babysitter!" gets one off the hook. And that's because the obligations that promises give rise to are pro tanto. It's not that there is no obligation there at all. Inabilities get one off the hook, but in a limited way—and some inabilities are logical and physical, whereas some involve prospective violations of more significant norms. They do not *void* the obligation to do what one has promised. But such promises are inevitably broken, and because of the existing obligation a moral debt is incurred. And there are norms governing the fulfillment of these moral debts.

The upshot of this view is that, in a way, one can have one's cake and eat it too. One has a pro tanto obligation to keep even impossible promises, though the obligation is overridden. Since these promises are inevitably broken they incur a moral debt. So, override does not mean utterly eliminate, instead, it puts pressure on the agent to do the best she *can*. When we make the claim that promises entail obligations we are committed to two things: one, that when S promises A to *x*, S has taken on a pro tanto obligation to *x* that can be overridden for practical purposes by an inability, but the inability does not eliminate the obligation; so, when S promises A to *x*, S is obligated to *x* to A, even when there are good reasons not to *x*; and "ought" does not imply "can," because the "ought" exists even when the agent can't. Promises, even ones one cannot perform, carry with them a commitment.

ACKNOWLEDGMENT

I would like to think the other participants in the Promising Conference organized by Hanoch Sheinman at Rice University for their very helpful feedback on this essay. I would also like to thank Hanoch Sheinman in particular for his very helpful written comments on an earlier draft.

NOTES

1. See Kagan (1989: 16–17) for more on the distinction.
2. Broadcast on Wolf Blitzer's *Situation Room*, August 7, 2008.
3. I discuss this paradox in Driver (1983).
4. An evaluational internalist holds that the moral quality of x (action, character trait, etc.) is determined by factors internal to agency, such as the agent's motives or intentions. For more on the distinction between evaluational internalism/externalism see Driver (2001).
5. I discuss these kinds of scenarios in Driver (2007).
6. For more on this example, and how it fails to capture the complexity of the Liar Paradox, see Sorensen (2006).
7. Stephen Darwall, "Demystifying Promises," this book. Darwall notes examples used by Gilbert (1990).
8. Sinnott-Armstrong (1984: 252).
9. Stocker (1971); Sinnott-Armstrong (1984).
10. Sinnott-Armstrong focuses on a critique of Martinich's solution, which is to deny that people sometimes make promises they can't keep.

11. Or, perhaps a cleaner case is "Alice promised to do x, even though she can't do x (and everyone is aware of this)."

12. Rawls (1955).

13. Scanlon (1990).

14. Kolodny and Wallace (2003).

15. This characterization is due to Stalnaker (1999: 47–63).

REFERENCES

Driver, J. 2007. "Dream Immorality." *Philosophy* 82: 5–22.

———. 1983. "Promises, Obligations, and Abilities." *Philosophical Studies* 44: 221–223.

———. *Uneasy Virtue*. 2001. New York: Cambridge University Press.

Gilbert, M. 1990. "Walking Together: A Paradigmatic Social Phenomenon." *Midwest Studies in Philosophy* 15: 1–14.

Grice, H. P. 1961. "The Causal Theory of Perception." *Proceedings of the Aristotelian Society*, supp., 35: 121–152.

———. 1981. "Presupposition and Conversational Implication." In P. Cole, ed., *Radical Pragmatics*. New York: Academic Press, 183–198.

Kagan, S. 1989. *The Limits of Morality*. Oxford: Oxford University Press.

Kolodny, N. and R. J. Wallace. 2003. "Promises and Practices Revisited." *Philosophy and Public Affairs* 31: 119–154.

Martinich, A. P. 1985. "A Solution to a Paradox of Promising." *Philosophia* 15: 117–122.

Rawls, John. 1955. "Two Concepts of Rules." *Philosophical Review* 64: 3–32.

Scanlon, T. M. 1990. "Promises and Practices." *Philosophy andPublic Affairs* 19: 199–226.

Sinnott-Armstrong, W. 1984. "'Ought' Conversationally Implies 'Can,'" *Philosophical Review* 93: 249–261.

———. 1987. "A Resolution to a Paradox of Promising." *Philosophia* 17: 77–82.

Sorensen, R. 2006. *A Brief History of the Paradox*. New York: Oxford University Press.

Stalnaker, R. 1999. "Pragmatic Presuppositions," In *Context and Content*. New York: Oxford University Press, 47–63.

Stocker, M. 1971. "'Ought' and 'Can.'" *Australasian Journal of Philosophy* 49: 303–316.

Chapter 8

The Value of Making and Keeping Promises

Michael Smith

Abstract

Consequentialists hold, quite in general, that what we are obliged to do are those things, among the alternatives available to us, that uniquely maximize value and minimize disvalue. But surely this cannot be right, some people say, because we may have an obligation to (say) keep a promise we made to someone whether or not doing so happens to maximize value and minimize disvalue. Fully understanding how we are able to put ourselves under an obligation to another person by making him a promise is, they think, thus the first step in a move away from a consequentialist analysis of obligation in general. But is this right? The issue turns on whether gaining a full understanding of how we are able to put ourselves under an obligation to another person by promising is a matter of coming to appreciate the special values produced by making promises. I will argue not just that it is, but that the opponents of this view are themselves committed to it by their own lights.

What is the value of making and keeping promises? In what follows I will describe and evaluate several different answers to this question. Equipped with one sort of answer in particular, my hope is that we might inch our way toward a better understanding of both promissory obligation and the long-standing dispute in moral philosophy between consequentialists and nonconsequentialists.

The essay divides into five sections. I begin by explaining the connection between understanding the nature of promissory obligation, on the one hand and the debate in moral philosophy between consequentialists and nonconsequentialists on the other (section I). Since consequentialist theories of obligation will occupy center stage in what follows, I next go on to offer some preliminary clarification of what it is for a theory to be consequentialist (section II). Equipped with this account of what it is for a theory to be consequentialist, I then describe and evaluate two accounts of the value of making and keeping promises and the consequentialist accounts of promissory obligation to which they give rise (section III). This leads to a further clarification of what it is for a theory to be consequentialist (section IV) and a description and evaluation of one last consequentialist account of promissory obligation (section V).

To anticipate, the moral of the essay is that consequentialists have the upper hand in the debate over the nature of promissory obligation. The argument given for this conclusion is, however, sufficiently general and abstract that it will require us to take no stand at all on what the value associated with promissory obligation is. The conclusion, in other words, is that promissory obligation should be understood in consequentialist terms no matter what value it is associated with.

I. CONSEQUENTIALISM, NORMATIVE REASONS, AND PROMISSORY OBLIGATIONS

As I understand it, the dispute in moral philosophy between consequentialists and nonconsequentialists is a dispute about the nature of permissibility and impermissibility. According to consequentialists, facts about permissibility and impermissibility reduce to facts about what people can do—that is, facts about the options that people have in the circumstances of action in which they find themselves—together with facts about the values of the outcomes of their doing the various things that they can do. The opponents of consequentialism, by contrast, deny that a reduction of this kind is possible.

Myself I think of this as a debate within serious metaphysics (Smith 2005)—the issue, as I understand it, is whether facts of one kind consist in facts of another—but that may just reflect my own realist leanings. Since irrealists have their own metaphysically less serious way of understanding talk of "facts" about permissibility and impermissibility, and hence their own way of understanding talk of the "reduction" of one set of facts to another, they too can presumably take sides in the dispute between consequentialists and nonconsequentialists, as I have characterized it. Despite the realist-sounding language, I therefore take it that this characterization of consequentialism in terms of its reductionist ambition is neutral on the issue of realism versus irrealism.

So understood, consequentialism is a broad church that allows for much disagreement, as consequentialists can and do differ among themselves about the precise nature of the reduction. But, at least when understood in this broad church way, it has always seemed to me that some sort of consequentialism just has to be correct. It has to be correct because consequentialism, so understood, dovetails so readily with an extremely plausible and widely held account of the nature of normative reasons, an account that Joseph Raz dubs the "classical" account (Raz 1999, p. 23) and a plausible conceptual truth about moral obligation. Let me explain the connection between these two ideas.

According to Raz,

> one approach to the explanation of agency, with origins in the writings of Plato and Aristotle, takes acting for a reason to be the distinctive and central case of human agency.... Reason is then explained in part by invoking value: valuable aspects of the world constitute reasons. (Raz 1999, p. 22)

According to the classical account, what it is for an agent to have a normative reason to act in a certain way is thus for there to be some value realized by his acting in that way.

John Mackie further explains what it is for something to have value, according to the classical account of normative reasons, as follows.

> Values themselves have been seen as at once prescriptive and objective.... Sidgwick [for example] argues that... what ought to be "must in another sense have objective existence: it must be an object of knowledge and as such the same for all minds"; but he says that the affirmations of this science "are also precepts," and he speaks of pleasure itself as "an end absolutely prescribed by reason." (Mackie 1977, pp. 23–24)

Sidgwick's idea is thus that something has value just in case—and here I paraphrase his idea of something's being "an end absolutely prescribed by reason"—there is a requirement of reason that we desire or approve or aim at it.

Though he doesn't trace the idea back to its classical origins, Thomas M. Scanlon holds a very similar conception of values.

> To value something is to take oneself to have reasons for holding certain positive attitudes toward it and for acting in certain ways in regard to it. Exactly what these reasons are, and what actions and attitudes they support, will be different in different cases. They generally include, as a common core, reasons for admiring the thing and for respecting it. (Scanlon 1998: 95)

Thus, according to Scanlon, to value something is, inter alia, to take oneself to have reasons for desiring or approving or aiming at it, from which it presumably follows that for that thing to be valuable is, inter alia, for there to be reasons for desiring or approving or aiming at it. On the assumption that reason requires us to be sensitive to such reasons as there for holding certain positive attitudes, Scanlon's idea and Sidgwick's thus amount to much the same thing.

If what Sidgwick and Scanlon say about the nature of value is along the right lines, then it should come as no surprise that, according to the classical account, what an agent has a normative reason to do is fixed by the values associated with his actions. For it follows from the fact that an agent's actions realize something of value that, to put it in the way I paraphrased Sidgwick, there is a requirement of reason that he desires or approves or aims at that thing. What better candidate could there be for what agents have normative reason to do than what they are required by reason to desire or approve or aim at? The dispositional theory of value and normative reasons that I myself have developed elsewhere is, of course, simply a further elaboration and refinement of this classical account (Smith 1994, 2005).

I said earlier that consequentialism dovetails well with a plausible account of normative reasons. It should now be clear why I said this. For when we add to the classical account of what it is for someone to have a normative reason the observation that is a contradiction in terms to suppose that an agent could have an obligation to act in a certain way without his having a normative reason to act in that way, it seems hard to resist the conclusion that facts about agents' obligations themselves consist in the very facts about the values of the outcomes of their actions that their normative reasons consist in. Facts about agents' obligations thus reduce to facts about their normative reasons, which, in their turn, reduce to facts about the values of the outcomes of the actions they can perform. And with the reduction of facts about obligation to facts about value in hand, the reduction of facts about permissibility and impermissibility to facts about value simply follows suit.

Notwithstanding the evident plausibility of consequentialism, when argued for along such lines, it is striking that so many philosophers who accept the classical account of normative reasons—Raz himself is an example (Raz 1986)—reject consequentialism. Moreover, several philosophers—Scanlon is a notable example (Scanlon 1998)—argue that promissory obligation in particular resists capture in consequentialist terms. Here, accordingly, we find the rationale for asking what value there is in making and keeping promises. For, to focus for the moment on the value of keeping promises, if an agent is obliged to keep the promises he makes, then, on pain of contradiction, that commits us to the conclusion that there is a normative reason for him to do so, and the fact that there is a normative reason for an agent to keep promises he makes commits us to the conclusion that there is some value realized by his keeping the promises he makes. But if this is right, then what is that value? And how does the resulting consequentialist account of promissory obligation, grounded in that value, compare to the accounts on offer that supposedly resist being fit into a consequentialist mould? A similar set of questions arises about the permissibility of making promises.

Before answering these questions it is important that we get clearer about what it is for a theory to be consequentialist. Earlier I said that consequentialists disagree among themselves about the exact nature of the reduction of facts about permissibility and impermissibility to facts about what agents can do and facts about the values of the outcomes of the things that they can do. Though some of these disagreements can safely be put to one side, others will need to be addressed. They will need to be addressed because, as we will see, some theorists think that these disagreements bear on the plausibility of consequentialism itself. It is important to see that this is a mistake, as only so will we get clear about the sorts of values that might be realized by making and keeping promises.

II. CONSEQUENTIALISM CLARIFIED

As I said, the major source of disagreement among consequentialists concerns the precise nature of the reduction of permissibility to value. Let me begin by describing some different aspects of this reduction and some of the different views that consequentialists might take.

(i) Maximizing Views versus Satisficing Views

Some consequentialists think that an act is permitted only if it maximizes value. Others disagree. They think that an act is permitted so long as it produces enough in the way of value; that maximization isn't required. This is the well-known debate within the consequentialist camp between *maximizers* and *satisficers* (Slote and Pettit 1984). For ease of exposition, I will assume that maximization is required in what follows. An act is permitted, according to the maximizers, just in case it one of the acts among an agent's options that maximizes value, and it is obligatory just in case it is uniquely permissible. But nothing I say will turn on this assumption. My arguments could all quite easily be recast if it turns out that satisficing is all that is required.

(ii) Monism versus Pluralism

Another disagreement among consequentialists concerns the number of values that are in play when we rank outcomes. Some consequentialists think that there is just one value—most famously, pleasure—while others think that there are many different values, all of which have to be weighed against each another in determining an overall ranking of outcomes. This is the well-known debate within the consequentialist camp between *monists* (Mill 1861) and *pluralists* (Moore 1903). For ease of exposition I will only ever talk about one value at a time. Though this may make it sound like I embrace some form of monism, what I have to say is in fact noncommittal on the issue of monism versus pluralism. Everything I say is meant to be consistent with the truth of pluralism.

(iii) Actual Outcome Views versus Expected Outcome Views

Another disagreement that arises within the consequentialist camp that can safely be put to one side is that between those who hold the *actual outcome* view (Railton 1984) and those who hold the *expected outcome* view (Jackson 1991). Consequentialists who hold the actual outcome view think that facts about the permissibility of an agent's actions are a function of the value of the actual outcomes of that agent's options, whereas those who hold the expected outcome view think that they are a function of the expected value of the outcomes of the agent's options. For ease of exposition, I will simply assume that facts about the permissibility of an agent's actions are a function of the value of the actual outcomes of his options in what follows. But, again, nothing I say will turn on this assumption. The arguments I give could all be recast in terms of the expected outcome view, if it turns out that that is the correct view to hold.

(iv) Commensurability Views versus Incommensurability Views

Another disagreement that can arise within the consequentialist camp is a disagreement among pluralists. Pluralists hold that outcomes differ from each other in various respects. They differ not just in how much of any particular value is instantiated, but also in which values are instantiated. Pluralists can therefore disagree among themselves about whether, notwithstanding these differences between outcomes, it is possible to provide a single ranking of outcomes from best to worst. Those pluralist consequentialists who think that outcomes can be ranked from best to worst hold that the different values that are instantiated in the outcomes are *commensurable* with each other. Those who think that they cannot hold that at least some values are *incommensurable*: that when different values are at stake there is sometimes no saying which outcome is better and which is worse.

This disagreement is a little more tricky, as some who oppose consequentialism do so precisely on the grounds that, though all normative reasons are grounded in facts about values, some values are incommensurable (Raz 1986). But it is difficult to see why the incommensurability of certain values is supposed to be a barrier to the truth of some sort of consequentialism. At most, what this shows is that facts about the permissibility and impermissibility of certain of an agent's actions are themselves relativized to options, all of which instantiate values that are commensurable. Certain of an agent's actions will therefore be permissible relative to one range of options, and others will be permissible relative to a different range of options, and there will be no fact of the matter about whether his actions are permissible or impermissible simpliciter: that is, relative to all of his options. Since this is still a reductionist doctrine—facts about the permissibility and impermissibility of the agent's actions still reduce to facts about the values of his options—it still qualifies as a form of consequentialism, at least as consequentialism was defined at the outset. The incommensurability of certain values thus seems to me to be no barrier to the truth of consequentialism.

(v) Global Consequentialism versus Local Consequentialism

One claim to which I am committed by my characterization of consequentialism, and which does affect the cogency of the arguments that follow, is that consequentialists cannot avail themselves of a rule-consequentialist account of promissory obligation. This is because, as I have characterized it, consequentialism is the view that an act is obligatory only if it is an act, among the agent's options, that maximizes value. This is an *act*-consequentialist account of what it is for an action to be obligatory. I must therefore deny the *rule*-consequentialist's suggestion that an act is obligatory only if it is permitted by the rules the acceptance of which is value maximizing, never mind about whether the act itself is value-maximizing (Hooker 2000).

Of course, rule-consequentialism of this kind still falls within an even broader consequentialist church than the one that I have identified, a church that shares a reductionist ambition much like the one I have spelled out. For, according to this kind of rule-consequentialism, facts about an agent's obligations still reduce, inter alia, to facts about the values of outcomes. It is just that the values in question are not the values of the outcomes of the various *acts* that the agent had available to him, but are rather the values of the outcomes of accepting the various alternative *rules* that might be accepted. But I think that this even broader consequentialist church is one to which we will be attracted only if we forget the argument for consequentialism that was outlined earlier. Rule-consequentialism of the kind just described implausibly breaks the connection between an agent's having an obligation to act in a certain way and his having a normative reason to act in that way.

In order to see that this is so, remember that, according to the standard view of what it is for an agent to have a normative reason to act in a certain way, his having such a reason amounts to there being something valuable realized by his acting in that way. To paraphrase Sidgwick, the agent must be required by reason to desire, or approve, or aim at whatever it is that is realized by his action. Bearing this in mind, the problem with the kind of rule-consequentialism just described should be clear. For there is no reason at all to suppose that there is any value realized by an agent's action when he acts in accordance with a rule the acceptance of which is itself value-maximizing. True enough, his acceptance of a rule requiring him to act in that way must be value-maximizing. He must therefore be required by reason to desire, or approve, or aim at the outcome of his acceptance of the rule. But his acting in accordance with that rule need not be value-maximizing. It may even be value-minimizing. (In this connection, it is useful to remember what J. J. C. Smart has to say about rule-worship [Smart and Williams 1973, p. 10].) The upshot is thus that, at least according to the kind of rule-consequentialism we have been considering up until now, an agent may have a normative reason *not to do* what he has an obligation *to do*. To my mind, this is a decisive objection to this kind of rule-consequentialism, as it shows that it entails a contradiction.

Assuming that I am right about this, it might be thought that a certain question becomes rather urgent. For aren't those who advance the sort of rule-consequentialism we have been considering right that consequentialism provides us with the resources to answer not just the question "Which are the acts among an agent's options that are value-maximizing?" but also the question "Which are the rules among those that we might accept that are value-maximizing?" And, if they are right about this, then aren't they also right that we need to decide which of these evaluands—acts or rules—is the appropriate evaluand in terms of which to account for facts about obligation?

The answer is that they are of course right that consequentialism provides us with the resources to answer questions about the value of both acts and rules. Indeed, consequentialism provides us with the resources to answer questions about the value of anything and everything that can be evaluated. But the correct conclusion to draw from this is not that one or another of these evaluands must therefore be privileged when it comes to understanding the nature of obligation. The correct conclusion to draw is rather that there are many different claims about obligation that we can make, one corresponding to each of the evaluands. The correct form of consequentialism is thus not some form of *local* consequentialism, according to which we must choose a privileged evaluand and then assess all others in terms of it, but rather *global* consequentialism (Pettit and Smith 2000).

According to global consequentialism, *which acts we ought to perform* is fixed by a comparison of the values of the outcomes of those acts as opposed to those we might have performed instead (this is *act*-consequentialism); *which rules we ought to accept* is fixed by a comparison of the values of accepting those rules as opposed to those we might have accepted instead (this is *rule*-consequentialism, properly conceived, as it is simply a view about which rules we ought to accept, not a view about which acts we ought to perform); *which motives we ought to have* is fixed by a comparison of the values of having those motives as opposed to those we might have had instead (this is *motive*-consequentialism); and so we could go on. These various forms of consequentialism—act, rule, motive, and so on—are thus not alternatives to each other, but are instead all elements of a global consequentialist outlook. This will be important in what follows.

(vi) Welfarism versus Nonwelfarism

Another debate within the consequentialist camp with which I will need to engage in what follows is the debate between *welfarists* and *nonwelfarists* (Sumner 1996). Welfarists hold that the only intrinsic value is well-being; that other putative intrinsic values, in so far as they are values at all, are either a part of well-being or a condition of well-being. Nonwelfarists deny that well-being is the only intrinsic value.

Perhaps the best known version of welfarism is hedonism, the view that the only intrinsic value is pleasure and that the only intrinsic disvalue is pain, and I will begin by assuming that welfarism of this kind is correct. But there are other versions of welfarism as well. Indeed, anyone who takes the plausible view that whether or not a life goes well or badly depends on more than just the amount of pleasure or pain enjoyed by the person whose life it is—those who hold that, for example, how much one achieves can affect how well one's life goes, independently of how much pleasure one gets from those achievements (Griffin 1988)—holds an importantly different version of welfarism. And nonwelfarism too comes in many different varieties. We will consider two such varieties in due course.

(vii) Neutral Values versus Relative Values

With welfarism clearly within our sights, we are in a position to identify a final debate within consequentialism with which I will need to engage, a debate that will loom large in what follows. This is the debate about whether values, be they welfarist or nonwelfarist, are by their nature *neutral*, or whether some values are *relative*.

As I understand it, to say that values are neutral is to make a claim about how the intrinsic value-making features associated with that value are properly to be characterized. Values are neutral when, in order to properly characterize the associated intrinsic value-making features, no mention of a specific agent or evaluator need be made. Values are relative, by contrast, when the proper characterization of the associated intrinsic value-making features requires the mention of an agent or evaluator. The intrinsic value-making features associated with the value of welfare provides a neat illustration of this distinction, an illustration that allows us to bring out the significance of this debate within the consequentialist camp.

Consider *hedonistic ethical egoism*. As I understand it, hedonistic ethical egoism is a consequentialist theory that holds that the only intrinsic value is welfare and that also holds that the intrinsic value-making feature associated with welfare is relative. This is because, according to hedonistic ethical egoism, the intrinsic value-making feature associated with the actions that I ought to perform is *my* pleasure, that associated with the actions you ought to perform is *your* pleasure, that associated with the actions someone else ought to perform is *his* pleasure, and so on: I ought to maximize *my* pleasure, you ought to maximize *your* pleasure, others ought to maximize *their* pleasure, and so on. We cannot properly characterize the value-making features in question if we do not mention agents or evaluators. *Hedonistic utilitarianism* differs from hedonistic ethical egoism precisely in that it holds that the intrinsic value-making feature associated with welfare is neutral: the intrinsic value-making feature associated with everyone's obligations is pleasure, without regard to whose pleasure it is. I ought to maximize pleasure without regard to whose, you ought to maximize pleasure without regard to whose, others ought to maximize pleasure without regard to whose, and so on.

Some philosophers think that hedonistic ethical egoism, so understood, is an incoherent position (Moore 1903). They point out that, on the assumption that hedonistic ethical egoism really is supposed to be a version of consequentialism, the effect of my actions on my pleasure can play a role in fixing what I ought to do only if my pleasure has value, and that the effect of your actions on your pleasure can play a role in fixing what you ought to do only if your pleasure has value. But they then go on to argue that, if just this much is agreed, then it is obscure why the effect of my actions on your pleasure doesn't likewise play a role in fixing what I ought to do as well as playing a role in fixing what you ought to do. The effect of my actions on your pleasure is, after all, an effect that my actions has on something that is admitted to be of value. To suppose that what I ought to do is a function of the effect of my actions on my pleasure alone is thus to suppose that what I ought to do is a function of the effect of my actions on only *some* of what's of value, not *all* of what's of value. And the same goes for the idea that what you ought to do is a function of the effect of your actions on your pleasure alone.

According to this line of argument, consequentialism is therefore committed to the view that if pleasure has value at all, then it has neutral value, not relative value: consequentialists who were inclined to accept hedonistic ethical egoism at first blush should, on reflection, reject that view in favor of hedonistic utilitarianism. And what goes for pleasure, conceived of as a relative value, goes for all of the other values that we might have thought were relative values too, for a similar line of argument will show that it is incoherent to combine consequentialism with the view that there are any relative values at all. The upshot, according to this line of argument, is that consequentialists must suppose that all values are neutral. If this is right then that has a very important impact on our main question. For if consequentialists must suppose that all values are neutral then they will have to say that the value-making features associated with promissory obligations are neutral too.

III. CONSEQUENTIALISM, NEUTRAL VALUES, AND PROMISSORY OBLIGATION

What would a global consequentialist account of promissory obligation grounded in neutral value look like? We get one possible answer to this question if we focus on the account of promissory obligation proffered by a welfarist theory like global hedonistic utilitarianism.

Note, to begin, that if global hedonistic utilitarianism is correct, then it is a contingent empirical matter whether an agent's keeping his promises is obligatory at all. This is because it will be a contingent empirical matter whether an agent's keeping any particular promise he makes will maximize pleasure (here the focus is on hedonistic *act-utilitarian*ism). Having said that, however, we must immediately add that, even if it isn't obligatory for an agent to keep all of the promises that he makes, it may still be the case that he ought to accept the rule that each person should keep all of the promises that he makes (here the focus is on hedonistic *rule-utilitarian*ism), and that it may also be the case that he ought to be motivated to keep all of his own promises (here the focus is on hedonistic *motive* utilitarianism). This is because the amount of pleasure that is caused by an agent's acceptance of the rule that he keeps his own promises, and that caused by his being motivated to keep all of his promises, may be quite different from the amount of pleasure that would be caused by any of the particular acts that accord with those rules or that he would be thus motivated to perform. To repeat, however, all of this depends on empirical contingencies.

Do matters look very different if we abandon welfarism and adopt instead some nonwelfarist account of neutral values? Suppose, for example, we adopt the most favorable nonwelfarist account of neutral value from the point of view of accounting for promissory obligation: suppose we hold that a kept promise is itself an intrinsic neutral value-making feature. Would matters look very different? The answer is that this would make some difference, but not all that much. For it would still be a contingent empirical matter whether an agent's keeping any particular promise he makes maximizes the number of kept promises. Perhaps there would be more kept promises if an agent were to ignore the promises that he makes and saw to it that others kept the promises that they make instead. If so, then he ought to ignore his own promises and see to it that others keep theirs. This too will depend on empirical contingencies. Moving to a nonwelfarist account of neutral values, even one that is most favorable to promissory obligation, thus leaves us with a consequentialist account of promissory obligation that is, in crucial respects, a lot like the account we get from the version of consequentialism that is committed to a welfarist account of neutral values.

Of course, this doesn't show that there is anything wrong with these accounts of promissory obligation. For all that we have said, one or another of these accounts of promissory obligation might be the correct one to adopt. Such will certainly be the case if the neutral values in terms of which these accounts of promissory obligation are given are the only values that there are. For in that case these neutrally characterizable outcomes are the only outcomes that reason is on the side of our desiring or approving of: we quite literally only have reason to care about our keeping our own promises to the extent that our keeping our own promises brings about such neutrally characterizable outcomes. Having said that, however, it must be admitted that neither of the accounts of promissory obligation described are accounts of the kind that we might have expected from a consequentialist *prior* to having any idea about what values there are. Moreover there is, I think, an important reason why we haven't been given an account of the kind that we might have expected. For what's remarkable about both of these accounts of promissory obligation, grounded as they in neutral values, is that an agent's obligations turn out not to be especially targeted on the promises that *he* makes. This is remarkable because promissory obligation, at least as ordinarily understood, *is* so targeted. As ordinarily understood, promissory obligation is such that I ought to keep *my* promises, you ought to keep *your* promises, and others ought to keep *their* promises; to suppose otherwise is to suppose that there is nothing distinctive about promissory obligation at all.

Ex ante, then, we might have expected a consequentialist account of promissory obligation to look for something distinctive about promissory obligation, and the obvious way for it to do this would be to model promissory obligation on the sorts of obligations postulated by hedonistic ethical egoism, rather than on those postulated by hedonistic utilitarianism, or any of its nonwelfarist counterparts. For the obligations postulated by hedonistic ethical egoism are structurally exactly like promissory obligations, as ordinarily understood. They too are targeted on features of the agents in question: I ought to maximize *my* pleasure, you ought to maximize *your* pleasure, and others ought to maximize *their* pleasure. What we might have expected from the consequentialist, then, prior to having any idea what values there are, is an account of what's distinctive about promissory obligation in terms of the particular *relative* value that is promoted by an agent's keeping the promises that he makes, just as hedonistic ethical egoism attempts to account for what's distinctive about our obligations vis-à-vis our own pleasure in terms of the distinctive relative value of our own pleasure. But, of course, this is exactly what the earlier arguments for the incoherence of relative values tell us cannot be done. There are no distinctive relative values promoted by an agent's keeping the promises he makes because there are no relative values full stop.

To sum up, if the argument for the incoherence of combining consequentialism with the view that some values are relative given earlier is correct, consequentialism looks like it will be unable to give an account of promissory obligation as being in any way distinctive. Though it may seem to be a distinctive feature of an agent's promissory obligations that they are targeted on the promises that he himself makes, this turns out to be a mistake, as according to accounts of promissory obligation grounded in neutral values, such obligations are never so targeted. To repeat, this isn't an objection to such accounts of promissory obligation. For if there are only neutral values then reason is only ever on the side of our desiring or approving of outcomes that are neutrally characterizable. Reason isn't on the side of our desiring or approving of anything that is targeted on ourselves. But it does suggest that a rather large burden is being carried by the earlier argument for the incoherence of combining consequentialism with the view that some values are relative. The question we must ask is therefore whether the argument is really convincing. If it is not really convincing—if there is some latent confusion or equivocation—then the way is clear to look again at whether there is some distinctive relative value promoted by an agent's keeping the promises that he makes.

IV. RELATIVE VALUES RECONSIDERED

Here is the crucial part of the argument given earlier:

> Some philosophers... point out that, on the assumption that hedonistic ethical egoism really is supposed to be a version of consequentialism, the effect of my actions on my pleasure can play a role in fixing what I ought to do only if my pleasure has value, and that the effect of your actions on your pleasure can play a role in fixing what you ought to do only if your pleasure has value. But they then go on to argue that, if just this much is agreed, then it is obscure why the effect of my actions on your pleasure doesn't likewise play a role in fixing what I ought to do as well as playing a role in fixing what you ought to do. The effect of my actions on your pleasure is, after all, an effect that my actions have on something that is admitted to be of value.

Despite its apparent plausibility, it seems to me that this step in the argument is crucially flawed. It is flawed because it proceeds without making explicit what it is for something to be of value. Yet when we do make that explicit, it becomes clear that the argument turns on a crucial equivocation (see also Smith 2003).

Let's once again follow Sidgwick's lead and say that something is of value if and only if and because there is a requirement of reason that we desire it, or approve of it, or aim at it. We might initially try formulating this claim as follows:

> ∀x (p is valuable iff and because x is required by reason to desire that p, or approve of p, or aim at p).

But a moment's reflection makes it clear this is at best a very sloppy formulation. What we have is here is a purported reduction of facts about value to facts about the desires, attitudes of approval, and aims that are required by reason. Desirers are therefore explicitly mentioned on the right-hand side, but where exactly are they mentioned on the left-hand side? The answer is that they must be mentioned at least implicitly in our talk of something's being valuable. To properly formulate the claim we should therefore make the mention of desirers on the left hand side explicit as follows:

> ∀x (p is valuable_x iff and because x is required by reason to desire that p, or approve of p, or aim at p).

This reformulation is required because it makes it explicit that the concept of something's being valuable is itself a relational concept. The subscript explicitly signals the relational element.

Armed with this account of what it is for something to be valuable, let's now reconsider the argument for the incoherence of relative value. According to hedonistic ethical egoism, in order to properly characterize the value-making feature that explains why I ought to maximize *my* pleasure, you ought to maximize *your* pleasure, and others ought to maximize *their* pleasure, we must mention an agent or evaluator: *my* pleasure in the case of my obligations, *your* pleasure in the case of yours, the *others* pleasure in the case of the others. They therefore conclude that the values in question are relative, not neutral, a conclusion we can formulate as follows:

> ∀x (x's pleasure is valuable_x)

or, equivalently given our paraphrase of Sidgwick,

> ∀x (x is required by reason to desire that x has pleasure, or to approve of x's having pleasure, or to aim at x's having pleasure)

But once we formulate their idea in this way, it becomes clear that the earlier argument for the incoherence of hedonistic ethical egoism turns on a crucial equivocation. For what follows from the fact that I ought to maximize my pleasure is not that my pleasure is valuable, but that my pleasure is valuable$_{me}$, and what follows from the fact that you ought to maximize your pleasure is not that your pleasure is valuable, but that your pleasure is valuable$_{you}$. And since it does not follow from the fact that my pleasure is valuable$_{me}$ and that yours is valuable$_{you}$ that your pleasure is valuable$_{me}$ or that my pleasure is valuable$_{you}$, so it follows that there is no way to make the equivocation innocent. Your pleasure simply isn't relevant to my obligations, nor is mine relevant to yours, because though reason is on the side of my desiring or aiming at my pleasure, it isn't on the side of my desiring or aiming at yours, and vice versa.

Is it surprising that facts about my obligations are fixed by what's valuable$_{me}$ and that facts about your obligations are fixed by what's valuable$_{you}$? The answer is that it isn't surprising at all, given that we are each obliged to do is, fixed by what we have normative reason to do, and what we each have normative reason to do is fixed by what we are each required by reason to desire, or approve, or aim at (or, to put the point in Scanlon's terms, what we would each desire or approve or aim at if we were maximally sensitive to all of the reasons that there are for desiring or approving or aiming at things). It simply reflects the fact that I may be required by reason to desire a different state of affairs to that which you are required by reason to desire: I may be required to desire that I have pleasure, whereas you are required to desire that you have pleasure. Absent some additional argument or consideration, it is thus simply false that either of us has any normative reason at all, hence any obligation, to bring about each other's pleasure. The quite general argument given earlier for the incoherence of relative value thus collapses.

V. CONSEQUENTIALISM, RELATIVE VALUES, AND PROMISSORY OBLIGATION

The way is therefore clear for a consequentialist to construct an account of promissory obligation grounded in distinctive relative values. But how might he go about doing this? How, in other words, might he try to identify the distinctive relative values that are realized by the fulfillment of our promissory obligations? The consequentialist's best strategy, I think, is to take a leaf out of the book of those who claim to construct nonconsequentialist theories of promissory obligation. Let me briefly illustrate the strategy I have in mind by looking at Scanlon's account of promissory obligation.

According to Scanlon, our obligation to keep the promises we make is explained by (very roughly) the impermissibility of our failing to meet the reasonable expectations that we knowingly create when we make promises.

Though these expectations are ones that we might create without explicitly making promises, promising is one conventional way such expectations can be created. He formulates this idea in the following principle, a principle he dubs "Principle F":

> If (1) X voluntarily and intentionally leads Y to expect that X will ϕ (unless Y consents to X's not doing so); (2) X knows that Y wants to be assured of this; (3) X acts with the aim of providing this assurance, and has good reason to believe that he or she has done so; (4) Y knows that X has the beliefs and intentions just described; (5) X intends for Y to know this, and knows that Y does know it; and (6) Y knows that X has this knowledge and intent; then, in the absence of special justification, X must ϕ unless Y consents to ϕ's not being done. (1998, p. 304)

Principle F is a nonconsequentialist principle, according to Scanlon, because we cannot explain why it is true simply by appealing to the value of the outcome of X's ϕ-ing. But is this true?

There is, I think, a real problem in supposing that it is true. After all, Scanlon presumably has to think that there is a reason for each person to want that (very roughly) when he knowingly creates certain reasonable expectations, he meets the reasonable expectations he thus creates. Each person has to think that there is such a reason because, absent such a reason, people would have no normative reason to do what Principle F tells them they must do. Scanlon's own Principle F would in that case break the connection between what agents are obliged to do and what they have normative reason to do. The trouble is, however, that if there is such a reason then it follows immediately that there is $\text{value}_{\text{each}}$ in each's meeting of the reasonable expectations each knowingly creates. This follows immediately because, to put the point in Scanlon's terms, all that p's being $\text{valuable}_{\text{each}}$ amounts to is each's having a reason to desire that p (or, in terms of our paraphrase of Sidgwick, all that p's being valuable amounts to is each's being required by reason to desire that p).

The upshot is that Principle F itself seems to presuppose that there is a nonwelfarist *relative* value in an agent's meeting of the reasonable expectations that he knowingly creates. The value in question is nonwelfarist because there is no reason to suppose that meeting such expectations contributes, as such, to the agent's well-being. And the nonwelfarist value in question is relative because the desires that there is reason for me to have concern the reasonable expectations that *I* knowingly create; the desires that there is reason for you to have concern the reasonable expectations that *you* knowingly create; and the desires that there is reason for others to have concern the reasonable expectations that *they* knowingly create. Moreover, Principle F's truth depends on the existence of such relative values because, as we just saw, the existence of such relative values is required for agents to have a normative reason to do what Principle F says that they must do. Far from Principle F's being a nonconsequentialist principle, then, it turns out that Principle F is itself an implicitly consequentialist principle. It is an implicitly consequentialist principle because the facts about obligation that it describes are all ultimately grounded in, and thus reduce to, facts about the relative value of agents meeting the reasonable expectations that they knowingly create.

Scanlon might reply that this argument is predicated on a false assumption about Principle F. He might suggest that the argument assumes, falsely, that Principle F is an ultimate moral principle. But, he might say, Principle F is not an ultimate moral principle, but is rather a principle that is derived from the ultimate *contractualist* moral principle. As he puts it elsewhere:

> in order to decide whether it would be wrong to do X in circumstances C, we should consider possible principles governing how one may act in such situations, and ask whether any principle that permitted one to do X in those circumstances could, for that reason, reasonably be rejected. (1998, p. 195)

Principle F, he might say, is a derived moral principle because it is one of the principles governing how one may act that no one could reasonably reject. What makes it the case that violations of Principle F are wrong is thus, ultimately, the fact that no one could reasonably reject acting in accordance with it.

The trouble with this reply, however, is that it has no affect on the cogency of the argument just given. For all it shows is that, though we do indeed have a reason to desire that we meet the reasonable expectations that we knowingly create, this desire is itself derived from something much more general that we have reason to desire, namely, that we each act only on those principles that no one could reasonably reject. But the fact that we each have a reason to desire this itself shows that the relative value that grounds the truth of Principle F is itself derived from a much more fundamental relative value, namely, the nonwelfarist relative value of acting in accordance with principles that no one could reasonably reject. This is another nonwelfarist value, because there is once again no reason to suppose that meeting such expectations contributes, as such, to an agent's well-being. And the nonwelfarist value in question is once again relative because what I have a reason to desire, at the most fundamental level, is that *I* act in accordance with principles that no on could reasonably reject; what you have a reason to desire, at the most fundamental level, is that *you* act in accordance with principles that no one could reasonably reject; and what others have a reason to desire, at the most fundamental level, is that *they* act in accordance with principles that no one could reasonably reject. What we all have a reason to desire, at the most fundamental level, is thus that we can justify *our own* conduct to others. Once again, it seems that Scanlon has no choice but to admit that there are such reasons, and hence to admit that there are such relative values, because, absent such reasons, and hence absent such relative values, we would have no normative reason to do what, according to the contractualist principle, we have an obligation to do: namely, to act in accordance with principles that no one could reasonably reject.

Note that this discussion of Scanlon's Principle F and of his more general contractualist principle are meant to be merely illustrative. All I have tried to indicate is how a consequentialist who has an open mind about the possibility of there being relative values that explain the distinctive nature of promissory obligation might go about trying to figure out what those relative values are. Nothing I have said shows that there is any relative value in agents' meeting the reasonable expectations that they knowingly create, and nothing I have said shows that there is any relative value in agents' acting in ways that they can justify to others either. What the discussion does suggest, however, is that, to the extent that we find Scanlon's Principle F and his deeper contractualist principle independently plausible, our finding them so amounts to our finding it independently plausible that there are indeed such relative values. To put the point somewhat contentiously and ambitiously, what the argument suggests is that the very best arguments for nonconsequentialism will all turn out, on closer inspection, to be arguments for consequentialism, albeit versions of consequentialism that are grounded in relative values that had hitherto escaped our attention.

ACKNOWLEDGMENT

An earlier version of this essay was presented at Promises and Agreements, a workshop held at Rice University, October 2008. I would like to thank all of workshop participants for their helpful comments during the workshop and Hanoch Sheinman for his very helpful written commentary.

REFERENCES

Griffin, James. 1998: *Well-Being: Its Meaning, Measurement and Moral Importance* (Oxford: Oxford University Press).

Hooker, Brad. 2000: *Ideal Code, Real World* (Oxford: Clarendon Press).

Jackson, Frank. 1991: "Decision Theoretic Consequentialism and the Nearest and Dearest Objection." *Ethics* 101: 461–482.

Mackie, J. L. 1977: *Ethics: Inventing Right and Wrong* (Harmondsworth, England: Penguin).

Mill, John Stuart. 1861: *Utilitarianism* (Toronto: University of Toronto Press).

Moore, G. E. 1903: *Principia Ethica* (Cambridge: Cambridge University Press).

Pettit, Philip, and Michael Smith. 2000: "Global Consequentialism." In Brad Hooker, Elinor Mason, and Dale E. Miller, eds., *Morality, Rules, and Consequences: A Critical Reader* (Edinburgh: Edinburgh University Press), pp. 121-133.

Railton, Peter. 1984: "Alienation, Consequentialism, and the Demands of Morality." *Philosophy and Public Affairs* 13: 134-171.

Raz, Joseph. 1986: *The Morality of Freedom* (New York: Oxford University Press).

———. 1999: "Agency, Reason, and the Good." In Raz, *Engaging Reason* (New York: Oxford University Press), pp. 22–45.

Scanlon, Thomas M. 1998: *What We Owe to Each Other* (Cambridge, MA: Harvard University Press).

Slote, Michael, and Philip Pettit. 1984: "Satisficing Consequentialism." In *Proceedings of the Aristotelian Society*, supp., 58: 139–176.

Smart, J. J. C., and Bernard Williams. 1973: *Utilitarianism: For and Against* (Cambridge: Cambridge University Press).

Smith, Michael. 1994: *The Moral Problem* (Oxford: Wiley-Blackwell).

———. 2003: "Neutral and Relative Value after Moore." In *Ethics*, Centenary Symposium on G. E. Moore's *Principia Ethica* 113 (), pp. 576–598.

———. 2005: "Metaethics." In *Oxford Handbook of Contemporary Philosophy,* edited by Frank Jackson and Michael Smith (Oxford: Oxford University Press), pp. 3–30.

Sumner, Wayne. 1996: *Welfare, Happiness, and Ethics* (Oxford: Clarendon Press).

Chapter 9

Act-utilitarianism and Promissory Obligation

Alastair Norcross

Abstract

Act-utilitarianism is often criticized for failing to account for the strength of promissory obligation. Worse still, it is not even clear that the institution of promising could exist in an act-utilitarian society. Rule utilitarianism is often claimed to be in a better position than act utilitarianism with respect to providing an account of the moral status of promising (or rather keeping one's promises). In fact, the move from act utilitarianism to rule utilitarianism is often motivated by the desire to justify the obligation to keep promises. However, the act utilitarian has multiple resources available to explain the moral status of promissory behavior. I argue that act utilitarianism provides a fully satisfactory account of the moral considerations relevant to promising.

The standard maximizing act-utilitarian account of rightness is attacked both for being too demanding and for being too permissive. The theory is said to be too demanding, because it counts the interests of all equally. Thus, if the $10 I propose to spend on a movie can produce more good for others than the good I will get from seeing the movie—which it undoubtedly can—I should forgo the movie, and spend the $10 on improving the lot of others. The theory is said to be too permissive, because it permits agents to break intuitively appealing moral rules whenever more good (on balance) will come from breaking them than from keeping them. In fact, it doesn't merely permit agents to break rules in such circumstances, but it demands that they do so.

One of the most common examples of this latter criticism concerns the rule that one should keep one's promises. Few philosophers, with the exception of some (hopefully) imaginary Kantians, claim that this rule has absolute force. *Of course* promises may be broken when enough is at stake. If I have promised to meet you for coffee in five minutes, but my CPR skills are required to keep a stranger alive until the medics arrive, I can, indeed must, break my promise to you. Even highly serious promises can be broken in exceptional circumstances. A promise of marital fidelity, probably the most serious promise most people will make, can be permissibly broken, if that is the only way to get information from a terrorist that will save the lives of thousands. However, the mere fact that *some* more good (on balance) will come from breaking the promise than from keeping it is not enough to justify breaking it. If this claim is correct, it would seem that act-utilitarianism is mistaken.

I shall argue in this essay that utilitarianism provides an appealing and satisfactory account of the moral status of promising, an account that makes the value of promising and promise-keeping entirely unmysterious. Rule-utilitarianism is often claimed to be in a better position than act-utilitarianism with respect to providing an account of the moral status of keeping one's promises. In fact, the move from act-utilitarianism to rule-utilitarianism is often motivated by the desire to justify the obligation to keep promises. However, the act-utilitarian has multiple resources available to explain the moral status of promissory behavior. I will argue that act-utilitarianism provides a better account of the moral considerations relevant to promising.

I. ROSS AND THE CLASSICAL CRITICISM

First, let's begin with the classic antiutilitarian argument concerning promising. W. D. Ross presents an example in which keeping my promise to A will produce 1,000 units of good for him, but I also have an alternative, involving breaking my promise to A, that will produce 1,001 units of good to B, to whom I have promised nothing.[1] The utilitarian, Ross claims, must endorse breaking my promise in this case, because I can do more overall good by doing so. Of course we can object that breaking the promise to A will also produce some units of bad, in the form of disappointment on the part of A and some loss of trust in me, so that it would take more than 1,001 units of good for B to justify breaking the promise. Ross accepts this, but argues that, nonetheless, there will be a point at which breaking the promise, even taking everything into account, will produce slightly more net good than keeping it.

The example by itself does not provide an argument against the utilitarian account of promising. We need to add two claims. First, the claim that utilitarianism judges the breaking of the promise to be right. Second, the claim that breaking the promise in this case is not right. The first claim follows from the maximizing act-utilitarian account of rightness. The example includes the stipulation that breaking the promise has better consequences (from the utilitarian point of view) than keeping it. But what of the second claim? Here we have a simple appeal to intuition. "How *can* it be right," we ask, "to break the promise in this case, just to produce a *smidgen* more good?" Although it may appear that this is a clear, and widely held, intuition, we need to be careful to distinguish between two very different intuitions that may be in play.

Most antiutilitarian arguments involve hypothetical cases described in moderate detail. Thus, we have the classic trolley cases, involving differing numbers of people trapped on tracks, a trolley whose runaway behavior is explained with varying amounts of detail, perhaps some large individual, whose girth may or may not be attributable to his own moral vices, leaning over a bridge, a driver or a bystander at a switch or someone else on the bridge with the large man, with varying amounts of information about the situation, and so on. The reader is typically encouraged to give the same intuitive verdict on the case as the author. Sometimes the reader is simply informed of the correct verdict (this is notably the case with Frances Kamm's examples, whose details render them totally unsuitable for generating intuitive reactions from anyone except Kamm herself). Alternatively, consider Thomson's famous violinist example and its variations. Such examples are supposed to engage our moral intuitions. Usually, we are asked to consider the option supposedly recommended by the target ethical theory, and to agree that it is morally unacceptable.

There are, of course, numerous problems with this methodology. Intuitions may be subconsciously swayed by morally irrelevant factors, or may be generated by prerational mechanisms that evolved to guide the behavior of our ancestors who faced a simpler environment and did not possess our abstract reasoning abilities.[2] For the sake of argument, however, I will ignore these problems, and suppose that an intuitive verdict on a hypothetical case is at least prima facie trustworthy. If, for example, utilitarianism says to do x in one of these cases, but I (we?) strongly intuit that it would be wrong to do x in this case, that is a significant strike against utilitarianism.

Now, consider Ross's example. This case is strikingly different from the standard examples that fill the pages of ethics journals. It contains very little in the way of details. In essence, the example can be boiled down to the following: imagine a situation in which breaking a promise will produce one-tenth of 1 percent more overall good than keeping it. Don't we agree that it would still be wrong to break the promise in this case? The problem is that the example presents an unstable mixture of a moderately detailed hypothetical case and statement of principle. If we agree that, in this case, it would be wrong to break the promise, to what are we responding? Is it to a *case* in which a smidgen more good will come of breaking a promise than of keeping it, or is it to the *principle* that one should keep one's promises, even in cases in which a smidgen more good will come from breaking them? If we think we are responding to a case, how can we be sure that it is really a case in which more overall good comes of breaking the promise than of keeping it? It is hard enough to compare alternatives in real cases. Hypothetical examples, even highly detailed, are even harder. Ross simply tells us to imagine a case that fits his requirements. We should be highly dubious, to say the least, that we have succeeded in this feat of imagination.

The considerations of the previous paragraph are a familiar line of defense against arguments that involve hypothetical cases. Utilitarians, in particular, rightly point out the uncertainty involved in judging that a particular hypothetical alternative has better consequences than its alternatives. They stress that the theory tallies with common sense judgments in most real world cases. The consequences of breaking most actual promises, once disappointed expectations and the negative effects of loss of trust have been considered, appear to be worse than the consequences of keeping them. It is difficult to describe a case in detail, such that it is obvious both that breaking the promise has better consequences than keeping it and that it would be wrong to break it. As Mill says:

> The important rank, among human evils and wrongs, of the disappointment of expectation, is shown in the fact that it constitutes the principal criminality of two such highly immoral acts as a breach of friendship and a breach of promise. Few hurts which human beings can sustain are greater, and none wound more, than when that on which they habitually and with full assurance relied, fails them in the hour of need; and few wrongs are greater than this mere withholding of good; none excite more resentment, either in the person suffering, or in a sympathising spectator. (*Utilitarianism*, ch. 5)

I am not claiming that it is impossible to come up with a suitable example. Perhaps some "desert-island" cases, involving deathbed promises, could be described in sufficient detail to convince us both that it really would do more good to break the promise and that such behavior would be wrong (in my experience with such attempts, the latter claim is the most dubious). However, even if no plausible example could be given that clearly involves a utility-maximizing breach of promise that is nonetheless intuitively unjustified, the utilitarian account of promising can be attacked on the grounds that the principle that promises should be kept, even when slightly more good can come of breaking them, is intuitively appealing. Indeed, this seems to be Ross's point, when he writes:

> When a plain man fulfils a promise because he thinks he ought to do so, it seems clear that he does so with no thought of its total consequences, still less

> with any opinion that these are likely to be the best possible.... What makes him think it right to act in a certain way is the fact that he has promised to do so—that and, usually, nothing more. That his act will produce the best possible consequences is not his reason for calling it right. (*The Right and the Good*, 17)

Of course, to insist that the reason promise-breaking is wrong has *nothing* to do with the consequences of such behavior, and thus to claim that utilitarianism is mistaken, is to beg the question against the theory. A more fruitful line of attack would be to challenge utilitarianism's ability to defend any kind of special moral status for promising. In fact, it might appear that utilitarians can't even consistently make promises. At the very least, making a promise involves something like an intention to get the promisee to believe that the promisor both intends to carry out the promise and will not fail to do so just because there is something a bit better she can do. But, if the promisor is a maximizing act-utilitarian, and the promisee knows this, wouldn't the promisee believe that the promisor will only keep the promise if there's nothing better to do? Further, if the promisor knows that the promisee knows her to be a utilitarian, she will know that her promissory declarations won't succeed in getting the promisee to believe that her intention is anything more than conditional on the absence of better alternatives. But, if she knows that she can't effect the relevant change in the promisee's mental states, she won't be able to intend to do so, and thus she won't be able to promise.

It appears, then, that the institution of promising couldn't exist in an act-utilitarian society. Is this embarrassing for act-utilitarianism? Perhaps the act-utilitarian should simply dismiss the institution of promising, and its attendant notion of promissory obligation, as a relic of a discredited moral theory, along with political obligation, desert, and the doing/allowing distinction. But this would be too hasty. There appear to be good utilitarian reasons to favor something like the institution of promising. The reasons are well enough known that there is no need for me to rehearse them here. Suffice to say that a world without the institution of promising (or something very much like it) is less likely to flourish than one with it. So it appears that an act-utilitarian society can't have an institution it has good utilitarian reasons to have, and thus that the theory is at least pragmatically self-defeating. This would, if true, be an unfortunate consequence for the theory.

II. THE RULE-UTILITARIAN GAMBIT

At this point, many a utilitarian may be tempted to experiment with rule-utilitarianism. I must confess that I engaged in such experimentation myself, along with many other forms of experimentation, when I was in college (since I have no plans to run for public office, I don't fear this admission coming back to bite me). Consider what is clearly the most thoughtful and well-presented version of the theory, Brad Hooker's:

> RULE-CONSEQUENTIALISM. An act is wrong if it is forbidden by the code of rules whose internalization by the overwhelming majority of everyone everywhere in each new generation has maximum expected value in terms of well-being (with some priority for the worst off).[3]

Although the question of which code would, if internalized, maximize utility is complex, it is at least highly plausible that such a code would include some kind of rule against breach of promise. As I said above, the arguments in favor of the utility-promoting role of the institution of promising are well known. Indeed, the strength of the utilitarian case, whether in the act or rule variety, for the value of the institution of promising has the distinct advantage of making the moral case for promising entirely unmysterious. So long as we recognize the intrinsic value of welfare, well-being, flourishing, or some related notion, it is obvious why promising is valuable. Contrast this with a nonconsequentialist approach. How, exactly, does promising manage to generate a moral obligation? Some nonconsequentialists, especially of the Kantian variety, will invoke the supreme mystery of their faith, respect. Others may talk of the intrinsic value of "assurance," or "authority." The problem, of course, is that it is hard to see how assurance or authority could have intrinsic value. It is easy to see why we judge them valuable. They are clearly tied to welfare. But this would generate only instrumental value. Likewise, the very notion of respect, unless tied instrumentally to welfare, remains either entirely mysterious or perfectly consistent with a utilitarian (or more broadly consequentialist) approach. A utilitarian may claim that the demand for equal consideration of interests embodied in her theory (and other consequentialist theories) is precisely what it means to respect individuals. It is only when I weigh your interests equally with the interests of all others whom I can affect that I adequately respect you. Nonconsequentialist constraints function to disallow the consideration of certain interests in certain circumstances. Thus they, at least sometimes, prevent us from respecting certain individuals.

According to rule-consequentialism, the moral status of an action, such as keeping or breaking a promise, doesn't depend on the consequences of that action, but on the consequences of internalizing a code of rules. A rule-consequentialist promisor could thus succeed in making a promise to a like-minded promisee, or even just to a promisee who believes the promisor to be a rule-consequentialist. So long as the promisee believes the promisor to be a rule-consequentialist who believes that the optimal code includes a rule against breach of promise, she will have reason to trust that the promisor will keep the promise. The promisor will not be disposed to evaluate the consequences of keeping the promise, and certainly not to break the promise merely to produce a smidgen more good than will come of keeping it.

Rule-consequentialism thus succeeds both in explaining the value of promising and in grounding the obligation to keep promises. The problem, of course, arises in cases in which the consequences of breaking a promise are better than those of keeping it. Hooker's answer to such cases lies in his disaster avoidance rule. No doubt, the optimal code will include a rule to avoid disasters, which can override other rules in the code. So, it won't be wrong to break a promise, if keeping the promise will lead to a disaster. What counts as a disaster will be relative to the seriousness of the promise. The more serious the promise, the greater the disaster to be avoided by breaking it. Although this gives the intuitively correct results (how could it not when it is phrased so loosely?), we still have to confront the familiar "rule-worship" objection. Presumably, the disaster avoidance rule does not say that just any comparative loss of utility counts as a disaster. If it did, then we would have act-utilitarianism, or at least a theory extensionally equivalent to it. So there must be cases in which more good would come of breaking a promise than of keeping it, but in which it would nonetheless be wrong to break it. Why would a utilitarian—someone who believes that well-being, or welfare, or flourishing (whether prioritarianly adjusted or not) is the only intrinsic good—believe that it is wrong to bring about more of the good rather than less *in any case*? The question is not whether a good utilitarian actually confronted with such a case would break a promise, or even would believe that it is right to break the promise. Perhaps a good utilitarian would not perform the requisite calculations in such a case, or would even do something she knows to be wrong (more on that shortly). The question is whether a utilitarian would believe of an option under the description "breaking a promise but maximizing the good" that it is wrong. Of course Hooker could reply that a rule-utilitarian could believe such a thing, because that is what rule-utilitarianism implies (that at least some optimal instances of rule-breaking are wrong). But that would simply beg the question against the criticism, which is that a utilitarian wouldn't be a rule-utilitarian.

There is, of course, a lot more to say about rule-utilitarianism, and, even after it is all said, there may be some who still believe it gives a better account of the moral status of promising than act-utilitarianism. However, I don't have world enough or time to say it all here. What I want to do now is to explain how act-utilitarianism can account for promising, and what it has to say about the commitment to keep promises even in circumstances in which a little more good would come of breaking them.

III. ACT-UTILITARIANISM AND "ONE THOUGHT TOO MANY"

Here, very roughly, is how the argument goes: if it is true, as it seems to be, that something like the convention of promising promotes overall well-being, a utilitarian would want such a convention to exist. In order for the convention to exist, individual agents must have commitments that include the disposition to keep promises even in cases in which somewhat more good would come of breaking them. Thus, a utilitarian would approve of the existence of such commitments in individual agents. Even though such commitments will sometimes lead agents to sacrifice utility, there would be less overall utility if the agents lacked those commitments.

So far, so good, but there might appear to be a difference between the case of me approving of *your* commitment to keep your promises and me approving of my own commitment. The point has been most notably pressed by Bernard Williams and Michael Stocker with respect to personal commitments to individuals, rather than to moral rules, but the worries might be thought to transfer. Williams describes a situation in which a man chooses to rescue his wife rather than some other person: "It might have been hoped by some (for instance, by his wife) that his motivating thought, fully spelled out, would be the thought that it was his wife, not that it was his wife and that in situations of this kind it is permissible to save one's wife." What is being criticized is not the agent's action, but his decision procedure: the conscious application of a principle of morality in a situation in which the agent should act simply on his natural affection. If the agent is a utilitarian, he doesn't simply act on his commitment to his wife, but he also justifies such a commitment on utilitarian grounds. This, according to Williams, leaves him with "one thought too many." The problem here is not just that the wife might have hoped that her husband's commitment to her would have provided the sole motivation for his action. Rather, it seems that the kind of conscious evaluation of his commitment that appears in Williams' example is actually inconsistent with having the commitment in the first place. What it is to have a strong commitment to someone is, in part, to be disposed to perform certain actions without subjecting either the actions or the disposition to independent moral scrutiny.

Do similar considerations apply to the commitment to keeping one's promises? Does the utilitarian who thinks to herself that a particular option is right, because it is the keeping of a promise, and the commitment to keep one's promises has utilitarian value, also have "one thought too many"? In fact, we might go further and question whether an act-utilitarian can coherently think such a thing at all. She can think that she should be *generally* committed to promise-keeping because of the general value of such a commitment, but she can't think that keeping promises (including this one) is for that reason *right*. She believes of any action that it's right just in case *it* maximizes the good. But this objection confuses the evidential sense of "because" with the constitutive sense. It is perfectly consistent for a utilitarian to think that the fact that an act is one of promise-keeping is evidence that it is right, without thinking that its rightness is constituted by its being an act of promise-keeping. Of course, it might be objected that the connection between promise-keeping and rightness is more than just evidential, and thus that the utilitarian fails to account for this. But that would simply beg the question against utilitarianism. Perhaps, though, the objection can be resurrected in a less question-begging form. Whether or not the connection between promise-keeping and rightness is more than just evidential, the utilitarian benefits of a general commitment to promise-keeping can only be (or at least are more likely to be) realized, if individual agents don't (usually) think of the connection as only evidential. The idea here is that an agent who thinks to herself "it's the keeping of a promise, which is evidence that it's right, because the general commitment to keep one's promises has utilitarian value," is always prepared to break her promise, if she sees that more good will come of it on this occasion. But the utilitarian value of the general commitment to keep one's promises depends in part on the commitment being robust enough to lead to keeping one's promise on at least some occasions on which more good could be done by breaking the promise. This seems to require that the agent not rehearse the utilitarian justification for having the commitment to promise-keeping on every occasion when the commitment might come into play. So the possibility of the act-utilitarian having one thought too many when it comes to decisions about promise-keeping threatens the theory again with pragmatic self-defeat.

The answer to this objection (like the answers to many other objections) is to be found in Sidgwick (just think of the trees that could have been saved, if only Williams, Stocker, and their ilk had read and properly understood the *Methods of Ethics*!). Speaking of the value of a special concern for one's "near and dear," Sidgwick cites many reasons why such concern has utilitarian value. "On these grounds," says Sidgwick, "the Utilitarian will evidently approve of the cultivation of affection and the performance of affectionate services."[4] Is Sidgwick recommending that, on every occasion, or even most occasions, on which an agent does or might feel the promptings of self-love or natural affections, he should mentally run through the arguments for cultivating such feelings in calculating what to do? I don't think so. He does not say so, and seems to imply the contrary. He defends "spontaneous beneficence," which could hardly exist if the agent were to subject his feeling to utilitarian assessment every time it prompted him to some action. He claims that "we feel that the charm of Friendship is lost if the flow of emotion is not spontaneous and unforced."[5] He stresses the connection between natural affection and the activities that it prompts in his claim that such activities are pleasurable because they are prompted by affection. Perhaps the clearest indication that Sidgwick didn't think that the utilitarian agent must always apply utilitarian reasoning is to be found in the following passage:

> [T]he doctrine that Universal Happiness is the ultimate standard must not be understood to imply that Universal Benevolence is the only right or always best motive of action...it is not necessary that the end which gives the criterion of rightness should always be the end at which we consciously aim: and if experience shows that the general happiness will be more satisfactorily attained if men frequently act from other motives than pure universal philanthropy, it is obvious that these other motives are reasonably to be preferred on Utilitarian principles. (413)

If, on a particular occasion, we do not consciously aim at Universal Happiness, we can hardly justify our actions on that occasion with reference to Universal Happiness. That is, we cannot, on that occasion, employ a conscious reasoning process that involves recognizing that certain justifications for what we are doing are utilitarian justifications and therefore to be heeded. If we take this view held by Sidgwick, together with a recognition that certain forms of motivation are valuable as direct motivations, we can see that a good utilitarian agent need not have one thought too many. This applies equally with respect to personal commitments and to commitments to moral rules such as the rule to keep one's promises.

IV. ESOTERICISM

At this point, we have to confront the dreaded specter of "esotericism." Both Williams and Stocker claim that utilitarianism is an "esoteric" theory, and that that is a problem for the theory. Williams is aware of the claim that utilitarianism might demand that moral agents not employ utilitarian reasoning on all occasions. Indeed, he regards this as a grave defect in the theory. He writes: "[I]t is reasonable to suppose that maximal total utility actually requires that few, if any, accept utilitarianism."[6] In which case, he claims, it is a matter for discussion whether "utilitarianism is unacceptable, or...no one ought to accept it."[7] Thus we are confronted with two different claims:

> FALSE: If utilitarianism is true, it would be best if at least most people didn't believe it to be true;
>
> DEFECT: The truth of FALSE exposes a defect in utilitarianism.

Williams claims that there are "some powerful reasons" for thinking that the prevalence of "utilitarian thinking as a personal and social phenomenon...could be a disaster."[8] However, his arguments show only that utility will probably not be maximized if every action is motivated by the conscious desire to maximize utility; they certainly don't show that utility can only be maximized if no one believes utilitarianism.[9]

Michael Stocker, in a discussion of maximization, also seems to endorse both FALSE and DEFECT:

> Maximizers hold that the absence of any attainable good is, as such, bad, and that a life that lacks such a good is therefore lacking. The basic moral psychological reason for denying this is that regret over the absence or lack is a central characterizing feature of narcissistic, grandiose, and other defective selves.[10]

Stocker admits that it may be argued that this shows, not that maximization is wrong, but that being a maximizer is itself not maximizing. He adds:

> I see it as a severe problem for a theory if, by its own lights, it cannot be embraced and followed.... What I have trouble in understanding is why we should be expected to think that a theory which is so esoteric as the one now in question is worth serious consideration as our ethical theory.[11]

What is Stocker claiming here? He moves from the possibility that being a maximizer may not be maximizing to the claim that maximization cannot be embraced and followed by its own lights. The tone of his remarks ("so esoteric as the one now in question") suggests a claim as extreme as Williams's claim that utilitarianism entails that no one believe it. But the evidence for this claim, that being a maximizer may not be maximizing, supports, at best, the claim that utility will probably not be maximized if every action is motivated by the conscious desire to maximize utility.

Although Stocker clearly seems to embrace DEFECT, he offers no argument for it. Even if it is true that utilitarianism requires that most people don't believe it, why should that count against the theory? The most we get from Stocker is the rather cryptic claim that such a theory would be "esoteric." Williams offers a little more, but his arguments for DEFECT seem to center on the mistaken impression that act-utilitarianism is solely concerned with "the situation of decision."[12] This is illustrated by the following piece of reasoning:

> [The direct utilitarian] tells us that the answer to the question "what is the right thing to do?" is to be found in that act which has the best consequences. But it seems difficult to put that to any use in this connection, except by taking it to imply the following: that the correct question to ask, if asking what is the right thing to do, is what act will have the best consequences.[13]

Thus Williams claims that the distinction between act-utilitarianism and other forms of utilitarianism is a matter of motivation. If this were the case, then FALSE, if true, would be a problem for act-utilitarianism. But it is obviously not true that act-utilitarianism is only concerned with motivation. Traditional utilitarian theory has, as its basic goal, the maximization of utility, and if this can only be achieved by no one believing the theory, then that is what the theory demands.

Williams predicts that utilitarianism will retire to the "totally transcendental standpoint from which all it demands is that the world should be ordered for the best, and that those dispositions and habits of thought should exist in the world that are for the best, leaving it entirely open whether those are themselves of a distinctively utilitarian kind or not."[14]

If we allow the utilitarian to specify what she means by "for the best," I don't think she would object to this formulation as a basic characterization of utilitarianism. Utilitarianism must leave open the question of which dispositions and habits of thought are "for the best." That doesn't mean that it cannot take a stand on the issue, just that it must always be prepared to change its view in the light of new psychological evidence. Not only may our knowledge of and opinions about human nature change, but human nature itself may change. The fact that utilitarianism can accommodate itself to such change should be seen as an asset of the theory, not a drawback.

V. WHAT'S SO BAD ABOUT ESOTERICISM?

Although neither Williams nor Stocker provides good reasons for believing DEFECT, it may seem plausible. Isn't there something strange in the suggestion that a particular moral theory requires that no one believe it? This certainly seems to violate what Rawls calls the "publicity condition" for a moral theory. Doesn't it seem right that if a moral theory is correct, it should be possible for everyone, or at least most people, to act as it prescribes and to believe that it is correct? Perhaps this is at least contingently true, but it is hard to see how it could be a necessary feature of the correct moral theory. Imagine that there are two deities, Bart, who is good, and Lisa, who is bad.[15] Imagine, further, that the correct moral theory is the following version of divine command theory:

> BARTISM An act is wrong iff it is forbidden by Bart, otherwise it is permissible.

Many people believe BARTISM and act on it. Many other people believe a false moral theory, LISANITY, which has the same structure as BARTISM, but which centers on the commands of Lisa. Both Lisa and Bart regularly appear to the people and issue their very different commands. There is nothing in the story so far to suggest that BARTISM could not be the correct moral theory. Suppose now that the people are getting better and better. In fact, most people now believe BARTISM and very few believe LISANITY. This annoys the hell out of Lisa, who desperately wants people to do what She says, so She works the following piece of trickery on the minds of the people. Every time Lisa appears to the people, they believe they are seeing Bart, and vice versa. Lisa, who, though evil, is also more powerful than Bart, also fixes Bart so that He is not aware of the people's reversed perceptions. Now most, if not all, people who believe in BARTISM will actually fail to act as it prescribes. Conversely, those who believe LISANITY will usually do what BARTISM requires. Has this exercise of evil power by Lisa rendered the previously true BARTISM false? This would be a very strange conclusion. If BARTISM was true before, it is still true now; it's just that now it's better if people believe LISANITY instead.[16]

It will be easier to see both the appeal and the failing of DEFECT, if we pause briefly to consider the role of moral theories, or at least one central aspect of their role. Both moral realists and antirealists (of various kinds) agree that moral theories are action-guiding in the following sense: they provide reasons for acting. If my moral theory contains a prohibition on coveting my neighbor's ass, I have a reason not to covet my neighbor's ass (I'm not sure whether coveting is a kind of action, but bear with me). But if, according to my moral theory, I shouldn't even believe my moral theory, how is it supposed to supply me with reasons? And if it can't supply me with reasons, how can it be a moral theory? The obvious answer to this is to point out that reasons don't have to be embodied in consciously held beliefs, or even unconscious beliefs, in order to apply. The smoker who doesn't believe that smoking is bad for her has the same reason to quit as the better informed (or less self-deceived) smoker. At this point, the moral antirealist will probably point out that the harmful effects of smoking are a matter of objective fact, whereas moral theories inhabit (according to him) an entirely different realm. The reasons supplied by moral theories are more like the reason I have for benefiting someone I care deeply about than the reason I have for quitting smoking. If I care deeply about Smith and you don't, I have a reason for benefiting Smith that simply doesn't apply to you. But this example can be modified to illustrate how moral theories can provide reasons for acting to those who don't accept them, even given moral antirealism. Suppose I care deeply about Smith and want her to be happy, above all else. However, I also know, from bitter past experience, that when I care deeply about someone, I become irrational, possessive, violent, and obsessive. In fact, everyone for whom I have cared deeply has suffered terribly as a result. Given that I really do want Smith to be happy, I judge that it would be better if I could get myself not to care about her at all. Perhaps I succeed in this endeavor, and no longer care about Smith. As a result, she is a lot happier than she would have been. My emotional commitment to Smith provided the reason for me to change my feelings, and continues to provide reasons for my behavior, even though such reasons are now inaccessible to me. This suggests that the assumption that moral antirealists must be committed to DEFECT stems from an impoverished view of how reasons for behavior can operate.

Now consider how a moral antirealist might view my example. Given the kind of being Bart is, and the kind of person I am, BARTISM is my chosen theory. My acceptance and advocacy of BARTISM express something deeply rooted in my character. But what if Lisa were tricking me in the manner described above? Even though I embrace BARTISM, I judge that, were Lisa to be tricking me, it would be better, according to my chosen theory, if I were to embrace LISANITY instead. Perhaps I am told that LISA will begin Her trickery tomorrow (the trickery will, of course, include erasing my memory of being told this). There is a rigorous course of drug and behavioristic treatment that I can undergo today. This treatment has a 95 percent chance of changing my character in such a way that I will embrace LISANITY. Given that I currently embrace BARTISM, I have a very good reason to submit myself to the treatment. The reason is supplied by BARTISM itself. I might regard it as regrettable that Lisa's power has driven me to this, but I don't consider BARTISM any less appropriate as a moral theory because of it. If the treatment is successful, and I come to embrace LISANITY (and therefore act as BARTISM requires), there is a very clear sense in which BARTISM is still providing me with reasons for acting, even though I would then believe otherwise.

There are good reasons, then, for believing both that FALSE is false and that DEFECT is false. Neither does the truth (or acceptability) of utilitarianism require that most people not believe it, nor would it matter if it did.

VI. SOPHISTICATED CONSEQUENTIALISM

Elsewhere[17] I have explored and defended a utilitarian approach to commitments to moral principles that expands on a seminal essay of Peter Railton. Although Railton's concern is with personal commitments, for example to one's spouse, the approach can be applied pretty straightforwardly to commitments to moral principles, such as promise-keeping. Railton argues that a good moral agent will have a "standing commitment to leading an objectively consequentialist life.... *Objective consequentialism* is the view that the criterion of the rightness of an act or course of action is whether it in fact would most promote the good of those acts available to the agent."[18] You can espouse values which can affect decision-making in a nonconsequentialist way, just so long as you are committed to removing those values that tend to produce bad results. This doesn't mean that you cannot be committed to nonconsequentialist values, even though you would attempt to remove them if you discovered that they were reducing overall utility (or some broader conception of good). You should probably be committed to removing, say, racial prejudice from your value system, but could be committed to a moral aversion to chemical and biological warfare, even though on some occasions such an aversion could result in a decision that was wrong from an objective consequentialist point of view. Railton calls this view "sophisticated consequentialism."

Consider an example involving the commitment to promise-keeping. John has made a promise, but confronts an option that will produce more overall good than keeping the promise, but not by a huge amount. Suppose John opts to keep his promise. John could be a sophisticated consequentialist who has both a standing commitment to leading an objectively consequentialist life and a nonconsequentialist commitment to keep his promises. If he had been able on this occasion to perform the objectively right action, he would have been less committed to keeping his promises. If he had been less committed to keeping his promises, perhaps he would have done less good in the long run.

In my example, it is not clear whether John's commitment to keep his promises overrides his commitment to act for the best on this occasion, or whether he simply doesn't employ consequentialist considerations. Railton's account of sophisticated consequentialism allows for both possibilities. Consider the following passage:

> individuals may be more likely to act rightly if they possess certain enduring motivational patterns, character traits, or prima-facie commitments to rules in addition to whatever commitment they have to act for the best. Because such individuals would not consider consequences in all cases, they would miss a number of opportunities to maximize the good.[19]

Railton is suggesting that a good sophisticated consequentialist will sometimes act directly on the promptings of certain commitments or character traits, without consulting consequentialism. This makes room for spontaneous or affectionate behavior. But Railton is not solely concerned with motivations that are either nonmoral or not opposed to moral motivations. He is not just arguing for the place of "moral holidays" in the life of a good consequentialist agent:

> Surely part of the attraction of these indirect consequentialisms is the idea that one should have certain traits of character, or commitments to persons and principles, that are sturdy enough that one would at least sometimes refuse to forsake them even when this refusal is known to conflict with making some gain—perhaps small—in total utility.[20]

To return to the example of John, it is consistent with the description of John as a sophisticated consequentialist that he knows that he could do more good by breaking his promise. Perhaps he knows this, but doesn't consciously entertain the belief. A consequentialist can, in any case, allow for the possibility of conscious conflict between commitments, or other motivations that are justified on consequentialist grounds, and the belief that the right action is the action that produces the best results. Let me illustrate this by filling in the details of John's promise:

John is devoted to his grandfather, who is bedridden. One day John tells his grandfather that he is going to take a trip to India, for which he has been saving his money. Grandpa becomes very excited and asks John to fetch a locked box from the closet. Grandpa opens the box with a key he wears on a chain around his neck. He takes out a jade figure of a three-headed wolf-sloth hybrid. He found this figure, he explains, in the ruins of a temple sacred to a little-known and long dead Jainist sect based about fifty miles from Mumbai. For years now he has been feeling guilty about removing the figure from the ruined temple, and would have returned it himself, if he had not been an invalid. Now that John is going to visit India, Grandpa finally has the chance to achieve the spiritual peace he craves before he dies. He tells John exactly where to go, and even draws a detailed map, and asks him to promise to return the figure to its rightful place. John, who is, as I said, devoted to his grandfather, readily promises. Once in India, John makes his way to the village located a couple of miles from the site of the temple. In the village market he drops his bag and the jade figure rolls out. A street vendor picks up the figure, examines it, and offers John a moderate sum for it. (Although the sum is moderate, it is fair. A friend of John examined the figure before he left the United States, and told him that the jade is of an inferior quality, and the figure is fairly common.) John refuses, telling the vendor it is not for sale. On his way out of the village, John meets a priest (fill in your favorite religious denomination) with a distressed expression. He runs the village orphanage, he explains. The shipment of food for the next week's meals has arrived, but half the food is spoiled. They have no money to replace the spoiled food, so the orphans will be especially hungry this week, unless some kind stranger could donate the requisite money. John is on a very tight budget, and has no extra money to spare. However, he realizes that, if he sold the figure to the street vendor, he would have just enough extra money to make up the shortfall in the orphans' meals.

Now I think there is little doubt that we would not blame John for refusing to sell the figure and thus break his promise, indeed it would probably be psychologically extremely difficult for him to break his promise, but I also think that the strongest moral reasons favor doing so. We may well feel that there would be something wrong with John if he could break his promise readily without any soul searching. We think that, as a matter of psychological fact, it would be difficult for someone with a morally appropriate commitment to keeping promises to break one in such circumstances, but it would nonetheless be right for them to do so. Just how difficult it is for John to break his promise may, and indeed should, vary according to the value of the alternatives. If, for example, the vendor offered him a considerable sum of money (change the example to make it a fair price), and that sum is, in this example, the amount needed to buy food that would make the difference, in this example, *between life and death* for the orphans, it should not be overly difficult for John to break his promise. In fact, if John clung to his promise in the face of the certain death of many orphans (or even one), he would have a morally perverse commitment to keeping his promises. Nonetheless, even in such a case, regret at breaking the promise would be appropriate. If John broke his promise without any regret or remorse, we would take that as a sign of a defective character, even though we realized that he had done the objectively right thing. The fact that John himself realizes that he has done the right thing does not diminish the appropriateness of regret or remorse on his part.

John can have a standing commitment to leading an objectively consequentialist life and have a moral commitment to keeping his promises, even though the objectively right thing to do may, on occasion, involve breaking his promises. John may even, in a calm hour, reflect on his commitment to keeping his promises and realize that there may be situations in which this will make it difficult, or even impossible, for him to do the right thing. Yet he may judge that the costs of trying to change his attitude to promise-keeping will outweigh the benefits.

VII. WHAT ABOUT SELF-DECEPTION?

Does the sophisticated consequentialist find herself engaging in self-deception? What are we to say of the first version of the example, in which John refuses to break his promise, because of his moral commitment to promise-keeping, even though he is aware that he will do more good by breaking his promise than by keeping it? If his choice to keep his promise is motivated by a moral commitment to keeping promises, must he not believe that he is doing the morally right thing? But in that case, how can he at the same time believe that the morally right thing is what does most good and that breaking the promise on this occasion would do most good? Must he not deceive himself into believing that keeping his promise on this occasion is the morally right thing to do?

One possible reply to this charge of self-deception is to claim that John doesn't even consider the consequences of breaking his promise. What it is to have a commitment to keeping promises is, at least in part, to be disposed to choose a course of action that doesn't involve breaking promises, without considering the consequences of this. The sort of person who has a commitment to keeping promises is the sort of person for whom the question of the consequences of such behavior doesn't arise.

This reply may be acceptable for a number of cases, and perhaps for more serious moral commitments, such as the commitment to not killing innocent people, but I think it is clear that it won't do as a general answer to the charge of self-deception. It is particularly implausible for the commitment to keep one's promises, as the second version of John's choice demonstrates. It is obvious that a commitment to keep one's promises without ever considering the consequences of breaking them would not be part of a good consequentialist character. The reply also won't apply to all applications of a more serious moral commitment. Suppose that John refuses to kill an innocent person on an occasion when he could do more good by doing so. Even if he doesn't consider the consequences of killing the innocent person at the time of making his decision, he may well reflect on his choice later. He may realize that he did the wrong thing. It is reasonable to suppose that he will at least consider the consequences if another choice involving killing an innocent person should arise. More important, though, is the possibility of conflicting commitments. An admirable moral agent may have a commitment to not killing innocent people, to saving the lives of innocent people, to increasing the level of welfare of suffering people, to keeping her promises, and so on. Given the variety of different commitments that John may possess, and the obvious possibilities for conflicts between them, it is hardly plausible to maintain that having a commitment to ϕing involves being disposed not to consider the consequences of not ϕing. Some commitments may be stronger than others. An admirable moral agent will be more likely to consider the consequences of breaking a promise than to consider the consequences of killing an innocent person. To adapt an example of Elizabeth Anscombe, a judge may be so strongly committed to not procuring the judicial execution of innocent people that she never actually considers the consequences of doing this in any particular case. Some people may have some commitments that never lead to a conscious conflict with the commitment to produce the best results, but it seems likely that most of the commitments that a consequentialist would endorse may sometimes lead to such a conscious conflict.

Despite the possibility that John's commitment to keeping promises will lead him to do something that he knows does not have the best results of all his available alternatives, I do not think that the charge of self-deception is justified. Consider John's commitment. Does this include the belief that breaking promises is always wrong, or even the belief that it is usually wrong? It is not clear that John's commitment needs to include any beliefs about what is right or wrong. It may include the belief that breaking promises is bad, either in itself or because of its consequences, but it is not even clear that this is needed. John may have many moral beliefs about breaking promises, but these need not be part of his commitment to not breaking promises.

John has a deep aversion to breaking promises. If he breaks a promise, he feels bad. Not breaking promises is one of the many projects around which he builds his life. John also has a deep desire to watch *The Simpsons*. If he misses out on an opportunity to watch an episode of *The Simpsons*, he feels bad. Watching *The Simpsons* is one of the many projects around which he builds his life. John's commitment to watching *The Simpsons* is not a moral commitment. So what makes his commitment to keeping his promises a moral commitment? Part of the answer to this lies in the etiology of the commitment. John was probably taught that it was morally wrong to break his promises. More important, John universalizes this commitment and tries to get other people to share it. John's aversion is not just to John breaking his promises, but to anybody doing that. If John meets someone who is not committed to keeping his promises, he will probably try to get him to share his commitment. On the other hand, John can have a deep commitment to watching *The Simpsons*, but not care in the least whether anybody else watches it. He may not even be inclined to spread his passion for what is undoubtedly one of the two finest products of Western civilization.

It is clear that a sophisticated consequentialist needn't engage in self-deception, even when she knowingly follows a commitment at the expense of producing the best outcome. One might also ask what would be so bad about self-deception anyway. I suspect that the answer is "not much," but I don't have space to go into that here. Nevertheless, isn't there something strange about the state of mind of someone who acknowledges that she is morally required, on consequentialist grounds, to do x, but admits that she is not going to do x? At least, isn't it strange to describe such a person as having a standing commitment to leading an objectively consequentialist life? However, such a commitment involves the disposition to attempt to change character traits that are overall harmful, not those that merely prevent one from maximizing utility on some occasions. At the very least, though, there seems to be a tension between the belief that x is morally required and a commitment to doing something other than x (such as keeping a promise). The tension may be diminished somewhat by rejecting the maximizing requirement in consequentialism. If John does not break his promise, he has not done the morally best thing, but he hasn't failed a moral requirement. Such a scalar approach to morality, which has ample independent motivation,[21] can be combined with the approach of this essay to give a more satisfying account of the utilitarian approach to moral rules, such as the rule to keep one's promises, than the maximizing sophisticated consequentialist approach. We should not, however, expect a moral theory to remove *all* the tension between our moral beliefs and commitments. Such tension is a fact of the moral life, not a problem for an account of morality. It is part of the richness of our moral lives that an admirable character involves commitments that conflict. A good life, even the best life, may involve often doing what is less than best.

NOTES

1. Ross, *The Right and the Good* (Oxford: Oxford University Press, 2002), 35.

2. It doesn't, of course, follow from the fact that an intuition is generated by such a mechanism (if it is) that it is mistaken. It should, however, greatly undermine our faith in such intuitions.

3. Brad Hooker, *Ideal Code, Real World* (Clarendon Press: Oxford University Press, 2000) , p. 32. Although Hooker calls his theory "Rule-Consequentialism," rather than "Rule-Utilitarianism," the differences aren't relevant to the present discussion.

4. Henry Sidgwick, *The Methods of Ethics,* 7th ed. (Indianapolis: Hackett, 1981), p. 431.

5. Ibid., p. 437.

6. Williams, *A Critique of Utilitarianism* in J. J. C. Smart and Bernard Williams, *Utilitarianism for and against* (Cambridge: Cambridge University Press, 1973), p. 135.

7. Ibid., p. 135.

8. Ibid., p. 130.

9. For more on this, see Alastair Norcross, "Consequentialism and Commitment," *Pacific Philosophical Quarterly* 78:4 (December 1997): pp. 380–403.

10. Michael Stocker, *Plural and Conflicting Values* (Oxford: Oxford University Press, 1990), p. 321.

11. Ibid.

12. Williams, *Critique of Utilitarianism*, p. 125.

13. Ibid., p. 125.

14. Ibid. p. 135.

15. See what I just did? You were expecting Lisa to be the good one, weren't you?

16. Although I talk of the "truth" of a moral theory, the example could be recast to apply to moral antirealist approaches.

17. "Consequentialism and Commitment."

18. Peter Railton, "Alienation, Consequentialism, and the Demands of Morality," *Philosophy and Public Affairs* 13, 2 (spring 1984), reprinted in Samuel Scheffler, ed., *Consequentialism and its Critics* (Oxford: Oxford University Press, 1988), p. 114.

19. Ibid. p. 120.

20. Ibid. pp. 118, 120.

21. See, for example, my "Reasons without Demands: Rethinking Rightness," in James Dreier, ed., *Blackwell Contemporary Debates in Moral Theory* (Oxford Blackwell Publishing, 2006); "Scalar Act-Utilitarianism," in Henry R. West, ed., *Blackwell Guide to Mill's Utilitarianism* (Oxford Blackwell Publishing, 2006; and "Good and Bad Actions," *Philosophical Review* 106, 1 (January 1997) pp. 1–34.

Chapter 10

Promises and Rule-Consequentialism

Brad Hooker

Abstract

The duty to keep promises has many aspects associated with deontological moral theories. The duty to keep promises is non-welfarist, in that the obligation to keep a promise need not be conditional on there being a net benefit from keeping the promise–indeed need not be conditional on there being at least someone who would benefit from its being kept. The duty to keep promises is more closely connected to autonomy than directly to welfare: agents have moral powers to give themselves certain obligations to others. And these moral powers, which enable promisors to create agent-relative obligations to promisees, correlate with rights the promisees acquire in the process, such as rights to waive the duty or insist on its performance. As a result of promises, promisees acquire (not only rights but also) a special status: the promisees are the ones wronged when promises to them that they have not waived are not kept. One more aspect of the duty to keep promises that is associated with deontological moral theories is that what actions the duty requires is at least partly backward-looking: what actions the duty requires depends on facts about the past, namely facts about what promises were made and then waived or not. This paper surveys these aspects of the duty to keep promises and then explores whether rule-consequentialism can be reconciled with them.

This essay begins by rehearsing what is unacceptable in various attempts to explain the duty to keep promises. From that discussion will emerge some aspects of the duty that are associated with deontology. The essay then turns to the question of whether rule-consequentialism offers a plausible justification of the duty to keep promises.

I. WHY THE DUTY OF FAIR PLAY IS NOT THE GROUND OF PROMISES

Rawls contended in *A Theory of Justice* that the duty of fair play underlies the duty to keep promises.[1] We live in a society where there is a recognized social practice of people's doing what they have promised to do (unless an excusing condition comes into play). This social practice provides the opportunity for enormous benefits.

Especially important, of course, is the benefit of diachronic cooperation. Suppose I help you to get in your crops today because of your promise to help me get in mine tomorrow. Were it not for the social practice of taking promises to create moral obligations that people generally honor, you would have had difficulty in convincing me that you would help me tomorrow if I helped you today. That is, you might not have been able to elicit my services today were it not for the social practice of taking promises to create moral obligations. This kind of case is extremely common. Hence, if there were no social practice of promising, very much less diachronic cooperation would occur, to the general detriment of everyone.

Rawls argued that if you willingly accept the benefits of a social practice, such as the social practice of making promises to others in order to get them to believe you will do certain things, then the duty of fair play requires you to do your part under the rules of the social practice, for example, keep the promises you have made.

The duty of fair play has been attacked for implying that keeping your promise to me is something you owe to *society at large*—or at least to those who collectively have sustained the social practice of making and keeping promises. *According to the duty of fair play*, if you break a promise you made to me, you have wronged society, or at least you have wronged the promise-keeping members of society. But here the duty of fair play is mistaken about promissory obligations, for keeping your promise to me is something you owe me, not anyone else.[2]

Because Nico Kolodny and Jay Wallace's "hybrid account of promising" retains an element of the fair play account, let me comment on their view here.[3] Suppose A and B live in a society where there is a social practice of doing X and being expected to do X (unless certain accepted excuses come into play) if one performs a certain kind of communicative act, such as saying "I hereby promise to do X." Suppose A now says to B, "I hereby promise you that I will do X." On Kolodny and Wallace's hybrid view, A has *two* moral reasons to keep his promise to B.[4] First, A's assuring B that A would do X gives A an obligation *to B*, and this is the first moral reason to keep the promise. The other moral reason A has to keep his promise to B comes from the obligation A has *to society* not to exploit and undermine the beneficial social practice.

I have qualms about two elements of the hybrid view Kolodny and Wallace have developed. First, from Scanlon, they have taken on board the focus on assurance as the main rationale for promising and promise keeping. I will say more about this below when I discuss David Owens's views.

Second, from Rawls, Kolodny and Wallace have retained the idea that the duty to keep promises is partly composed of, or at least depends crucially on, an obligation *to society* to keep promises. Well, suppose you are a promise-keeping member of the society that contains many other people including A and B. Are you *necessarily wronged* when A fails to keep his promise to B? No, you aren't the one with a moral right or claim against A that he keep his promise. When A fails to keep his promise to B, B is the one wronged, not necessarily anyone else. A reflection of this point can be seen in the fact that, even when a promise should be broken because something very much more important arises, the promisee is the one owed an apology and perhaps compensation; society is not owed an apology or compensation.

Information/Expectation/Assurance Accounts of Promising Are Inadequate

A common view is that the point of the social practice of making promises is to give information, expectations, and assurances to promisees. However, David Owens's essays on promising argue persuasively that the Information/Expectation/Assurance account of promising is at least very incomplete if not completely wrong.[5] Admittedly, people very often seek promises from others so as to get assurance that certain actions will be done and others not done. Yet *sometimes* promises *do not* induce confident expectations in promisees (but the promises are still valid). And confident expectations that certain things will be done or not done can *sometimes* be induced by means other than promising. As Owens forcefully argues, what valid promises necessarily do is confer authority—I would prefer to say rights—on promisees.[6]

Very often this is what promisees want: the right to have the promisor keep the promise unless the promisee cancels the promise. Suppose I construct a machine that will torture me if I do not give to you my three best seashells.[7] By constructing that machine and showing it to you, I give you utter assurance that I will give you my three best seashells. However, my giving you information about what I will do, and even very confident expectations about what I will do, does not constitute, and thus is not sufficient for, my having promised. What is constitutive of my promising you my best seashells is not your feeling assured that I will transfer them to you but your acquiring *the right* to have me transfer the seashells to you.[8]

Act-consequentialism (Unless Very Gimmicky) Seems a Nonstarter

The Information/Expectation/Assurance account of promising aligns normally with act-consequentialism. Agent-neutral act-consequentialists point to the benefits people derive from having the confident expectations and assurance they get from other people's promises. If you have your heart set on getting my three best seashells, and I promise them to you, you are overjoyed. When I break my promise, you are heartbroken. Furthermore, other people are unnerved by my revealing myself to be untrustworthy. Finally, in breaking the promise, I make it less likely that people will do deals with me in the future. In all these ways, things go less well when people break their promises. Agent-neutral act-consequentialists appeal to such facts in explaining why promises should normally be kept.[9]

But as W. D. Ross pointed out and has often been repeated ever since, common-sense moral conviction holds that a promise should be kept even when on balance slightly more agent-neutral good would come from breaking it.[10] Suppose I give the three best seashells to a passing stranger rather than keep my promise to give them to you. Suppose that, on balance, my giving them to the stranger really does produce slightly more agent-neutral good, and in advance had slightly higher expected agent-neutral value. Nevertheless, in breaking my promise, I did wrong. You would complain that my promise gave you the right to decide what happened to the seashells. By making the promise to you, I transferred to you the right to decide what happens to them.[11] Or so holds common-sense morality.

The idea that promising creates duties to do things other than maximize the good (except in the special case where the promise *is* a promise to maximize the good) and the idea that promising involves transferring a right from the promisor to the promisee are ideas that I think any moral theory must accommodate if it is to be plausible. As I see it, the first question is which moral theory fully accords with our most confident ideas about moral (including promissory) obligations. Only if more than one theory coheres with our most confident ideas about moral obligations will we turn to the question of which moral theory identifies a foundational principle that unifies these obligations.[12]

Let me expand on this line of thought. Some philosophers hold to the very abstract and general idea that the point of morality is the maximization of agent-neutral good. And many philosophers hold that this abstract and general idea supports the agent-neutral act-consequentialist account of moral wrongness: An act is wrong if it produces less (expected) agent-neutral value than some alternative act. But agent-neutral act-consequentialism and any idea that leads to agent-neutral act-consequentialism look counterintuitive when we focus on cases where agent-relative obligations and prerogatives come into play. To be sure, when agent-relative obligations and prerogatives do not come into play, it is irrational for the agent to choose what he or she can see is a lesser agent-neutral good over a greater agent-neutral good. But the agent's (agent-relative) promissory obligations can be decisive, at least in cases where a little more agent-neutral good would result from breaking the promise, and even in cases where quite a lot more agent-neutral good would result from breaking the promise.

Some philosophers are inclined to build enough into the value theory of act-consequentialism to make it accommodate deontological morality.[13] Suppose that act-consequentialism accords intrinsic disvalue to promise breaking and rights violations. Suppose it also recognizes agent-relative and time-relative value and disvalue. If act-consequentialism does these things, and if it is fine-tuned in other ways, maybe it can assimilate not only our intuitive views about when promises must be kept and when they are rightly broken but also our view about making up to the promisee for broken promises.

Even if the project of trying to configure act-consequentialism so that it does not conflict with settled moral convictions is successful, the resulting theory seems to me unlikely to constitute a significant gain. This sort of approach has to *postulate* so much (e.g., agent-relative value, desert, etc.) in order to squeeze everything into act-consequentialism that the resulting theory is left *explaining* very little.[14] (I surmise that Michael Smith's contribution to this book puts forward act-consequentialism as a framework for discussing moral theories rather than a particular moral theory or even particular family of moral theories. So Smith's is a form of act-consequentialism so broadly characterized as not to attempt to explain the features of morality.)

Furthermore, agent-relative act-consequentialism disavows one of the main attractions of traditional consequentialism, namely commitment to agent-*neutral* impartiality at the foundational level (sometimes called the level of first principle). Why? Well, common-sense moral conviction holds that the duty to keep promises is either completely or almost completely agent-relative. Your duty is to keep *your* promises; it is not your duty to keep any other agent's promises (except perhaps in special cases, which I will return to below). The agent-relative duty to keep promises can be fully accommodated by act-consequentialism only if act-consequentialism accords agent-relative value to promise keeping. But any theory that posits agent-relative value at the foundational level does not have the kind of impartiality we want to see at that level, that is, impartiality that in no way privileges people or projects specially connected to the agent.[15]

II. SIX DEONTOLOGICAL ASPECTS OF THE DUTY TO KEEP ONE'S PROMISES

The duty to keep one's promises is paradigmatically deontological. I have already mentioned many of these elements. But let me pull the points together by making a list.

First, the wrong done to you if I fail to keep my promise is not necessarily a loss in welfarist terms. Suppose my promise was simply to hand over to you my best three seashells. I didn't promise to make you better off in terms of welfare. The content of my promise was not that I would hand over to you my three best seashells *only if* this would benefit you. So my promise gives me a moral reason for action even if my keeping the promise would have no impact on your total welfare. Admittedly, my promise to you is nullified if both my keeping it would not benefit you and there is an understanding between us that you mean to waive the promise if my keeping it would not benefit you. And admittedly, even if the promise has some pro tanto force, the promise should be overridden if keeping it would conflict *very sharply* with your welfare or perhaps with someone else's. Where to draw the line between situations in which promises that should be overridden and ones in which promises should not be overridden is notoriously difficult and may be indeterminate. Nevertheless, clearly the promise can be morally binding even when my keeping it would cost me somewhat more than you would benefit from my keeping it.

Furthermore, a promise can be morally binding even when no one would benefit from its being kept. Consider, for example, promises made to people before they died about what would be done after they die. Arguably, such promises are morally forceful, but keeping them might benefit no one. This is most clearly true if there cannot be posthumous benefits and harms. I am not sure whether there can be posthumous benefits and harms. But I am sure that promises made to people about what one will do after they die can be morally forceful even if no one would benefit from their being fulfilled. More generally, promises can be morally forceful even when the promisee is, though alive and kicking, not going to benefit from the promise's being kept.

This antiwelfarist idea seems implicit in a common complaint against act-utilitarian and more broadly act-consequentialist approaches to promising. The complaint is that the distinctive *wrongness* in breaking a promise is *not* primarily the *loss in welfare* for the promisee or for others. There is always a pro tanto moral reason to promote welfare, but it is distinct from the moral reason not to break one's promises.

Second, while the duty to keep one's promises is not (at least on the face of it) self-imposed, the promises one makes generate self-imposed duties. So the duty to keep promises ties in with deontologists' (or at least Kantian deontologists') emphasis on autonomy and self-ownership.

For example, Fried wrote,

> In order that I be as free as possible, that my will have the greatest possible range consistent with the similar will of others, it is necessary that there be a way in which I may commit myself. It is necessary that I be able to make non-optional a course of conduct that would otherwise be optional for me. By doing this I can facilitate the projects of others, because I can make it possible for those others to count on my future conduct, and thus those others can pursue more intricate, more far-reaching projects. If it is my purpose, my will that others be able to count on me in the pursuit of their endeavor, it is essential that I be able to deliver myself into their hands more firmly than where they simply predict my future course.[16]

The third characteristically deontological element of the duty to keep promises is the backward-looking nature of this duty. What one has a duty to do can depend on facts about the past, including facts about one's own past, especially facts about what one has promised.

Perhaps there are some things one is required to do now because of promises one *needs* to make, or is *likely* to make, or perhaps only *might* make *in the future*. For example, the duty to *keep* one's promises should prevent me from *making* promises I cannot or simply will not keep. Furthermore, the content of my promise might have pointed to various variables in the future, such as when I promised you yesterday that tomorrow I will provide whatever breakfast you want tomorrow. Still, what promissory duties I have depends essentially if only partly on the past—that is, on what promises I have made.

The fourth deontological element in the duty to keep one's promises is agent-relativity. *You* do not have a duty to keep *my* promises. Nor do you have a duty to ensure that I keep them. And I have no duty to keep your promises and no duty to ensure that you keep them.

Admittedly, there might be some cases where someone has a pro tanto duty to keep someone else's promise. An example might be that Emma's boss at Sunshine Corporation promises her a year-end bonus as a reward for her excellent performance. Then her boss is replaced by a new boss. Well, the new boss has a pro tanto duty to Emma deriving from the old boss's promise. Another example might be that the Earl of Wessex promises that his son will marry the Duke of Wiltshire's daughter. Some people think the son has a pro tanto obligation deriving from the father's promise. Yet another example might be that the government of Canada promises that Canada will protect Canada's allies in Afghanistan, and this promise gives Canadian citizens some duty to support such protection.

We might think such examples are not counterexamples to the thesis that promissory obligations are agent-relative. For we might think that these examples show that, while promissory obligations are always agent-relative, sometimes agents are multi-individual collectives. If we think that companies, families, and political entities can be agents, then we have to accept that agents can be collectives. That promissory obligations are relative to collective agents might be suggested by the fact that only some people have an obligation to Emma deriving from her old boss's promise: rather, only those with authority over Sunshine Corporation's money have this promissory obligation. Likewise, unless we are in the Earl's family, we have no promissory obligation to make sure the Earl's son marries the Duke's daughter. And only Canadians have a promissory obligation to support Canada's protection of its allies in Afghanistan.

On the other hand, we might accept that, in exceptional cases, there can be promissory obligations where the agent with the obligation is no part of the agent who made the promise (the two aren't both members of some collective agent). But I stress that such cases are exceptional if they exist at all. In all but these exceptional cases, promissory obligations are agent-relative, though often the agent to whom they are relative is a collective one. To avoid clutter, for the rest of this essay, I will ignore the possible qualifications to the claim that all promissory obligations are agent-relative.

The fifth deontological element is that the duty to keep promises is correlative to rights held by those to whom the promise was given. Again, when I promise you my three best seashells, I confer on you the right to this promise's being kept. My promise gives you the authority to decide whether I hand them over to you or not.

That the right to the three seashells I promised you is a right of yours brings out the sixth characteristically deontological element in the duty to keep one's promises. If I do not keep the promise, there is someone with a special reason to complain, someone who has been wronged. The one wronged if I don't keep the promise is the one to whom I gave the promise, and the one who has the right to insist that I keep the promise, namely you.

The rest of this essay addresses the question of whether rule-consequentialism offers a plausible justification for the duty to keep one's promises.

III. RULE-CONSEQUENTIALISM AND PROMISES

Rule-consequentialism selects rules by their consequences and evaluates acts by the rules thus selected. Rule-consequentialism should be formulated in terms of rules whose *consequences have the greatest expected value*. The expected value of a rule is calculated by multiplying the values of possible consequences of the rule times the probabilities of those possible consequences, and then adding the products of these multiplications together. There are lots of difficulties about how to best characterize this "expected value" formulation of rule-consequentialism. There is also a debate about whether an "actual value" formulation might be better. But I cannot go into such matters here.

If rules are to be selected by the (actual or expected) value of their internalization, should this be *agent-neutral* value (such as welfare for everyone, equality, or getting everyone above some threshold of sufficiency) or *agent-relative* value (such as the agent's own welfare and the welfare of those specially connected to the agent)? Assessing rules in terms of agent-neutral value has much to be said for it. There is an appealing and natural form of impartiality in assessing possible rules in terms of the benefits and harms *for everyone*, not merely for the agent or some subset of everyone. So rule-consequentialism is best formulated in terms of assessing rules in terms of agent-neutral impartial value.

Rule-consequentialism should be formulated in terms of the expected value of the *internalization* of rules, not merely in terms of the expected value of *conformity* with rules. Although conformity with rules is hugely important, the process of internalizing rules and their ongoing acceptance can have consequences in addition to conformity with them. Another important aspect of the difference between assessing mere conformity and assessing internalization is that assessing conformity ignores the costs of getting the rules internalized. Suppose that *conformity* with rule A would have *slightly* greater expected value than conformity with rule B. But suppose also that the time, effort and other costs involved in getting rule A *internalized* would be *much* greater than those involved in getting rule B internalized. These additional consequences *should* be counted in a rule-consequentialist assessment of possible rules. Thus, rule-consequentialism is better formulated in terms of internalization of rules than in terms of mere conformity with rules.

Thus formulated, rule-consequentialism holds that an act is morally permissible if it is allowed by the rules whose widespread internalization (including the costs of getting them internalized) has the greatest expected value. Usually, "widespread internalization" is interpreted as "full internalization by a large percentage of people." Permissibility is determined by rules selected by the expected value of their internalization by *a collection of people*, not merely internalization by *the individual agent*. In this sense, rule-consequentialism is typically put forward as a "collective" rather than "individual" form of consequentialism.

There are other complications, but in order to avoid repeating what I have argued elsewhere, I will now just state my own preferred form of rule-consequentialism:

> An act is wrong if it is forbidden by the code of rules whose internalization by the overwhelming majority of everyone everywhere in each new generation has maximum expected value in terms of well-being with some priority for the

> worst off. The calculation of a code's expected value includes all costs of getting the code internalized. If in terms of expected value two or more codes are better than the rest but equal to one another, the one closest to conventional morality determines what acts are wrong. (Hooker (2000: 32))

One of the classic early outlines of rule-consequentialism—so early, in fact, that the act-/rule- terminology hadn't even been coined yet—was John Rawls's "Two Concepts of Rules" (1955).[17] And Rawls's essay illustrated the difference between act- and rule-consequentialism by contrasting their approaches to promising. According to act-consequentialists, the permissibility of breaking a promise depends on whether breaking it has at least as much expected value as keeping it. According to rule-consequentialists, the rules defining the social practice of promising are assessed in consequentialist terms, but the permissibility of breaking a promise depends on these rules.

Imagine one possible social practice that allows promisors to break promises whenever the promisors believe doing so would produce greater agent-neutral value. Imagine an alternative possible social practice that allows promisors to break promises whenever they believe doing so would be better for the promisees, even if only a little better. The rule-consequentialist holds that the contours of the moral duty to keep promises are determined by whichever of these *or alternative rules* about promising are such that their internalization by the overwhelming majority of agents has the highest expected value.

IV. OBJECTIONS AND REPLIES

Let me close by discussing two attacks on the rule-consequentialist justification of the social practice of making and keeping promises. Both of these attacks appear in Fried's book. I discuss the first attack here and the second in section VI.

The first is an attack that claims rule-consequentialism is unsatisfactory throughout—that is, unsatisfactory not only with respect to the requirement to keep one's promises but also with respect to more or less every other moral requirement. This attack contends that rule-consequentialism is either incoherent or collapses into extensional equivalence to act-consequentialism (Fried (1981: 16)).

Rule-consequentialism is incoherent if it holds that there is an overarching and overriding commitment to maximize expected value but then requires one to stick to some rule even in a case where doing so won't maximize expected value. But if rule-consequentialism avoids the incoherence objection by *not* requiring one to stick to some rule even in a case where doing so won't maximize expected value, then rule-consequentialism collapses into extensional equivalence with act-consequentialism.

For three or four decades, this general attack on rule-consequentialism was widely taken to be successful. But rule-consequentialism can be formulated in a way that makes it invulnerable to this attack. Of course, such a formulation will have to avoid both incoherence and collapse. I take these up separately in the following few paragraphs.

Collapse

Rule-consequentialism does not collapse into extensional equivalence with act-consequentialism if rule-consequentialism is formulated in terms of internalization of rules instead of in terms of mere conformity with rules. As rules multiply in terms of number, complexity, or demandingness, their internalization costs increase. Admittedly, the expected value of conformity with them can also increase. But, at some point, the extra costs of internalizing additional rules, additional complexity of rules, and additional demandingness of rules outstrips the extra benefits of conformity with them. So rule-consequentialism formulated in terms of internalization will resist indefinite multiplication of rules, indefinite increases in their complexity, and indefinite strengthening of their demandingness. Settling on rules that are limited in terms of number, complexity, and demandingness, rule-consequentialism avoids collapse into extensional equivalence with act-consequentialism.[18]

Incoherence

That reply to the collapse objection has been around since Richard Brandt's essays in the 1960s. What came much later was a persuasive reply to the incoherence objection, the objection that rule-consequentialism is incoherent in on the one hand holding that there is an overarching and overriding commitment to maximize expected value but on the other hand requiring one to stick to some rule even in cases when this won't maximize expected value. In order to reply to this objection, we need to distinguish the theory of rule-consequentialism from the psychology of the agent who embraces the theory.

Does rule-consequentialism, that is, the theory itself, contain an overriding commitment to maximize expected value? The theory contains a principle for selecting rules (i.e. in terms of the expected value of their internalization) and the principle that the rules thus selected determine moral wrongness. There is nothing necessarily incoherent in evaluating codes of rules differently from acts. It is often the case that different kinds of things should be judged by different criteria.

Now must an agent who embraces rule-consequentialist theory have an incoherent psychology? Consider an agent who not only has an overriding moral commitment to maximize expected value but also is morally committed to following rules even when this won't maximize expected value. Such an agent *is* incoherent.

But a rule-consequentialist agent could have a different psychology. This might contain, as its fundamental moral motivation, an overriding moral commitment to act in ways that are impartially defensible. It might also contain the belief that complying with impartially justified rules is impartially defensible, and the belief that rule-consequentialism is the best account of impartially justified rules. An agent with that fundamental moral motivation and these beliefs would be a rule-consequentialist agent. But she would not have an overriding commitment to maximize the good.[19]

V. THE FOUNDATION OF RULE-CONSEQUENTIALISM

So the most influential general objections to rule-consequentialism are unsuccessful. There may, however, be new objections that prove fatal. I think the most likely such objection would be one that shows rule-consequentialism to have implausible *implications*. What I think is less likely is that rule-consequentialism can be shown to have implausible *foundations*.[20]

What is rule-consequentialism's foundation? Different philosophers give different answers to that question. My own answer is that what makes rule-consequentialism attractive is that it starts from *impartial* assessment of alternative possible *public* codes of moral requirements, permissions, rights, and so on. It then proclaims that the code it endorses for "public consumption" (i.e. for internalization by the public) is what agents should follow and what determines right and wrong.[21]

I admit that rule-consequentialism is not the only theory that begins with *impartial* assessment of alternative possible rules or principles. Nor is it the only theory that takes right and wrong to be determined by the best *public* code. Contractualism also has these virtues. What I think makes rule-consequentialism superior to contractualism, if in fact they don't dovetail, is that rule-consequentialism is better at according with our confident moral convictions about some cases.

VI. PROMISING

But does rule-consequentialism accord with convictions about the institution of promising? Fried acknowledges: "there is obvious utility in rules establishing and enforcing promissory obligations" (1981: 16). However, he contends, "the obligation to keep a promise is grounded not in arguments of utility but in respect for individual autonomy and in trust."

I agree with Fried that the obligation to keep a promise is not grounded in the utility of keeping that particular promise. Rather, the rule-consequentialist position is that the obligation to keep a promise is grounded in the utility of rules establishing and enforcing promissory obligations. An essential feature of the rules establishing promissory obligations is that the particular obligations one has because of the combination of a general duty to keep one's promises and one's autonomous commitments are self-imposed. In this way, the source of a duty to do X can be one's autonomous promise to do X. But, at a deeper level, rule-consequentialism explains why an autonomous promise can create an obligation, that is, because of the expected utility of having a social practice enabling the creation of self-imposed obligations.[22]

Earlier I accepted that typically individual promissory obligations (1) are not contingent on benefits to the promisee or others, (2) are self-imposed (autonomy), (3) are backward-looking in the sense that they depend on events in the past, (4) are agent-relative, (5) confer rights on particular others, and (6) give only some others (the promisees) the status of being wronged if the promise isn't kept. These are all deontological aspects of promissory obligations. I will now argue that rule-consequentialism embraces all six deontological features.

Some of these elements go together. In particular, obligations cannot be *self*-imposed without being agent-relative. Furthermore, with respect to not only the idea that promissory obligations are self-imposed and the idea that they are agent-relative but also the idea that promissory obligations depend on an event in the past, a social practice that didn't have these elements just wouldn't be a social practice of promising. To claim that rule-consequentialism endorses the social practice of promising is to claim that rule-consequentialism endorses a social practice of taking *past* events of telling others "I promise to do such and such" to generate *self-imposed, agent-relative* duties to do what was promised.

In contrast, consider a possible social practice in which the duty to keep an individual promise is always conditional on the promisee's benefiting from the keeping of the promise. Such a social practice would be recognizable as a social practice of promising. So if rule-consequentialist thinking reaches the conclusion that individual promissory obligations are not contingent on benefits to the promisee or others, its path to this conclusion must involve more than conceptual claims about promising.

Let us compare two possible social practices. The first is a possible social practice in which the duty to keep an individual promise is always conditional on the promisee's benefiting from the keeping of the promise. The second is a possible social practice exactly like the first except that there is no such condition on the duty to keep an individual promise. Which of these two possible social practices is likely to have higher expected value?

A number of different considerations point to the conclusion that the social practice with the greater expected value is the one in which the duty to keep a promise is not dependent on there being a benefit to the promisee if it is kept.

First, as I have already mentioned, many promises have a point other than benefiting the promisee. In the most straightforward and familiar case, the promisee asks for the promise because the promisor's keeping it would benefit someone else. For example, you ask me to promise that, if you die before your great-grandchildren are born and if I live long enough, I will pass on your diaries to your great-grandchildren, in the expectation that they will benefit from the information contained therein.

Or the promisee might ask for the promise because the *promise* itself would produce benefits whether or not *keeping it* would produce some additional benefit. An example might be that, in front of Jill's parents, Jack promises Jill he will always wear something black if she dies before he does. The reason he makes this promise is to show Jill's parents how much he loves her. Let us suppose that Jack, Jill, and her parents all know that his wearing black after she died, that is, *his keeping the promise*, would not itself benefit Jill or her parents. Nevertheless, he makes the promise and *his making it* makes Jill's parents happy. (Compare the way that making a convincing threat can have considerable advantages even if keeping it would have none.)

Those two kinds of cases where one person seeks a promise from someone else for some reason other than a benefit to the promisee from the promise's being kept are important. As we have seen, making a promise can produce benefits other than benefits to the promisee of the promise being kept. Furthermore, scope for autonomy is less if one can make morally binding promises only where keeping the promise would benefit the promisee.

Another disadvantage of a public moral rule that promises are morally binding only where keeping them would benefit the promisee is the insecurity of promises this would induce. Keeping a promise is very often disadvantageous to the promisor. Promisees need assurance that promisors do not have too much room for talking themselves into believing that their promises aren't binding. Promisees would not have much confidence that promises to them would be kept if they knew that promisors would feel released from their promises whenever they convinced themselves that keeping the promise would not benefit the promisee. Although of course promisees typically want the right to cancel the promise where keeping it would disadvantage the promisee, having that right is entirely compatible with also having the right to insist that the promise be kept even when the promisor says or even sincerely believes that keeping the promise wouldn't benefit the promisee.

I turn now to the thesis that rule-consequentialism agrees that promises confer rights on promisees. A practice that gives promisees rights has greater expected value than an alternative practice that gives promisors duties but does not give rights to promisees. As David Owens argues, people can benefit from having transferred to them certain kinds of authority over other people's behavior. Such authority typically takes the form of waivable rights to others' doing or not doing certain things. Admittedly, with respect to some kinds of rights, there may be greater benefit in these rights' being inalienable, or unwaivable. But, with respect to promissory obligations, promisees will typically have greater authority over promisors' behavior if the promisees can waive their rights to have the promises kept. This greater authority is likely (generally though not in every last case) to generate greater benefit to the promisees without disadvantaging the promisors at all. Hence rule-consequentialism supports the idea that promises confer rights on promisees.

Now, can rule-consequentialism account for the point that the promisee is the one wronged by a broken promise? The promisee's status as the potential wrongee seems a concomitant of the promisee's moral rights to waive the promise in advance of the time at which it is to be kept and moral right to an apology and perhaps compensation if the promise is not kept. It does seem natural that, if promisees have rights because of and over the promises that have been made to them, promisees are the ones wronged if promises to them aren't kept.

Yet, while the promisee is wronged if the promise isn't kept, there is room for discussion about whether some others might also be wronged. Suppose you obtain from me the promise that I will give your diaries to your great-grandchildren (who may not be born at the time I make the promise). Suppose these diaries will be very valuable because of the secrets you recorded and the brilliance of your everyday observations. However, suppose I then break my promise to you (e.g.) by giving the diaries straight to a collection or archive. In doing this, I have wronged you and deprived your great-grandchildren of a valuable asset. Since your great-grandchildren were the intended beneficiaries of the promise you obtained from me, perhaps they too were wronged by my breaking the promise. It certainly seems that they have a morally legitimate grievance against me, and I owe them an apology and compensation.

Whether the promisee is the *only* one who can be wronged by a broken promise seems to me intuitively unclear. Perhaps here is an area where rule-consequentialist assessment of alternative possible rules can help us see how to improve an element of our social practice. We should hold on to the connection between the status of being a potential wrongee and the having of rights to waive the promise and rights to redress. But then we might observe that a social practice where *intended beneficiaries* of promises joined *promisees* in having special claims on promisors—such as rights to waive the promises and rights of redress if the promises aren't kept—would probably have better consequences than a social practice in which *only the promisees* have such special claims. Some legal systems have made this innovation, presumably because it is psychologically easier to enforce an obligation where there is a living potential legal wrongee than where there is not. There seems to be the same reason for revising our social practice so as to give to intended beneficiaries the status of being potential moral wrongees.

CONCLUSION

If the arguments in this essay are sound, rule-consequentialism endorses all six of the deontological elements present in promissory obligations. My final suggestion was that rule-consequentialism favors extending from promisees to intended beneficiaries both the status of being potential wrongees and the rights associated with that status.

ACKNOWLEDGMENT

This essay was presented at Rice University, the Universities of Reading, Edinburgh, and Missouri-Columbia, Tulane University, Queen's University Belfast, and Trinity College Dublin. The essay benefited from comments from Ruth Abbey, Andre Ariew, Elaine Beadle, Bruce Brower, Rona Burger, Sarah Chant, Eric Chwang, Jennifer Culbert, Shane Coutland, Jonathan Dancy, Alison Denham, Joseph Diekemper, David Evans, Ian Folland, Chris Gadsden, Gerald Gaus, Max de Gaynesford, Margaret Gilbert, Jonathan Gorman, Claire Horisk, Stan Husi, Robert Johnson, Martha Klein, Kok Yong Lee, Xiaofei Liu, Cynthia Macdonald, Graham Macdonald, Elinor Mason, Matt McGrath, Andrew Melnyk, Alasdair Norcross, David Owens, Michael Pratt, Anna Raustol, Jonathan Riley, Philip Robbins, Deborah Roberts, Connie Rosati, Oliver Sensen, Michael Smith, Philip Stratton-Lake, Richard Velkey, Jeremy Watkins, and Paul Weirich. Seth Joseph Kurtenbach, Doug Portmore, Hanoch Sheinman, and Peter Vallentyne sent to me written suggestions about the essay that resulted in huge improvements.

NOTES

1. Rawls (1971: 344–350). See also Rawls's "Justice as Fairness," esp. pp. 60 and 63 in Rawls (1999), and Prichard (1949).

2. On the idea that the promise is owed to the promisee, see Ross (1930: 22); Warnock (1971: 30); MacCormick (1972), Atiyah (1981: 71–74, 86); and Scanlon (1998: ch. 7).

3. Kolodny and Wallace (2003).

4. Kolodny and Wallace (2003: 152–54).

5. Owens (2006) and (2007).

6. Also important in this context are the end of Hart (1955); and the end of Scanlon (1978).

7. See Foot (2001: 45), and the discussion of Foot in Owens (2007).

8. What Fried says of the law of contract can be largely transposed to the morality of promising: "the law of torts and the law of property recognize our rights as individuals in our persons, in our labor, and in some definite portion of the external world, while the law of contracts *facilitates our disposing of these rights* on terms that seem best to us." Fried (1981: 2), italics added.

9. See, for example, Alastair Norcross's essay in this book and Mason (2005).

10. Ross (1930: 34–39). See also Atiyah (1981: 70–79).

11. Atiyah writes, "to break a promise on the ground that this will do more harm [good?] than good [harm?] is to redistribute good from the promisee who is entitled to it, to others who are not. If this sort of redistribution is to be permitted, at the sole discretion of the promisor (however well motivated and reflective), why should the promisor not be just as morally entitled to break into the promisee's house and rifle the contents for the benefit of some deserving charity?" (1981: 86).

12. For more on moral methodology, see sections 1.2–1.6 of Hooker (2000).

13. See, as a leading example, Portmore (2003, 2007, 2008).

14. I say more about these ideas in Hooker (2009). For carefully argued replies to my attacks on agent-relative act-consequentialism, see Doug Portmore's *Commonsense Consequentialism* (forthcoming).

15. I explain the point in Hooker (2010 a).

16. Fried (1981: 13).

17. I describe "Two Concepts of Rules" as an early *outline* of rule-consequentialism, *not* as an *endorsement* of a rule-consequentialist *morality*.

18. Hooker (2000: sec. 4.2).

19. Hooker (2000: sec.4.3; 2007: 514–519).

20. See the discussion in Sheinman (2011: ch. 7).

21. I defend these claims in Hooker (2010 b). See also Hooker (forthcoming).

22. For some possible objections to rule-consequentialism concerning other possible worlds, see Doug Portmore (2009).

REFERENCES

Atiyah, P. S. 1981. *Promises, Morals, and Law*. Oxford: Clarendon Press.

Foot, P. 2001. *Natural Goodness*. Oxford: Oxford University Press.

Fried, C. 1981. *Contract as Promise*. Cambridge, MA: Harvard University Press.

Hart, H. L. A. 1955. "Are There Any Natural Rights?" *Philosophical Review* 64: 175–191.

Hooker, B. 2000. *Ideal Code, Real World: A Rule-consequentialist Theory of Morality*. Oxford: Clarendon Press.

———. 2007. "Rule-consequentialism and Internal Consistency: A Reply to Card." *Utilitas* 19: 514–519.
———. 2009. "Up and Down with Aggregation." *Social Philosophy and Policy* 26: 126-147.
———. 2010 a. "When Is Impartiality Morally Appropriate?" in J. Cottingham, B. Feltham, and P. Stratton-Lake (eds.), *Partiality and Impartiality: Morality, Special Relationships and the Wider World*. Oxford: Oxford University Press: 26–41.
———. Forthcoming. "Egoism, Partiality, Impartiality," in R. Crisp (ed.) *Oxford Handbook on the History of Ethics*. Oxford: Oxford University Press.
———. 2010 b. "Publicity in Morality: Reply to Katarzyna de Lazari-Radek and Peter Singer." *Ratio* 23: 111–17.
Kolodny, N., and Wallace R. Jay. 2003. "Promises and Practices Revisited." *Philosophy and Public Affairs* 31: 119–154.
MacCormick, N. 1972. "Voluntary Obligations and Normative Powers I." *Proceedings of the Aristotelian Society* 46: 59–78.
Mason, E. 2005. "We Make No Promises." *Philosophical Studies* 123: 33–46.
Owens, D. 2006. "A Simple Theory of Promising." *Philosophical Review* 115: 51–77.
———. 2007. "Duress, Deception, and the Validity of a Promise." *Mind* 116: 293–315.
Portmore, D. 2003. "Position-relative Consequentialism, Agent-centered Options, and Supererogation." *Ethics* 113: 303–332.
———. 2007. "Consequentializing Moral Theories." *Pacific Philosophical Quarterly* 88: 39–73.
———. 2008. "Dual-Ranking Act-Consequentialism." *Philosophical Studies* 138: 409–427.
———. 2009. "Rule-consequentialism and Irrelevant Others." *Utilitas* 21: 368–76.
———. Forthcoming. *Commonsense Consequentialism*. New York: Oxford University Press.
Prichard, H. A. 1949. "The Obligation to Keep a Promise." in Prichard, *Moral Obligation*. Oxford: Clarendon Press: 169–79.
Rawls, J. 1955. "Two Concepts of Rules," *Philosophical Review* 64: 3–32. Reprinted in Rawls 1999: 21–46.
———. 1958. "Justice as Fairness," *Philosophical Review* 67: 164–94. Reprinted in Rawls 1999: 47–72.
———. 1971. *A Theory of Justice*. Cambridge, MA: Harvard University Press.
———. 1999. *Collected Essays*. Cambridge, MA: Harvard University Press.
Ross, W. D. 1930. *The Right and the Good*. Oxford: Clarendon Press.
Scanlon, T. M. 1978. "Rights, Goals, and Fairness." In S. Hampshire (ed.), *Public and Private Morality*. Cambridge: Cambridge University Press: 93–111.
———. 1998. *What We Owe to Each Other*. Cambridge, MA: Harvard University Press.
Sheinman, H. Forthcoming. *Promise, Agreement, Practice: An Essay in Social Philosophy*. New York: Oxford University Press.
Warnock, G. J. 1971. *The Object of Morality*. London: Methuen.

Chapter 11

Demystifying Promises

Stephen Darwall

Abstract

The traditional problem of promising is to explain how it is possible to place oneself under obligation by expressing one's will to do so. A second problem is how it is possible to become obligated to another person *by so expressing one's will. The major attempts to explain promissory obligations-consequentialist, Rawls's, and Scanlon's-all fail to account for this "directed" or "bipolar" obligation, whether or not they can explain promissory obligations* simpliciter. *By appreciating bipolar obligations' second-personal character and promising as a second-personal phenomenon, however, it is possible to account for promising is a species of a genus,* transactions, *in which parties acquire new obligations to and rights against one another through interactions that presupposes their mutual accountability and their sharing a common basic second-personal authority. Other examples are consent, agreement, accepting an invitation, and acceding to a request.*

> To breed an animal with the *right to make promises*–is not this the paradoxical task that nature has set itself in the case of man?
>
> Nietzsche

Promises appear shrouded in mystery. We promise in the standard case by uttering words whose significance is to place us under an obligation in saying those very words. It is not generally puzzling that we can come to be obligated by what we say. I might say something that hurts your feelings, thereby incurring an obligation to apologize and make amends. Or I might utter words to get you to expect that I will do something and incur an obligation not to frustrate the expectations I have intentionally created. But promising is different from both of these. In these latter cases, becoming obligated is not intrinsic to what I say or do. In J. L. Austin's terms, it is a *perlocutionary* aspect of the speech act I perform, a further consequence I cause *by* so speaking. In promising, however, incurring an obligation is something we do *in* saying "I promise"; it is part of what Austin called the speech act's *illocutionary force*.[1] We *undertake* rather than simply incur an obligation when we promise.

The puzzle is how we can come to be obligated just in saying words whose meaning is to make us so obligated. This can seem a kind of word magic, getting morals out of meanings, or an "ought" from an "is," as John Searle famously tried to do (Searle 1964). I can come to be obligated through saying, "I promise," only if those to whom I say it take me to be successfully placing myself under an obligation to them in saying those words. But how can they justifiably believe that? How can my saying I am placing myself under an obligation to them make it the case that I actually am?

Similarly, to promise is voluntarily to *undertake* an obligation. This is different, again, from doing something that brings about an obligation as a consequence, as one comes to be obligated to apologize by saying something hurtful or to do something because one encouraged someone to believe one would. But how exactly does one undertake an obligation? How can the obligation *itself* be brought into existence, seemingly at will?

Hume famously noted that promises purport to involve a "*willing* of that *obligation* which arises from the promise" and that this is not "only a conclusion of philosophy, but is entirely conformable to our common ways of thinking and of expressing ourselves, when we say that we are bound by our own consent, and that the obligation arises from our mere will and pleasure" (1978: 516). For his part, Hume found this idea not just puzzling but absurd, since, he thought, we can no more make an obligation come into being at will than we can will a change in the "motions of the heavens" (517). At most, we can "feign" the willing of an obligation, as Hume regards priests as doing when they feign a "transubstantiation" of unleavened bread into the body of Christ while performing the sacrament of Holy Communion (522, 524).

Hume's own reasons for thinking that promising is too mysterious for words, at least for sober secular ones, derive from his moral sentimentalism. An obligation, for Hume, is a sentiment of approbation toward an "obligatory" motive or state of character, in the first instance, and, by extension, toward acts these motivate or express. We approve of fidelity, disapprove of infidelity, and thereby feel an obligation to keep promises. Since we cannot change our sentiments at will, we can but feign a voluntary undertaking of an obligation when we promise.

We don't have to be moral sentimentalists, however, to find the idea of willing an obligation mysterious. Theological voluntarists believe that God can will moral obligations into being. But we are not God, and it is not clear, in any case, how even God can do that. Moreover, God's capacity to create obligations at will is thought to derive from a superior authority he has over his creatures; by command he creates specific obligations that they then have to him. In promising, however, one purports to bind *oneself to others*. The distinctive obligation created by promise is a "directed" or "bipolar" obligation *to the promisee* (Gilbert 2004, Thompson 2004). How is that something it is possible to do at will or simply by expressing one's will?[2]

I believe we can understand how it is indeed possible to obligate oneself to another by expressing a will to undertake that very obligation by appreciating what I will call promising's *second-personal* character. As I shall argue, promising is but one example of a variety of undertakings in which one person comes to be obligated to another in a new and distinctive way by virtue of a second-personal interaction with that person. Since, as I shall argue, these undertakings are always mutual in the sense of presupposing a mutual recognition of an authority shared by both participants, I will call them *transactions*.[3] In *The Second-Person Standpoint*, I argue that presuppositions of second-personal engagement in general commit us to a fundamental answerability to one another and to recognizing our common capacity to obligate ourselves to each other through transactions of various sorts of which promising is but one specific instance. Before I begin to discuss both the general phenomenon and promising as a special case, however, I would like to say something about other approaches that end up demystifying promises only by making them less distinctive than they actually are. In my view, they not so much explain the apparent mystery as explain it away by reducing promising and its distinctive obligation to something else.

I. PRACTICE-BASED ACCOUNTS: HUMEAN/MILLIAN AND RAWLSIAN ACCOUNTS

One kind of approach of which this is true is any that attempts to ground the obligation to keep promises in the benefits of promising as a useful social practice. This might be done in a utilitarian or consequentialist fashion, following Hume, Mill on justice and rights, and Rawls's "Two Concepts of Rules" (Hume 1978, Mill 1998: ch. 5, Rawls 1955). Or it might be pursued in the way Rawls does in *A Theory of Justice*, by arguing that failing to keep promises amounts to unfairly "free riding" on the efforts of others who do their fair share in maintaining a mutually advantageous practice (Rawls 1971: 344–347). Whatever their differences, practice-based accounts of both kinds share a common vulnerability: they cannot adequately explain the distinctive way promises obligate a promiser *to a promisee*.

Hume's own account is a good example. Hume treats fidelity to promises as one of three central instances of the "artificial" virtue of justice. Justice is "artificial" because it requires ongoing social practices that are established by "convention," by which Hume means a mutually advantageous convergence of individual wills to abide by the "rules" of just practices of property, promise, and contract so long as others do. Given these practices' manifest benefits, everyone has powerful prudential reason to enter into and maintain them. Hume calls this self-interested motive the "natural obligation" to justice (1978: 498). The "moral obligation" to be just, and so to keep our promises, by contrast, derives from sympathy with the public benefits that are produced by the practice (498–499).

There are familiar problems with trying to ground an obligation to conform to desirable social rules in the good consequences of the practice they help constitute. There would be no need for rules of this kind unless they required actions that cannot be justified by *those actions'* beneficial consequences, *either* for the agent or for society at large. To be useful, rules of promising must require fidelity in at least some cases where neither self-interest nor the public interest would recommend keeping the promise. It may happen, as Hume himself imagined, that not fulfilling a promise to repay a loan to a "seditious bigot" would free one to use the money for a better purpose, either for oneself or for the public at large (1978: 497). But if they did not require us to keep promises in cases like this the rules of promising would not enable us to fix expectations in the beneficial ways they do.

Suppose, however, that this problem can be circumvented and that considerations of overall good somehow recommend keeping one's promise even in such cases, indeed, that they do so in every case where we intuitively feel (let us suppose correctly) that an obligation to keep a promise exists. Even if it could deliver an extensionally adequate account in this sense, there would still be at least two ways in which a consequentialist account of the kind we are imagining might be found wanting. One is simply that without some explanation of why we are morally *obligated* to produce overall good in general, we would still be lacking an account of the obligation to keep promises in particular. On the assumption we have just stipulated, the desirable consequences of the practice of promise-keeping would uncontroversially provide a moral reason, arguably a weighty moral reason, to keep our promises. But it would remain unclear why this would make keeping our promises morally *obligatory*. After all, even Mill held that what is obligatory, or morally wrong not to do, is, as a conceptual matter, what we are appropriately held responsible and blamed for not doing, that is, where a failure to comply would be *culpable* unless adequately excused.[4] Without some showing that we are responsible for producing overall benefit and rightly blamed for failing to do so without adequate excuse, it would therefore remain unclear how the social benefits of promise-keeping would ground a moral obligation to keep promises.

In *The Second-Person Standpoint*, I argue that this feature of obligation reveals what I call the concept's irreducibly *second-personal* character. Moral obligations are what we are appropriately held morally *accountable* for doing by ourselves and others; blame and other instances of what Strawson called "reactive attitudes," like indignation and guilt, are, as a conceptual matter, the fitting response to unexcused moral wrong (Darwall 2006: chs. 4–5, Strawson 1968). Holding someone accountable in the requisite sense invariably involves, I argue, an implicit *address* of a putatively legitimate demand to someone that purports to make a claim on that person's will and conduct. Since any address is necessarily *to an addressee*, reactive attitudes are in this sense second-personal. They always involve the implicit address of a purportedly legitimate demand to their objects. (Since one can address such demands to oneself [as, for example, in the feeling of guilt], "second person" in this sense does not entail "second party." An address can be second personal without being to someone else.) Moral obligations are thus what we can legitimately demand of one another and ourselves as representative moral persons or, as we might also put it, as representative members of the moral community. If we are morally obligated to keep our promises, therefore, this must be something we are accountable to one another for doing. Any attempt to ground the obligation to keep promises, like any attempt to ground a moral obligation of any kind, must therefore explain why morality *demands* the conduct in this sense.[5]

Since I am not concerned to defend a second-personal account of moral obligation in general here, however, we can put to one side any defects a consequentialist practice-based account of the moral obligation to keep promises might have on this score. Nevertheless, even if it could succeed in providing a convincing account of promissory obligations simpliciter, such an account would not yet explain how by promising the promiser comes to have a distinctive obligation *to the promisee*. Promissory obligations are a paradigm of the kind Michael Thompson calls "bipolar" and Margaret Gilbert terms "directed" (Thompson 2004, Gilbert 2004). When a promiser fails to keep a promise without adequate justification, she not only does wrong or violates a moral obligation simpliciter. She also *wrongs the promisee* and violates her obligation *to him*. Even if a consequentialist practice-based account could explain the wrongness simpliciter of breaking promises, it would not yet explain why it wrongs the promisee.

As Gilbert has stressed, a promise gives a promisee rights against the promiser, and therefore a distinctive standing, authority, or sovereignty in relation to the promiser and her will (Gilbert 2004: 83, 86–90; see also Watson 2009). When A promises B to do X, B thereby acquires an ensemble of rights against A. Most obviously B acquires the right that A do X, but B also acquires the right to release A from her promise, to insist that A act as promised, to object if A doesn't, to hold A accountable in ways that others do not have standing to do (even if they do have standing to blame or morally disapprove of B), for example, by demanding an apology, to seek compensation, to forgive, and so on. Joel Feinberg made a similar point about ("claim") rights in general when he pointed out that to have a right to something, like the performance of a promised action, is to have an authority or standing to demand or claim it from those against whom one holds the right (Feinberg 1980). In promising, a promiser gives a promisee an ensemble of rights and, therefore, the standing to make certain demands of him and to hold him answerable in certain ways.

As I shall elaborate further below, the standing anyone has as *a representative person* to hold himself and others responsible for violations of moral obligations simpliciter through what Strawson calls "impersonal" reactive attitudes like indignation and moral blame is related to the different standing we also have *as individuals* to demand that others respect and not violate our own individual rights in particular. It is the latter standing we presuppose in *personal* reactive attitudes, like resentment, or even gratitude, which we feel, respectively, as if from a victim's or beneficiary's point of view.[6] The conceptual connection between these two standings is that it is a conceptual truth that to wrong someone is, other things equal, at least, to do moral wrong simpliciter.[7]

If this is so, then it would seem that adequate accounts of moral obligation *period* and of "bipolar" or "directed" obligations (obligations *to*) of the sort created by binding promises should go hand in hand. Below, I shall suggest how such accounts might be provided. My current point, however, is that a consequentialist practice-based theory of promissory obligations simpliciter would not yet account for their bipolar character, that is, the way promises create a distinctive obligation and authority of the promisee with respect *to* the promiser.

Now this judgment might seem at best premature since the relevant rights and standings would seem to be able to be defined *within* the practice of promising. Surely the practice that would be most beneficial would be one whose rules accord the relevant standings and rights. Why, then, would a practice-based consequentialist account of promissory obligations simpliciter not simply generate an account of obligations *to the promisee* as a theoretical consequence? The problem is that if promisees' rights and standings are defined *internally* to a practice then, *on the consequentialist's own view*, they do not yet entail any moral obligation. So we get no entailment from the proposition that A violated B's right (and so wronged B) as defined by rules *internal* to the practice to the proposition that A violated a moral obligation simpliciter, even other things being equal. The consequentialist will be the first to point out that rights and standings that are defined *internally* to a practice are in themselves morally neutral, since the practice might be either laudable or objectionable, having beneficial consequences or harmful ones. The practice of apartheid in South Africa gave whites *practice-defined* rights and authorities that blacks did not have; these were part and parcel of what the practice was. But the consequentialist will rightly insist that no genuine moral obligations or rights flowed from these practice-defined rights and authorities.

The only sensible route for a consequentialist, it seems, is the one that Mill took, namely to hold that *moral* rights are based in the desirable consequences of their social protection, that is, that a given moral right holds if, and only if, a practice with the relevant practice-defined right would have good or the best consequences (relative to any competing practice). "To have a right," Mill wrote, is "to have something which society ought to defend me in the possession of." And if anyone asks "Why it ought?" Mill continues, "I can give him no other reason than general utility" (1998: ch. 5). Taking this route, however, will saddle a consequentialist practice-based account of bipolar obligations *to* promisees with a problem closely related to the one we noted above for consequentialist accounts of moral obligation simpliciter.[8] In its current guise, the problem is that A's actually having an obligation to B, and therefore B's actually having a right against A, cannot plausibly derive simply from the fact that it would be *desirable* for us to *treat* A and B *as though* they actually had these respective rights and obligations. This is an instance of the same "wrong kind of reasons problem," what I call "Strawson's Point" in *The Second-Person Standpoint*, that I pointed out above in connection with consequentialist accounts of obligation simpliciter.

That an action would be desirable, even morally desirable, does not entail that it is morally obligatory, since a reason (of the right kind) for desiring something is not automatically a reason (of the right kind) to warrant the reactive attitudes through which we hold people responsible and blame them for doing something without adequate excuse. Strawson argued in "Freedom and Resentment" that the desirable consequences of treating people as if they are morally responsible for some action does not provide a reason of "the right *sort*" for practices of moral responsibility "as we understand them" (1968:72, 74). It does not provide a reason of the right kind for thinking their actions *culpable*. Reasons of the right sort must be able to support the distinctive attitudes through which we hold ourselves and others responsible (impersonal reactive attitudes, in this case). Taken by themselves, desirability considerations can only rationally support desire, not the reactive attitudes that, as a conceptual matter, are distinctively involved in judgments of moral obligation and responsibility.

An exactly similar point holds with rights and bipolar obligations *to*, and the reason it does is because these also conceptually involve distinctive attitudes (*personal* reactive attitudes, in this case) that differ from desire. That it would be desirable, even morally desirable, to treat someone as having a right cannot entail that the person actually has that right. For example, part of what it is for a promise to give a promisee the right to expect performance, to demand apology for nonperformance, and so on, is for it to make him warranted in *resenting* nonperformance owing to his having the authority to demand performance. But from the fact that there are reasons to desire, even from the moral point of view, a practice in which individuals are treated as having this authority and warrant it simply does not follow that they actually do have it. This obstacle, which seems to face any purely consequentialist practice-based theory of rights in general, is one that will also apparently afflict any such account of promissory obligations *to promisees* in particular.[9]

II. RAWLS'S ACCOUNT

A practice-based account of the kind Rawls proposes in *A Theory of Justice* can provide a more satisfying explanation of the obligation simpliciter to keep promises than consequentialist versions, but it seems to face the same obstacle they do in explaining any distinctive obligation *to promisees* and promisees' correlative promissory rights. Justice as fairness stresses the mutually advantageous character of the practice of promising, not just its overall aggregate benefits, and a resulting duty of reciprocity or fair play to do one's fair share when one benefits from others doing theirs. Failing to keep promises amounts to "free riding," accepting the benefits of others playing their practice-defined roles while not playing one's own.

Justice as fairness is primarily a political conception, as Rawls emphasizes even more strongly in his later writings. But Rawls suggests in *A Theory of Justice* a related general theory of moral right and wrong, which he calls "rightness as fairness" (1971: 111). And he explicitly there discusses certain specific moral duties, both the natural duty to support just institutions and duties that derive from the "principle of fairness." According to the latter, if one voluntarily accepts the benefits of a just practice, then one incurs an obligation to do one's part. Rawls treats promissory obligations as falling under this principle (344–348). So long as the practice of promising is fair and assigns practice-defined rights and obligations by rules or principles that any participant could endorse from an impartial position of ignorance of how the practice's benefits are likely to fall on her *individually*, participants have a moral obligation to do their fair share if others do theirs.

Rawls rarely discussed the metaethics of moral obligation, but in his Dewey Lectures, he sounded a theme that enables us to connect justice as fairness, the moral duty to support and play one's role in just institutions and practices, and so the practice of promising, to the metaethical aspect of moral obligation to which I pointed above. Rawls said that justice as fairness conceives of persons as "self-originating source[s] of valid claims" (1980: 546). I propose we interpret Rawls's idea as entailing that it is because everyone has the same *fundamental* authority to make claims on one another *at all* that each can come to have *practice-defined* standings to make claims on each other when the practice-defined rights and obligations can be codified by rules that all can endorse as equal persons with the same equal basic authority. Failing to play one's practice-defined role when others play theirs amounts to insisting on one's own standing (which justifies one's own practice-defined rights) while failing to recognize theirs (which equally ground their practice-defined rights). In this way, justice as fairness is rooted in an ideal of *reciprocity* that itself derives from the idea that every person has the same fundamental authority to make (reciprocal) claims of one another.[10] When we enter into just practices like promising and accept the benefits of practice-defined standings to make demands on others, we have an obligation to reciprocate, to do our fair share in turn.

I said earlier that moral obligations are, as a conceptual matter, standards we are aptly held responsible for violating, by ourselves and others, through reactive attitudes like guilt, indignation, and moral blame. And I mentioned also that reactive attitudes are distinguished from other critical responses by their "second-personal character," that is, by their invariably involving an implicit address of a putatively legitimate claim or demand. Moral obligations are what we can legitimately demand and hold ourselves and one another responsible for (Darwall 2006). But if this is right, and if a requirement to keep promises can be rooted in the idea that all persons have the same equal authority to make claims of one another at all, then there is an obvious line of thought leading to the proposition that there is a moral obligation to keep our promises. Free riding, taking advantage of the practice by accepting the benefits of others playing their practice-defined roles while failing to play one's own, is evidently something we can legitimately demand that people not do, since it plainly violates, and so disrespects, the authority we all have to demand reciprocity, that is, reciprocal respect of our equal basic authority to make claims on one another.[11]

In this way, a Rawlsian practice-based theory can provide a plausible account of the moral obligation to keep promises simpliciter. But can it adequately explain the obligation a promiser has *to a promisee*? I shall argue below that the Rawlsian idea that persons are self-originating sources of valid claims is fundamental to any satisfying explanation of promissory obligations, including obligations to promisees. However, *Rawls's own* account of the obligation to keep promises via the "principle of fairness" cannot adequately account for the ensemble of promisees' rights and correlative bipolar obligations of promisers, since it focuses on unfair treatment not distinctively of promisees, but of *all* who do their fair share by playing their roles in a mutually advantageous practice.

According to Rawls's account, the wrongness of breaking a promise consists in unfairly free riding on those who do their part in maintaining the practice, namely, all who follow the rules at cost to themselves. Promising is a cooperative scheme involving all persons, and everyone who cooperates by keeping promises has a legitimate claim that others be prepared to shoulder the costs by keeping promises at some cost to themselves also. This will frequently include the promisee, of course, but not in any distinctive way. We might imagine, for example, that the promisee actually has a history of shirking his own promissory obligations. But this wouldn't automatically cancel, or even diminish, any directed or bipolar obligation arising from a promise made to him, especially if the promiser were to know about this.

The only way any obligation *to* the promisee (and her correlative right) can come into Rawls's account is as *practice-defined* obligations and rights that are morally neutral in themselves. They can acquire moral or *de jure* normativity only through advantages that the practice provides for all who participate in it. Rawls's account is similar in this way to consequentialist practice-based accounts. Roles, rights, and obligations that are defined within a practice have no inherent validity or moral standing; they derive any genuine or *de jure* normativity from, as it were, the outside—from the aggregate benefits the practice produces, according to consequentialist approaches, or from the mutual benefits of a cooperative enterprise that everyone has a duty of fairness to promote and do their part in, according to Rawls's approach.[12] On Rawls's account, any non-practice-derived obligations and rights connected with promising are to or against anyone who participates in the practice, not to or against the promisee or the promiser distinctively.

III. SCANLON'S ACCOUNT

Scanlon argues against practice-based accounts of both consequentialist and Rawlsian varieties that it is unnecessary for an established practice to exist in order for promises, or their moral equivalent, to take place and obligate. Scanlon presents cases where there is no ongoing practice and argues that it is possible in such cases for people to undertake to give one another assurances of future conduct that create obligations of fidelity, whether or not we choose to call such extraconventional acts "promises."[13]

Scanlon's argument depends on a general contractualist argument and, more specifically, his claim that it would be unreasonable for anyone to reject the following principle, which he calls *Principle F*:

> If (1) in the absence of objectionable constraint, and with adequate understanding (or the ability to acquire such understanding) of his or her situation, *A* intentionally leads *B* to expect that *A* will do *X* unless *B* consents to *A*'s not doing so; (2) *A* knows that *B* wants to be assured of this; (3) *A* acts with the aim of providing this assurance, and has good reason to believe that he or she has done so; (4) *B* knows that *A* has the beliefs and intentions just described; (5) *A* intends for *B* to know this, and knows that *B* does know it; and (6) *B* knows that *A* has this knowledge and intent; then, in the absence of special justification, *A* must do *X* unless *B* consents to *X*'s not being done. (Scanlon *1998*: 245)

We may stipulate that these conditions are all satisfied in standard promises. Scanlon's claim then is that the wrongness of breaking promises can be explained by the wrongness of violating Principle F. We should note, however, that Principle F might be reasonably interpreted to contain notions, such as that of "consent" and "providing [an] assurance," that are already second-personal and presuppose obligations of the sort involved in promising, which the reasonable unrejectability of Principle F is supposed to explain.[14] As we ordinarily understand it, one can only consent to others doing things they would otherwise be obligated to one not to do, and an assurance would seem to involve the assumption of an obligation to the assured that is similar, if not indeed identical, to any involved in promises. So interpreted, therefore, Principle F can hardly feature in any explanation of the existence of a promissory obligation. I shall argue, however, that if we interpret consent and assurance in non-second-personal terms, Principle F can indeed be reasonably rejected.

Consider, first, cases where one intentionally or negligently causes someone to expect that one will do something. Scanlon argues persuasively that obligations arise in such cases. If the other has not yet relied on the expectation, then one has some obligation to correct the expectation if it is mistaken. And if the other has relied on it, then one has some obligation to fulfill the expectation or to compensate the other if it will be unfulfilled.

Promises are, of course, different. If one promises to do something and the other has not yet relied on an expectation that one will do it, one cannot simply disabuse her of the expectation if one wishes not to do what one promised. The other has a remaining valid claim to one's doing what one promised and not just to due notice of nonperformance or to compensation of the costs of reliance.

Principle *F* attempts to capture this through a complex set of conditions connected to providing assurance. But the idea of assurance can be interpreted in two different ways. A *causal* interpretation of providing assurance would be: causing someone to be assured that something will happen, say, that one will do something. According to a *second-personal* interpretation, on the other hand, providing or giving someone an assurance involves a second-personal act of *assuring*, that is, a putatively claim-giving address to another of the same genus as promise (that may indeed be the very same thing as a promise).

Interpreted second-personally, Principle F is compelling, but, as I see it, that is itself explained by the kind of account of (second-personal) *transactions*, of which assuring and promising are both species, that I shall sketch presently. Without such an account, the fact that no one could reasonably reject Principle F is impotent to provide a complete explanation of the obligations that promisers have to promisees, even if F is interpreted second-personally. But if we interpret Principle F in non-second-personal, causal terms, it is simply not compelling. Whatever obligations are created by causing someone to be assured by satisfying conditions (1) through (6) need not include, as a second-personal assurance or promise must, the obligation to perform the assured action (rather than simply to provide due notice of non-performance or compensation of reliance costs).

To see the first point, that Principle F must already presuppose and so cannot explain the obligations that promises create if it is interpreted in second-personal terms, note Scanlon's use of "consent" in condition (1). Like the idea of *giving assurance*, consent is also a second-personal idea. It is conceptually impossible to consent to someone's doing something unless one already has the standing or authority to demand that he or she not do it. To consent is precisely to waive or voluntarily restrict this authority. So something can cause someone to be assured that one will do *X* unless she *consents* to one's not doing *X* only if it also brings about her having the authority to demand that one do *X*. It follows that if we take "consent" in condition (1) literally, Principle F must presuppose and so cannot explain the obligation to promisees that promises create.

Suppose, however, that we understand Principle F non-second-personally. For "providing an assurance" we substitute "causing to be assured." And instead of requiring that *B* be assured that *A* will do *X* unless *B consents* to *A*'s not doing *X*, we say that *B* is assured that *A* will do *X* unless *B* expresses a wish that *A* not do *X*. So interpreted, Principle F is not plausible. To see this, we need only imagine cases in which someone leads another to expect that he will do something, unless the other wishes him not to, and that it is *very* unlikely he will change his mind, with all of Principle F's knowledge and intention conditions satisfied, but in a way that explicitly cancels any implication that he intends to place himself under any obligation to do it in the very unlikely instance he *does* change his mind. Suppose, for example, that for whatever reason the person in whom one wishes to cause the assurance is someone who wishes not to be bound to one by a promissory obligation (and would reject a promise if one tried to make it to her). Even so, such a person might want to be assured that one will in fact do something and one might seek to cause such an assurance, with all of Principle F's conditions satisfied, but in a way that explicitly cancels any suggestion that one would consider oneself obligated to perform in the very unlikely event one did change one's mind. To make such a case most convincing, we will need to make the likelihood of a change in mind extremely small. But there is no reason, consistently with satisfying the conditions specified in F, that we cannot make that likelihood as small as we like.

It seems impossible *to assure* someone one will do something (second personally) while simultaneously canceling such an implication. But it certainly seems possible to cause someone to believe (and so, in a non-second-personal, causal sense, to have an assurance) that one will do something in a way that satisfies all of the clauses of Principle F while simultaneously canceling any implication of obligation to perform in the unlikely event of a change in mind.

For example, suppose I want you to be assured that I will attend your party (although only if you continue to want me to). And suppose that I know that, for whatever reason, you really don't like other people to be beholden to you through promises.[15] I could say to you something like the following with the relevant (Principle F–like) intentions: "I intend to attend your party and the chances that I will do so are 99.99 . . . percent (but only if you continue to want me to). There is almost no chance that I will change my mind. However, were I to do so and informed you before you relied on my earlier intention, I would consider myself under no obligation to come. Nonetheless, there is almost no chance of this happening." It seems clear that in saying this, I might cause you to be assured in a way that satisfies clauses (1)–(6) of Principle F, but that it would be false that, were I to change my mind, I would be obligated to come to the party. I conclude, therefore, that if we interpret Principle F in non-second-personal terms, it is indeed one we could reasonably reject.

It is important to appreciate, however, that *even if* Scanlon were right and Principle F were not reasonably rejectable, the most this could show is that there is an obligation to keep promises simpliciter. It still would not show that the promiser was obligated *to the promisee.*

Promises have an essentially second-personal character that Principle F cannot capture when it is interpreted in causal terms. It is part of the very idea of a promise or a genuinely second-personal assurance that the addresser gives the addressee to understand that she thereby has a claim to the addresser's following through. Moreover, as I shall show presently, when I promise or assure someone that I will do something, I must already be authorizing the other to presuppose that she and I share a second-personal authority to make claims of, and be accountable to, one another.

IV. PROMISING AS SECOND PERSONAL (I)

In the next section, I shall illustrate how promising is but one species of a genus of second-personal *transactions* in which one person comes to have an obligation *to* another by virtue of a second-personal interaction. Before that, however, we should clarify the second-personal character of promising itself.

To begin with the most obvious point, promises are always *to* some person or persons. There must be a *promisee* who is given by virtue of the promise an ensemble of rights and prerogatives she would otherwise not have had. But it is also important, as I shall be arguing presently is true of all transactions, that it is part of the very idea of a promise that the *promisee already* has some rights and prerogatives (hence some (second-personal) authority to make claims and demands) with respect to the promiser, as indeed with respect to every other person, independently of the promise. In particular, the (would be) promisee has the authority to refuse to accept a promise. A promise's existence is conditional on its acceptance (or at least not being rejected) by the promisee. I simply cannot make a promise to you if you refuse to accept it.

In this way, a promise is like a gift; it must be accepted or not rejected to be given at all.[16] Otherwise, I will have no more than tried to promise (or give a gift). Various other rights and prerogatives derive from the would-be promisee's authority to reject the promise. Just as it is part of the very idea of a gift that it cannot be forced on someone, so also does a would-be promisee have standing to demand that he be genuinely free to reject it—that his acceptance not be forced, manipulated, extracted by deception, and so on.

But the promisee is not the only one with a standing that is implicitly recognized in promising. In accepting a promise, a promisee recognizes an authority the promiser has as well. Not just any being has the "right to make promises."[17] When we accept a promise from someone, we treat him as having the authority or "normative power" to make promises and thereby become answerable to us in the distinctive way that promisers are to promisees.[18] We treat him, moreover, as responsible for his own conduct more generally and implicitly accord him authority as someone having this competence. This is far from trivial. We do not treat very young children as having this standing, for example. Accepting a promise involves entrusting an action to someone and giving him the responsibility for doing it. If we accept someone's promise and subsequently try to usurp control by offering extra incentives or even doing the promised thing ourselves, the promiser may be entitled to object though our conduct might otherwise have been permissible.

Moreover, just as promises presuppose an authority on the part of the promisee—for example, to be able to consider whether to accept the promise without coercion, manipulation, or fraud—one that is independent of any relation brought about by the promise, so also do they presuppose a similar authority on the part of the promiser. Although no one is bound to accept promises from others, it is part of the very idea of a promise that it is freely given—otherwise, promisers could hardly purport to undertake any obligation in giving them. So just as promising presupposes mutual recognition of the promisee's authority freely to accept or reject a promise, so also does it presuppose mutual recognition of the promiser's authority freely to give it. Of course, it may happen that a promise is extracted or accepted through some violation of either of these authorities, through coercion, say, or manipulation. But it nonetheless remains the case that to interpret a transaction as a promise, we must see it as one in which the parties have an authority that was thereby violated and that they have standing to hold the other accountable, object, and so on. Promises under such conditions may not completely "misfire," as Austin put it, but they nonetheless constitute an "abuse" in his terms (1962: 18). They violate "felicity conditions" that are part of our very idea of the speech act.

V. SECOND-PERSONAL TRANSACTIONS

In these ways, promises are but one species of the genus we are calling *transactions*. What species of this genus have in common is a kind of interpersonality, mutuality, or reciprocity. Transactions take place at all only if there is the relevant uptake from both parties, and they presuppose a common authority both parties have to demand free participation and therefore that both parties are mutually accountable for participating on these terms.[19]

One kind of transaction, which I discuss more fully in *The Second-Person Standpoint*, is *agreeing* in what Margaret Gilbert calls the "everyday" sense that is involved when two people decide to do something together (Gilbert 1990, Darwall 2006: 198–201). For two people genuinely to take a walk together, Gilbert argues, there must be at least an implicit invitation and uptake between the parties that, having taken place, obligates them to one another, so that neither may simply depart from the agreement unilaterally and both have standing to hold the other accountable should he do so. It is possible for the parties to an agreement to become subsequently obligated to one another *through* their agreement, however, only if they are already obligated to one another in some more fundamental way independently of it (Darwall 2006: 198–201). Specifically, the parties can become so obligated only because their agreeing presupposes that they already have a common (second-personal) authority, which grounds obligations to one another that exist independently of the agreement (including not to force the other to do what she is being invited to agree to do). The parties to the agreement both presuppose that this authority simply includes the standing or normative power to undertake new obligations to one another through the agreement.

For a Gilbertian agreement to take place there must be some implicit second-personal address between the parties (an implicit invitation and uptake or acceptance). But consider what is involved in second-personal interaction of this kind. It is part of the very idea of an invitation that the invitee is free to reject it if she chooses and that the issuer of the invitation has no authority to force the invitee to do what he is inviting her to do, that is, that any such use of force would be illegitimate and so a violation of the invitee's authority. If someone puts a gun to your head and threatens to pull the trigger unless you give him your wallet, he has thereby made it impossible for himself to invite you to do so and therefore for your giving him the wallet to be something you *agree* to do in the relevant sense. Genuine invitations and their acceptance are only possible within a second-personal space that itself presupposes that inviters and invitees are already obligated to one another in this more fundamental way.

It follows that *acceptings of invitations*, whether they give rise to Gilbertian agreements or not, are another species of transaction. If I accept your invitation to a party, I thereby have some obligation to you to come, to give you timely notice if I can't, and so on. And you acquire thereby an authority to hold me responsible if I don't come, don't give you timely notice, and so on. If I violate my obligation to you, then I violate an obligation period, at least other things being equal, and so I do something that anyone—you, me, or anyone else—has standing to blame me for if I have no excuse. But you acquire a distinctive standing, as the person *to whom* I am obligated, to object, resent, and, perhaps, forgive violation. And, again, it is possible for you to acquire this authority, which is created by my accepting your invitation, only if you and I already are obligated to one another in some more fundamental way. The issuing and acceptance of an invitation is a second-personal transaction that itself presupposes that the transagents already have the authority to enter (freely) into the transactional relation and are therefore already accountable to one another prior to the invitation, for example, for not forcing the potential invitee to do what she is being invited to do.

Accepting or *acceding to a request* is another species of transaction with the same second-personal structure. It is intrinsic to the concept of request that the person of whom a request is made is free not to accede to it and that she will acquire some new obligation to the requester to perform as requested if she does so accede. The freedom not to accede or not does not simply consist in a permission simpliciter or even a permission with respect to the requester. In order to be in the normative position to accede to and thereby become obligated by a request, one must already have a claim against the requester not to be forced either to accede to it or to do as one is requested.

Yet another example is *allowing* or giving *consent*. This always involves some implicit second-personal transaction between the person allowing or giving consent and the person allowed or to whom consent is given (Ripstein 2009: 111–126). In consenting to someone's doing something, we thereby give her authority to do it and to hold us accountable if we attempt to impede her in various ways. This of course presupposes that we had the authority so to authorize her, but also that we were free not to do so, hence that we had the authority to demand that she not so act without our consent, to hold her accountable if she does, and so on. Although it may be harder to see, the person consenting must also presuppose that the person soliciting consent has an authority independently of any she might be given by consent. Just as the giving of consent must be free, so also must the solicitation. I cannot *consent* to your doing something if you have not requested consent at least implicitly.[20] If I attempt to force you to solicit my consent, I violate an authority any consent I might give you must presuppose.

VI. SECOND-PERSONAL AUTHORITY, SECOND-PERSONAL ADDRESS

Promising is but one species of transaction in which the transagents create new obligations to one another, but presuppose that they are already both accountable to one another and have an authority to create these new obligations, independently of any obligation they acquire through the transaction. In the final section, I will return to promising as a species of this genus. Before that, however, I need to say something more about what grounds the fundamental authority, *equal basic second-personal authority*, that transactions presuppose generally, including the authority to create new bipolar obligations through the transaction.[21] After all, someone might object, it is all well and good to show that promises are a species of a genus whose nature is such that *if they validly take place at all*, then the parties to them must have the authority to create the new obligations they inherently involve. But we don't yet know how it is possible for these new bipolar obligations to be created unless we know what makes it the case that the parties really have the authority their transactions presuppose. Maybe there are no valid promises or transactions generally. Maybe all transactions "misfire" because the authority they presuppose simply does not exist.

Although I can hardly rehearse the argument here, in *The Second-Person Standpoint* I argue that all beings having the psychic capacities necessary to enter into second-personal relations (*second-personal competence*) share a common authority (equal basic *second-personal authority*) to make claims and demands of one another at all. To put the same point in other words, all persons (second-personally competent beings) are *mutually accountable*. Rawls put what I argue to be the same point when he said that to be a person is to be a "self-originating source of valid claims" (1980: 546).

I make the argument in two stages. I argue, first, that the address of any putatively valid claim or demand at all from the second-person standpoint is committed simultaneously to the common second-personal competence of addresser and addressee alike, and to their sharing a common basic authority to make claims and demands of one another by virtue of this shared competence. It follows that if there are any legitimate claims or demands, hence any obligations *to* or claim rights against, at all, then all persons must share a common basic authority, which makes them mutually accountable and grounds those more specific claims and demands.

To see how this more fundamental authority, should it exist, must ground the authority to enter into transactions, consider the role of consent in such familiar claim rights as those of autonomy and property in one's own body. It is simply part of what it is to have the right to control access to one's own body, for example, that one can waive it by consent. But consenting just *is*, again, a second-personal engagement in which two parties undertake new obligations to and rights against (and hence new accountability relations regarding) one another that are rooted in a shared common basic authority and mutual accountability.

Even if an argument along these lines can establish that a shared basic second-personal authority (mutual accountability) is a presupposition of the second-person standpoint, however, a further skeptical challenge might be mounted, since someone might simply deny that there any valid claims or demands whatsoever. I respond to this challenge by arguing that second-personal reasons are no worse supported than those of *any* other kind, but we can ignore a skeptical challenge of this kind for present purposes (Darwall 2006: 277–299). If we are entitled to assume that any moral obligations exist at all, and if moral obligations are themselves legitimate demands, it will then follow from the line of argument to which I just referred that we all share a basic second-personal authority that makes it possible for us to undertake new obligations to and rights against one another through transactions.

VII. PROMISING AS SECOND PERSONAL (II)

But what, finally, about the specific character of promissory obligations within the genus of transactions more generally? Explaining how it is possible to assume new obligations to and rights against others through transactions goes some of the way toward accounting for promissory obligations, but only some way. We will have not fully accounted for the distinctive obligations created by promising until we account for what is distinctive about this species.

Although promising is a second-personal transaction, which requires, like others, reciprocal recognition of a shared authority to assume new obligations and rights through the transaction, promising is clearly more one-sided than, say, accepting an invitation, acceding to a request, or making an agreement. In promising, there is no quid pro quo, as there is in agreement, and a promise need not be solicited, whereas one can only accept an invitation or accede to a request that has been made. But those differences actually carve out quite nicely what is distinctive about promising. As I see it, we reserve 'promise' and its synonyms for a transaction where the assumed obligation of performance need be conditional on no future action (unlike an agreement) or any past action (like a solicitation) of the addressee.[22] Once we have explained how transactions obligate in general, there is no mystery in explaining how it is possible to do the *kind* of thing that promising is. But if we can explain the assumption of new obligations that are conditional on an addressee's performance (agreement) or solicitation (request or invitation), there is no special problem about explaining the assumption of new obligations that need be conditional on neither of those. 'Promise' and its synonyms, I propose, are words we use to express to promisees that the obligations *to* them we are assuming are unconditional to them in these ways (although not necessarily, of course, that they are incapable or being overridden or otherwise defeated).[23] When you and I interpret what I am doing as giving you a promise, we therefore both take me to be undertaking to assume such an obligation. And since we reciprocally recognize me as having the authority to bind myself to you in transactions generally, we are entitled to conclude that I have thereby really placed myself under a promissory obligation to you.

But what on the second-personal account I am proposing determines the dimensions and weight of promissory obligations, including what kinds of considerations can override and defeat them? In conclusion, I would like to say something about how a second-personal approach can be fit with a contractualist normative moral theory within which such questions might be settled. I argue in *The Second-Person Standpoint* that the defense I there provide of equal second-personal authority (again, on Rawls's formulation, that each person is a "self-originating source of valid claims") provides a grounding of the right sort for a contractualist moral theory. It accounts for the kind of reason we have for complying with our obligations to one another in a way that explains its distinctive character and does not reduce it something else (Darwall 2006: 300–322; see also Watson 2009). If this is so, then a second-personal approach to explaining the character, weight, and extent of promissory obligations might fairly be called Scanlonian or "Rawlsian," even if it differs in certain crucial respects from Rawls's and Scanlon's own accounts.

NOTES

1. Austin 1962: 99–131. Austin calls the plain meaning of an uttering the *locutionary* aspect. The quotation in the epigraph is from Nietzsche (1989: 57).

2. Actually, if God can obligate us by command, he can create a bipolar obligation that we have *to* him. In Darwall 2006, I argue that theological voluntarism is best interpreted in terms of second-personal authority, but that it is unstable, since the conditions of second-personal address entail a commitment to a common fundamental second-personal authority that we share with God owing to our common second-personal competence, that is, our ability to enter into relations of mutual accountability at all.

3. Gary Watson uses this term in a similar sense in Watson 2009, e.g., at 157.

4. "We do not call anything wrong, unless we mean to imply that a person ought to be punished in some way or other for doing it; if not by law, by the opinion of his fellow creatures; if not by opinion, by the reproaches of his own conscience" (Mill 1998: ch. 5).

5. Watson also notes this shortcoming of consequentialist accounts (2009: 162–163).

6. What Strawson calls "impersonal" reactive attitudes we might also call "third-party" attitudes, though not "third-personal" attitudes, since like any reactive attitude, third-party indignation or moral blame invariably involves the second-personal element of address. We might then call "personal" reactive attitudes "second-party" attitudes.

7. Thus, just as the concepts of moral obligation, right, and wrong are conceptually related to that of the blameworthy, so also are the concepts of obligations *to* and (claim) rights against conceptually related to those of moral obligation, right, and wrong, and through them, to the concept of the blameworthy. If something is morally obligatory then it is a conceptual truth that it would be blameworthy if done without excuse, and if something would be a violation of an obligation *to* someone (a claim right she holds), then it is a conceptual truth that, other things being equal, it would be wrong and a violation of a moral obligation simpliciter. Hence it is a conceptual truth that violations of obligations *to* and rights against are, *other things being equal*, blameworthy if done without excuse. A violation of a claim right or obligation *to* is wrong simpliciter, absent some *justification*. And a violation of moral obligation simpliciter is blameworthy, absent some excuse. So a violation of an obligation to or a claim right against is blameworthy, absent some justification *or* excuse. I am indebted here to discussion with Jules Coleman and Daniel Friedrich.

8. To be clear, I don't mean to be suggesting that one could not maintain a consequentialist theory of either obligation simpliciter or (bipolar) obligations *to* without

running afoul of this problem. The point is just that some argument must be provided that links the desirability of a practice to the (second-personal) propositions that we have authority, as representative moral persons, to *demand* of one another that we follow optimific practice rules (obligation simpliciter) and/or that we have standing, as individuals, to demand that others follow such rules when they accord practice-defined rights *to us* ([bipolar] obligations *to*).

9. See, however, the previous note.

10. In Darwall 2006: ch. 12, I argue that this idea of equal "second-personal authority," as I there interpret it, provides the most adequate grounding for contractualism.

11. Gary Watson makes similar remarks regarding the grounding of contractualism in reciprocal or "mutual recognition and its relation to promissory obligations" (Watson 2009: 165–167).

12. An important difference between consequentialist and Rawlsian accounts that can be exploited in developing the latter in the direction I will propose is that whereas consequentialists treat the practice as having only instrumental value, it is open to a Rawlsian to build on the fact that the practice itself expresses relations of mutual respect that are as fundamental to justice as fairness and other contractualist views.

13. This section draws heavily on Darwall 2006.

14. As Watson notes, it is a curious fact that philosophers have focused so much on the mystery of promise as opposed to other transactions like givings of consent (Watson 2009: 160).

15. I am indebted here to discussion with Tim Mulgan. Sara Protasi reminds me that lovers are frequently in this situation with one another—wanting to say assuring things but without the usual trappings of formal promises or assurances.

16. But see Watson 2009: 156. In the end, I doubt there is any substantive issue between Watson and me here, since he agrees that any promissory obligation depends on acceptance or lack of rejection.

17. Of course, Nietzsche has in mind a "right to stand surety for himself" that, in his view, only those who are genuinely autonomous and have gotten beyond morality can have.

18. For the notion of a "normative power" in this context, see Raz 1977. Watson's account of promissory obligations, which shares central aspects with the one I provide here, is also offered in terms of normative powers. I prefer to talk of the *authority* of promiser and promisee, since the relevant standing involves the power to affect normative space in fundamentally second-personal ways, i.e., to affect accountability relations, and therefore, second-personal reasons. As I argue in Darwall 2006 and 2009, the idea of practical authority (indeed, of the very idea that Raz has been focusing on) is a fundamentally second-personal notion.

19. I discuss the conceptual relation between practical authority and accountability in Darwall 2006 and 2009.

20. Perhaps one might consent in advance to others' doing something should they wish to. But this would also seem to presuppose others' authority, for example, to will autonomously.

21. Cf. Gary Watson's claim that the normative power to bind ourselves through promising is "integral to our conception of our moral standing" (Watson 2009: 164–165).

22. And, perhaps, where the parties take the resulting obligation to meet some rough standard of importance or weight.

23. Unless, of course, the condition is brought explicitly into the content of the promise.

REFERENCES

Austin, J. L. 1962. *How to Do Things with Words*. Cambridge, MA: Harvard University Press.

Darwall, Stephen. 2006. *The Second-person Standpoint: Morality, Respect, and Accountability*. Cambridge, MA: Harvard University Press.

———. 2009. "Authority and Second-personal Reasons for Acting." In *Reasons for Action*, David Sobel and Steven Wall, eds. Cambridge: Cambridge University Press, pp. 134–154.

Feinberg, Joel. 1980. "The Nature and Value of Rights." In *Rights, Justice, and the Bounds of Liberty*. Princeton, NJ: Princeton University Press.

Gilbert, Margaret 1990. "Walking Together: A Paradigmatic Social Phenomenon." *Midwest Studies in Philosophy* 15: 1–14.

———. 2004. "Scanlon on Promissory Obligation: The Problem of Promisees' Rights." *Journal of Philosophy* 101: 83–109.

Hume, David. 1978. *A Treatise of Human Nature* Ed. L. A. Selby-Bigge. 2nd ed. Rev. P. H. Nidditch. Oxford: Oxford University Press.

Mill, John Stuart. 1998. *Utilitarianism*. Ed. Roger Crisp. Oxford: Oxford University Press.

Nietzsche, Friedrich. 1989. *On the Genealogy of Morals and Ecce Homo*. Trans. and ed. Walter Kaufmann and R. J. Hollingdale. New York: Vintage Books.

Rawls, John. 1955. "Two Concepts of Rules." *Philosophical Review* 64: 3–32.

———. 1971. *A Theory of Justice*. Cambridge, MA: Harvard University Press.

———. 1980. "Kantian Constructivism in Moral Theory." *Journal of Philosophy* 77: 515–572.

Ripstein, Arthur. 2009. Force and Freedom: Kant's Legal and Political Philosophy. Cambridge, MA: Harvard University Press.

Scanlon, T. M. 1998. *What We Owe to Each Other*. Cambridge, MA: Harvard University Press.

Searle, John. 1964. "How to Derive 'Ought' from 'Is.'" *Philosophical Review* 73: 43–58.

Strawson, P. F. 1968. "Freedom and Resentment." In *Studies in the Philosophy of Thought and Action*. London: Oxford University Press.

Thompson, Michael. 2004. "What Is It to Wrong Someone? A Puzzle about Justice." In *Reason and Value: Themes from the Philosophy of Joseph Raz*, R. Jay Wallace, Philip Pettit, Samuel Scheffler, Michael Smith, eds. Oxford: Oxford University Press.

Watson, Gary. 2009. "Promises, Reasons, and Normative Powers." In *Reasons for Action*, David Sobel and Steven Wall, eds. Cambridge: Cambridge University Press, pp. 155–178.

Chapter 12

Promises and Trust

Daniel Friedrich and Nicholas Southwood

Abstract

In this article we develop and defend what we call the "Trust View" of promissory obligation, according to which making a promise involves inviting another individual to trust one to do something. In inviting her trust, and having the invitation accepted (or at least not rejected), one incurs an obligation to her not to betray the trust that one has invited. The distinctive wrong involved in breaking a promise is a matter of violating this obligation. We begin by explicating the core notion of "inviting someone to trust one to do something", suggesting that it involves signaling to the other individual one's recognition of the importance the relevant action has for her, and one's willingness to license her to have faith or optimism in one's character with regard to the performance of that action. We then turn to a defense of the Trust View, arguing that it has considerable appeal in its own right, that it is distinct from and superior to three similar accounts (T.M. Scanlon's Assurance View, Judith Jarvis Thomson's Reliance View and David Owens' Authority View), and that several objections to it can be answered.

I. INTRODUCTION

It is natural to suppose that what makes promises morally distinctive has something to do with the ways in which they involve trust. Just what this comes to is not entirely clear. Gary Watson speaks of promising as "entitling others to take one's utterance as trustworthy" (2004: 61). David Hume says that by breaking a promise, the promiser "subjects himself to the penalty of never being trusted again" (2000: 335). Dori Kimel proposes that by keeping a promise "a promiser can rehabilitate her reputation as a trustworthy person" (2003: 20).

We suggest that in making a promise the promiser invites the promisee to trust her to do something. In inviting the promisee's trust, and having the invitation accepted (or at least not rejected), the promiser incurs an obligation to the promisee not to betray the trust that she has invited in promising. In breaking the promise, she violates this obligation. Such a view has been hinted at elsewhere.[1] But it has not been developed in any detail. Our aim in this essay is to do just that.

We begin, in section II, by simply spelling out the "Trust View," as we call it, in more detail. In section III, we say something about its appeal, focusing in particular on its considerable explanatory power. In section IV, we show that it compares favorably with three rival theories—the Assurance View of T. M. Scanlon, the Reliance View of Judith Jarvis Thomson, and the Authority View of David Owens—theories to which it bears important affinities but to which we argue it is ultimately superior. In section V, we defend it from several objections.

II. THE TRUST VIEW

Suppose that Albert has been unfaithful to his wife, Berta. She is deeply hurt. He is full of remorse. He sincerely promises her that he will be unerringly faithful henceforth. According to the Trust View, in promising to Berta that he will be faithful to her, Albert invites her to trust him to be faithful to her. In virtue of inviting her to trust him to be faithful to her, and having the invitation accepted (or at least not rejected), Albert incurs an obligation not to betray the trust that he has invited in Berta. The wrong involved in his breaking his promise, if he chooses to do so, is a matter of his violating this obligation, that is, of his betraying the trust that he has invited.

At the heart of the Trust View is the idea of *inviting someone to trust one to do something*. To explicate this idea, consider first what it means for someone to *trust* one to do something.[2] For someone to trust one to do something she must have a certain *faith* or *optimism* in one's character insofar as one's doing it is concerned. Suppose that Berta believes that Albert will be faithful to her simply out of fear (perhaps serial infidelity is punishable by death in their society) or greed (perhaps the considerable matrimonial assets are in her name alone). In neither case does it seem appropriate to say of Berta that she "trusts" Albert to be faithful to her. To trust Albert to be faithful, she must regard him in a certain light, namely, as someone disposed to be moved by certain kinds of reasons: a recognition of the value of their marriage, a concern for her happiness, a respect for her as his wife, and so on.

It is important not to confuse trusting one to do something with trusting one simpliciter. Trust simpliciter seems to require a relatively all-encompassing faith or optimism in one's character. Those whom an individual trusts simpliciter are those whom she is prepared to view in a generally positive light. Trusting one to *do* something, in contrast, involves a form of faith or optimism that is more limited, since it is tied to the performance of some particular action or actions. It is quite possible for someone to have this more limited kind of faith or optimism in one's character without trusting one simpliciter. A generally suspicious client, who would not dream of trusting one to keep a personal secret, might still trust one to look after his finances. A bitter ex-wife, whose faith in one's character has been irredeemably damaged in the course of an acrimonious divorce, might nonetheless trust one to look after the children.

It seems crucial to someone's trusting one to do something that the thing she is trusting one to do has a certain *importance* for her. Suppose that Albert and Berta's marriage is an open one, or merely a marriage of convenience, and that Berta could not care less how or with whom Albert spends his nocturnal hours. In such a case, it would be decidedly odd to speak of Berta's "trusting" Albert to be faithful. For her to trust him to be faithful, she must have something at stake; his sexual conduct must be of some importance to her; she must be in some measure vulnerable to his unfaithfulness.

This brings us to the idea of *inviting* someone to trust one to do something. In issuing such an invitation, one is in effect signaling to the other individual one's recognition of the importance that the relevant action has for her, and one's willingness to be moved on that basis, to license her to have the requisite faith or optimism in one's character with regard to the performance of that action. Issuing an invitation to trust is thus not simply, or even primarily, a matter of trying to *get* her to trust one. Rather, it represents, first and foremost, a kind of *overture* to the other individual to be party to a certain kind of relationship—an overture that has the character of an offering, or even a gift, inasmuch as one's willingness to be party to the relationship, potentially onerous to oneself, is itself grounded in one's recognition of what is important to her.

An invitation to trust, like any other invitation, can be accepted or rejected. It may be that in response to Albert's invitation to trust him to be faithful in the future, Berta rejects the invitation, saying, "There is no way I will ever trust you again." However, if she accepts (or perhaps at least does not reject)[3] the invitation, then it seems their relationship is relevantly transformed. Were he to err again, he would not only have done something he knows she wants him not to do. Rather, he would have betrayed the trust he had invited.

According to the Trust View, then, in promising the promiser makes the aforementioned kind of overture to the promisee, displaying her willingness, conditional on the promisee's acceptance (or nonrejection) of the overture, to be party to a certain kind of relationship with the promisee, namely one in which the promisee has a certain faith or optimism in the promiser's character that the promiser will perform some action that is of importance to the promisee. In so doing, and having the overture accepted (or not rejected), the promiser incurs an obligation to the promisee not to betray the trust she has invited. The distinctive wrong involved in breaking a promise is precisely a matter of violating this obligation.

III. SOME VIRTUES OF THE TRUST VIEW

Having done something to clarify the Trust View, we shall now turn to the task of defending it. There are, we think, many considerations that can be adduced in its favor. One notable virtue is that it is admirably faithful to our pretheoretic sense of what is involved in making and breaking promises. Consider, for example, the phenomenology associated with being on the receiving end of a broken promise. When someone has broken a promise to us, we feel let down, used, taken advantage of—as if the promiser has betrayed the trust she has invited in us. Or again, consider the ways in which the language of trust is deployed within the practice of promising. We often make promises simply by saying "I will X. Trust me."[4] Promises are often accepted and rejected by saying things like "OK, I trust you," "Sorry, I just don't trust you." When a promise has been broken, promisees will often say things like "You have betrayed my trust," "You asked me to trust you, and you have let me down," "Don't bother asking me to trust you again."

In addition to having considerable intuitive plausibility, the Trust View also has impressive explanatory power. First, it offers a compelling explanation of certain "formal" features of promises. Take the fact that genuine promises involve actions that promisers take promisees to want promisers to perform. The mafia boss's utterance to the informant—"I promise that I'll make you regret this"—is a threat, not a genuine promise. The Trust View explains why this is so. Inviting someone to trust one to do something involves a recognition by the would-be trustee of the importance of the action to the would-be truster. In contrast, the mafia boss is completely indifferent to what is of importance to the informant. Far from inviting his trust, he is signaling his intention to make the informant's life as unpleasant (and as short) as possible.

Or take the so-called uptake requirement—the fact that for a promise to exist it must be somehow "accepted" (or at least not "rejected").[5] The Trust View offers a straightforward explanation of why this should be so. According to the Trust View, promising involves issuing an *invitation* to the promisee to trust her to do something—an invitation that, like any invitation, can be accepted or rejected.

Or take the standards of competence that must be met by both would-be promisers and promisees. Individuals who are severely cognitively limited or impaired, such as infants and the severely mentally disabled, are plainly unable to make promises. Nor are we able to make promises to them in turn. The Trust View explains why. Issuing invitations to trust and accepting or rejecting such invitations involve an appreciation of the complex dynamic of the trust relationship: the importance of certain things to the would-be truster; the role of faith or optimism in the would-be trustee's character; the idea of a commitment to do something potentially onerous. Clearly, individuals who are severely cognitively limited or impaired will not be able to grasp these complex ideas and will consequently be unable to issue or accept an invitation to trust.

Or consider the background conditions that must be met in order for promising to be possible. Promising seems to presuppose a certain minimum background of trust. In circumstances in which trust is wholly absent—think of the nastiest kind of Hobbesian state of nature—promising seems to be impossible. Once again, the Trust View explains why this should be so. It is part of the logic of invitations that they presuppose at least some chance of being accepted. If one knows that one's frail elderly great-great-grandmother cannot leave her hospital bed, then even if one sends her the stock "invitation" to one's wedding one is not so much inviting her to attend as trying to make her feel part of what is going on. Similarly, if one inhabits a state of nature in which one knows that there is no prospect of being trusted to perform some action, then it seems impossible to issue a genuine invitation to trust.

The Trust View also offers a persuasive account of the *point* of promising. What promises do, according to the Trust View, is to relevantly modify one's relations with others by licensing others to have faith and optimism in one's character with regard to the performance of actions that are of importance to them. In some cases, such as in Hume's famous example of the farmers who require one another's help to harvest their crops, such a modification is largely of instrumental value. What the farmers want is to be able to rely on one another's assistance. Inviting trust (and having the invitation accepted) helps to achieve this end by transforming their relationship from one in which they were virtual strangers into one in which they have put their characters on the line, one in which they have made a valuable overture to one another and had the overture accepted. If either farmer fails to help the other, he will not simply be failing to do something that he knows the other wants. He will now also be violating the terms of the relationship that he has sought to bring about.[6]

The modification in one's relations with others may also go beyond being merely of instrumental value. This may be true in circumstances where trust has been damaged (as in the case of Albert and Berta). In such circumstances, promises can play an important role in helping to repair trust that once existed but that has been somehow compromised or called into question.[7] Even in circumstances where trust is relatively plentiful, inviting trust may have important expressive value, namely, the value of expressing to a would-be truster that one is in some sense putting her first; that one is acknowledging what is important to her; and that one is willing to license her to expect one to act on that basis.

Perhaps most important, the Trust View is also capable of explaining certain core aspects of the distinctive *obligation* that we incur in making promises and violate in breaking them. Consider, for example, what Stephen Darwall calls the special "second-personal" character of promissory obligation: the fact that the obligation to keep a promise is owed specifically to the promisee, and that when you break a promise you are wronging the promisee in particular, rather than merely committing a wrongful action.[8] According to the Trust View, promising involves bringing into existence a special kind of relationship between promiser and promisee. In making a promise, it is specifically the promisee whose trust one has invited; and in breaking a promise, it is specifically the promisee whose trust one has betrayed.

Or again, consider the special *stringency* of promissory obligation. A number of philosophers have noted that the obligation to keep a promise can typically only be dissolved by the promisee's releasing the promiser from the obligation. It cannot be dissolved, for example, merely by the promiser giving timely warning of nonfulfillment or some kind of compensation after the event.[9] This is exactly what the Trust View predicts. It is clearly an essential feature of the trust relationship that performance of the very action that one is trusting another individual to perform is required to express adequate fidelity to the relationship. Suppose that Albert were to inform Berta that, notwithstanding having previously invited her to trust him to be faithful to her, and having the invitation accepted, he has decided to have another affair after all. Or suppose that he were to go ahead and have the affair, and then seek somehow to compensate Berta. This would hardly constitute honoring the trust he invited in her. Indeed, it would be incontrovertible proof that the faith and optimism in his character that he had invited was badly misplaced.[10]

The Trust View, then, possesses many important virtues. In addition to having substantial intuitive plausibility, it can explain various "formal" features of promising, the point of promising and core aspects of the distinctive obligation that we incur in promising. It is, in short, a view with considerable appeal.

IV. THE TRUST VIEW CONTRASTED: ASSURANCE, RELIANCE, AND AUTHORITY

Appealing as it is, one might nonetheless wonder whether the Trust View really represents a genuine alternative to, and improvement on, certain of its rivals. In particular, there are several other theories that have loomed large in the recent literature on promises to which the Trust View bears an important resemblance. It will be useful to say something about how it differs from these rival theories, and why we should think it is superior to them.

The Assurance View

Consider, first, T. M. Scanlon's influential version of the Assurance View (1998: ch. 7).[11] This holds that the wrong involved in breaking a promise is a matter of violating an obligation that we incur to the promisee in virtue of creating in her a particular kind of assurance that we shall perform or refrain from performing some action.[12] Scanlon's Assurance View has evident affinities with the Trust View. Inviting trust and creating assurance are obviously closely related.[13] This can be seen by the fact that they typically go together. In promising to pick up Donna's kids from school, her neighbor Chris will typically be *both* inviting Donna to trust him to pick up the kids *and* creating assurance in Donna that he will do so.

Nonetheless, the Trust View and the Assurance View remain importantly different. First, creating assurance need not involve any invitation to trust. Suppose that Wilko, the barman of the Dingo's Jaws, has heard on the grapevine that Gazza, a popular local and occasional drinking buddy at the Dingo, has been interviewed for a job in Wagga Wagga. When Wilko asks him outright if the rumors are correct, Gazza tells him sincerely that he has no desire to live in Wagga Wagga, and that even if he is offered the job he won't take it.[14] In doing so, Gazza might very well be intentionally and voluntarily creating assurance in Wilko that he will not take the job. However, it need not be true that he is inviting Wilko to trust him not to take the job. Inviting trust, as we have seen, involves licensing the other to have faith or optimism in one's character with regard to some action. And it may be wholly inappropriate to describe Gazza's conduct in this way. He may be simply imparting information to Wilko, telling Wilko something he knows Wilko wants to hear, and making it reasonable for Wilko to have a certain belief about his future plans.[15]

Second, we can also invite someone to trust us to do something, and have the invitation accepted, without creating assurance. Suppose that when Albert asks Berta to trust him to be faithful, Berta responds, "Look, Al. I know you're sincere. But I'm just not convinced that you won't do it again.

Even so, I'll give you one last chance. If you screw up, don't ever bother to ask me to trust you again." Though Albert has had his invitation to trust him to be faithful accepted, he has not succeeded in creating assurance in Berta that he will be faithful.[16]

The Trust View represents a significant improvement on the Assurance View. As the example of Gazza and Wilko shows, where assurance is created in the absence of an invitation to trust, it is simply implausible to suppose that the kind of obligation that is involved in making a promise is brought into existence.[17] Though Gazza creates assurance in Wilko that he will not move to Wagga Wagga, he is plainly under no obligation to Wilko not to move. Suppose that the job is offered to him and, on reflection, he changes his mind and decides that he should like to go to Wagga Wagga after all. It would be preposterous to insist he is under an obligation to Wilko to decline the job. He might be under an obligation to let Wilko know that he has changed his mind, that what he said previously no longer holds. But the idea that he is bound to stay put just because he told Wilko about his future plans cannot seriously be maintained. Since Gazza does not invite Wilko to trust him to stay put, the Trust View, unlike the Assurance View, is not committed to this implausible claim.

Moreover, as the example of Albert and Berta shows, the kind of obligation that is involved in making a promise can arise in contexts where no assurance has been created. By promising that he will be faithful to her, Albert is obligated to keep his promise, whether or not he succeeds in assuring Berta that he will do so. If he commits additional infidelity, Albert can hardly defend himself by citing his failure to assure her. This seems wholly beside the point. Promises without assurance remain binding. The Assurance View is unable to explain the obligation to keep non-assurance-generating promises. Since cases like Albert's nonetheless involve an invitation to trust that is accepted, the Trust View has no comparable difficulty.

The Reliance View

Next, consider Judith Jarvis Thomson's version of the Reliance View,[18] according to which the wrong involved in breaking a promise is a matter of violating an obligation that we incur to the promisee in virtue of inviting her to rely on one to do something, and having the invitation accepted (or not rejected). Thomson's Reliance View is importantly similar to the Trust View. Both views involve the notion of an invitation that can be accepted or rejected. Moreover, trust and reliance appear, at least on the face of it, to be much closer than trust and assurance, say.

Once again, however, it is important to be clear about where the two views differ. First, inviting someone to rely on one to do something does not entail inviting her to trust one to do it. Suppose that two felons on death row are desperate to escape from a maximum-security prison. Each requires the help of the other to do so. Each has a lot to gain from cooperating and nothing to gain from not cooperating. So each invites the other to rely on him to help the other escape, and each accepts the other's invitation. Yet neither felon need invite the other to *trust* him to help the other escape. Trust involves faith or optimism in another's character. But the two felons may be wholly unconcerned with the quality of one another's character. It may be that all they care about is being able to successfully execute the plan to escape in the knowledge that the other will do his part. For that it is enough that they know that their interests are perfectly aligned and that each has strong self-interested reasons for cooperation.[19]

Second, nor does inviting someone to trust one to do something entail inviting her to rely on one to do it. Suppose that Emily is sitting by the side of her dying husband, Frank. Suppose, moreover, that it has long been Frank's heartfelt wish that Emily seek reconciliation with their estranged daughter, Gabriela. Emily has stubbornly resisted for forty years. But seeing her beloved husband struggle and realizing that this might be her last chance to express her love to him, she suddenly reaches a decision. Taking his hand and looking into his eyes, she says, "I am going to sort things out with Gabriela. Trust me." Visibly relieved, Frank says "Thank you," and dies. It is clear that in this case Emily has invited Frank to trust her to make amends with their daughter. But it does not seem plausible to say that she has invited him to *rely* on her making such amends. To rely on someone to do something is to make plans on the basis that she will do it. But both Frank and Emily know that Frank is well and truly beyond making any further plans.

Once again, the Trust View is superior to the Reliance View in certain respects. As the example of the felons shows, invitations to rely that are not accompanied by corresponding invitations to trust do not suffice to create the kind of obligation that is involved in making a promise. Although the felons plausibly incur *some* obligation, the obligation lacks the special stringency of promissory obligation. To see this, suppose that, after the felons' invitation to rely has been issued, and accepted, but before any actual reliance has taken place, one of the felons changes his mind, and informs the other that he is not prepared to go through with their plan to escape. Under these circumstances, it seems that the initial obligation of fulfillment is wholly dissolved, and that the second felon is in no position to insist otherwise. Compare this to the obligation to keep a promise. As we have seen, promissory obligation can typically only be dissolved by the promisee's releasing the promiser. Giving timely warning does not suffice to dissolve the obligation to keep a promise. Giving timely warning may, of course, induce a promisee to release the promiser. It may also be preferable to simply not doing as one has promised. But the fact remains that a promisee is entitled to insist that a promiser does as he has promised. So, while each of the felons has certainly invited the other to rely on her to help the other escape, and had the invitation accepted, they do not incur the kind of obligation that we incur in making a promise. This is exactly what the Trust View predicts, since there is no invitation to trust. But it constitutes a counterexample to the Reliance View.[20]

Moreover, as the example of Emily and Frank shows, the kind of obligation that is involved in making a promise can arise in contexts where no invitation to rely is made. Recall Emily's words to her dying husband: "I am going to sort things out with Gabriela. Trust me." As we saw, Emily is not plausibly construed as inviting Frank to *rely* on her to sort things out with Gabriela. Even so, it seems that she is still subject to the kind of obligation involved in making a promise. Were she to fail to attempt to effect a reconciliation with Gabriela, we would take her to have wronged Frank, and to have made herself subject to the kind of moral censure that is appropriate in the case of breaking a promise. But since there is no invitation to rely, the Reliance View, unlike the Trust View, cannot explain the presence of the relevant obligation.

The Authority View

While creating assurance and inviting reliance bear a close resemblance to inviting trust, they are normatively thinner in ways that make attempts to ground promissory obligation in them correspondingly less compelling. Recently, David Owens has advanced a theory that is based on another normatively rich notion, the notion of *granting authority*.[21] According to Owens, under normal circumstances, each individual has sole authority over at least many areas of her life. It is typically our business and our business alone, whether we go to a party and when we leave it, whether we have a glass of wine with our meal, whether we help our neighbors move house, and so on. It is not up to others to decide whether we do these things. What promising does, on Owens's view, is change this. In promising to drive you home from the party whenever you want, I grant you the authority to decide when I shall leave the party. It is now no longer simply up to me to decide when I may make my exit. Were I to ignore your request to leave, I would have wronged you by failing to respect the authority I have granted to you. According to Owens, the wrong involved in breaking a promise, then, consists in violating an obligation to which one is subject in virtue of having granted someone the authority to decide how one shall act.[22]

How are the Trust View and the Authority View different? First, granting someone the authority to determine what one shall do obviously does not entail inviting her to trust one to do it. Suppose that Henry has been unable to find matrimonial felicity on his own, and so decides to seek the help of the renowned Indira, giving her absolute authority to choose the woman he will marry. As a result, whom he will marry is now solely up to Indira. She has the authority to decide who he is to marry. Clearly, though, Henry has not invited Indira to *trust* him to do anything. In ceding authority, he is not concerned with what is of importance to her. Quite the contrary. Both are moved by what is of importance to *him*, namely, to find a suitable marriage partner. Nor is he signaling that he is willing to license Indira to have faith or optimism in his character. Indeed, both may think that such faith or optimism is wholly unwarranted.

Second, inviting someone to trust one to do something need not involve granting her authority. Recall the case of Emily's inviting Frank to trust her to make amends with Gabriela. The idea that Emily is also thereby granting Frank *authority* to require her to make amends with Gabriela seems very odd indeed. What we are trying to do when we grant authority to another individual is to license her to make decisions about how we are to act. But Emily and Frank know that he will not be around to make such decisions. It would thus be utterly pointless to attempt such a transfer of authority in Frank's case.

Once again, the Trust View represents an improvement on the Authority View. As the case of Henry and Indira shows, granting someone authority to determine what one shall do is not sufficient for incurring the kind of obligation involved in making a promise. If Indira exercises her authority and instructs him to marry the beautiful Jessica, he would not be wronging *Indira* were he to ignore her command. She may be angry at his foolhardiness, or complain about his erratic and inconstant behavior, but she cannot complain that he has violated an obligation to her, the kind of obligation that he would have incurred had he promised her to marry whomever she chooses. This creates a serious problem for the Authority View. The Trust View, in contrast, stands unscathed, since Henry does not invite Indira to trust him to do anything.

Moreover, as the case of Emily and Frank shows, there are obligations of the kind involved in making a promise that an appeal to granting authority cannot explain. Emily does not grant Frank authority to decide how she is to act. In contrast, the Trust View provides a compelling explanation of the obligation that is involved in making promises to those on their deathbeds. Emily does invite Frank to trust him to sort things out with Gabriela, even though he will not be around to see her carry out his wishes.

***

We have contrasted the Trust View with three rival theories that have loomed large in the recent literature. We have argued not only that the Trust View is genuinely distinct from the Assurance View, the Reliance View, and the Authority View but also that it is superior to them in certain important respects. Inviting trust is both more and less than creating assurance, inviting reliance, and granting authority. And the ways it is more and less, we have argued, are crucial to its ability to provide a more plausible theory of promissory obligation.

V. OBJECTIONS

Let us now consider several objections to the Trust View. First, it might be said that inviting trust is ubiquitous in human communication, and that the Trust View consequently implies an absurd inflation in our obligations. Whenever we assert something, and/or tell someone something, we invite her to trust us. Indeed, assertions and/or tellings might be thought to have the general form "p; trust me."[23] But it is plainly false, so the objection goes, that, simply by asserting, or telling someone, that p we thereby incur an obligation to make it the case that p. Thus, when Keith tells Lena that "Sweden has a population of 20 million," he certainly incurs no obligation to make it the case that Sweden has a population of 20 million.

As it stands, the objection can be quickly answered. The Trust View holds that the kind of obligation involved in making a promise arises specifically when we invite someone to trust us with regard to our future conduct. And Keith's conduct is not at issue when he tells Lena that Sweden has a population of 20 million. However, the objection can be reformulated. Suppose we focus narrowly on communicative actions that concern the future conduct of the speaker. Thus, suppose that Lena tells Keith: "I'm going to Sweden in May." We might say that she has invited him to trust her merely by performing an act of telling. But she is surely under no obligation to go to Sweden in May.

We concede that there may be an interesting sense in which Lena can be said to have invited Keith's trust about something that concerns her future conduct. However, it is not the sense on which the Trust View is based. Call the kind of trust at play in assertion and telling "epistemic trust." To epistemically trust someone involves something like having confidence in her epistemic position with regard to some proposition. To invite someone to have epistemic trust in one with regard to a proposition, in turn, involves something like licensing her to have such confidence in one with regard to that proposition, and to hold one to appropriately demanding epistemic standards. In contrast, the Trust View is based on a kind of "practical trust," a notion of trust that is essentially tied to character and reasons for action. To trust someone in this practical sense is to have faith or optimism in her character as regards the performance of an action that is of importance to one. To invite someone to trust one in the practical sense, it is not enough simply to license confidence in one's epistemic position, nor, indeed, to license her to hold one to appropriately demanding epistemic standards. Rather, it involves licensing her to have a certain faith or optimism in one's character–in a sense, to hold one to certain standards of good character. Cases of mere assertion or telling therefore do not involve inviting trust of the right sort. And so they do not pose a problem for the Trust View.

Second, a related worry may arise as a result of the ubiquity of inviting trust in human relationships. It might be argued that, in the context of participating in certain relationships, we are constantly implicitly inviting individuals to trust us to do certain things. For example, lovers may interact in ways that seem to constitute invitations to trust one another to be faithful, to look after one another, to act with compassion, and so on. And although in such cases genuine obligations are surely in play, it might be said that they are different from the particular kinds of obligations involved in promise-making.

Now we are unsure whether the obligations in such cases really *are* fundamentally different. However, the Trust View can be developed in different ways, depending on which of these options one finds more palatable. If the obligations are fundamentally the same, then the notion of an invitation to trust ought to be understood in a relatively loose way, so as to include the more implicit and diverse ways we can knowingly encourage the creation of trust. But if the obligations are fundamentally different,[24] then the notion of an invitation to trust ought to be understood in a relatively strict sense, such that it involves something like an explicit speech-act.[25] Either way, the Trust View has the resources to accommodate this concern.

Third, it might be objected that the Trust View squares poorly with the possibility of promising in intimate relationships, where trust is already plentiful. In such relationships, an invitation to trust might seem at best superfluous, at worst rather offensive. This might seem to have the objectionable consequence of limiting the domain of application of promises to relatively impersonal contexts.[26]

Even in extremely trusting intimate relationships, trust is seldom absolute. We might trust our lovers to look after our children, but not to stick to the agreed-on budget. We might trust them to defend us when we are not present to a large degree, without trusting them absolutely to do so. Far from being obsolete, invitations to trust can therefore continue to play a significant role in intimate relationships. To be sure, there may be something inappropriate about invitations to trust in circumstances where trust really is absolute. But the same can be said about promising. Suppose that one's partner has, and has always had, absolute trust in one to be faithful to her. In that case, it would be decidedly odd to say to her, as one is going out the door one evening, "Goodbye, darling. I promise you that I'll be faithful to you tonight."

Doing so would very likely have the perverse consequence of calling into question the very trust that, according to the Trust View, promising is meant to be promoting. If anything, then, it is virtue and not a vice of the Trust View that it explains what is inappropriate or deficient about promising in contexts of absolute trust.

VI. CONCLUSION

The notion of trust is frequently appealed to in passing in discussions of promissory obligation. Our aim here has been to develop in greater detail a view that locates the wrong involved in breaking a promise is the violation of an obligation that we incur by inviting another individual to trust us to do something, and having the invitation accepted (or not rejected). We have argued that the Trust View has considerable appeal in and of itself. We have shown how it is distinct from, but also superior to, three prominent rivals to which it bears some resemblance. Finally, we defended it from several objections. More remains to be said. But we hope we have done enough to show that the Trust View is a view that deserves to be given serious consideration.[27]

NOTES

1. We first proposed the Trust View as an improved modification of T. M. Scanlon's Assurance View in Southwood and Friedrich (2009). Baier (1986: 245), Kimel (2003: 26–27), and Shiffrin (2008: 517–519) also appear to be sympathetic to something very much like the Trust View.

2. There is considerable disagreement among philosophers about just what trust involves. Cf. Baier (1986), Hieronymi (2008), Holton (1994), Jones (1996). We intend the following to be relatively neutral.

3. We shall remain neutral about whether acceptance of the invitation is required or whether mere nonrejection suffices.

4. See Scanlon (1998: 306). Of course, this is not to say that we *always* make promises by explicitly employing the language of trust, simply that we *often* do so.

5. See e.g. Thomson (1990: 298); Owens (2006: 73).

6. This might be thought to be too quick. As we have noted, being confident that someone will do something simply because one takes her to have self-interested reasons for doing it is not the same as trusting her to do it, since the latter requires having a certain faith or optimism in her character. It might be objected that this feature of the Reliance View means that it cannot explain how Hume's farmers could come to trust one another and thus to be able to rely on one another's assistance. To respond to this worry, let us distinguish two interpretations of Hume's case. The first interpretation holds that, although only narrowly self-interested reasons are operative in their initial interaction, Hume's farmers are in principle sensitive to other reasons—for example, the reason not to betray another's trust. On this interpretation, the Trust View obviously has no difficulty explaining the possibility of trust between the

farmers. The second interpretation holds that Hume's farmers remain responsive throughout solely to narrowly self-interested reasons. In that case there would indeed be no basis for one farmer's trusting the other to do something. Assuming that this fact is transparent to the farmers, the Trust View entails that the farmers could not resolve their quandary by making promises. Put another way, the Trust View entails that promising is pointless or impossible if people are (transparently) exclusively self-interested. This strikes us as the intuitively correct result. We are grateful to Hanoch Sheinman for pressing us to be clearer on this point.

7. Recall Hume's remark that by breaking a promise the promiser "subjects himself to the penalty of never being trusted again" (2000: 335), and Kimel's remark that by keeping a promise "a promiser can rehabilitate her reputation as a trustworthy person" (2003: 20).

8. See Darwall (2010) (chapter 11 of this book). See also Darwall (2006a: 214) and (2006b: 203–208) as well as Scanlon's critique of Hume's practice-based account (1998: 314).

9. Scanlon (1998: 301).

10. To be sure, giving timely warning or offering compensation may be preferable to simple nonperformance. But it would still be falling short of living up to the trust one has invited.

11. Earlier proponents of something much like the Assurance View include Sidgwick (1874), MacCormick (1972) and Narveson (1971). Contemporary philosophers who draw on Scanlon's account include Kolodny and Wallace (2003), Pratt (2003, 2004), and Watson (2004).

12. More precisely, for the assurer to give the assuree the kind of assurance that generates the relevant obligation of fulfilment is for the assurer to voluntarily and intentionally create in the assuree an expectation that the assurer will X, where the assurer's X-ing is something that the assurer takes the assuree to desire or value and wants to be assured of; and both the assurer and the assuree know that the assurer has the aforementioned intentions and beliefs, they both know that they know it, and both know that they know that they know it, and so on ad infinitum. See Scanlon (1998: 304). Notice that in the context of his discussion of the "value of assurance" and especially the discussion of Harold and the "Guilty Secret," Scanlon appears to come close to suggesting that assurance is factive, i.e. that it involves not merely having a belief but having a *true* belief about the assurer's future conduct. However, since the proponent of the Assurance View is committed to the claim that all paradigmatic promises create assurance on the part of promisees, this would entail that it is impossible to break a paradigmatic promise. If assurance entails true belief, then a paradigmatic promise that one will X entails that one will X. If one fails to X, then one will have failed to make a paradigmatic promise, since the promisee will have failed to have a true belief that one will X and thus have failed to have been assured that one will X. We shall therefore assume that "assurance" is not to be understood as factive.

13. Indeed, many authors simply conflate the two. A good example is Watson (2004: 70), who writes: "I have been working with an oversimplified picture of the connection between assertion and assurance, between assertion and trust. In pressing the parallels between promising and asserting, I said at one point that both assertions and promises can be glossed as, "P; trust me." This gives the impression that the function of assertion is, like promising, to provide assurance."

14. We present a more detailed version of this example in Southwood and Friedrich (2009).

15. That we can create assurance without inviting trust should be unsurprising. Assurance is a normatively thinner attitude than trust. To have assurance that someone will do something is simply to have a belief about a state of affairs that one wants to obtain. It is therefore consistent with B's being assured that A will do X that B believes that A will do X for any number of reasons—that she will make a lot of money if she does X, that she is afraid of doing otherwise, that her tyrannical parents will see to it that she does X, or whatever. At bottom, creating assurance is about information—information that can be useful and desired, but information nonetheless. Inviting trust, on the other hand, centrally concerns expressing one's willingness to be party to a certain kind of relationship—a relationship of trust. Trust seems to preclude certain reasons. In order to trust you to do something, it is not enough that I think you will do it out of self-interest or fear. Rather, I must see you as being disposed to be motivated by certain kinds of consideration, namely, those that support my faith or optimism in your character with regard to the action in question.

16. At a first glance, this might strike one as rather strange. How is it possible to have an invitation to trust accepted without assurance being created? One might, of course, insist that it is enough that the invitation be not rejected. But assuming that acceptance is required, there are two possible avenues open to the proponent of the Trust View. One is that accepting an invitation to trust one to do something requires trusting one to do it; but that trusting one to do something does not require believing that one will do it. For example, if trust is an affective, noncognitive state, as a number of philosophers have argued, then it should not be surprising that one can be in the relevant affective state without holding the associated belief. (Proponents of affective accounts of trust include Becker [1996], Jones [1996], and Lahno]2001]). For a different approach to trust that also aims to leave room for the possibility of trust without the associated belief, see Holton [1994]). On this picture, in accepting Albert's invitation, Berta might actually be said to come to trust Albert. The other possibility is that, even if trusting one to do something does require believing that one will do it, someone can accept an invitation to trust one to do something without actually coming to trust one to do it. On this view, what Berta would be doing in accepting the invitation is something like giving Albert a chance to *earn* her trust, to prove he can be trusted, even though she does not actually trust him at present. In doing so, she might be moved by a desire to restore their relationship and to reestablish the trust that has been lost.

17. For a detailed defense of this claim see Southwood and Friedrich (2009). See also Owens (2006) and Shiffrin (2008).

18. Thomson (1990). An earlier and somewhat different version of the Reliance View was proposed by MacCormick (1972).

19. It is also worth noting in this context the oft-made observation that reliance can only be disappointed, whereas trust can be betrayed (Baier [1986: 235], Holton [1994: 66]).

20. Could one avoid this objection by modifying the Reliance View so as to claim that the kind of obligation involved in promising only comes to exist once *actual* reliance has come into play? The problem with such a view is that it would entail that it

is not wrong to break a promise that has not (yet) actually been relied on. For criticism of this claim, see Sheinman (2000) and Pratt (2004: 20–23).

21. Owens (2006) and (2007).

22. Note, the notion of "authority" figures at two crucial junctions in Owens's theory: authority is what we grant someone in making a promise, and our interest in authority is said to explain the "function" of promising. We are doubtful of the latter claim, but will here focus only on the former.

23. Cf. e.g. Watson (2004); Hinchman (2005).

24. Of course, this is consistent with claiming that the obligations have a lot in common, and that this is so because they are tied to morally significant ways of creating trust.

25. Nodding in response to a request, for example.

26. Some philosophers are happy to concede that there cannot be promising among intimates. See Markovits, chapter 13 of this book.

27. We are grateful to Hanoch Sheinman for useful comments on an earlier draft of this article and to many friends and colleagues for discussion that has been invaluable in helping us to develop the Trust View. Southwood's research was carried out under Australian Research Council Discovery Grant DP0663060 "Norms, Reasons, and Values".

REFERENCES

Baier, Annette. 1986. "Trust and Antitrust." *Ethics* 96: 231–260.

Becker, Lawrence C. 1996. "Trust as Noncognitive Security about Motives." *Ethics* 107: 43–61.

Darwall, Stephen. 2006a. Contractualism, Root and Branch: A Review Essay. *Philosophy and Public Affairs* 34: 193–214.

———. 2006b. *The Second-Person Standpoint: Morality, Respect, and Accountability*. Cambridge, Mass.: Harvard University Press.

———. 2010. "Demystifying Promises." In H. Sheinman (ed.), *Promises and Agreements: Philosophical Essays*. New York: Oxford University Press.

Hieronymi, Pamela. 2008. "The Reasons of Trust." *Australasian Journal of Philosophy* 86: 213–236.

Hinchman, Edward S. 2005. "Telling as Inviting to Trust." *Philosophy and Phenomenological Research* 70: 562–587.

Holton, Richard. 1994. "Deciding to Trust, Coming to Believe." *Australasian Journal of Philosophy* 72: 63–76.

Hume, David. 2000. *A Treatise of Human Nature*. Oxford: Oxford University Press.

Jones, Karen. 1996. "Trust as an Affective Attitude." *Ethics* 107: 4–25.

Kimel, Dori. 2003. *From Promise to Contract: Towards a Liberal Theory of Contract*. Oxford: Hart.

Kolodny, Niko, and Jay Wallace. 2003. "Promises and Practices Revisited." *Philosophy and Public Affairs* 31: 119–154.

Lahno, Bernd. 2001. "On the Emotional Character of Trust." *Ethical Theory and Moral Practice* 4: 171–189.

MacCormick, Neil. 1972. "Voluntary Obligations and Normative Powers I." *Proceedings of the Aristotelian Society* 46: 59–78.

Markovits, Daniel. 2010. "Promise as an Arm Length Relation." In H. Sheinman (ed.), *Promises and Agreements: Philosophical Essays*. New York: Oxford University Press.

Narveson, Jan. 1971. "Promising, Expecting and Utility." *Canadian Journal of Philosophy* 1: 207–233.

Owens, David. 2006. "A Simple Theory of Promising." *Philosophical Review* 115: 51–77.

———. 2007. "Duress, Deception, and the Validity of a Promise." *Mind* 116: 293–315.

Pratt, Michael. 2003. "Promises and Perlocutions." *Critical Review of International Social and Political Philosophy and Public Affairs* 6: 93–119.

———. 2004. "Promising and Promissory Obligation." Ph.D. diss., University of Sydney.

Scanlon, T. M. 1998. *What We Owe to Each Other*. Cambridge, MA: Harvard University Press.

Sheinman, Hanoch. 2000. "Contractual Liability and Voluntary Undertakings." *Oxford Journal of Legal Studies* 20: 205–220.

Shiffrin, Seana Valentine. 2008. "Promising, Intimate Relationships, and Conventionalism." *Philosophical Review* 117: 481–524.

Sidgwick, Henry. 1874. *The Methods of Ethics*. London: MacMillan.

Southwood, Nicholas, and Daniel Friedrich. 2009. "Promises beyond Assurance." *Philosophical Studies* 144: 261–280.

Thomson, Judith Jarvis. 1990. *The Realm of Rights*. Cambridge, MA: Harvard University Press.

Watson, Gary. 2004. "Asserting and Promising." *Philosophical Studies* 117: 57–77.

Chapter 13

Promise as an Arm's-length Relation

Daniel Markovits

Abstract

Many have argued that promising and loving are mutually sympathetic. In fact, they are not. Promises characteristically arise among strangers and the promise relation is opposed to intimacy. *Thus, the formal structure of promissory recognition is incompatible with the formal structure of recognition among intimates. Whereas promissory recognition takes as its object the generic humanity of the promisee, the recognition involved in intimacy takes as its object the humanity of the promisee as it receives a particular, contingent expression in her distinctive person. Moreover, whereas promissory recognition is cabined by the* ex ante *intentions of the promising parties, the recognition involved in intimacy must adjust to* ex post *developments, which evolve in the shifting sands of the intimate relationship. Both these differences entail that promises characteristically arise at arm's length. Indeed, the legal practice contract - commonly thought a degenerate case of promise - in fact represents promise's highest expression.*

Do promises characteristically arise among intimates or among strangers? Philosophers have, increasingly, taken the former view, for example associating promises with trust, which is a cognate of intimacy, or even directly with intimacy itself. See Shiffrin (2008). Even pluralists about promising, who take the more modest view that promises figure in all manner of interpersonal relations, accept intimacy as one of promise's natural habitats. See Sheinman (2004). I shall argue for the very different view that promises characteristically arise among strangers and, indeed, that the immanent structure of the promise relation is in itself distancing, which is to say *opposed to intimacy*. Although both intimacy and promising involve persons' recognizing others as persons, the formal structures of the two types of recognition are very different. Indeed, the formal structure of promissory recognition is in an important way incompatible with the formal structure of recognition among intimates.[1] Thus promissory recognition is thin, whereas the recognition involved in intimacy is thick: whereas promissory recognition takes as its object the generic humanity of the promisee—her perspectival nature, or personality, simpliciter—the recognition involved in intimacy takes as its object the humanity of the promisee as it receives a particular, contingent expression in her distinctive person. Moreover, whereas promissory recognition is cabined by the ex ante intentions of the promising parties, that is, their intentions when the promise is created, the recognition involved in intimacy must adjust to ex post developments, which evolve in the shifting sands of the intimate relationship. Both these differences entail, I argue, that promises characteristically arise at arm's length. One of the argument's implications, which I take up briefly at its end, is that the legal practice contract—commonly thought to fall somewhere between being a marginal and a degenerate case of promise—in fact represents promise's highest and most complete expression.

I.

Promises create obligations. Thus it is one of the banalities of promising that a promisor may not break her promise simply because, as things have turned out, breaking it has become best overall. (See e.g. Rawls, 1955; Raz, 1977.) Moreover, promises confer the authority to demand performance of the promised acts specifically on promisees. (See e.g. Raz, 1977: 227–28; Darwall, 2006: ch. 8.). Promises, one might say, *shift* the moral right to decide whether or not to do the acts that they name from promisors to promisees.

Promising therefore involves a form of recognition: to promise to someone is to respect her as a person—to acknowledge her moral personality—in a particular way. Certainly our ordinary practices of promising make clear that only persons can receive promises.[2] We are inclined, when confronted with a promise to a creature other than a person, to attribute the promise to a category error: either to an excessively sentimental anthropomorphizing of the object, as when an owner promises a bone to her dog; or simply to madness. The mechanics of promising give this intuition a practical expression. Promises must be accepted before promissory obligation arises, and only persons possess the power of acceptance (indeed, this power is no less a mark of moral personality than the power to promise itself).[3] Finally, the legal orders that have grown up around promise also follow this line. Contract law requires both offer and acceptance before a legal obligation arises, and only persons possess the capacity to accept.[4]

This intuitive account of promissory recognition may, moreover, be made precise.[5] When a person makes a promise, she forms intentions in favor of certain ends—the ends associated with the promised performance—that are also available to her promisee. Moreover, the promisee, on whose acceptance the creation of the promissory obligation depends, is not merely drafted into the service of the promisor's pursuit of these ends.[6] Instead, she is engaged by the promise and takes up the promisor's engagement by also forming intentions in favor of the ends associated with the promised performance—specifically, the intention to vindicate her promissory rights and correlatively also not to act in ways that would undermine these rights. The ends of a promisor therefore coincide with those of her promisee, at least with respect to the promised performance. Moreover, the connection between the promisor's and promisee's ends is no mere coincidence, and the overlap in their ends is not just incidental. Instead, the promisor, through her promise, intends to entrench her pursuit of the ends announced by the promise and to refuse to defect from these ends unless the promisee releases her. She intends, in effect, to give the promisee authority over her ends—to pursue, within the sphere of the promise, only ends that the promisee also affirms. She intends, one might even say, to become obligated to the promisee to render the promised performance.[7] And finally, insofar as the promisor honors the promise—insofar as she refuses to deviate from the promised performance without obtaining a release from the promisee—she carries out the intention not to defect and actually confers this authority over her ends to the promisee.

A promisor therefore intends, within the sphere of the promise, to defer to her promisee and indeed to subordinate her ends to her promisee's will. And through this subordination—through placing her ends in his hands—the promisor comes to take the promisee's ends as her own and, moreover, to treat him, his will, as an end.[8] In this way, the promise underwrites a form of respectful recognition by the promisor of her promisee.

The promise, through the performance that it describes, specifies the precise intentions and ends that the promisor shares with her promisee and in this way fixes the terms on which she engages him and treats him as an end in himself. A subsequent breach of the promise (when it is truly a breach[9]) abandons these shared ends in favor of other ends that cannot be shared with the promisee, because they are inconsistent with the ends that the promisee has in fact adopted in conjunction with the promise. The promisor, through her promise, invites her promisee to fix his intentions in a particular way, and the promisee, by accepting, so fixes his intentions. A subsequent breach involves adopting intentions and pursuing ends that the promissory intentions foreclosed.

The breach therefore does more than merely return the promisor and promisee to the status quo ante, in which they were strangers. Strangers do not share ends and do not treat each other as ends in themselves, but they may at any moment come to do so. The breach of the promise, however, presents an obstacle to such sharing between the promisor and promisee. The breach entails that, at least with respect to the promised performance, the two adopt *inconsistent* ends. The breaching promisor does not just unmake but instead actively *betrays* the recognition established by the promise; and she pursues ends, through her breach, that do not just depart from but instead *contradict* her promisee's ends. Her breach therefore forecloses possibilities for sharing ends that previously existed and imposes conflict in their place. Moreover, a breach has this consequence even (and in just the same way) in the case of pure promissory obligation–that is, in the cases of promises that have not produced any reliance or even expectations in their promisees.[10] The breach expresses incompatible intentions, and hence produces estrangement, based exclusively on its involving a denial of the promisee's authority, which is the opposite of recognition, and thus entirely apart from the promisee's reliance or subjective expectations concerning the promisor's conduct.

This remains so, moreover, even when the promisor made her promise honestly–actually intending to pursue the ends that her promise named and to defer to her promisee's authority in respect of these ends. To be sure, the breach of an honest promise is unlike a lying promise in that the breaching promisor (unlike the lying promisor) does not manipulate her promisee–she does not treat him merely as a means.[11] But this consideration does not exhaust the moral significance of the breach, because the failures of recognition are not exhausted by the disruption of the will that occurs when one person, employing force or fraud, treats another merely as a means. The parties to a broken promise, even one with an honest beginning, become more distant than strangers: the promisee has, though the promise, fixed his intentions in way that is incompatible with the promisor's breach. And the breaching promisor therefore denies (at least in respect of the promise) the personality of the promisee, closing herself off to him, so that the parties to the promise become incapable of recognizing each other. The parties to a broken promise become actively *estranged* from each other.[12] And this estrangement explains why not only making lying promises but also breaking honest promises is morally wrong.

One might summarize this by saying that promises render persons practically open to one another. Without promises, their wills would remain separated (just as their minds would remain separated without truth telling). Moreover, when promises are broken, persons' wills become isolated (just as their minds become isolated when they lie, including even when the lie fails). But when a person makes and keeps promises, she may overcome her separation from her promisees, and respectfully recognize them, by submitting to their authority (within the scope of the promise) and taking their ends as her own.[13] Promises, Seana Shiffrin recently observed, "involve... the transfer of a party's power to change one's mind to another party, and so a consolidation of the power to determine what the two parties will do," and in this way "enable... a fully first-personal perspective on joint activity" (2008: 516). As Hannah Arendt once said, promise-making and promise-keeping arise "directly out of the will to live together with others in the mode of acting and speaking" (1958: 246).

II.

Promising is of course not the only way one person might directly recognize another—not the only way she may open herself up to his moral personality. One other familiar form of recognition is intimate love, at least where intimacy and love are understood not in terms of a drive, desire, or even benevolence but rather, as on the model recently articulated by David Velleman, in terms of the lover's regard for her beloved's humanity (1999).[14] To love someone, on this model, is to perceive, clearly and vividly, his moral personality and to open oneself up to him in light of his personality. A lover develops what Velleman, borrowing from Kant, calls *Achtung* for her beloved—she both notices and values his moral personality. Perhaps the nearest English translation is to say that a lover *appreciates* her beloved for his humanity.

We ordinarily close ourselves off from the vividness of other persons' particular moral personalities—the immediacy of their constituting points of view that are just as rational, complete, distinctive, and free-standing (as Kant would say, "self-existent" [1964: 4:437])[15] as our own—even though we know in some vague and general sense that they are indeed persons. We must do so, because even if it is possible for us always to act in ways that are consistent with the equal moral status of other persons—that is, to treat them never merely as means and always also as ends in themselves[16]—we cannot always act in full appreciation of the separate and distinctive humanity of every person whose status we respect. Always to appreciate all other personalities in this way—not merely to acknowledge that they are personalities but to appreciate their perspectives in fully vivid detail—would literally overwhelm our own perspectival capacities. If we always took on the perspectives of all others with the same intensity and sensitivity that we devote to our own, we would no longer possess sufficient mental or intentional resources to live from our own perspectives.[17] This is why our efforts to ensure that we act only in ways that are consistent with the humanity of others, for example by testing the maxims of our actions against some principle of unanimous acceptance, inevitably abstract from the particularity of the perspectives of the persons whose acceptance they insist on. (This is illustrated in Rawls's veil of ignorance, although the illustration involves an analogic leap, as Rawls was not after principles to regulate individual conduct.) We must, as Velleman writes, engage in "self-protection" against other persons, "draw[ing] ourselves in and clos[ing] ourselves off from being affected by [them]" (1999: 360).[18]

But although we must close ourselves off from fully appreciating the personalities of many, and indeed most other persons, we need not (and indeed if we are to be healthy, cannot) close ourselves off from *all* others. And when we love another person, we depart from this ordinary practice of self-protection. "Love," as Velleman says, "disarms our emotional defenses; it makes us vulnerable to the other" (360). Many of our defenses against being overwhelmed by the perspectives of others are ways of not fully perceiving their perspectives (even as we act consistent with the fact of them)—they are cases of what Velleman has called "contrived blindness" (361). Love lifts this blindness, "with the result that we really look at [our beloved], perhaps for the first time, and respond emotionally in a way that's indicative of having really seen him" (361). In particular, love makes a person sensitive and responsive to her beloved's perspectival capacity; it involves a commitment to taking on his point of view and making it as immediate for her as her own (at least, as immediate as her capacity for love allows).

Love is therefore, Velleman observes, "essentially an attitude toward the beloved himself" (1999: 354). Like promising, love is a form of respectful recognition of the moral personality of another, a vivid appreciation of the value inhering in the beloved. Moreover, love is literally a vulnerability to the personality of the beloved; it is an openness to *sharing* one's perspective with the beloved. Indeed, where it is fully achieved, love produces a fusion of personalities,[19] reflected in the various commonplace ways of speaking (familiar at least since Aristophanes' speech in the *Symposium*) that suggest that the beloved *completes* the lover.

III.

Promisors and lovers therefore both recognize, and in some way open themselves up to, the moral personalities of their promisees and beloveds. This makes it natural to ask about the relationship between the forms of recognition involved in promise and in love. Answering this question will help, moreover, to determine whether promises characteristically arise among intimates or at arm's length.

One line of argument proposes that the two forms of recognition are sympathetic to each other and indeed complementary. A recent proponent of this view is Seana Shiffrin, who claims that "the power to make binding promises…is an integral part of the ability to engage in special relationships in a morally good way, under conditions of equal respect" (2008: 485). (Shiffrin's argument mentions "special relationships," but both the examples of special relationships that she provides, which center on friendship and family, and the title under which the argument proceeds, "Promising, Intimate Relationships, and Conventionalism," make clear that what makes the relationships special is that they are *intimate*.) Shiffrin argues that "being able to promise plays a role in forestalling some morally undesirable dynamics within special relationships and in reinforcing an important aspect of equality within them" (498). Shiffrin has in mind cases in which the parties to an intimate relationship are unequally situated with respect to an action that will importantly influence their lives and their relationship: perhaps, as in one of Shiffrin's examples, two persons whose friendship substantially depends on living near each other contemplate moving together to a new city under conditions in which the move matters more to the happiness of one than the other; or perhaps, as in another example, a parent and child contemplate some activity (an outing or a treat) that matters intensely to the child but that the child cannot, because he is only a child, pursue without the parent's cooperation (503–504, 509–510).

Shiffrin believes that the inequality in these and similar cases threatens to undermine the intimacy of the persons involved: the vulnerable party may come to feel powerless and frustrated. This may lead him self-protectively to suppress the desires that render him vulnerable; or, employing an opposite strategy, he may accept or even initiate exploitative side-arrangements designed to induce the powerful party to act in the ways he desires; or, he may threaten to impose new costs on the more powerful party if she fails to act as he desires; or, he may simply dwell on his disappointment, and broadcast it to the powerful party, in the hope that guilt or shame will lead her to act as he wishes (2008: 504). All of these responses, Shiffrin is surely correct to observe, distort the relationship. They render it "fraught," as she says, and may even "sour" it, as the powerful party falls into carelessness or callousness and the vulnerable party falls into self-denial, exploitation, resentment, or even just pleading or nagging (504). It seems that there is no way, given the inequality that Shiffrin imagines, for the two to retain their intimacy on egalitarian, respectful terms.

Things would be very different, Shiffrin thinks, if the parties could promise. In that case, the powerful person could promise the vulnerable person that she would do as he wished (in the relevant respect). In this way, says Shiffrin, "the power to promise provides an important way to manage vulnerability" that will otherwise skew the interactions even of well-disposed, mutually sympathetic persons in a manner that makes morally good, egalitarian intimacy impossible (2008: 509). A promise, in cases like those just imagined

> does not just increase the likelihood [that the powerful party will do what the vulnerable one wishes] but actively affirms [the vulnerable party's] status as a free person, capable and worthy of exercising sound judgment about what is to be done. [The powerful party's] relinquishment *and* transfer of that power to [the vulnerable party] works to neutralize aspects of the situations' hazards and to restore an equal standing between [the parties] in this local domain. (507)

Overcoming these hazards, moreover, promotes intimacy, since it enables persons confronted with the hazards

> to navigate around the fact that they are not identically motivated and may not always share the same agenda. The ability to promise provides a crucial tool to permit mutual engagement among equals, who are nevertheless distinct and diverse, without either party feeling the pressure to homogenize. (506)

Finally, this connection between promising and intimacy is, for Shiffrin, very close indeed. Although she sometimes writes as if promises are merely a tool (perhaps one among many) that may be deployed to produce or sustain intimacy—that they "facilitate healthy dynamics within relationships" (496)—Shiffrin in fact thinks that the relationship between promising and intimacy is much closer. Promise, for Shiffrin, is not just useful for intimacy; it is essential. Thus, she says that "[o]ur capacity to conduct our relationships in a morally decent way depends on our having the power to promise (as well as related, derivative powers of commitment)" (499). The closeness and necessity of this connection between promise and intimacy is driven home by the purpose to which Shiffrin directs this observation. In the very next sentence, she writes: "Therefore, given our noncontingent capacity [for intimacy] and its dependence on the power to promise, we must have the power to promise" (499). Shiffrin is making a transcendental argument. She is proposing that one of the side-benefits of her account of promising is that it lays to rest a worry, originally raised by Hume (1978: 455, 524) and elaborated by David Owens (in his contribution to this book) that persons lack the normative power to create obligations in the way promising seems to involve, that is, directly by intending to do so. Shiffrin seeks to defeat this worry by drawing an inference back from observed intimacy to the conditions of its possibility, arguing that among these conditions is the power to promise. The connection between promising and intimacy therefore must be, for Shiffrin, itself "noncontingent."

IV.

I believe that the true relationship between promise and love is very different. Although promising and love are both forms of recognition and respect, they are not nearly so sympathetic as Shiffrin's view supposes but are rather, in important respects, opposed.

To be sure, achieving intimacy requires that the intimates make some sort of commitment to each other. Love—a vivid and particularized appreciation of the personality of the beloved—cannot actually happen at first sight, and achieving love takes not just time but effort and also devotion, which amounts to an inclination to overcome the self-protective instincts that get in the way of love and the inevitable misunderstandings that seem, at first, to validate such self-protection. This effortful pursuit of intimacy may, moreover, be conceived of on the model of a commitment to the beloved and the love relation. And this commitment may in certain instances, including perhaps in some of the instances that Shiffrin describes, involve promises that insulate the relationship from some of the self-protective tendencies that threaten to undermine it. But the commitment *need* not involve promising nor any "derivative powers," as Shiffrin supposes (2008: 499). It may involve no more than a simple intention—perhaps on the model of the intention in favor of mutual support that figures in Michael Bratman's account of shared cooperative activity (1999: 103, 105)[20]—to continue pursuing the intimate relation, and the appreciation that constitutes its intimacy, even in the face of unanticipated roadblocks. (The lover might intend to pick up the relationship, as it were, if it falters, including even if it falters because her beloved has dropped the ball.) Moreover, and more significantly, even if promising can serve as a useful *instrument* in establishing intimacy, it is *in itself* inimical to intimacy. Even if Shiffrin is right to suppose that promises may in certain special cases enable love by eliminating obstacles to intimacy associated with various forms of inequality, these cases do not establish the close conceptual relation between promise and intimacy that Shiffrin imagines. Rather the more powerful promisors in the examples are incapable of spontaneously responding to their promisees in the open and vulnerable way that love requires: they remain blind to their promisees and do not yet love.[21] And while a promise may cabin the results of such blindness, and so may have the consequence of enabling persons eventually to love, *the promise in itself is not a case of seeing the promisee in the way—with the vividness—that love requires.* Once true love has been achieved, promises between lovers wither away; and making new promises introduces a distance, a form of alienation even, into the love relation. Indeed, the genetic structure of promissory recognition is impersonal and in this sense *opposed* to intimacy. Promises prototypically do not promote intimacy, but rather an arm's-length relation.

To see why, begin by observing that the forms of recognition associated with promise and with love are phenomenologically very different.

Most obviously, love is rival in a way promise is not. To be sure, our capacity for promising is not infinite, so that promises can compete with one another. Certain promises, made to some persons, foreclose making other promises to other persons: for example, a person's promise to devote her entire work energies to the success of one employer's business renders a further promise to work for a second employer a fraud. Indeed, such competition among potential promising partners is among the core features of the markets in which contractual promises (which I shall in a moment hold up as the highest expression of promise quite generally) arise. But a person's capacity to promise becomes exhausted only in certain substantive areas, that is, with respect to promises that have a certain subject matter. (In the example, this subject is the allocation of a person's economic production.) The formal pattern of recognition associated with promising is nonrival, which is to say that when a promisor recognizes one person in the way of promising, this does not reduce her capacity for promissory recognition of others. (Thus, the promisor in the example remains free to make any number of promises to the second employer, including even a promise to work for him should her relationship with the first employer come undone.) Indeed, there are some promises that may be made literally to all of humanity, or at least to all persons who accept them. A simple and familiar example, also drawn from the field of economic activity, is the promise associated with a creative commons license for a text or image, under which a creator promises all persons that they may reproduce her work as long as they make certain similar promises with respect to any of their own work in which it figures.

Things are very different in the case of love—which does display rivalry directly among persons, and indeed does so in virtue of the formal structure of recognition that love involves. A person cannot love all others appreciatively, that is, in the manner that I have described. Indeed, she cannot even be *open* to loving all others—our heart's arithmetic, our capacities for appreciation and vulnerability, will not allow it. Accordingly, to love someone is (among other things) to foreclose loving others.

Even if love involves an appreciation of universal humanity as it is rendered particular in the personality of the beloved, this appreciation remains in important ways tied to the specific beloved. Certainly, one cannot distribute the appreciation of universal humanity outside of the love relation, as it were, so that to love one person is not to love humanity in all its expressions. Indeed, and quite to the contrary, to see universal humanity in the idiosyncrasies of one person is to become blinded to how the different idiosyncrasies of another person might reflect universal humanity in different, and perhaps even opposed, ways. As Velleman says, "we discriminate in love" because

> the value we do manage to see in some fellow creatures arrests our emotional defenses to them, and our resulting vulnerability exhausts the attention that we might have devoted to finding and appreciating the value in others (1999: 372).

Accordingly,

> we are constitutionally limited in the number of people we can love; and we may have to stop short of our constitutional limits in order to enjoy the loving relationships that make for a good life (372).[22]

Our capacity for new love is not, of course, eliminated by the love we already display, and we can always fall in love again. It is rather that we cannot, past a point, sustain the appreciation that is constitutive of love for more than a certain class of persons all at once; after a point, to fall into a new love is to fall out of an old one. This is so, moreover, simply in virtue of the formal structure of the appreciation that love involves, and is therefore not limited to the case of loves with a certain substantive content. (The special place that popular perceptions accord jealousy in the life of specifically sexual love is misleading in this connection, not least since jealousy is rivalry approached from the point of view of the beloveds, whereas the structural limits on love that I have in mind apply from the point of view of the lover.) All love is rival. Promising, again, is not rival in this way.

This difference, which appears on the face of the immediate experience of promise and love, is moreover only the most obvious expression of a deep structural difference between the two relations. It is related to the deeper difference as phenotype to genotype.

Thus promissory recognition takes as its object the purely generic nature of the promisee—the promisee's intentional capacity, his personality simpliciter. Promising is an example of the form of respect that Kant says arises when we "subordinate[] our will to a mere concept or idea," so that a promisor's respect for her promisee is "a response to something that [she] know[s] about him intellectually but with which [she has] no immediate acquaintance." (Velleman 1999: 371). Loving recognition, by contrast, takes as its object the beloved's particular personality—the expression that universal humanity achieves in the distinctive traits that make the beloved not just a person, but the person who he is.[23] The fact that love is rival while promise is not is merely an expression of this deeper difference between the two relations. We can promise many but love only a few because we can recognize generic will wherever it appears, but our perceptual capacities lack the bandwidth to recognize will's particular expression in more than a few cases. Or, to change metaphors only very slightly, we lack the *resolution* to recognize personality in all but a few persons with the vividness that love requires. It is not that loving respect is a more intense or committed form of promissory respect. Rather, it is that loving recognition arises in a broader spectrum than promissory recognition: we promise in black and white, but we love in color.

Velleman is therefore wrong to suggest that promise and love may be arrayed along a single dimension of increasing recognition—to regard "respect and love as the required minimum and optional maximum responses to one and the same value" (1999: 366). Certainly, a promisor may be more faithful to her promisee than a lover is to her beloved: the promisor may be less easily tempted to defect than the lover, and in that sense the recognition in a promise may exceed that in a love. The difference between promise and love concerns the quality of the recognition that the two relations involve; promisors and lovers recognize in different ways. That the difference between promise and love is qualitative rather than quantitative is reflected also in the natural responses persons make to betrayals of the relations, which may, in appropriate circumstances, each be as serious or substantial as the other. Nevertheless, the two types of betrayal will always be qualitatively very different. A betrayed promise leaves the disappointed promisee upset and angry, but gives her no grounds for doubting whether the promise was real to begin with. The betrayal of a love is very different in this respect. It leaves the betrayed lover feeling as if she misunderstood the beloved who betrayed her in a way that calls the love itself into question—hence the commonplace sense, following the breakup of a romance, that the romance itself was an illusion and the commonplace utterance, "I guess I never really knew him." These are natural and appropriate responses: the betrayed love was constituted by the betrayed lover's vivid appreciation of her beloved's person, and the betrayal shows that this appreciation was, literally, mistaken—that it misunderstood what was being appreciated.

This difference between the morphologies of promise and love may be explained, moreover, not just figuratively and generally, but in literal detail. Because the recognition in promise is purely generic, the substance of promissory obligation is not fixed by the promissory form. That is, promises may take on many substances, including contradictory ones, and they need not, in particular, be fair or morally wholesome in order to sustain promissory recognition.[24] The substance that particular promises do take on is fixed not by the promissory form, nor even by the promissory form applied to the personalities involved in the particular promise in question, but by the contingent and indeed discretionary intentions of the parties at the point of making the promise, so that the only way to get a particular substance into promissory obligation is directly to choose it. Promises are therefore not just formally but in their substance *purely* the creatures of the intentions of the parties.

They are complete ex ante, from the moment of their creation, and have no independent lives of their own.[25]

Things are very different in love, where the substance of love relations is relatively more fixed by the loving form. Because the recognition involved in love is particular—because what is recognized is not the beloved's purely generic perspectival capacity but rather that capacity as it receives distinctive expression in the person who he is—loving recognition does have a required substantive content. To be sure, love can have many, substantively various expressions—the polite and the unruly family may both be loving, and a person's very different loves for her parents, her spouse, and her children may all and equally be true. But the varieties of love are more narrowly cabined than the varieties of promise, and love's content is not contingent and discretionary in the way promise's content is. Rather, the content of love is significantly constrained by the nondiscretionary ways the particular personalities of the participants in the love relation give distinctive expression to universal humanity. True love must in some sense answer to the nature of the beloved, which is not up to the lover, and to the conditions of understanding and appreciating the beloved as the particular person who he is. (This is the philosophical analogue to the advice text's commonplace that a lover should not try to change her beloved. The point is not just that the effort will fail, although it might well, but that it is inimical to love.) The substance of the obligations of love is, moreover, therefore not fixed at the point of falling in love, or indeed at any point, but instead adapts to the exigencies of the love relation, as the lovers themselves develop the ways generic personality is given distinctive expressions through their lives. (This is why we say that a marriage is for better or for worse.) Whereas persons' generic personality (that is, the generic perspectival capacity that constitutes them as persons, and which all persons equally possess) is a fixed feature of their nature, persons' particular personalities (the ways perspectival capacity is rendered distinctive in the persons who they are) are ever-changing, complex, and indeed unpredictable; they are too complex and unpredictable for one person fully to appreciate another all-at-once with the specificity that love requires. Love must thus be shifting and flexible—the vivid and particular appreciation of the beloved, by which love is constituted, requires an ongoing openness to changes in the beloved and even to the possibility that details of the beloved's peculiar manifestation of universal humanity come newly to the lover's attention. Loving appreciation, being a species of awareness, responds to forces that stand apart from the intentions of the lover, and love therefore does not arise or persist at the discretion of the lovers. (Something like this can occur even at the outset of a love relation, as in the experience of falling in love without meaning to, or even against one's will.) Love is never complete ex ante but rather necessarily takes on a life of its own, growing and changing ex post. Persons lack the perceptual capacities to love in any fashion other than as they go along.

These features of the comparative anatomy of promise and love may be collected in the observation that promise establishes a much thinner relation than love.

Promisors engage their promisees' pure personalities—that is, the generic perspectival capacities in virtue of which promisees are like all other persons. One person can appreciate another's generic perspectival capacity simply by treating his freely formed intentions as authoritative. (Because only persons can freely intend—because a free will is constitutive of personality—someone who gives over her freedom to another treats the other as possessing a personality that is in its perspectival capacity equivalent to her own.) Moreover, because persons have privileged epistemic access to their own intentions, one person may (at least in general) treat another as constituting an authoritative perspective simply by deferring to his expressed intentions. (Exceptions to the general rule—for example, cases in which a promisee suffers a temporary loss of her deliberative capacity or freedom, or simply misunderstands the nature of the promise she is owed—arise only at the margins of promise, and indeed often involve broader pathologies of rationality.) Accordingly, promissory appreciation may be rendered complete at the moment of promise, by shifting decisional authority over an action whose performance is antecedently discretionary in the promisor, to make the performance discretionary in the promisee. And that, of course, is precisely what promises actually do—it is just another way of characterizing the promisor's core commitment to perform her promise (quite apart from her private judgment concerning whether or not performance is all-things-considered for the best) unless released by her promisee.

The love relation, by contrast, is thick. Love requires the lover to engage her beloved's distinctive personality—that is, vividly to appreciate the peculiar way generic perspectival capacity receives expression in the particular person who he is. Appreciating another's particular personality in the way that love requires involves a very different set of attitudes and intentions from those associated with promise. Most important, a person does not have nearly so privileged an access to the way his peculiar life renders generic moral personality particular as he does to his bare intentions. (Self-knowledge is famously as difficult as knowing another, and self-love raises the same problems of vivid appreciation as love of others.) And accordingly, loving appreciation does not involve anything like the deference that promissory appreciation does. A lover must be enthralled by her beloved, of course, but she must also remain vigilant in fashioning and refining her own perspective on the love relation; she must pursue her appreciation of the working out of her beloved's generic personality in the distinctive details of his life, from her own point of view. Thus it is not just possible but natural and proper (indeed, a commonplace of the romantic imagination) for a lover to know her beloved in some respects better than he knows himself. Loving appreciation is therefore ever-changing, and in particular changing according to the internal growth dynamics of the lover's and not just the beloved's personality.

To be sure, a lover must allow her beloved's perspective on himself to figure prominently in her dealings with him. But it will figure not on the promissory model of deference—that is, to exclude her own perceptions of what respecting his humanity requires—but rather on the model of a fusion of perspectives or even of shared judgment—that is, to inform and instruct her appreciation, and indeed as one of the things about him that she appreciates. (Whereas a promisor need be no more than conscientious toward her promisee, a lover must be *fascinated* by her beloved. And whereas conscientiousness may be achieved impersonally, fascination occurs distinctively from one's own point of view.) In this sense, and in contradistinction to promise, the demands of love are, quite literally, not up to the beloved to determine. Whereas promissory appreciation *shifts* authority, loving appreciation *shares* it.

V.

Promise and love are in all these respects clearly very different. But it remains to determine what to make of the differences between them—in particular, whether the forms of recognition involved in promissory and intimate relations are complementary or in tension with each other. I believe that there exists a tension between promise and love. On the one hand, promissory obligations cannot be successfully created between persons who truly love each other, at least not within the scope of their love. On the other hand, insofar as lovers succeed at establishing promises between them, their promises crowd out their love.

To be sure, promise and love are not strictly incompatible. To begin with, lovers might employ promise to coordinate their activities in areas of their lives in which they lack the energy or inclination to achieve the vivid appreciation that characterizes the rest of their loving relations. Sometimes these will be trivial promises, adopted for cases in which the game isn't worth love's candle. Thus a wife may promise her husband that she will put gas in the car on the way home from work; or a father may promise a child that if she sleeps through the night, he will give her a treat for breakfast. In other cases, the promises are not trivial at all, but rather concern spheres of action and interest that the lovers self-consciously exclude, or carve out, from their intimate relations. A lover who has assumed a job that gives her authority over her beloved's work conditions may promise him that she will recuse herself from any decisions concerning his professional life.[26] Moreover, promises may even create space for intimacy to grow, by eliminating vulnerability and clearing away mistrust in the manner Shiffrin imagines, so that promise may be a path into love (although surely not the only path). But these possibilities concern the consequential or extrinsic interactions between promise and love. And even if the two relations can make room for each other or indeed support each other causally, they remain intrinsically—which is to say, in their immanent structures—opposed. Where love involves an emotional opening up or intimacy or vulnerability, promising closes off vulnerability. Promise is in its immanent structure opposed to intimacy; and promises characteristically arise at arm's length.

It is tempting to find the source of this tension in the fact that where a promisee loves his promisor, this will motivate him to release his beloved-promisor from any promises that she has made, just as soon as performance of the promises ceases to be best from the promisor's point of view. At the very least, one might think, a promisee who stood on his promissory rights even in such a case would not love his promisor well, and that a loving promisee therefore has a reason not to accept the promise. But while this may indeed be so—although I do not wish here to argue the question either way—such considerations approach the relationship between promise and love literally from the wrong perspective. They suggest only that there is a difficulty in making a promise to a loving promisee—that the *promisor's* promise is in tension with the *promisee's* love. But observations along these lines, even if they are well taken, do not yet establish the claimed tension between promising and loving—they do not establish any tension between promissory and loving recognition in the same person, from the point of view of the lover/promisor. The question is not whether promising is consistent with *being loved*, but rather whether it is consistent with *loving*. Answering "no" requires showing that to promise one's beloved is to take his pure, generic personality as determinative of one's conduct and thus to foreclose appreciating his particular personality in that manner that love requires. In that case, a promisor would indeed treat her promisee in a fashion inconsistent with loving him.

Perhaps the clearest illustration of the tension between promise and love arises in the case in which the intimacy between promisor and promisee is total. Thus, a person cannot successfully make promises to herself. At least where a person knows and appreciates her own humanity, which his to say displays self-love, she will find it literally impossible to shift decisional authority away from her promisor-self to her promisee-self as promissory recognition requires. She will find it impossible because, being totally intimate with herself, she will be unable to recognize herself as a generic personality, which is constituted by the general capacity to form intentions entirely apart from the specific intentions that she forms. A person's promise to herself cannot shift decisional authority to another person in the manner that promising requires—that is, to a person who is recognized generically for her intentional capacity rather than particularly for the intentions that make her who she is. A person simply cannot appreciate herself in this generic way—her self-love and the specific appreciation that it involves obscures her generic personality from herself. To herself, she is always and necessarily not just a person, but the person who she is. (The problem with promising to oneself is thus not the familiar problem that there is no way for the promisee-self to commit not to release the promisor-self from her obligations, but rather the novel problem that the very idea of *shifting* decisional authority by deferring to one's own purely generic will is a nonsense because one confronts one's own will in a necessarily particular mode, so that one's substantive intentions are front and center, and therefore that promissory appreciation is impossible in the case of promises to oneself.) At the very least, a person can achieve promissory recognition of herself only by distancing her promisee-self from the self that she occupies as promisor, as happens, for example, in the cases in which promises to "future selves" are understood in terms of an agent's efforts to achieve temporal coordination within her life on the model of interpersonal coordination among several agents at a single point in time. A person's promise to herself can therefore sustain promissory obligation only in gaps that appear (perhaps, that she has herself opened up) in her self-love.

Promises made within ordinary intimate relations—relations between a lover and her beloved—moreover, raise analogous difficulties. Indeed, the tension between promise and love is quite general and may be read more or less directly off the earlier account of the differences between loving and promissory recognition. That account, recall, emphasized that whereas a promisor appreciates her promisee's purely generic personality (the perspectival and intentional capacities that he possesses in common with all persons), a lover appreciates her beloved's distinctive personality (the peculiar way these capacities work themselves out in the person who he is). This entails, as I observed, that whereas promissory recognition, shifts decisional authority, is complete ex ante, and remains purely formal (so that the substantive content of promissory obligation is entirely a creature of the discretionary intentions of the parties), loving recognition *shares* decisional authority, must always be adjusted as the relationship develops ex post, and includes *substantive* requirements (so that the content of love is substantially fixed by the peculiar characters that make lovers the persons who they are).

These distinctions make plain that to love someone is to appreciate him in a manner that is incompatible with the manner of appreciation required in promising. Whereas a promisor abdicates responsibility for managing the subject-matter of her promise by shifting decisional authority in this area to her promisee, who is sovereign over his intentions to insist on or release the promise, a lover must rather be prepared to follow her own perceptions of her beloved's character where they lead, including even against his own perceptions (since his self-knowledge is not authoritative for her, although it may of course equally not ignore it). Whereas a promisor cabins her engagement with her promisee ex ante by the terms of her promise—and indeed obligates herself to restrain the natural tendency to adjust her conduct toward him in light of reasons that arise out of subsequent developments—a lover must remain open to constant revisions as her love relation develops ex post. And whereas a promisor may determine the shape of her promissory engagements by the free play of her will, a lover must accept that her engagement with her beloved must adjust itself to accommodate both their unchosen natures. It is not just that promise *falls short* of love in each of these respects—that promissory recognition does not involve the open-ended or vivid vulnerability to the particular humanity of the other that constitutes love—but rather that promising *forecloses* love, or at least *gets in love's way*. A promisor engages her promisee's generic personality, to be sure. But she also pursues, within the realm of the promise, and through the deference that the promise involves, a willful self-blinding to the particularity of her promisee; she abdicates the enterprise of knowing, really knowing, her promisee in the vivid detail that love would involve.[27] Contrariwise, promissory obligation cannot get going within love's scope, because a lover cannot, in light of her antecedent appreciation of her beloved, relinquish his fate to his choices in the manner that promissory appreciation requires. Just as when we confront ourselves, we necessarily confront our beloveds also in their particularity, as the persons who they are.

A familiar example—companionate marriage—illustrates the extreme difficulty of making promises within a love relation and that this difficulty increases as the relation becomes more expansively and completely loving. Certainly it is intuitively plain that if the reason why a wife remains faithful to her husband, or cares for him in a time of need, or performs any of the other myriad acts that a loving and intimate marriage involves is just that she recognizes that she is bound by her marriage vow, then her marriage is in serious trouble. Moreover, things would only get worse if she sought to give herself additional reasons to support her husband by making him further promises, say, a new promise to be faithful, made on the eve of a business trip. The general considerations adduced above explain why a marriage is in trouble in such a case. The husband wants his wife's fidelity and support not because she has promised but because she loves him. That is, he does not want her to act because she has an impersonal regard for his generic will which leads her to recognize his authority over her as her promisee—it will, after all, be worse rather than better for the marriage if she asks him to release her from her vows before betraying them.[28] Rather, the husband wants his wife to be faithful and supportive because she appreciates—vividly and specifically, which is to say, lovingly—his needs given the person who he is, and because she has opened herself up (by removing the self-protective blindness that shields her from the analogous particularity of others) to the claims associated with his needs.[29] Insofar as the promise becomes the basis for her actions, the wife treats her husband as she would a stranger, and not as her beloved.[30]

This account of marital obligation, moreover, receives support from the historical development of the marriage relation. Thus as companionate (that is, fully intimate and loving) marriage has emerged, over the last century or so, the marriage promise has receded from its once-central place in the institution and certainly no longer constitutes the marriage relation.[31] In a fully companionate marriage, the marital promise, far from being the ground of the relation, is quite literally an afterthought—just the public record of a relation that has existed, privately, on other grounds. (The relation may even have long ceased to be purely private, as when the partners openly cohabited before marriage.) I suspect, finally, that the inadequacy of promise as a basis for marital intimacy has always been recognized in at least some way. Common law marriage, which required no vows, recognized that promise is not a necessary basis for the marital relation. And even the old marriage vows implicitly acknowledged that promise cannot be a sufficient basis. The terms of marriage, after all, were not variable at the discretion of the parties (so that the marriage relation, unlike the promise relation, was never purely a creature of the parties' intentions),[32] and the marriage vows self-consciously acknowledged that they could not fix, ex ante, the content of a marital commitment that must develop organically ex post according to particular requirements of the organic growth of the distinctive personalities involved in the marriage, which is to say, for better or for worse.

VI.

The distinctions I have been drawing between love and promise suggest where one might look to find the highest and most complete expression of promissory appreciation. In particular, they suggest that promise's highest form will be achieved not in personal promises—which are embedded in intimate relations whose own immanent structure, I have argued, competes with promissory appreciation–but in promises among strangers, that is, among parties whose engagement arises entirely at arm's length. Contract may be understood as the legal elaboration of arm's-length promising. I therefore conclude by identifying three respects in which contract represents an especially impressive case of promissory appreciation. This suggestion, of course, runs directly counter to the commoner view that contract is at best a marginal and at worst a degenerate case of promise.

Before turning to the respects in which contract establishes the highest form of promissory recognition, it is worth pausing briefly to observe that contractual promises do indeed establish the form of recognition associated with promises more generally. Even this may surprise some. The parties to contracts, after all, are unlike the parties involved in many personal promises in that they generally enter into their relations with purely self-interested motivations. Indeed, the parties to contracts generally face strategic circumstances in which these motives lead them to compete, as each tries to get the best deal that she can: buyers press for low prices, for example, and sellers for high ones. Moreover, the law permits the parties to contracts to carry these self-interested motivations with them into the interstices of their contractual relations. Thus contract partners are typically each unwilling, when the other stumbles and places the success of the joint activity in jeopardy, to shoulder *any* uncompensated increases in their shares of the burden of the joint activity. This is especially true of discrete contracts, whose legal structure characteristically accepts such uncooperative participants. As a general matter, a material breach by one party to a contract (even if it is innocent)[33] relieves the other of its obligation of return performance.[34] Finally, the law *never* requires a disappointed promisee to catch a stumbling promisor and (shouldering the burden herself) ensure that the contemplated performance occurs.

But although contracting parties are motivated by opposed interests and retain these interests even within the contract relation, they nevertheless pursue their interests, insofar as they pursue them through contract, in a way that involves recognizing each other's personalities as authoritative in just the manner I have described. I have elsewhere elaborated in detail the precise pattern of recognition that contracts involve (Markovits 2004), and so I provide only a brief sketch here. To begin with, the intentions and actions of the parties to a contract are not just correlated but coordinated; they do not merely coincide but rather, to use Hume's phrase, "have a reference to" each other (1978: 490). Moreover, the character of this reference may be spelled out quite precisely. Thus contracts are characteristically established by an exchange of promises, in which each party intends to join in the performance of the exchange; each party intends her participation in the performance to support the other's; and, because even the simplest contract cannot be administered as pre-packaged coordination but instead requires constant adjustment in the face of unanticipated contingencies, the parties adjust their performance to be mutually responsive. Borrowing Michael Bratman's formulation, to which this account of the morphology of contract obviously owes a substantial debt, one can say that contracts involve a pattern of intentions in the parties to them in which these intentions are self-consciously *interlocking*: "each agent must have intentions in favor of the efficacy of the intentions of the other. In this way, each agent must treat the relevant intentions of the other as *end-providing* for herself; for each intends that the relevant intentions of the other be successfully executed" (1999: 102). Finally, and crucially, contract adds to this interlocking pattern of intentions the additional feature that each party adopts an intention not to defect from the performance that the contract describes—not to abandon the promised performance unless released. In this way, the parties to contracts form intentions not just in favor of the activity that constitutes contractual performance but also in favor of each other.[35] These are the promissory intentions not to defect—not to abandon the promised performance unless released. Rather than intending just that the intentions of her promisee succeed, a contractual promisor intends, in effect, to give her promisee authority—not just moral but also legal—to require her to promote the success of his intentions. She intends, within the sphere of the contract, to subordinate her will to her promisee's, and she comes, in this way, to treat her promisee, and not just the joint activity of the contract, as an end in himself. And when she does so, she recognizes the personality of her contract partner, taking his intentions (within the sphere of the contract) as authoritative.

These observations establish that contract involves the characteristic form of recognition associated with promise *in spite of* the self-interested motives contracting parties bring to their engagements. I am after a more striking claim, however, namely that self-interested contracting represents the highest form of promise—the form that most completely realizes the recognition in which the morality of promise is grounded. Indeed, I shall suggest that contract establishes the highest form of promise *because of* the arm's-length rather than intimate character of contractual promises—that is, because of the self-interestedness with which the parties approach their contracts. It is not that the moral light of promise, whose natural precincts lie in intimate relationships, manages to illuminate even the dark and inhospitable domain of self-interested contracting. Rather, self-interested contracting most completely realizes the forms of recognition in which the morality of promise is grounded. It does so in three ways.

First, the self-interestedness of the parties to contract—their arm's-length interaction—makes it natural for each party to a contract to recognize the pure and free-standing personality of the other: the parties to contracts recognize one another exclusively in virtue of their wills, the fact that they each constitute an independent perspective and are capable of forming and acting on intentions. In this way, the self-interest that motivates parties to contracts prevents one party's sympathetic concern for the other from interfering with the authority that her promissory engagements accord to his intentions.

As the earlier account of the tension between love and promise illustrated, paternalism—a practice in which a person imposes her own judgments on the person whom she paternalizes and that represents a direct affront to the forms of recognition and respect out of which the morality of promise arises—is natural in promises among intimates. As I have explained, promissory recognition in intimate relations is always compromised by the imperatives of intimacy—the promisor-lover's sense that she knows her beloved-promisee potentially better than he knows himself and her commitment, as lover, to act on this knowledge even against the deference she might owe, as promisor, even to his misguided or self-destructive intentions. By contrast, paternalism is quite alien to contract. Thus there is no analog, in the practice of personal promising, to the strikingly rigid rule of freedom of contract, which serves to protect persons' capacities to enter into whatever contractual relations they wish, without regard to their wisdom or prudence.[36] And within the contracts that persons have made, the law almost categorically rejects the practice, common in personal promising, of insisting that promisors take responsibility for their promises' impacts on promisees and subject their promises to regular reassessment, from their own points of view, concerning their attractiveness. The law effectively never imposes on the parties alterations of the terms of an agreement that one party has come to regret.

In both these ways, the law insistently supports the authority of contractual promisees to govern their contractual arrangements untrammeled by the interferences of meddling promisors. And by doing so, it accords promisees authority that is based simply on their possessing personality and is in particular not cabined by their promisors' perceptions of their interests or indeed of any peculiar features of their personalities. Contract therefore insists that the arm's-length promises it recognizes display precisely the form of recognition that intimacy threatens.

Contract represents the highest and most complete form of promise in a second respect also, which is connected to the fact that contracts involve reciprocal promises. Anglo-American contract law achieves this result through the consideration doctrine, which requires that a legally valid contract include not only offer and acceptance but also a bargained-for exchange—that each party to a contract must make a promise to the other and, moreover, that each of these promises must (at least conventionally) have induced the other.[37] This introduces an egalitarian element into contract, which is absent from promise simpliciter. The egalitarianism is not substantive, of course. Even as contract law insists on the fact of a bargain as a pre-requisite for legal enforcement, it expressly makes no effort to police the adequacy of the bargain.[38] A contract might allocate all of the contractual surplus to one party or the other and still be supported by adequate consideration.[39] But the formal equality of the contract relation survives such substantive inequality. The consideration doctrine requires each party to the contract to obligate itself to the other, so contracts necessarily involve authority on both sides. Moreover, by requiring not just an exchange of promises but also an exchange in which each promise induced the other, the consideration doctrine selects for promises in which reciprocal authority is not just *granted* but also, because it was sought on each side, actually *exercised*.

Through this formal reciprocity requirement, contract secures a crucial condition of recognizing the personality of others that may be absent from one-sided promises.[40] In particular, a person cannot engage others as persons by appreciating them in a manner that involves a retreat from her own humanity, a denial of her own personality. In order for recognition to be a good, it must be not just an appreciation of the personality of the other but also an expression of the personality of the agent herself. This is immanent in the very idea of recognition—in the idea of seeing oneself in the other—an attitude that involves not just an appreciation for the other but an assertion of self for the other to reflect.

Formally one-sided promises, for this reason, fail to achieve the good of recognition. Indeed, they may affirmatively undermine recognition and therefore suppress the appreciation of humanity. This possibility arises in connection with promises whose text or subtext includes the thought that while the promisor might obligate herself to the promisee, she lacks the capacity to *receive* promises from him because she is incapable of the authority over him that receiving such promises would require. The promises involved in (a highly stylized version of) the Hobbesian social contract are perhaps like this—through them, the personalities of the subjects are subsumed in a sovereign (think of the image on the frontispiece of the first edition of *Leviathan*) whose absolute authority makes it impossible for him to make binding promises in return. Other illustrations perhaps include the promise of unconditional obedience made by the slave to his master in Hegel's dialectic and the promise associated with a religious vow made to an omnipotent god. Promises such as these involve not recognition (and its combination of appreciation for the personality of the other and assertion of the personality of the self) but rather self-denial—the promisor does not express her personality so much as retreat from or even repress it. (This is a practical analogue of the suggestion, associated with Feuerbach, that the religious believer projects her capacities onto a god as a way of denying that she possesses them herself.)[41] And for this reason, such promises are detached from the human interest that underwrites promissory obligation (at least in its pure form), so that if they bind, they do not do so on the model of promise proper. By insisting, through the consideration doctrine, on promissory reciprocity and the formal equality of status such reciprocity engenders, contract denies the law's imprimatur to arrangements that constitute promises only in this degenerate sense.

The third and final respect in which contract represents the highest form of promise involves the fact that contract is a species of positive law. Insofar as the parties to promises (and especially to reciprocal promises) come to share ends and to recognize each other as authoritative with respect to the promised performance, their promise establishes a set of common reasons—a kind of public reason—between them. But for promises that have moral force only, this public reason remains, one might say, intangible or purely abstract. It has no independent constituency, no concrete expression in the world, but rather depends for its practical efficacy on the continued engagement of the parties and, critically, on their continued agreement concerning what conforming to the public reasons established by the promise requires. (The parties must agree not only *that* they are bound by the promises but also *what* the promises bind them to.) The legal recognition associated with contract changes this, and gives the public reason associated with contractual promises a concrete, tangible existence. In particular, the law establishes an agent—the court—who reasons not from the point of view of the promisor or of the promisee, but rather from the point of view of the contract, which it embodies, as it were.[42] And the parties to contracts agree to give the court the authority not just to declare what their contractual obligations are but also to enforce them. In both these respects, contract perfects the recognition associated with promise: it protects the publicity of promissory recognition against the inevitable encroachment of the parties' peculiar and contradictory views concerning what authority they have given each other; and it (relatedly) supports promissory recognition by creating third party enforcement, which proceeds from this public point of view. Contract law, one might say, does for private promises what the social contract—or constitutional law—does for public principles of justice.[43] And in this sense also contract represents promise's highest expression.

ACKNOWLEDGMENT

I would like to thank the participants in the Rice conference on the philosophy of promising, and in particular Hanoch Sheinman, who organized the gathering and edited this book, and without whose efforts the arguments here would have come out much worse.

NOTES

1. Even those who acknowledge that the norms of intimate relationships may compete with promissory norms (see, for example, Kimel, 2007) have not proposed, much less elaborated, a general conflict between the essential natures of promissory and intimate relations. Certainly they have not found this conflict in the distinction between two incompatible forms of recognition.

2. Insofar as organizations (for example, corporations) can make and accept promises, then this is because they are endowed by law with artificial personality.

3. The connection between moral personality and promissory capacity has a long history in philosophy and indeed in law. In philosophy, it is rendered most vivid in Nietzsche's remarks that "To breed an animal *that is permitted to promise*—isn't this precisely the paradoxical task nature has set for itself with regard to man? isn't this the real problem *of* man?" and that a person who possesses promissory capacity holds "his kick in readiness for the frail dogs who promise although they are not permitted to do so" (1998: Second Essay, sec. 2). The connection between legal personality and promise was for a long time expressed in legal rules that deprived human beings whose personality the law did not recognize—slaves and women—of contractual capacity. Even today, the law acknowledges this connection when it denies certain classes of human beings contractual capacity. See American Law Institute (1981), secs. 12–16). Notice, moreover, that human beings, for example minor children, may lack contractual capacity but nevertheless sue and be sued in tort, so that having contractual capacity indicates a higher legal status than merely enjoying the right not to be harmed (Keeton et al. 1984: sec. 134; Famsworth 1999: sec. 4.4).

4. See American Law Institute (1981), sec. 22.

5. The brief discussion that follows borrows heavily from my earlier effort to elaborate the patterns of recognition that promises involve in Markovits (2004).

6. If there were no acceptance requirement, so that a promisor could draft her promisee into the service of her ends, then promising would not necessarily involve respect or recognition, but could be a form of manipulation. This point has been noted by Fried (1981: 41).

7. The last two ways of characterizing promissory intentions, which build the idea of obligation (or its cognates) into these intentions, raise the specter that the theory is circular—that the account of recognition out of which the theory derives its defense of promissory obligation builds the very obligation that it is meant to generate into the promissory intentions from which it begins. This is a false worry, however, because the account of recognition can be fully elaborated without any reference specifically to obligation, using simply a promisor's intentions not to defect from her promise unless released by her promisee. Once recognition has been explained in this way, using the language of obligation going forward becomes a harmless concession to expository ease.

8. It is worth pointing out, in light of the complication mentioned in the previous note, that this account of the promissory relation does not depend on characterizing the promisor's intentions in terms of obligation or any of its cognates. All the elements of the promissory relation appear even if promising is characterized simply in terms of a promisor's intentions not to defect from the promised performance unless she is released from the promise.

9. That is, when the circumstances do not excuse the promisor from performance under either the express or implied terms of the promise.

10. The account of promising developed here therefore addresses what David Owens, in his contribution to this collection, calls the problem of the "bare wrong." I have addressed this problem (in the version articulated by Hume) in greater detail elsewhere (2004: 1442–1446).

11. This claim must be approached cautiously, because the distinction between making a lying promise and breaking an honest promise cannot be drawn formally. A promise that was honestly made may become a lying promise when a promisor develops a secret intent to breach that she does not disclose in order that the promise might continue to encourage her promisee to complete his own agreed-on performance. (An installment buyer, for example, might form an intention not to pay for goods that she had intended to pay for when she bought them but keep this intention secret from her sellers in order that they deliver the goods.) A once-honest promisor who forms such a secret intention to deceive her promisee becomes a lying promisor, and uses him merely as a means, just as surely as a promisor who lies from the start.

12. Here it is instructive to notice the difference between the moral character of nonperformance that constitutes a breach of promise on the one hand and nonperformance connected to a promisee's waiver of her promissory rights on the other. In this alternative case–in which the promisee releases the promisor from any duties that arose under the promise–the relation that was invited by the promise is not so much betrayed as abandoned, and the status quo ante in which the promisor and promisee were strangers is simply restored.

13. Promising, by uniting the wills of the parties in pursuit of shared ends, may even be said to serve as a private analogue to the public practice of lawmaking–as a private act of collective self-governance. The analysis that I am conducting of the respectful private community of promising may be said, therefore, to parallel the republican analysis of the respectful community of citizenship.

14. Velleman is concerned not just to characterize the peculiar form of appreciation that he has in mind but also to argue that it better captures what we commonly call love than more familiar conceptions, which, as Velleman says, "tend to conceive of [love] as having an aim, in the manner of a Freudian drive" (351). Velleman attributes this view of love to a host of philosophers, including Rawls and Nozick (352).

I set aside the question whether Velleman is right about what we commonly call love. It is enough, for present purposes, that Velleman has identified and characterized a form of recognition that accompanies a certain form of intimacy that we can recognize from our own experience, regardless of whether or not this is distinctive to love in the ordinary sense of the word. Indeed, nothing in my argument would change if it turned out–as may be the case–that certain forms of hatred, or at least resentment, involve the same formal structure of appreciation as love (although with an opposite affect) and therefore also constitute a style of intimacy. If I succeed in arguing that promise is incompatible with love, it will likely not seem a challenging extension to argue that it is incompatible with hatred, also.

15. Velleman also cites to this language, which he uses to emphasize that even though the lover acts for the sake of his beloved, he does not act in pursuit of effectuating any aim (1999: 356). Thus Velleman observes that "[s]elf-existent ends [such as a person's humanity] are the objects of motivating attitudes that regard and value them as they already are," whereas "other ends are the objects of attitudes that value them as possibilities to be brought about" (357). Thus, "the fact that a person is a self-existent end just consists in the fact that he is... a proper object for reverence, an attitude that stands back in appreciation of the rational creature he is, without inclining toward any particular results to be produced." My purpose in turning to the self-existence of moral personality is related to this thought but importantly different. I emphasize that the features of persons that make them proper objects for reverence also make it essential to close oneself off from most persons, most of the time.

16. This account of the equal moral status of persons obviously has its roots in Kant's injunction: "Act in such a way that you always treat humanity, whether in your own person or in the person of any other, never simply as a means, but always at the same time as an end" (1964: 429). This command identifies what O'Neill has called "two separate aspects to treating others as persons" (1989: 13). First, a person should never treat others merely as means to his own ends; and second, he should always treat others also as ends in themselves. The first principle, which insists that other persons are never simply *available* to an agent for her own use, is important to be sure, but not in the present context, which instead focuses on the second (separate) idea that persons must always treat others as ends in themselves. This has sometimes been thought to announce merely that each person should "enhance [other persons'] prospects for the successful exercise of their agency," including "by directly assisting [them] in their pursuit of [their] ends" (Guyer, 2000: 148). But this way of speaking does not quite capture Kant's idea, which is that in order to treat others as ends in themselves it is not enough to act just *in support of* their ends, assessed from one's own point of view. Rather, one must support the ends of others *for the sake of* their personalities, which requires deferring to their judgments and intentions concerning these ends. The forms of recognition involved in promising establish precisely this deference.

17. Keats proposed that poets characteristically do open themselves up to others generally in this way, displaying what he called "negative capability," with the result that they lose any distinct personalities of their own. As he wrote, "[i]t is a wretched thing to confess; but it is a very fact that not one word that I ever utter can be taken for granted as an opinion growing out of my identical nature–how can it be when I have no nature?" (1970: 158). I have elsewhere elaborated on a sense in which adversary lawyers, who must open themselves up to their clients' perspectives, face a similar threat to their own personalities (Markovits, 2008).

18. Velleman writes specifically of *emotional* self-protection. But the scope of the self-protection is much broader than the association with feelings or sentiments suggests. I suspect that Velleman would not disagree with this, and that he intends *emotional* to convey a broader idea than the word's standard usage.

19. This fusion can (and probably should) leave each personality room for independent expression. That lovers are united through their love does not mean that they retain no life outside their love.

20. Bratman in fact speaks of a "commitment" to mutual support (103). Note that the "commitment" Bratman identifies is a practical commitment *to the joint activity*; it is not *to the other participants in the activity*.

21. We may see this by noting the difference between his response and the response of the true lover, who acts toward her beloved in ways that are incomprehensible save by reference to her love. She exposes herself to the personality of her beloved and spontaneously adjusts to what she sees in ways that cannot be rendered comprehensible save through love's lens—through the thought that she acts, as it were, in the grip of his charisma. This is what we mean when, confronted with a lover's inexplicable sacrifices in the face of, to us, an unappealing beloved—"I don't know what she sees in him."

22. Some remarks by Velleman suggest that he would embrace still narrower limits on our capacity for love, under which the range of others that a person can appreciatively love is limited not just by her loves but also by her prior nature or character. Although I do not argue the point here, I am inclined to think that universal humanity shines more vividly through individual idiosyncrasy than this restriction allows, and that persons are, commensurately, open to finding love even in unexpected places. Love's power over us is just an expression of the powerful claims that the personalities of others make on our attention. No lesser power than love itself, it seems to me, can obscure these claims.

23. As Velleman observes, this feature of love is connected to the fact that falling in love involves overcoming our emotional defenses. As Velleman says, "[t]he manifest person is the one against whom we have emotional defenses, and he must disarm them, if he can, with his manifest qualities. Grasping someone's personhood intellectually may be enough to make us respect him, but unless we actually *see* a person in the human being confronting us we won't be moved to love; and we can see the person only by seeing him in or through his empirical persona" (1999: 371).

24. I set aside the question whether the content of a promise may be so profoundly immoral—so disrespectful of humanity—that it is incompatible with the formal structure of promissory recognition. Promises in which one party sells herself into slavery may have this character, as may promises in which two persons agree to wrong a third (although this is a harder case, because the disrespect is directed outside the promise-relation, and I do not want to deny that there might, as it were, be honor among thieves).

All that is needed for the argument in the text is that promises may depart from morally ideal terms and still remain perfectly good promises (which establish promissory recognition and promissory obligation just as surely as their more ideal counterparts). The terms of valid contracts, for example, are not limited by any notion of a "just price."

25. Promises may, to be sure, be modified, including over the course of their performance. But these modifications themselves have a promissory form, which is to say that their substance is also fixed by the intentions of the parties, ex ante, which now refers to the moment of *their* creation.

26. Such cases pose the question whether the vivid appreciation that love requires can endure the lover's commitment to avoiding matters that will inevitably impact her beloved's distinctive personality even in the areas of his life that her love affirmatively

engages. It seems likely, in the example, that the beloved's workplace triumphs and frustrations will receive expression in his personal life, and it will be difficult for his lover to appreciate this expression if she maintains her self-imposed exile concerning its causes. But this difficulty is not my main target, since the tension between love and promise that it takes up turns on the substance of particular promises and loves rather than, as in the argument that I am pursuing, on the incompatibility between the *form* of loving and promissory recognition.

27. Shiffrin recognizes the feature of promising that accounts for this tension. As she says, promises make persons "able to commit to a course of action, without valuing it as the promisee does" (2008: 496). To the contrary, a promisor must, for purposes of her performance, remain agnostic about the nature or importance of the promisee's valuing the performance, leaving that entirely for the promisee. She may not, in other words, indulge in the modes of appreciation that constitute love.

28. It will be worse for the marriage because, by asking him to release her, she is not just betraying her own love (since she could not make the request if she possessed a lover's vivid appreciation for its effects) but also attempting to exploit his love for her.

29. This thought bears a rough resemblance to Bernard Williams's well-known observation that a man who, facing a choice between rescuing a stranger and his wife, chooses his wife on the grounds that she is his wife and it is impartially permissible for him to prefer his wife has had, from her perspective, one thought too many (1981: 18). In each case, the beloved wants the grounds of her lover's conduct to lie in her particularity and its effect on him, and not in the generic personality that she shares with all other persons, and that affects him as anyone's personality might.

30. This distinction may make a practical difference to how the wife acts. Consider, for example, a case in which the wife can honor her marital obligations of support only by abandoning the more pressing needs of others. She might be a surgeon, for example, who can meet her husband's reasonable needs for emotional support only by abandoning an operation to a less experienced and less skilled colleague. If the basis of her husband's claim over her sounds in promise, then his releasing her from her promise in this case dispositively settles the question what she ought to do, namely perform the surgery. But if her duty of support sounds in her love, then her husband's protestations that she should take care of her patient do not release her from her duty of support, since her loving knowledge of him and his needs may exceed his self-knowledge and so endure even in the face of his efforts at self-abnegation. The second model, I believe, much more nearly accords with the lived experience of marriage than the first.

31. Shiffrin at one point cites Kant's argument for the necessity of marriage as an example of the way promise might support intimacy in the face of inequality (2008: 508). But this example depends on a model of marriage—one that makes heavy weather of gender differences concerning the attractions and burdens of sexual relations—that is very different from the companionate, truly loving account discussed in the main text. As Shiffrin herself acknowledges, Kant may have "unduly pessimistic about the necessity for legal relations" to resolve gender differences regarding sex (508).

32. Notwithstanding the increased prominence of antenuptial agreements, they still are not. Although antenuptial agreements do allow the parties to a marriage to

customize the outcomes that will follow the dissolution of their marriage relations, these agreements do not render the terms of the marriage itself discretionary, or make the marriage purely a product of the parties' intentions. Antenuptial agreements and their analogs do not so much constitute the marriage relation as fix its outer limits (by specifying what each party will receive on exiting the marriage). Antenuptial agreements carve a more individualistic space out of the intimacy of the marriage, on the model that I developed earlier. Thus, even as antenuptial agreements (and indeed agreements more generally between parties to an intimate relationship) are enforceable, agreements to *establish* an intimate relationship generally are not recognized by contract law (Williston 2008: vol. 7, sec. 16.23).

33. Contractual liability, after all, is strict liability.

34. See American Law Institute (1981), sec. 237.

35. This distinguishes contract from joint intention simpliciter, at least on Bratman's model. There, the entire interlocking intentional structure depends wholly on each participant's individual interest in the activity. Even though the participants in joint intention intend to adjust to each others' intentions, each participant's adjustments answer exclusively to her own engagement with the activity. The participants do not intend to subordinate themselves to *each others'* wills. And joint intentional and even shared cooperative activity therefore do not involve recognition in the sense that I have described. It should therefore come as no surprise that when Bratman turns to applying his model of joint intention to promising, he finds the foundations of promissory obligation in the morality of harm (1999: 130–141).

36. The law does of course include doctrines that review, and sometimes even override, contracting parties' apparent intentions. Many of these rules—for example, rules concerning duress, fraud, misrepresentation, and even unconscionability (especially insofar as unconscionability is understood, as it increasingly is, to require procedural defects in contract formation)—are designed to ensure that contracting parties' intentions are free rather than the product of manipulation. Others—for example rules concerning illegality—are designed to prevent persons from using contract as a tool for harming others in ways that the law deems impermissible. Neither set of rules seeks to override a party's intentions in the service of the parties' own interests, and so neither is paternalistic. Indeed, insofar as contract law does embrace paternalism, for example in the rule that contracts for the provision of personal services will not be specifically enforced, it does so in the service not of promoting contracting parties' interests but rather of safe-guarding their freedom over time. Even here, therefore, contract law supports the patterns of respectful recognition that I am describing.

37. See American Law Institute (1981), sec. 71.

38. See American Law Institute (1981), sec. 71, cmt. c.

39. The prototypical such case involves contracts of sale in perfectly competitive markets, in which the equilibrium price is competed down until all of the surplus goes to the buyers.

40. This feature of recognition is rendered vivid in Kant's Formula of Humanity, for example, which takes a broad view of the injunction always to treat humanity as an end in itself. This requirement applies, as Kant takes pains to point out, to every expression of humanity, "whether in *your own person* or in the person of any other" (Kant 1964: 429, italics added).

41. Perhaps this is why, as Jeremy Kessler has pointed out to me, many religions understand such vows on the model not of promise but of love.

42. Shiffrin is right that promise involves "a consolidation of the power to determine what the two parties will do" and therefore "enables a fully first-personal perspective on joint activity" (2008: 516). But whereas in promise this perspective exists at the pleasure of the parties, as merely a creature of their intentions, in contract it exists even apart from them.

43. Cf. Waldron (1996).

REFERENCES

American Law Institute (1981). *Restatement (Second) of Contracts*. Philadelphia: American Law Institute.

Arendt, H. 1958. *The Human Condition*. Chicago: University of Chicago Press.

Bratman, M. E. 1999. "Shared Cooperative Activity." In *Faces of Intention*, 93–108. Cambridge: Cambridge University Press.

———. 1999. "Shared Intention and Moral Obligation." In *Faces of Intention*, 130–141. Cambridge: Cambridge University Press.

Darwall, S. 2006. *The Second-person Standpoint*. Cambridge, MA: Harvard University Press.

Farnsworth, E. A. 1999. *Farnsworth on Contracts* 3rd ed. Aspen.

Fried, C. 1981. *Contract as Promise*. Cambridge, MA: Harvard University Press.

Guyer, P. 2000. *Kant on Freedom, Law, and Happiness*. Cambridge: Cambridge University Press.

Hume, D. 1978. "Of Morals." In *A Treatise of Human Nature*. Oxford: Oxford University Press. Book III, pp. 455–621.

Kant, I. 1964. *Groundwork of the Metaphysics of Morals*. Trans. H. J. Paton. New York: Harper and Row.

Keats, J. 1970. "Letter to Richard Woodhouse, October 27, 1818." In R. Gittings (ed.), *Letters of John Keats*, 157–158. New York: Oxford University Press.

Keeton, W. et al. 1984. *Prosser and Keeton on Torts*. 5th ed. West Group St. Paul, Minnesota.

Kimel, D. 2007. "The Choice of Paradigm for a Theory of Contract: Reflections on the Relational Model." *Oxford Journal Legal Studies* 27(2): 233–255.

Markovits, D. 2004. "Contract and Collaboration." *Yale Law Journal* 113: 1417–1518.

———. 2008. *A Modern Legal Ethics: Adversary Advocacy in a Democratic Age*. Princeton: Princeton University Press.

Nietzsche, F. 1998. *On the Genealogy of Morals*. Trans. M. Clark and A. J. Swensen. Indianapolis: Hackett.

O'Neill, O. 1989. *Constructions of Reason: Explorations of Kant's Practical Philosophy*. Cambridge: Cambridge University Press.

Rawls, J. 1955. "Two Concepts of Rules." *Philosophical Review* 64: 3–32.

Raz, J. 1977. "Promises and Obligations." In P. M. S. Hacker and J. Raz (eds.), *Law, Morality, and Society*, 210–228. Oxford: Oxford University Press.

Sheinman, H. 2004. "Are Normal Contracts Normal Promises?" *Oxford Journal of Legal Studies* 24: 517–537.

Shiffrin, S. 2008. "Promising, Intimate Relationships, and Conventionalism." *Philosophical Review* 117: 481–524.

Velleman J. D. 1999. "Love as a Moral Emotion." *Ethics* 109: 338–374.

Waldron, J. 1996. "Kant's Legal Positivism." *Harvard Law Review* 109: 1535–1566.

Williams, B. 1981. "Persons, Character and Morality." In *Moral Luck: Philosophical Essays 1973-1980*: 1-19. Cambridge: Cambridge University Press.

Williston, S. 2008. *Williston on Contracts*. 4th ed. West Group. St. Paul, Minnesota.

Chapter 14

Sidgwick on Promises

David Phillips

Abstract

Sidgwick believes that his own proto-utilitarian axioms satisfy criteria for self-evidence, while the principles of common-sense morality, including the particularly apparently compelling principle requiring fidelity to promises, do not. Sidgwick presents his argument for this claim in Book III of the Methods. *Important predecessors like Whewell and successors like Ross, who share Sidgwick's commitment to epistemic intuitionism but develop deontological moral theories, disagree. I articulate Sidgwick's argument, but suggest that it fails; its official version, directed against Whewell, is vulnerable to a charge of unfairness; and its unofficial version cannot establish Sidgwick's view against Ross's. Sidgwick is central to the development of the familiar contemporary theoretical contrast between utilitarianism and deontology; he aspires, as many utilitarians do, to argue for utilitarianism broadly on the grounds of its superior rationality; but his own attempt to argue for it in this way is a failure.*

The approach to ethics Sidgwick calls "dogmatic intuitionism" or "common-sense morality" has two key features.[1] One is epistemic: a commitment to self-evident moral claims, to moral intuitions;[2] the other is moral theoretic: the idea that what is self-evident is general rules, rather than judgments about particular cases. What then requires further clarification is the nature of these rules, and the extent to which they exclude consideration of consequences. Sidgwick's general line is that it is characteristic of the Common-Sense Moralist to hold that *some* kinds of actions are right (or wrong) in themselves independent of consequences (or, strictly, independent of any consequences except those involved in the definition of the kind of act in question). This moral-theoretic idea is important in the tradition of recent moral philosophy. For it is to capture it that C. D. Broad introduces the term "deontology" in its modern philosophical sense:[3]

> The only criticism that I wish to make at this point is that [Sidgwick's] division does not seem to rest on any very clear principle. The name "Intuitionism" seems to suggest an epistemic principle of classification, and the opposite of it would seem to be "Empiricism." On the other hand, the opposition of Egoistic and Universalistic Hedonism to Intuitionism rests on a quite different basis, viz., on whether some types of action are *intrinsically* right or wrong, or whether the rightness or wrongness of actions always depends on their conduciveness to certain *ends*. This of course is not an epistemic question at all. And this cross-division leads to needless complications in Sidgwick's exposition...I would therefore propose the following amendments. I would first divide ethical theories into two classes, which I will call respectively *deontological* and *teleological*. Deontological theories hold that there are ethical propositions of the form: "Such and such a kind of action would always be right (or wrong) in such and such circumstances, no matter what its consequences might be." (1930: 206)

Sidgwick takes the rule "I ought to keep my promises" to be a paradigm, especially initially appealing rule of common-sense morality:

> Moralists have generally felt [peculiar confidence] in...[the duty of fulfilling express promises and distinct understandings]...and it certainly seems to surpass in simplicity, certainty, and definiteness, the moral rules that we have hitherto discussed. Here, then, if anywhere, we seem likely to find one of those ethical axioms of which we are in search. (ME: 352–3)

But, famously, he argues that no such rules satisfy the four criteria of self-evidence he lays out in ME 3.11 ("Review of the Morality of Common Sense").[4] By contrast, he argues in 3.13 ("Philosophical Intuitionism"), there are genuinely self-evident principles that support or constitute utilitarianism, and that do satisfy the criteria. Sidgwick's conclusion is articulated in a passage from late in 3.13:

> I know by direct reflection that the propositions, "I ought to speak the truth," and "I ought to keep my promises,"–however true they may be–are not self-evident to me; they present themselves as propositions requiring rational justification of some kind. On the other hand, the propositions, "I ought not to prefer a present lesser good to a future greater good," and "I ought not to prefer my own lesser good to the greater good of another," do present themselves as self-evident; as much, (*e.g.*) as the mathematical axiom that "if equals be added to equals the wholes are equal." (ME: 383)

Call the argument summarized here, that the principles of common-sense morality (including "I ought to keep my promises") do not satisfy the criteria, while Sidgwick's favored protoutilitarian principles do, "the criterial argument."[5]

In this essay I examine the criterial argument, focusing on the rule about promising. I claim that the argument fails: Sidgwick can make no fair and compelling case for the self-evidence of his own favored principles which does not also make it self-evident that I ought to keep my promises. Tracing the vicissitudes of Sidgwick's argument will also provide a useful way in to the treatment of promising in the broader intuitionist tradition.

I. THE CRITERIAL ARGUMENT

a. The Four Criteria

The four criteria and their role are introduced at the start of book 3 chapter 11 of *Methods*:

> There seem to be four conditions, the complete fulfilment of which would establish a significant proposition, apparently self-evident, in the highest degree of certainty attainable: and which must be approximately realised by the premises of our reasoning in any inquiry, if that reasoning is to lead us cogently to trustworthy conclusions. (ME: 338)

In abbreviated form, the criteria are:

(1) The terms of the proposition must be clear and precise (ME: 338).
(2) The self-evidence of the proposition must be ascertained by careful reflection (ME: 338).
(3) The propositions accepted as self-evident must be mutually consistent (ME: 338).
(4) The proposition must be universally accepted (ME: 341—Sidgwick himself gives here no canonical formulation of this condition).

b. The General Strategy of Argument against the Self-evidence of Common-sense Morality

In an important passage in ME 3.11, Sidgwick sketches the general reasons why the principles of common-sense morality fail to satisfy the criteria:

> Now if the account given of the Morality of Common Sense in the preceding chapters be in the main correct, it seems clear that, generally speaking, its maxims do not fulfil the conditions just laid down. So long as they are left in the state of somewhat vague generalities, as we meet them in ordinary discourse, we are disposed to yield them unquestioning assent, and it may fairly be claimed that the assent is approximately universal—in the sense that any expression of dissent is eccentric and paradoxical. But as soon as we attempt to give them the definiteness which science requires, we find that we cannot do this without abandoning the universality of acceptance. We find, in some cases, that alternatives present themselves, between which it is necessary that we should decide; but between which we cannot pretend that Common Sense does decide, and which often seem

> equally or nearly equally plausible. In other cases the moral notion seems to resist all efforts to obtain from it a definite rule: in others it is found to comprehend elements which we have no means of reducing to a common standard, except by the application of the Utilitarian—or some similar—method. Even where we seem able to educe from Common Sense a more or less clear reply to the questions raised in the process of definition, the principle that results is qualified in so complicated a way that its self-evidence becomes dubious or vanishes altogether. And thus in each case what at first seemed like an intuition turns out to be either the mere expression of a vague impulse, needing regulation and limitation which it cannot itself supply, but which must be drawn from some other source: or a current opinion, the reasonableness of which has still to be shown by a reference to some other principle. (ME: 342–3)

The strategy of argument characterized here involves (a) refining the principles of common-sense morality so that they render a clear verdict on every case, which Sidgwick takes to be required to satisfy the first (clarity and precision) criterion, then (b) arguing that the new clearer and more precise versions of the principles then fail to satisfy either the second condition, requiring a genuine appearance of self-evidence, or the fourth condition, universality of acceptance.

c. The General Strategy Applied to Promising

This strategy is exemplified in Sidgwick's treatment of promising. As is typical, there are three discussions: first, and at most length, in the relevant (sixth) chapter ("Laws and Promises") of the third book ("Intuitionism")—ME 3.6; then, second, drawing explicitly the conclusion that no principle about promising is self-evident in the relevant (sixth) section of the third book's eleventh chapter ("Review of the Morality of Common Sense)—ME 3.11, sec. 6; then, third and finally, in the treatment of the "positive relation" between utilitarianism and Common-Sense Morality in the third chapter ("The Relation of Utilitarianism to the Morality of Common Sense") of the fourth book ("Utilitarianism")—ME 4.3.

Begin with the discussion in ME 3.6, sec. 9. Sidgwick there concludes:

> It appears that a clear *consensus* can only be claimed for the principle that a promise, explicit or tacit, is binding, if a number of conditions are fulfilled: viz, if the promiser has a clear belief as to the sense in which it was understood by the promisee, and if the latter is still in a position to grant release from it, but unwilling to do so, if it was not obtained by force or fraud, if it does not conflict with definite prior obligations, if we do not believe that its fulfillment will be harmful to the promisee, or will inflict a disproportionate sacrifice on the promiser, and if circumstances have not materially changed since it was made. If any of these conditions fails, the *consensus* seems to become evanescent, and

> the common moral perceptions of thoughtful persons fall into obscurity and disagreement. (ME: 310–11)

Sidgwick thus points to a number of possible problem cases where it is either not clear that a promise has properly been made (as in some cases of force or fraud) or where, though a promise has been made, it is not clear whether it remains binding (as in cases of promises to the dead, or promises whose fulfillment turns out, in unforeseen ways, to inflict disproportionate sacrifice on the promiser).

In 3.11, sec. 6, Sidgwick draws explicitly from these problem cases the conclusion that the principle that "promises ought to be kept" is not self-evident:

> Now we saw that the notion of a Promise requires several qualifications not commonly noticed to make it precise: but this alone is no reason why it may not be fitly used in framing a maxim, which when enunciated and understood will properly claim universal acceptance as self-evident....
>
> But the case is different with the other qualifications which we had to discuss. When once the question of introducing these has been raised, we see that Common Sense is clearly divided as to the answer. If we ask (e.g.) how far our promise is binding if it was made in consequence of false statements on which, however, it was not understood to be conditional; or if important circumstances were concealed; or if we were in any way led to believe that the consequences of keeping the promise would be different from what they turn out to be; or if the promise was given under compulsion...or even if...we now see that fulfillment will entail on us a sacrifice out of proportion to the benefit received by the promise...different conscientious persons would answer these and other questions in different ways: and though we could perhaps obtain a decided majority for some of these qualifications and against others, there would not in any case be a clear *consensus* either way. And, moreover, the mere discussion of these points seems to make it plain that the confidence with which the "unsophisticated conscience" asserts unreservedly "that promises ought to be kept," is due to inadvertence; and that when the qualifications to which we referred are fairly considered, this confidence inevitably changes into hesitation and perplexity. (ME: 353–4)

Finally and again characteristically, in 4.3, Sidgwick claims that utilitarianism properly resolves the problems and perplexities:

> [All the qualifications and exceptions] turn out to be as clearly utilitarian, as the general utility of keeping one's word is plain and manifest. (ME: 444)

d. The (Putatively) Self-evident Axioms

In 3.13, Sidgwick articulates principles he does take to meet the criteria. At the beginning of the crucial, positive, part of the chapter, he writes:

> There are certain absolute practical principles, the truth of which, when they are explicitly stated, is manifest; but they are of too abstract a nature, and too universal in their scope, to enable us to ascertain by immediate application of them what we ought to do in any particular case; particular duties have still to be determined by some other method. (ME: 379)

There are four such principles.[6] Sidgwick does not clearly identify a canonical formulation of any of them. The first, he says, "seems to be more or less clearly implied in the common notion of "fairness" or "'equity," [and] is obtained by considering the similarity of the individuals that make up a Logical Whole or Genus" (ME: 380). One formulation is

> It cannot be right for A to treat B in a manner in which it would be wrong for B to treat A, merely on the ground that they are two different individuals, and without there being any difference between the natures or circumstances of the two which can be stated as a reasonable ground for difference of treatment. (ME: 380)

The second and third "emerge in the consideration of the similar parts of a Mathematical or Quantitative Whole" (ME: 381). The second involves the good on the whole of a single individual. One formulation is:

> "That Hereafter *as such* is to be regarded neither less nor more than Now." (ME: 381)

The third, which emerges from thinking about "Universal Good rather than the "Good on the Whole" of a single individual" (ME: 382) is that

> The good of any one individual is of no more importance, from the point of view (if I may say so) of the Universe, than the good of any other. (ME: 382)

From this third, together with one extra principle, the self-evident element in utilitarianism ("the maxim of Benevolence") can be deduced:

> And it is evident to me that as a rational being I am bound to aim at good generally,—so far as it is attainable by my efforts,—not merely at a particular part of it.
>
> From these two rational intuitions we may deduce, as a necessary inference, the maxim of Benevolence in an abstract form: viz. that each one is morally bound to regard the good of any other individual as much as his own, except in so far as he judges it to be less, when impartially viewed, or less certainly knowable or attainable by him. (ME: 382)

This is not a complete derivation of utilitarianism. The hedonist component of utilitarianism, the claim that the good is happiness, is yet to be established. Sidgwick's argument for hedonism is to be found in 3.14. But, as Sidgwick presents the argument in book 3, that appears to be the only further step that is required. The argument is otherwise complete. This is clear at least two points at the end of 3.13:

> Utilitarianism is thus presented as the final form into which intuitionism tends to pass, when the demand for really self-evident principles is rigorously pressed. In order, however, to make this transition logically complete, we require to interpret "Universal Good" as "Universal Happiness." (ME: 388)

And a little earlier, and not so clear on the character of the work remaining to be done:

> I find that I arrive, in my search for really clear and certain ethical intuitions, at the fundamental principle of utilitarianism. (ME: 387)

II. THE UNFAIRNESS OBJECTION

Sidgwick interprets criterion I, the clarity and precision criterion, as requiring that the dogmatic intuitionist's principles be made precise enough to give determinate verdicts in every case. Then he argues that the principles, made precise in this way, always fail to meet some one or more of the other three criteria. But he does not seem to hold what he takes to be genuinely self-evident principles to the same standard. As we saw, in introducing his favored principles, he says they are

> of too abstract a nature, and too universal in their scope, to enable us to ascertain by immediate application of them what we ought to do in any particular case; particular duties have still to be determined by some other method. (ME: 379)

So, the objection has it, Sidgwick insists that common-sense principles meet a standard of determinacy from which he exempts his own favored utilitarian principles.[7] And that is unfair.

I just raised the objection in a way that suggests that, while the putative axioms of common-sense morality do not satisfy the criteria, Sidgwick's own preferred axioms do not satisfy them either. Interestingly, this is not the way Alan Donagan, the most prominent (and the only?) William Whewell sympathizer in recent philosophical literature, presses the objection. While concerned to make the charge of unfairness, he urges that the problem in Sidgwick's treatment is his failure to recognize that, properly and sympathetically treated, the putative axioms of common-sense morality *do* (or, better, *will*) satisfy the criteria.

> [The intuitionist moralists'] formulations, definitions, and explanations for the most part varied in such ways as to admit of being taken for approximations, in different degrees, to the true system they were seeking; and to encourage them in the hope that by persevering they might find it.... The intuitionists did not claim that all the precepts of any system then existing fully satisfied the four conditions Sidgwick laid down, but only that many of them approximated to doing so. And they might fairly have objected to Sidgwick's fourth condition as

> being prejudicially rigorous: Even were the ideal intuitionist system to be discovered, it might be expected that some informed eccentrics would be found to dissent from parts of it.
>
> Sidgwick's elaborate campaign against intuitionism was therefore misdirected. It gained its objectives; but they were not defended, and the intuitionists were left unmolested in the positions they did defend. To dislodge them, Sidgwick had to show, not that their method had not yet led to the complete success they looked for, but that it could not. (Donagan 1992: 129)

On this point I am more in sympathy with Sidgwick than Donagan. If we allow the issue to be whether there are any problem or borderline cases, where it is not clear whether a promise is binding, or anyway where it is much less clear whether it is binding than it is that promises made in ordinary paradigm cases are binding, then Donagan's optimism seems to me quite misplaced. To this extent I sympathize with C. D. Broad's view that

> Anyone who reads the relevant chapters in Sidgwick will agree that the extreme form of Intuitionism which he ascribes to common-sense cannot be maintained. (1930: 217)

The better way to press the objection, I believe, is the way I initially did: to object to the unfair leniency of Sidgwick's treatment of his own putative axioms, rather than to the unfair harshness of his treatment of the putative axioms of the common-sense moralist. The problem again is that in allowing his own preferred axioms to be

> of too abstract a nature, and too universal in their scope, to enable us to ascertain by immediate application of them what we ought to do in any particular case

Sidgwick exempts utilitarianism from a requirement, derived from the clarity and precision criterion, which is crucial to his attack on the axioms of common-sense morality.

How might we respond, on Sidgwick's behalf, to the objection put this way? The best thing to try is to argue that, properly understood, Sidgwick's axioms are clear and precise, and render a verdict in every case. Sidgwick thinks, as we have seen, that the axioms together lead to utilitarianism with the addition of just one further (non-self-evident) claim, hedonism.[8] And utilitarianism, it might be claimed, does satisfy the clarity and precision criterion.

This is not, however, a promising response, for two main reasons. First and most important, suppose we allow that Sidgwick's axioms plus hedonism equal utilitarianism. Sidgwick's own careful examination of utilitarianism does not suggest that *it* satisfies the clarity and precision condition, interpreted as requiring generating a determinate verdict on every case. The way to see this is to consider Sidgwick's careful and thorough treatment of the difficulties of hedonistic measurement in book 2, combined with some of his observations about utilitarianism in book 4. He there allows for serious problems in measuring and comparing different kinds of pleasures and pains across times and persons, and for important ambiguities as to whether utilitarianism requires us to consider average or total happiness. Given these perplexities and ambiguities, it is hard to see how Sidgwick could fairly claim that utilitarianism is completely determinate in a way the principles of common-sense morality are not.

Moreover, second, this possible response involves another kind of potential unfairness. The common-sense moralist is required to get determinacy *for every individual principle*, without either being allowed to consider principles as a set, or by helping herself to non-self-evident principles, like hedonism, to produce determinacy. By contrast, the utilitarian is being allowed to offer determinacy generated by a combination of multiple putative axioms together with a non-self-evident principle.

Thus, I think, Sidgwick's official argument really does turn out to be unfair. The initial objection against it succeeds.

III. SIDGWICK, ROSS, AND THE UNOFFICIAL ARGUMENT

This, though, is not the end of the story. For, at more than one place, Sidgwick sketches a different (as I will often say, "unofficial") version of the criterial argument, one that does not depend on (unfairly) requiring the common-sense moralist to meet a standard of determinacy from which the utilitarian is exempted. Two striking passages suggest such an alternate argument. One I have already quoted:

> I know by direct reflection that the propositions, "I ought to speak the truth," and "I ought to keep my promises,"—however true they may be—are not self-evident to me; they present themselves as propositions requiring rational justification of some kind. On the other hand, the propositions, "I ought not to prefer a present lesser good to a future greater good," and "I ought not to prefer my own lesser good to the greater good of another," do present themselves as self-evident; as much, (*e.g.*) as the mathematical axiom that "if equals be added to equals the wholes are equal." (ME 383)

What is striking in the current connection about this passage is that the principles of common-sense morality here denied to be self-evident are not the complex, precise versions that are the output at the end of book 3, but the simple, imprecise versions that are the input at its beginning. The response to the critic's charge of unfairness that this passage suggests Sidgwick might make is that *even in this simple form* the propositions of common-sense morality fail to meet the second criterion, which requires that they have the genuine appearance of self-evidence.

Another relevant passage comes from "Professor Calderwood on Intuitionism in Morals." There Sidgwick writes:

> If then the practical issue between the Intuitional and Utilitarian methods be thus precisely raised: if the question be put, whether in respect of certain kinds of conduct our moral faculty furnishes us with self-evident imperatives, which ought to be obeyed without regard to consequences, we have next to consider how this question is to be decided. Here, if I could trust my own moral faculty alone, as it acts at present, I should say that no further test is needed than the Cartesian, if rigorously applied. If I ask myself whether I see clearly and distinctly the self-evidence of any particular maxims of duty, as I see that of the formal principles "that what is right for me must be right for all persons in precisely similar circumstances" and "that I ought to prefer the greater good of another to my own lesser good:" I have no doubt whatever that I do not. I am conscious of a strong impression, an opinion on which I habitually act without hesitation, that I ought to speak truth, to perform promises, to requite benefits, &c., and also of powerful moral sentiments prompting me to the observance of these rules; but on reflection I can now clearly distinguish such opinions and sentiments from the apparently immediate and certain cognition that I have of the formal principles above mentioned. (Sidgwick 1876: 565).

But now the question arises just how to understand what I have called "the unofficial argument." Two related features are clear from what we have said so far: first, the argument does not involve interpreting the clarity and precision condition as requiring a determinate verdict in every case. And, second, it allows the dogmatic intuitionist's axioms to be relatively simple axioms like "I ought to keep my promises." As Sidgwick presents it in the passage from "Professor Calderwood," the alternative to the official argument is just an appeal to apparent self-evidence, whose problematic character Sidgwick clearly notes. But it need not be just this. It is presumably also possible to conceive an appeal to the four criteria that does not involve the problematic insistence on clarity and precision as complete determinacy found in the official argument. But clearly much more needs to be said to spell out how such an argument will work.

It is also important to see that, once we move from the official to the unofficial argument (however that unofficial argument is more fully conceived), we introduce a new and important deontological opponent—Ross. Rossian deontological intuitionism explicitly and by design does not meet Sidgwick's clarity and precision condition, interpreted as requiring complete determinacy. For Ross, famously, the only self-evident principles are principles of prima facie duty. When an action falls under more than one such principle, and these principles tend in opposite directions, its moral status can be determined only by a kind of balancing, whose results are never self-evident.

Though Sidgwick, of course, never directly encountered Ross's position, it provides a natural way to flesh out the view of the opponent Sidgwick conceives when he sketches the unofficial argument. And, once we allow that, it is striking to contrast Sidgwick's and Ross's views about what is apparently self-evident. For Sidgwick, as we have seen, principles like "I ought not to prefer my own lesser good to the greater good of another" are apparently self-evident in a way principles like "I ought to keep my promises" are not. Ross, critiquing Moore, strikingly disagrees:

> If we are told . . . that we should give up our view that there is a special obligatoriness attaching to the keeping of promises because it is self-evident that the only duty is to produce as much good as possible, we have to ask ourselves whether we really, when we reflect, *are* convinced that this is self-evident, and whether we really *can* get rid of our view that promise-keeping has a bindingness independent of productiveness of maximum good. In my own experience I find that I cannot, in spite of a very genuine attempt to do so; and I venture to think that most people will find the same, and that just because they cannot lose the sense of special obligation, they cannot accept as self-evident, or even as true, the theory which would require them to do so. In fact it seems, on reflection, self-evident that a promise, simply as such, is something that prima facie ought to be kept, and it does *not*, on reflection, seem self-evident that production of maximum good is the only thing that makes an act obligatory. (Ross 1930: 39–40).

The challenge issued in this passage from Ross makes it clearer that we need to flesh out the unofficial argument: If the deontological intuitionist's principles cannot be rejected on the ground of indeterminacy, on what ground can Sidgwick reject them? In order to decide whether Sidgwick's unofficial argument is more defensible than his official argument, we need to flesh out the idea that his preferred axioms have the genuine appearance of self-evidence in a way the deontological intuitionist's preferred axioms do not. To do this, the obvious strategy is to explore more fully Sidgwick's own account of the source and character of the self-evidence of his preferred axioms, to see if this supplies a way to distinguish his preferred axioms from the putative axioms of the common-sense moralist, particularly the axiom about promising.

As we have already noted, Sidgwick's account of the self-evidence of the formal principle of utilitarianism (that is, of utilitarianism minus hedonism) is developed in 3.14. To see just why Sidgwick takes this principle to be self-evident, we need to examine the relevant passages in more detail. Begin with the seventh-edition version:

> So far we have only been considering the "Good on the Whole" of a single individual: but just as this notion is constructed by comparison and integration of the different "goods" that succeed one another in the series of our conscious states, so we have formed the notion of Universal Good by comparison and

> integration of the goods of all individual human—or sentient—existences. And here again, just as in the former case, by considering the relation of the integrant parts to the whole and to each other, I obtain the self-evident principle that the good of any one individual is of no more importance, from the point of view (if I may say so) of the Universe, than the good of any other; unless, that is, there are special grounds for believing that more good is likely to be realised in the one case than in the other. And it is evident to me that as a rational being I am bound to aim at good generally,—so far as it is attainable by my efforts,—not merely at a particular part of it.
>
> From these two rational intuitions we may deduce, as a necessary inference, the maxim of Benevolence in an abstract form: viz, that each one is morally bound to regard the good of any other individual as much as his own, except in so far as he judges it to be less, when impartially viewed, or less certainly knowable or attainable by him. (ME 382)

Other passages help clarify Sidgwick's view of the character of the argument. The first edition is particularly illuminating here. As Sidgwick there clearly explains, like the argument for the principle of equity, the argument for the principle of benevolence involves articulating a requirement of impartiality built into a concept. And it is supposed to be directed against a certain kind of egoist:

> It must be distinctly explained that here, as in the case of Equity, we must start with some ethical judgment, in order that the rule may be proved; and, in fact, the process of reasoning is precisely similar in the two cases. There, an individual was supposed to judge that a certain kind of conduct was right and fit to be pursued by others towards him: and it was then shewn that he must necessarily conceive the same conduct to be right for all other persons in precisely similar circumstances: and therefore judge it right for himself, in like case, to adopt it towards any other person. Similarly here we are supposed to judge that there is something intrinsically desirable—some result which it would be reasonable for each individual to seek for himself, if he considered himself alone. Let us call this the individual's Good or Welfare: then what Clarke urges is, that the Good of any one individual cannot be *more* intrinsically desirable, *because it is his*, than the equal Good of any other individual. So that our notion of Ultimate Good, at the realization of which it is evidently reasonable to aim, must include the Good of *every* one on the same ground that it includes that of *any* one. This seems to be as much a self-evident truth as the principle of Equity. (Sidgwick 1874: 360)

And, in the first edition, Sidgwick worries explicitly about the argument's consequent possible triviality:

> And here, perhaps, I may seem to have laboriously executed one of those circles in reasoning before noticed.... When, at the end of a long and careful examination of the apparent intuitions with which Common Sense furnishes us, we collect the residuum of clear and definite moral knowledge with which the operation has left, we find the same problem facing us. We seem to have

> done nothing: and in fact we have only evolved the suppression of Egoism, the necessary universality of view, which is implied in the mere form of the objective judgment "that an end is good" just as it is in the judgment that "an action is right." (Sidgwick 1874: 364)

In order to see whether this account of the self-evidence of the axioms of utilitarianism distinguishes them from the putative axioms of the common-sense moralist, we should ask: can a parallel story be told about the self-evidence of those putative axioms of common-sense morality?

Consider again the example of promising. The deontologist does seem to be able to say about promising something importantly parallel to what Sidgwick says about rightness and goodness. Just as a kind of universality is part of the concepts of objective rightness and goodness, so it is part of the concept of a promise that promises create obligations. Sincere employment of the concept of a promise therefore commits one to the existence of the obligations promises create.

Of course, someone can avoid commitment to the existence of promissory obligations by refusing sincerely to employ the concept of a promise. But this does not undermine the parallel to Sidgwick's own favored axioms. For, famously, on Sidgwick's own account, the same is true of the concept of objective goodness: the consistent egoist, by refusing sincerely to employ this concept, can avoid commitment to the existence of objective reasons:

> If the Egoist strictly confines himself to stating his conviction that he ought to take his own happiness or pleasure as his ultimate end, there seems no opening for any line of reasoning to lead him to universalistic hedonism as a first principle; it cannot be proved that the difference between his own happiness and another's happiness is not *for him* all-important. (ME: 420)

Thus the deontological intuitionist can respond effectively to the unofficial argument, fleshed out using Sidgwick's own account of the self-evidence of his own favored axioms. The parallel is not exact in all respects: the conceptual commitments on which Sidgwick relies involve a kind of universalizing, while the conceptual commitment involved in the concept of a promise does not rely on universalizing. But there is a parallel in the crucial relevant respect: I am committed to the idea that I ought (ceteris paribus) to keep my promises by sincere use of the concept of a promise, just as I am committed to the importance of the good of others by the sincere use of the concept of objective goodness.

IV. CONCLUSIONS

Sidgwick believes that his own protoutilitarian axioms satisfy criteria for self-evidence, while the principles of common-sense morality, including the particularly apparently compelling principle requiring fidelity to promises, do not. Important predecessors like Whewell and successors like Ross, who share his commitment to epistemic intuitionism but develop deontological moral theories, disagree. In ME 3, Sidgwick presents what I have called his "criterial argument" for his view. I have claimed that this argument fails; its official version, directed against Whewell, is vulnerable to a charge of unfairness; and its unofficial version cannot establish Sidgwick's view against Ross's.

Sidgwick is central to the development of the familiar contemporary theoretical contrast between utilitarianism and deontology; he aspires, as many utilitarians do, to argue for utilitarianism broadly on the grounds of its superior rationality; but his own attempt to argue for it in this way is a failure.[9]

NOTES

1. Unless otherwise specified, references to Sidgwick are to Sidgwick (1907), (hereafter ME).

2. Sidgwick's argument for the epistemic component is to be found at ME 97–8. done. It is discussed interestingly in a number of the essays collected in Stratton-Lake (2002) including Crisp (2002).

3. For a nice account of the history here, see Louden (1994).

4. I will treat the criteria here as criteria for self-evidence, criteria whose purpose is to decide whether claims we take to be self-evident really are. Not everyone regards the criteria in this way. An interesting alternative view is to be found in Shaver (1998).

5. There is controversy about just how to understand Sidgwick's moral epistemology and just how the argument for utilitarianism against intuitionism that is our focus here fits into that epistemology. We can abstract from that controversy here, because on almost anyone's view what I here call "the criterial argument" is an important part of Sidgwick's reconciliation of intuitionism with utilitarianism. Important treatments of these issues include Singer (1974), Schneewind (1977), Brink (1994), and Shaver (1998).

6. I get the number 4 here by following Sidgwick in taking there to be principles of justice, prudence, and benevolence, and taking seriously his suggestion that the maxim of benevolence follows from two other self-evident principles. There are other interpretive possibilities, but nothing crucial for current purposes turns on the question how many self-evident principles we count.

7. Crisp also raises this problem: (2002: 74).

8. That Sidgwick thinks hedonism not self-evident is suggested by his treating it in a separate chapter (ME bk. 3, ch. 14) looks fine rather than in the key chapter on philosophical intuitionism, and by his not listing it among his axioms. I do not want to deny, though, that it would be *possible* to try interpreting Sidgwick as thinking hedonism self-evident.

9. That Sidgwick aspires to argue for utilitarianism and sees himself as a utilitarian is clear. It is of course important to note that arguing for utilitarianism is not the *Methods*' primary purpose, as he makes clear in the first chapter, especially ME

14. But he does there also acknowledge that he is "led to discuss the considerations which should . . . be decisive in determining the adoption of ethical first principles" (ME: 14); and he clearly gives, and endorses, the argument I consider here, an argument that is central to his reconciliation of utilitarianism with common-sense morality on the utilitarian's terms.

REFERENCES

Brink, David. 1994. "Common Sense and First Principles in Sidgwick's Methods." *Social Philosophy and Policy* 11: 107–113.

Broad, C. D. 1930. *Five Types of Ethical Theory*. London: Routledge and Kegan Paul.

Crisp, Roger. 2002. "Sidgwick and Intuitionism." In Stratton-Lake 2002: 56–75.

Donagan, A. 1992. "Sidgwick and Whewellian Intuitionism." In Schultz 1992: 123–142.

Louden, Robert B. 1994. "Towards a Genealogy of '*Deontology*'" *Journal of the History of Philosophy* 34: 571–592.

Ross, W. D. 1930. *The Right and the Good*. Oxford: Oxford University Press.

Schneewind, Jerome. 1977. *Sidgwick's Ethics and Victorian Moral Philosophy*. Oxford: Oxford University Press.

Schultz, Bart. 1992. *Essays on Henry Sidgwick*. Cambridge: Cambridge University Press.

Shaver, Robert. 1998. *Rational Egoism: A Selective and Critical History*. Cambridge: Cambridge University Press.

Sidgwick, H. 1907. *The Methods of Ethics*. London: Macmillan.

———. 1874. *The Methods of Ethics*. 1st ed. London: Macmillan.

———. 1876. "Prof. Calderwood on Intuitionism in Morals." *Mind* 1: 563–566.

Singer, Peter. 1974. "Sidgwick and Reflective Equilibrium." *Monist* 58: 490–517.

Stratton-Lake, Philip. 2002. *Ethical Intuitionism: Re-Evaluations*. Oxford: Clarendon Press.

Chapter 15

Contractarianism and Emergency

Yitzhak Benbaji

Abstract

This paper offers a contractarian interpretation of the laws of war, in which the moral standing of the laws of war follows from their being terms in an actual *agreement between states for the regulation of the conduct of combatants in the battlefield. The paper illustrates this "actual contract" account to elucidate one of the most important laws of war, namely the exemption states have from the basic prohibition on direct attack against civilians in cases of emergency—the so-called* emergency exemption. *The group of civilians protected by the basic prohibition is surprisingly large; it includes rulers, political activists, and supportive citizens who might well be culpable for the unjust threat posed by their aggressive state. On the proposed contractarian account, the immunity of those civilians is conventional; in point of fact, states and soldiers have undertaken the duty to avoid attacking culpable civilians in order to immunize their own civilians from direct attack. This paper shows that the conventional contractarian account illuminates the special permission assigned to just states in extreme circumstances. Extreme circumstances are those in which the contract that immunizes culpable civilians collapses. That is, it can be known* ex ante *that, in these circumstances, a rationally-led state has no reason to prefer rule-governed war to total war. This is the case if a defeat in a rule-governed war would result in dehumanization, enslavement, or systematic murder.*

I. NONCOMBATANT IMMUNITY AND THE SUPREME EMERGENCY EXEMPTION

The term "just war theory" may relate to two distinct theories of the laws of war. The first theory explores the current positive and customary legal regulations that govern warfare, as well as the convictions and principles that underlie them. The second is a theory of the morality of wars, investigating which wars are moral, what is the moral behavior within wars, and in particular the extent to which the contemporary laws of war reflect morality.

Consider first the structure of the international legal system of the laws of war. It is comprised of two branches: (1) *jus ad bellum*—a code that specifies the circumstances in which states are permitted to initiate or respond to armed attacks, but largely ignores the important question of *how* armies may engage in armed conflicts; (2) *jus in bello*—a code that specifies what one might legally do *in* war, complementing the *just ad bellum* code. International law treats the *jus in bello* and the *just ad bellum* codes as entirely independent systems: a state that initiates an aggressive war is condemned by international law as having committed a crime against peace, which is the most serious crime under international law; but this condemnation finds no echo in the *in bello* code. Indeed, the *in bello* regulations are designed to apply to soldiers independently of the cause for which they are fighting. The legislator determines the duties of belligerents irrespective of the justness of their cause.[1]

The *jus in bello* code is complex, but its basic features are quite simple. It contains a fundamental prohibition on direct killing of innocents or defenseless individuals such as civilians and prisoners of war, thus conferring on noncombatants almost absolute immunity from direct attacks in wars. In addition, it contains a fundamental permission: subject to constraints such as necessity and proportionality (to be discussed later), soldiers possess a legal right to kill and maim enemy combatants. These rules are *egalitarian*, in the sense that they do not discriminate against soldiers fighting an unjust war (unjust combatants) and do not privilege soldiers fighting a just war (just combatants). In other words, the *jus in bello* code commands two kinds of equalities, between civilians and between soldiers, while rejecting an asymmetrical law of war encapsulated in the motto "The more justice the more rights."[2] These equalities are possible because of the logical independence between the *in bello* and the *ad bellum* codes.

On the contractarian interpretation of the laws of war, the morality of the war convention follows from two facts: first, states actually agreed on them; second, decent states whose aim is minimizing the harm inflicted on innocents in wars would agree on them. Wars are construed by this contract as a clash between *armies* rather than as a clash between *peoples* or *states*. The fundamental duty to which combatants are subject is a straightforward implication of this conception of war. The group of immunized civilians is large; it includes rulers, political players, and supportive citizens who might be culpable of the unjust threat that their aggressive state poses. On the contractarian account, the immunity of these culpable civilians is conventional; states and soldiers undertake the duty to avoid attacking them in order to immunize their own civilians from direct attack in war. This essay revisits the contractarian interpretation (for which I argued in Benbaji 2008: sec. 3 and 2009) in order to analyze a well-known restriction on the scope of noncombatant immunity.

According to Michael Walzer, the presumption against direct or intentional killing of civilians collapses in the face of an imminent catastrophe or moral disaster.[3] Walzer's standard example is the terror bombing of German cities at the beginning of World War II. There was a time in which the unlimited spread of Nazism's dehumanizing rule had been a real, substantial threat. Thus, the bombings were justified *if*, as Churchill argued, they were absolutely necessary for eliminating the Nazi threat.[4] The contractarian account of the disparity between extreme and regular circumstances is simple: the laws of war are terms in a fair and mutually beneficial agreement between decent states that *collapses* in extreme circumstances.

The essay is structured as follows. Sections II and III revisit the moral framework by which the contractarian interpretation of the rules of war is articulated, with special emphasis on its complicated relations with consequentialism. Section IV shows that this contractarian framework can adequately explain the supreme emergency exemption (hereafter "the Exemption"). This section further shows that the contractarian elucidation is better than the competing account offered for the Exemption in the literature.

II. THE THEORETICAL FRAMEWORK: CONTRACTARIANISM AND RIGHTS CONSEQUENTIALISM

This section sketches the framework on which the contractarian account of the laws of war is based. The morality I sketch here makes an explicit distinction between the realm of rights and the sphere of justification; it characterizes an overlooked tension between these distinct systems, as well as two points of interaction between them.

II.1. The Realm of Rights versus the Sphere of Justification

Implicit in almost any moral theory is the fundamental distinction between the *realm of moral rights* and the *sphere of impartial justification*.[5] Basic rights are liberties to act in one's legitimate self-interests, claims against others not to violate one's legitimate interests, and rights to take defensive measures against violators of these claims. In exercising one's right to property or to protect one's life one does not *enforce justice* in the distribution of harm, or bring about an outcome that involves *less evil*. The right to life, body, health, and happiness—rights that are entailed by the basic moral fact that persons own themselves—are rights to be partial; they entitle the right-holder to act in his or her legitimate self-interest.

In contrast, impartial justification—and, in particular, lesser-evil considerations—are grounded in an impartial evaluation of consequences. Acting in a certain way is prima facie justified if the act brings about an outcome that contains less evil than all other available outcomes. Whether a complete list of factors can be drawn to determine how bad an outcome is all things considered, and what their relative weight is vis-à-vis each other, remains an open question. It would nevertheless be safe to assume that among other things, the overall badness of an outcome is determined by the number of people undeservingly harmed in this outcome, and the magnitude of the harm they suffer. I shall discuss other factors later.

The two-tiered morality that is constituted by the realm of rights and the sphere of impartial justification is *moderate*: there are circumstances in which one has the right to act in one's own self-interest even if, on impartial consideration, exercising this right would turn out to be *un*justified. Moderate morality asserts that acting for the greater good is always justified impartially, but claims that in many circumstances, one has a right to act in one's interest. That is, a morality that takes rights seriously does not require unqualified impartiality.

II.2. Contractarianism: Conventional Rights and Justified Rules

Having characterized the tension between the realm of rights and the sphere of justification, I shall now describe the first point of interaction between them: moral rights and duties are generated by the tacit acceptance of impartially justified rules. Let me explain.

Possessing rights typically involves the power to waive them, in order to gain other (more beneficial) rights. A microlevel case in which basic moral rights are redistributed is particularly revealing. We are under duty not to violently attack each other. By entering the ring, a boxer waives this claim against a violent attack and, in return, gains a right/privilege to attack his opponent. Note that the redistribution of rights in the boxing ring is generated by an explicit acceptance of rules that command this redistribution. The boxers' consent is communicated by their entering the ring. It is usually assumed that the convention governing boxing is considered by *both* parties to be fair and ex ante mutually beneficial; we can therefore safely presume that the boxers consented to be attacked by each other.

Following the so-called Lockean view,[6] I shall assume that an exchange or redistribution of rights explains the moral standing of the norms that govern the political society. A person relinquishes ownership of an article (say) by freely giving up his claim on it—he sells it, gives it as a present, and so on. But explicit consent or a well-informed waiver of rights do not tell the whole story about how rights are redistributed in a community. Suppose that Mary unknowingly lost an article she owns, such that she did not waive her claim on it. The article has no identifying marks; she will not be able to prove her ownership. Within Mary's community, the legal system allows the finder of a lost article without identifying marks to appropriate it. Suppose that this finders-keepers rule meets three conditions: (a) it is fair: since many will deceptively allege the article to be theirs, the fairest way to proceed is to allow whoever finds the lost article first to acquire it; (b) ex ante, that is, from the rulemaking standpoint, an outcome in which this treatment of lost articles is accepted is good for everyone, as a prohibition to use the article would be a waste; (c) since it is commonly known in Mary's community that commonly following the rule would be to everyone's benefit, the rule is, in fact, commonly followed.[7]

A rule that meets the first two conditions is *impartially justified*, just like rules such as (the *mala prohibita*) "Drive on the right-hand side," or (the *mala in se*) "Do not harm innocents." For an outcome in which these rules are commonly followed is better for everyone than any other feasible outcome. Importantly, such rules ought to be justified along another dimension. A rule is justified only if "the pattern of human rights fulfillment it tends to produce [if it is commonly followed] is superior to the pattern that its best feasible alternatives would tend to produce" (Pogge 1992: 55).That is, an outcome in which the rule is commonly followed contains the best pattern of the fulfillment of human rights.

Is Mary's claim to the article denied merely for *pragmatic* reasons, on this account? The simple answer is that the very distinction between the moral and the pragmatic is unstable. The rule that determines the distribution of burdens and benefits with respect to lost articles is accepted in the community to which Mary belongs, by virtue of its being fair and mutually beneficial. That is, individuals are expected with *moral* reason to conform to it. The moral standing of such expectations follows from (what contractarians take to be) a fundamental moral truth: a person is wronged if he is treated in a way to which he has a legitimate objection. That is, the explanation of the wrong I've done you makes an essential reference to your standing to complain. I shall assume that the very fact that I was expected with moral reason to behave in accordance with a fair and mutually beneficial rule yet failed to do so gives the person I've harmed a reason to complain. This, I suggest, should be formulated in the moral rights discourse; for as Jay Wallace argued recently, bipolar claims and directional duties are ethical concepts that belong firmly within the family of moral ideas that are accessible from a second-personal standpoint.[8]

These sketchy remarks make clear that the expectations that entrenched rules generate and maintain are of moral significance only if the rules themselves are impartially justified; they wouldn't be binding if there is a considerably better set of rules. On the Lockean account I employ here, one cannot bind oneself to unjust norms any more than one can bind oneself morally to commit murder. This is why the expectations generated by a law ordering blacks to sit at the back of public buses have no moral standing. In contrast, impartially justified rules constitute a point of interaction between the sphere of impartial justification and the realm of rights. By tacitly accepting such rules, members of a community allow for the redistribution of their moral rights and duties that these rules command. They gain the *conventional* rights that the rules assign to them, and they lose the *preconventional* or *natural* rights that the rules deny them.

Interestingly, this point of interaction between the realm of rights and the sphere of impartial justification preserves the tension between these systems. For, as a matter of conceptual possibility, there might be a justified violation of a justified rule. If seriously harming one person (a victim) would save ten others from death, then harming the victim might be justified even if this involves violation of the rule that prohibits harming the innocents. The fact that the victim's right is violated in these circumstances is also very significant. A morality that takes rights seriously does not require total impartiality, and, since the victim's right was violated, she might be entitled to eliminate a justified threat against her even when the outcome of that threat would be less evil.

II.3. Consequentialism: The Aggregation of Rights Violation

A second point of interaction between the realm of rights and the sphere of impartial justification, concerns the role that rights violations play in measuring how bad an outcome is. As it is usually understood, the value that consequentialism recommends maximizing is determined by factors such as the total sum of (opportunities to) welfare/resources and fairness in distribution of welfare/resources. "Utilitarianism of rights" adds another irreducible factor, namely: the violation of rights in a given outcome, which Amartya Sen (1982) insists cannot be reduced or cashed out in terms of welfare or resources.

Sen's conception of rights contrasts with Robert Nozick's. According to Nozick, rights are *agent-relative side constraints*; they limit the scope of the morally available actions of an individual in specific circumstances. They present themselves to the agent simply as a limit to *her* conduct. Therefore, on Nozick's view, an agent ought to be concerned exclusively with her own observance of the constraints. To illustrate, suppose that by violating Y's property right you prevent X from violating the property rights of many others, or from violating Z's right to life. On the side constraint conception, these facts are irrelevant to what *you* ought to do. In violating Y's property right, you are using him as a means to a further end, and this is impermissible, even if your end is preventing the violation of Z's right to life by others, or minimizing the violation of rights by others. Nozick then explicitly rejects Sen's approach: "The side constraint view forbids you to violate... moral constraints in the pursuit of your goals; whereas the view whose objective is to minimize the violation of these rights allows you to violate rights (the constraints) in order to lessen their total violation in the society" (1974: 29).

Sen's conception of rights attaches normative significance to the *extent* to which rights are violated. It views rights violation as a measurable quantity. The importance of this measure is manifest in what I shall call "first-personal conflicts of rights." In such cases, an agent faultlessly finds herself in a situation in which she must choose between two or more rights violations. How would a perfectly moral agent deliberate in such situations? Necessarily, she would form judgments such as the following: violating X's right to life is worse than violating Y's property right; and also violating X's right to life is (roughly) Z times as bad as violating X's right to X's body. In short, she is guided by considerations of rights utilitarianism, under which the normative considerations employed by moral agents in first-personal conflicts of rights shape lesser-evil considerations.

Therefore, the extent to which an outcome is bad depends on the extent to which the outcome in question contains rights violation. This is measured by the number of individuals whose rights are violated and the number and weight of the violated rights. That is, the two-tiered morality sketched here takes rights seriously also by insisting that the disvalue of an outcome depends not only on the aggregate undeserved harm that it involves but also on the extent to which rights are violated by the harmful actions. Hence, all else being equal, preventing the harmful violation of rights ought to take *some* priority over preventing harms that do not involve violation of rights.[9] Rights consequentialism insists that rights violation is not just one of several considerations; it is a weightier consideration than the others.

Finally, rights consequentialism presents the additional factor of rights violation as irreducible: the extent to which rights are violated is not entailed by facts concerning the other factors that determine how bad an outcome is. To illustrate this point, consider a well-known example. A and B suffer from a terminal disease. We face two outcomes, O1 and O2, in which A dies and B lives. In both outcomes, a physician gives B the only lifesaving pill he has. Outcomes O1 and O2 are identical except for the *way* they were obtained: O1 is the result of a fair draw, while O2 is the result of B's bribing the physician, that is, a violation of A's rights. Therefore, O2 contains a rights violation and is worse than O1 (Peter Diamond's example discussed in Temkin 1994: 368–371). We can formulate this with two propositions about the value of outcomes:

(i) All else being equal, an outcome that contains harms involving rights violations is *much* worse than outcomes containing the same amount of harm but no rights violation.
(ii) All else being equal, violation of the rights possessed by people of a certain group is worse (a) the larger this group is, (b) the weightier these rights are, and (c) the more rights are violated.

I concluded the previous section by observing that the tacit acceptance of well-entrenched rules shapes the distribution of rights in a community, and that a person is entitled to the benefits that such rules command to her. I further noted that a violation of a justified rule (and the violation of the conventional right that the rule commands) might be justified by lesser-evil considerations. Rights consequentialism implies, however, that ceteris paribus, breaking a rule is worse—or *less* justified—if it involves a violation of a conventional right.

II.4. Inclusive Ought Propositions

The two-tiered morality I have sketched requires an inclusive, normative concept that is sensitive to facts about rights and duties on the one hand and about impartial justifications on the other. I shall use schemes of the sort "X ought, all things considered, to A."

The two-tiered morality is moderate by virtue of one of its constituents: the realm of rights. It implies that as a matter of conceptual possibility, X might have a right (to self-defense, say) even if X ought, all things considered, to waive it. Suppose that in order to survive, a victim has to kill five people who *innocently* pose a threat to him. Unlike lesser-evil conceptions of self-defense, a moderate morality of self-defense might assert that the victim has a right to kill the five in self-defense, while being under obligation to waive this right: he has a right to be *partial* even if morality requires impartiality. But the reverse holds as well: suppose that by acting in a certain way, X brings about an outcome that involves less evil (such that impartially considered, X's action is justified by lesser-evil considerations.) Still, it might be the case that X ought *not* to act in this way. For example, it is widely believed that firefighters ought to save those who paid for their services. They ought to do so even in circumstances in which they can save a larger group of people to whom they bear no contractual duty.

III. THE WAR CONVENTION: A CONTRACTARIAN ACCOUNT

Walzer's interpretation of the received war ethic is usually understood as preconventional. On this reading, he argues that the war convention implements the morality of self-defense, which permits killing responsible attackers in self-defense yet prohibits killing innocent bystanders in self-preservation. Thus, the *in bello* code permits killing soldiers yet strictly forbids a direct killing of civilians, because soldiers are responsible attackers, whereas civilians are innocent bystanders. Noncombatant immunity is simply "a reaffirmation of the morally foundational 'no-harm' principle. One ought generally not to harm other persons. Non-combatant immunity says one ought, most emphatically, not to harm others who are themselves not harming anyone. This is as fundamental, and as straightforward, and as nearly non-controversial, as moral principles can get" (Shue 2003: 742).[10]

This interpretation of the legal equalities of soldiers and civilians has recently come under attack by critics whom I shall label "purists."[11] Purists simply deny that soldiers posses an equal moral right to participate in wars or—more specifically—to kill in self-defense in war. Purists observe that with respect to killing soldiers, the received *in bello* rules are much more permissive than the preconventional morality of self-defense. The convention permits killing *nonthreatening* and *just* combatants; it permits, in other words, killing soldiers who do not contribute to the war effort and hence pose no threat, as well as soldiers who exercise their right of self- and other-defense and hence did nothing by which they lost their right to life. (These soldiers are not, as McMahan puts it, "liable to defensive killing.") Purists complain that the war convention denies the liability of engaged civilians: political leaders who initiate the war, scientists who develop new military technologies, and civilians who import munitions. They are noncombatants, and hence according to the *in bello* code, they are immune from direct killing in war. Arguably, most versions of the morality of self-defense would, however, regard those civilians as liable to preventive killing.[12]

Another aspect of the laws of war that purists criticize is the rule of proportionality within wars (i.e., "*in bello* proportionality"). The rule permits causing proportionate collateral damage to innocent enemy civilians. A collateral damage inflicted on enemy civilians is justified only if the evil it prevents is greater. Yet, as purists are quick to observe, such a "lesser-evil-based proportionality" rule prohibits any collateral damage that *un*just combatants might inflict on innocents. By causing collateral damage to civilians, unjust combatants aim at causing a further evil, that is, the victory of the unjust side.[13] Indeed, lesser-evil-based proportionality is *necessarily* asymmetrical—it permits only the just side to inflict collateral damage in certain circumstances.

Interestingly, McMahan admits that unjust combatants' participation in war should not be criminalized (if they fought in accordance to the *in bello* rules) despite the fact that they have no right to kill, and that their killings are, in principle, disproportionate. He nevertheless insists that the immunity from legal persecution is *merely* a legal right that is conferred on soldiers for pragmatic reasons: the law treats them *as if* they were equal. Similarly, from the perspective of the preconventional morality of self-defense, civilians who contribute to the wrongful threat that their state poses might well be morally liable to defensive killing. The law, however, prohibits attacking them. Once again, the law equalizes the status of morally unequal individuals.

Responding to the purist challenge, I elsewhere suggested a different moral interpretation of the *in bello* code that relies heavily on the framework that I sketched in section II.[14] On the contractarian interpretation, the equalities legislated by the war convention (i.e., the equality of soldiers vis-à-vis each other and the equality of civilians vis-à-vis each other) do not reflect preconventional moral equalities. Rather, the rules that command these equalities constitute a set of fair, mutually beneficial and hence, impartially justified rules. By accepting the rules, the parties *generate* the moral equalities between soldiers and civilians. Soldiers tacitly accept these rules, and since they are justified, their acceptance by soldiers allows for a redistribution of their preconventional rights and duties.

I shall illustrate this contractarian account by arguing for the possibility and justifiability of a rule I label "symmetrical *in bello* proportionality." In principle, I suggest, states agree on rules of combat that command disregarding facts about desert, guilt, and (preconventional) liability. The question is, of course, how the rule of proportionality, which permits military actions whose good effects outweigh their bad effects and prohibits actions that fail to meet this condition, can be detached from lesser-evil considerations. How can proportionality avoid appealing to facts concerning liability and culpability?

The contractarian answer is as follows: symmetrical proportionality is built on a conventional definition of the good effect of a military action: the value of an aerial bombardment that is exercised by the army of a state S (viz., what is considered the "good" effects of the military attack) is the anticipated military advantage gained by it, which is determined by the extent to which the bombardment contributes to S's victory. In other words, armies and their soldiers are entitled to treat their own victory *as if* it is good in and of itself. The conventionally negative effects of a military action are also conventionally defined as the harm it causes to enemy soldiers and civilians. In effect, soldiers are required to treat enemy soldiers as if they were *innocent* attackers, however culpable they are for the unjust war they are fighting. And they are required to treat enemy civilians as if they are innocent bystanders, whatever their political commitments and contribution to the military effort may be. These conventional definitions follow from the decision that states made to separate the final military end of the warring armies (viz., victory) from the final political ends aimed at by the warring states.[15] Symmetrical proportionality might therefore prohibit inflicting collateral damage even if it is fully justified by lesser-evil considerations. Indeed, symmetrical proportionality might prohibit harming engaged civilians who significantly promote the unjust aim of the aggressive state.

The symmetrical proportionality rule is justified (in the sense defined in section II) if and only if ex ante—namely, from the standpoint of the relevant rulemaking institution—it is better for everyone involved than lesser-evil-based proportionality. To see why this is indeed so, consider first a pilot fighting a just war who has been ordered to bomb a munitions factory, knowing that if he bombs that factory, the explosion will kill a group of innocent civilians. The bombing meets the asymmetrical (lesser-evil-based) proportionality condition. The pilot suspects, however, that the attack is disproportionate; so he would refuse to kill any civilians, unless he is convinced that his suspicion is baseless. Lesser-evil-based proportionality might therefore be counterproductive—it compromises the ability of states to fight just wars.

Purists tend to think that in the usual case, the justness of a military action is manifested to soldiers. I doubt that. But let us grant, for the sake of argument, that a war's just cause, as well as the lesser-evil proportionality of a military action, are accessible when a full-blooded war is in progress. Still, there are many just military objectives that states aim to achieve before or after a war, and many other missions they are required to fulfill during peacetime. These military activities involve posing risks, and their lesser-evil proportionality may be controversial. For security reasons, the information that validates the justness of the objectives in question cannot be revealed to all combatants taking part in the military campaign.

Suppose, however, that these arguments against lesser-evil proportionality fail: being governed by this rule will not compromise states' ability to wage just wars, or the ability of soldiers to serve just aims. Still, the lesser-evil proportionality rule would be counterproductive, because unjust combatants usually do not know that the war they are fighting is unjust. In the usual case, both sides believe that they are serving a just aim. A second, and more popular, argument against asymmetrical proportionality takes this to be a self-evident truth: soldiers tend to believe that they are in the right. The argument further presumes that the rules of war are conceived as enforceable by self-help: intentional violation of the laws of war by one side gives the other a right to proportionate retaliation.[16]

It follows from these two assumptions that under an asymmetrical *in bello* regime, any aerial bombardment (say) exercised by one side involving collateral damage would be considered by the other a violation of *in bello* proportionality. The second assumption thus implies that such an attack would invite retaliation in kind. As a result, "war's violence quickly spirals even higher."[17] Indeed, a war governed by asymmetrical rules "is prone to illegitimate escalation of targets" and consequently "increases the risks to both parties, without any compensating advantage."[18] Therefore, if asymmetrical proportionality is a rule of war, then war's violence in general and rights violation in particular would increase. Wars governed by asymmetrical proportionality tend to be total.

Since symmetrical proportionality seems to be the only alternative to lesser-evil-based proportionality, the argument against the latter suggests that the former is an impartially justified rule. It follows from the morality developed in section II that if states, civilians, and soldiers accept symmetrical proportionality either explicitly or implicitly, they are under moral duty (toward their enemy) to conform to it. Soldiers fighting a war are under *moral* duty to disregard facts about guilt, desert, and liability. In return, they gain a right to the same treatment by the enemy.

Thus, the killing of civilians who are preconventionally liable to defensive killing constitutes a violation of *in bello* proportionality and, therefore, a violation of the *moral* right these civilians have against being directly attacked in war. Moreover, the immunity of totally innocent civilians is explained within this framework by appealing to two importantly distinct moral facts. Most fundamentally, innocents have the natural preconventional right to life; they have done nothing to justify its loss. In addition, they acquired a further *conventional* right not to be directly or collaterally harmed. Thus, the mutual acceptance of symmetrical laws of war conventionalizes and considerably strengthens noncombatant immunity.

IV. ELUCIDATING THE SUPREME EMERGENCY EXEMPTION

So much for the contractarian conception of the war convention. In this section I shall exploit this approach to the morality of the laws of war in order to elucidate the notion of emergency and for justifying the special permissions that statesmen have in supreme emergency situations. Indeed, as Walzer's moral interpretation of the laws of war is usually understood, it cannot explain the unique features of the supreme emergency exemption. On the other hand, the Exemption is elegantly elucidated within the contractarian framework I have just described.

IV.1. Lesser Evil and the Exemption

Consider first the moral conviction that grounds the Exemption. In Churchill's view, which he expressed as early as September 1940, the Allies' area bombings in Germany in World War II were necessary, despite the fact that they involved the killing of innocent civilians: "the bombers alone provide the means of victory," he said.[19] Walzer notes that "Churchill's statement suggests a certainty to which neither he nor anyone else had any right";[20] he could have "no clear notion of what the probabilities were or even how they might be calculated given our present knowledge."[21] Moreover, it is doubtful whether Great Britain faced a threat of defeat when it began launching area bombing in Hamburg and other German cities. There is evidence indicating that, when the bombings began, Churchill had no reason to fear total defeat. Moreover, historians argue that Churchill could realize that the bombings would achieve no military value: they may have demoralized the German population, but the collaboration with the Nazi regime remained intact, enduring to the war's very end.[22]

It should be recalled that we assume, for the sake of the argument, that Churchill was correct with respect to the facts. In that case, Walzer convincingly argues, the terror bombing of German towns and cities would have been justified. Churchill initiated a massive violation of the basic prohibition of the *in bello* code. But "Nazism is an ideology and a practice of domination so murderous, so degrading even to those who might survive, such that the consequences of this final victory are literally beyond calculation, immeasurably awful."[23] The circumstances that obtained in World War II were special, and "in [these] special circumstances—the strict status of civilians that normally prevents their being directly attacked in war" is no longer relevant.[24]

As the above quotes make clear, for Walzer (and following him, for Rawls),[25] it would have been permissible to bomb the German cities, even if the Nazis had fought World War II in accordance with the rules of war. It was the end result—the horrific consequences of Nazi victory—that had to be prevented by all available means. Indeed, it is the postbellum murderous regime that the Nazis would have established that justifies the killing of innocent Germans, if these killing were necessary for preventing it. Walzer's argument for the Exemption is, therefore, an argument from consequences. As he would acknowledge, a strictly Kantian, radically anticonsequentialist absolutist morality would reject the Exemption. Yet absolutist morality is implausible: it implies a requirement to avoid lying, even if by so doing one would save the life of an innocent person. The slogan " 'do justice even if the heavens fall' has never seemed to me a plausible moral position" (Walzer 1977: 229).

Alas, the lesser-evil elucidation of the Exemption faces two difficulties. Consider a case in which the Allies could have chosen between killing thousands of innocent Germans and killing thousands of innocent Swedes. Both groups were innocently obstructing the Allies' access to Hitler, whose killing at this stage would have prevented the war. According to proponents of the Exemption, they ought to have killed the Germans rather than the Swedes. But lesser-evil considerations show no sensitivity to these distinctions. If—as proponents of the Exemption argue—it was justified to kill innocent Germans by bombing Hamburg, it would have been justified *exactly to the same degree* to kill the Swedes by bombing Stockholm. But this does not sound right: the Exemption should discriminate against the Germans, even if they are totally innocent.[26]

A deeper difficulty with the lesser-evil interpretation is that it threatens the logical independence of the *jus in bello* and the *jus ad bellum* codes and, as a result, also the moral equality of civilians under the traditional morality of war. To see why, observe that exponents of the Exemption assert that, if proved necessary for preventing Nazi mass murder and dehumanization, a direct killing of tens of thousands of innocent people was justified. By this logic, directly killing a proportionally small group of innocent civilians of an aggressive state in order to prevent a minor evil that would result from the victory of that state would be justified. The reason is straightforward: if a massive killing of civilians to prevent a massive murderous dehumanization is permissible, then a limited killing of civilians to prevent an equally limited murderous dehumanization is permissible as well. From a consequentialist—lesser-evil—perspective, the immunity of civilians depends on the justness of the war that their state is fighting.

But, thus understood, the lesser-evil interpretation would support the doctrine that "the truth about war rights is best expressed in terms of a sliding scale: the more justice, the more rights."[27] It would support a sliding scale that erodes the traditional convention bit by bit, implying that "the rights of the righteous are enhanced, and those of their enemies devalued."[28] Indeed, as I noted at the outset, the just war doctrine strictly denies any such relation between *jus in bello* (the governing conduct of war) and *jus ad bellum* (determining the culpability for initiating the war). The *in bello* rules that govern the conduct of soldiers in wars do not depend on the justness of the cause for which they fight. In particular, soldiers have no right to kill civilians. This injunction stands even if those soldiers are fighting a defensive war that justly aims to prevent the (minor) evil that would probably result from the victory of their aggressive enemy.

Walzer acknowledges that the argument from extremity threatens the independence of the two codes. He nevertheless believes that, ultimately, it allows for a merely "sudden breach of the convention," and only "in the very last minute," just before the imminent catastrophe occurs:

> The reasons...have to do with the nature of the rights at issue and the status of men and women who hold them. These rights...cannot be eroded or undercut; nothing diminishes them; they are still standing at the very moment they are overridden: that is why they have to be *overridden*...[The statesman] has no choice but to break the rules: he confronts at last what can meaningfully be called necessity. (Walzer 1977: 231)

Walzer's argument here does not really address the challenge posed by his own sliding scale objection. For the lesser-evil considerations seem to apply to extreme *and* regular circumstances alike. In both types of circumstances, rights "cannot be diminished" and "they are still standing at the very moment they are overridden." Still, since a greater evil is prevented, the lesser-evil considerations to which Walzer appeals in explaining the Exemption justify overriding the rights of innocents in regular circumstances.

IV.2. Defining Extreme Circumstances

The contractarian account resolves the sliding scale objection, by creating a clear disparity between extreme and regular circumstances. To see why, note that decent states submit to surrender, even if they can win a war only by committing systematic violations of the *in bello* rules, and even in circumstances in which the violation of the *in bello* code will bring about better moral results. Why did just states subject themselves to such restrictions? Specifically, are states authorized to undertake the duty to avoid violating symmetrical proportionality (i.e., avoid harming culpable civilians for example), in cases in which such harm is impartially justified by lesser-evil considerations? Do they have the moral authority to bring about the morally suboptimal end result, even if this exacts high costs on their own innocent citizens?

I shall not answer these tough questions here. I am raising them in order to point to one important advantage of the contractarian account. On this account, the laws of war bind decent states only if entering the contract was in their interest (i.e., in the interest of the citizens that they represent) at the time at which they entered it. That is, rationally led states accept the *in bello* code if the expected utility they and their citizens gain by entering the agreement is sufficiently great.

This fact entails a rigorous definition of extreme circumstances, and an illuminating explanation for why noncombatant immunity is much weaker in these circumstances but not in others. Circumstances are extreme if it can be known ex ante that in these circumstances a rationally led state has no reason to prefer rule-governed war to total war. This is the case if a defeat in a rule-governed war would result in enslavement and/or systematic murder, and/or ethnic cleansing of the community in question. It follows that the *jus in bello* agreement is morally binding only in cases in which states predict with sufficient certainty that "[w]hatever happens to [the] two armies, whichever one loses or wins, whatever the nature of the battles or the extents of the casualties, the 'peoples' on both sides must be accommodated at the end."[29] By stipulation, in extreme circumstances this condition is not met—the very existence of the just state and the way of life of the communities that this state protects, are seriously threatened.

The disparity between regular circumstances of war and extreme circumstances is clear: in the latter circumstances, soldiers and civilians of the aggressive state lose all *conventional* rights that they possess in the former. For just states have never committed themselves to follow the restrictive *in bello* rules under the threat of total extermination. Consequently, in fighting against enslavement and ethnic cleansing, states are subject to natural preconventional duties *only*; they are free from any restriction whose *sole* source is the laws of war.

This analysis of extremity might be put in more general terms. The system that separates *in bello* from *ad bellum* codes by commanding states, armies, and soldiers to disregard lesser-evil considerations in combat regulates only conflicts in which the surrender of the enemy grants the victor the power it had sought; that is, the power to determine how the resources for which it fought will be distributed. The surrender ends the violence because the victor needs no further use of violence; the victor has achieved its (just or unjust) objective. Put differently, in a war regulated by the war convention, the end of both sides is (presumed to be) morally reasonable: self-defense and/or appropriation of resources, territory, and political power to which the parties may or may not be entitled. Only under such conditions can a commitment to follow the rules imposed by the *jus in bello* code be rationalized in terms of the self-interest of decent states. But a war whose aim is the extermination of a people undercuts the contractarian basis of the laws of war, even if the evil aggressor fights in accordance with the *in bello* rules.[30]

IV.3. Contractarian Norms in Extreme Circumstances

There seems to be a norm that is tacitly accepted in the society of states, whose objective is minimizing the *risk* that supreme emergencies will obtain. This is revealed by the approach of the society of states to nuclear deterrence (especially during the Cold War period). The facts are well known: in the Cold War years, a "balance of terror" was produced by a mutual conditional threat of indiscriminate slaughter that Western and Communist countries posed to each other. Indeed, Western governments intended to kill fully innocent people in Eastern Europe, in case their own citizens were attacked with nuclear weapons by Communist countries. Is the threat morally defensible? Walzer's answer seems to be positive:

> it is not tolerable that advances in technology should put our nation, or any nation, at the mercy of a great power willing to menace the world or to press its authority outwards in the shadow of an implicit threat.... Against an enemy actually willing to use the bomb, self-defense is impossible, and it makes sense to say that the only compensating step is the (immoral) threat to respond in kind. Hence any state confronted by a nuclear adversary...and capable of developing its own bomb is likely to do so, seeking safety in a balance of terror. Mutual disarmament would clearly be a preferable alternative but it is available only to the two countries working closely together, whereas deterrence is the likely choice of either one of them alone.[31]

Walzer describes in this passage a simple prisoner dilemma situation, in which all parties prefer mutual nuclear disarmament to a balance of terror. Yet each party prefers to a mutually disarmed world, a situation in which it alone possesses both conventional weapons and weapons of mass destruction. Our interest in an "unequal" distribution of power makes the best outcome (viz., a world that is free of weapons of mass destruction) unstable, and hence unfeasible. Therefore, the dominant strategy of each state is to produce or acquire weapons of mass destruction and/or to secure the protection of a state that possesses nuclear capabilities.[32] Indeed, in a world of sovereign and suspicious states, deterrence might be the only rational way to cope with the technological reality created after Hiroshima. If this is the case, morally restrained, rational, and self-interested individuals who live in a world that is burdened by the availability of nuclear technologies would strongly prefer being protected by weapons of mass destruction to living in a state that provides no such protection.

How does this justify the credible mutual threats by which the balance of terror is sustained? An answer to this question, I submit, would appeal to the fact that these killings are *permitted* by an impartially *justified* rule that is tacitly accepted within the society of states. In a world burdened by the existence of extremely destructive conventional and nonconventional weapons, the murderous intentions of evil leaders can be cheaply and easily executed. In such a world, the Exemption is ex ante a mutually beneficial norm: if the rule that allows a direct attack on civilians in extreme circumstances is accepted, citizens have a strong reason (of narrow self-interest) to prevent evil leaders—with murderous intentions of enslavement and ethnic cleansing—from coming to power. The argument is simple: under such a regime, if our ruler is so evil that he intends to eliminate a nation and we let him remain in power, we leave ourselves open to indiscriminate killing by our adversaries in war. Therefore, we would have strong incentive to make sure that our rulers will not support an extermination of another nation. In other words, citizens are more likely to struggle for the minimal decency of their state, in a world in which a supreme emergency exemption is a universally accepted norm. Under a threat of total war—in which states are constrained only by preconventional morality—the risk of enslavement and ethnic cleansing is reduced.

Note that we have *no* parallel reason to expose ourselves to total wars, in order to generate a stronger incentive for preventing governments from becoming aggressive. For, as opposed to enslavement and ethnic cleansing whose evilness is easily recognized by all, wars are inevitably marked by *reasonable* disagreements over the justness of their cause. Requiring from citizens to block crimes against peace would therefore be ineffectual.

States have not *explicitly* accepted an exemption that allows directly violating the right to life of innocents. This legislation contradicts the commitment of the liberal law to human dignity. Morally restrained states cannot expose innocent citizens who faultlessly fail to preserve the minimal decency of their government to (direct) killing, just as such states cannot threaten harming children in order to deter their parents, even if this turns out to be very effective. Still, it is commonly known to virtually all statesmen and to most mature and well-informed civilians that under a regime in which the Exemption is accepted, the likelihood that a regime would become murderous is sharply reduced. And in tolerating and imposing the threats that maintain the balance of terror, the society of states effectively acknowledges the authority of the Exemption.

IV.4. Elucidating the Exemption

The following observations—for which I have argued in the previous sections—are sufficient for elucidating the Exemption: (a) in supreme emergencies the *in bello* contract is null and void; (b) states and statesmen tacitly accepted the supreme emergency exemption; and (c) the Exemption is commonly known to be a justified norm. Conjoined to the two-tiered morality I have sketched in section II, these three propositions entail a contractarian and consequentialist disparity between extreme and regular circumstances.

Consider the Exemption from the contractarian standpoint: which rights are possessed by a just state facing supreme emergency and the just combatants fighting against enslavement and extermination? Which duties do they bear in such circumstances? First, and maybe most important, just parties facing supreme emergencies reacquire the right to be guided by lesser-evil considerations in general, and by *a*symmetrical proportionality in particular; the *in bello* agreement commanding states and armies to treat civilians as if they are innocent bystanders is null and void. Therefore, as the immunity from killing in war of *culpable* civilians is solely conventional, in committing the killings of such civilians, just combatants violate no right that these civilians hold against them.

Now, the group of *culpable* citizens who are preconventionally liable to defensive killing is relatively large. Adult citizens are not exempted from the duty to do whatever they can to prevent an evil government from posing a threat of ethnic cleansing. This group of engaged civilians includes the rulers, people who have actively supported them, and those who could have removed these rulers from power but failed to do so.

The right to life of fully innocent civilians "still stands," and "nothing can diminish it." Yet the rule allowing states to employ the supreme emergency exemption is tacitly accepted within the society of states. Therefore, in directly killing the fully innocent, just combatants violate the rights of these individuals, but not any claim that the *evil state* holds against them. A state that poses an existential threat to another nation loses its legitimacy.

So much for the fundamental rights-based disparity between extreme and regular circumstances; consider now the Exemption from a consequentialist perspective. If all other things are equal, lesser-evil considerations are more likely to justify direct killing of fully innocent civilians of the aggressive states in extreme circumstances, and less likely to justify killing innocents in nonextreme circumstances. This is because a killing of *one* innocent citizen of the evil state in a supreme emergency involves a violation of fewer and less weighty rights. Therefore, it is not as bad as a single killing of a totally innocent person in regular circumstances.

To see why, observe that a killing of an innocent civilian of the evil state in extreme circumstances involves violation of fewer rights, as she has no *conventional* right against being treated in accordance with *asymmetrical*, lesser-evil-based proportionality. And it involves a violation of less weighty rights, as the right to life of innocent citizens of the evil state is weakened by virtue of the common knowledge that states tacitly accept the rule that allows such killing, and by virtue of the fact that the rule allowing it is a justified norm.

The difficulties that the lesser-evil justification faces are thus dissolved. Why is only a sudden breach of the convention permissible, and why only in the very last minute, when a morally horrific catastrophe is about to occur? What's the difference between extreme and regular circumstances? Our answer runs as follows: although consequentialism of rights (on which the Exemption is based) supports "the more justice the more right" ethics of war, it is in the shared interest of states and of the individuals they represent in regular circumstances of war to be governed by a set of rules of conduct that is entirely irresponsive to lesser-evil considerations. However, the *in bello* agreement does not apply to supreme emergencies, where states face extermination or enslavement. Hence, states facing this predicament are not under conventional duty to disregard lesser-evil considerations; they bear no *conventional* duty to avoid attacking noncombatants.

Our second question was how a lesser-evil-based Exemption can discriminate between innocent citizens of the evil state and citizens of the neutral states; Why is it preferable that citizens of the evil state, rather than neutrals, would be killed if killing innocents of one of these groups is necessary for eliminating the threat of total extermination? The account presented here implies a simple answer: an exemption that discriminates against citizens of the evil state reduces the risk that supreme emergencies will obtain. As such, it is tacitly accepted within the society of states, and known to citizens of the evil state to be justified. The common knowledge of these facts somewhat weakens the rights of citizens of the evil state.

CONCLUSION

I have sketched in this essay a morality that supports the special permission to kill innocent civilians in supreme emergencies, based on a contractarian analysis of the laws of war. The contractarian interpretation reverses the usual (and perhaps natural) order of justification: this contractarian analysis does not reflect a preconventional moral equality of soldiers and civilians. Rather, the legislation is justified independently, by the fairness of the rules and by the mutual advantage that the acceptance of the rules secures. Indeed, states adopt a norm that commands disregarding lesser-evil considerations in combat, because it is both mutually beneficial (in terms of self-interest) and fair (in terms of rights violation).

The contractarian interpretation grounds a theory of extremity. The supreme emergency exemption is compelling, because lesser-evil considerations support it. True, these considerations cannot distinguish between extreme and regular circumstances of war: lesser-evil considerations might justify direct killing of innocent civilians in nonextreme circumstances as well. Yet the traditional convention that outlaws killing civilians justifiably instructs armies and soldiers to disregard lesser-evil considerations in combat. That is, it is better in terms of welfare and of human rights fulfillment if lesser-evil considerations are disregarded in combat. Extreme circumstances are such that just states have no reason to prefer rule-governed wars, in which lesser-evil considerations are disregarded, to total wars. Thus, a state facing extermination and/or enslavement is not subjected to any *conventional* duty, because in such circumstances the *in bello* agreement is null and void. I further argued that supreme emergencies erode specifically the immunity to killing of the innocent citizens of the evil state. For it is commonly known that the society of states, whose aim is to minimize the risk that supreme emergencies will obtain, tacitly agrees that war in extreme circumstances will be total. This common knowledge weakens the right of citizens of the evil state against attack in supreme emergencies.[33]

NOTES

1. This and other statements about the international law are all drawn from Dinstein (1988: 156–162).

2. Interestingly, Rawls was attracted to this view: "When a country's right to war is questionable...the constraints on the means it can use are all the more severe" (1971: 379), quoted in Walzer (1977: 229).

3. Walzer (1977, chap. 16). For a defense of a modified version of the Exemption, see Primoratz (2004, and 1997 at pp. 231–233) for a powerful critique see Coady (2004a and 2004b).

4. Walzer (1977, pp. 251–255).

5. See also Benbaji (2005: sec. 4). Compare Waldron (1993: chap. 10).

6. I am relying on Simmons (1999) here.

7. See also Benbaji (2008: sec. 3.A).

8. This sketch is indebted to Lewis (1969: 97–100) and to Darwall (2005), Wallace (2007), and Watson (2007).

9. Cf. Arneson (2001).

10. This moral interpretation has been espoused by a number of philosophers, such as Elizabeth Anscombe, Thomas Nagel, Jeffery G. Murphy, and Michael Walzer, and most recently by Igor Primoratz. See Primoratz (2007) for exposition and citations.

11. I focus on McMahan (2004, 2009).

12. As Primoratz concedes, "The way the Hague and Geneva conventions provide for the protection of civilians is in line with this view, although the scope of the category is wider: civilians are contrasted with combatants, and the latter are those, and only those, who openly carry arms, either at all times or at least at the time they are fighting or preparing to do so" (Primoratz 2007: 40).

13. "How...could a Nazi soldier weigh the harms he would cause to enemy combatants [or to enemy noncombatants] against the end of victory by the Nazis without assigning any value to the victory?" (McMahan 2004: 715).

14. An earlier version of the contractarian elucidation can be found in Walzer: "Military conduct is governed by rules [which] rest on mutuality and consent" (1977: 37); and Thomas Hurka: "By voluntarily entering military service, soldiers on both sides freely took on the status of soldiers and thereby freely accepted that they may permissibly be killed in the course of war" (2007: 210).

15. See Benbaji (2009: 604).

16. Kutz (2008: 75).

17. Ibid., 78.

18. Ibid., 78.
19. Quoted in Walzer (1977: 250).
20. Ibid.
21. Ibid.
22. Garrett (1993: 10–11) quoted and discussed in Coady (2004a: 781–782).
23. Walzer (1977: 253).
24. Ibid., 262.
25. Rawls (1999: 98–99).
26. This difficulty is developed by Statman, and it grounds his alternative conception of the Exemption. See Statman (2006).
27. Walzer (1977: 229). Interestingly, the early Rawls seems to accept the sliding scale. He says, "When a country's right to war is questionable . . . the constraints on the means it can use are all the more severe" (Rawls 1971: 379, quoted in Walzer 1977: 229).
28. Walzer (1977: 229).
29. Walzer (2006: 4).
30. It should be noted that Walzer's claim is stronger than the one I advance here. He argues for the following biconditional: the Convention collapses (and thus statesmen are authorized to deliberately kill innocent people), *if and only if* the circumstances are extreme. My argument establishes the sufficient condition to which Walzer commits himself: if the circumstances are extreme, the Convention collapses. Whether it collapses in other circumstance I leave as an open question. Let me note, however, that Walzer's necessary condition seems plausible for epistemic reasons: only in extreme circumstances can the just side know for sure that a total war is preferable to abiding by the Convention.
31. Walzer (1977: 273–274); this is of course a very controversial position. See e.g., Lackey (1984) who claims that that the intentions that are necessary for nuclear deterrence are immoral, and moreover that they are as immoral as the act itself.
32. This is true of a morally constrained state, S1. For, suppose that S1's superior military force enables it to appropriate resources to which it is entitled. Its relatively weak rival S2—which unjustly acquired these resources—would rationally fear that S1 is *un*constrained by morality. This fear would cause S2 to surrender unconditionally. S1 would thus appropriate the resources to which it is entitled, without any violence.
33. For extremely helpful comments I would like to thank Dave Barnes, Roger Crisp, David Heyd, Seth Lazar, David Miller, Daniel Schwartz, Hanoch Sheinman, Naomi Sussmann, Daniel Statman, David Rodin, Michael Walzer, Alex Yakobson, Tomasz Żuradzki, and the audiences in the Justice, Culture and Tradition Conference in honor of Michael Walzer (Institute for Advanced Study, Princeton), The Uehiro Centre Seminar (Oxford University) and the Seminar for Political Philosophy (the Hebrew University).

REFERENCES

Arneson, R. 2001. "Against Rights." *Philosophical Issues* 11: 172–201.

Benbaji. Y. 2005. "Culpable Bystanders, Innocent Threats and the Ethics of Self-Defense." *Canadian Journal of Philosophy* 35: 585–622.

———. 2008. "A Defense of the Traditional War Convention." *Ethics* 118: 464–495.
———. 2009. "The War Convention and the Moral Division of Labor." *Philosophical Quarterly* 59: 593–618.
Coady C. A. J. 2004a. "Terrorism, Morality and Supreme Emergency." *Ethics* 114 (2004): 772–789.
———. 2004b. "Terrorism and Innocence." *Journal of Ethics* 8: 37–58.
Darwall, S. 2005. *The Second Person Standpoint: Morality, Respect and Accountability*. Cambridge, MA: Harvard University Press.
Dinstein, Y. 1988. *War, Aggression, and Self-Defence*. Cambridge: Cambridge University Press.
Garrett, S. A. 1993. *Ethics and Airpower in World War II: The British Bombing of German Cities*. New York: St. Martin's Press.
Hurka, T. 2007. "Liability and Just Cause." *Ethics and International Affairs* 20: 199–218.
Kutz, K. 2008. "Fearful Symmetry." in David Rodin and Henry Shue (eds.), *Just and Unjust Warriors: the Moral and Legal Status of Soldiers*. New York: Oxford University Press: 69–86.
Lewis, D. 1969. *Convention*. Cambridge, MA: Harvard University Press.
Lackey, D. P. 1984. *Moral Principles and Nuclear Weapons*. Totowa, NJ: Rowman & Allanhald.
McMahan, J. 2004. "The Ethics of Killing in War." *Ethics* 114: 693–733.
———. 2009. *Killing in War*. Oxford: Oxford University Press.
Primoratz, I. 1997. "The Morality of Terrorism." *Journal of Applied Philosophy* 221–233.
———. 2004. "State Terrorism and Counterterrorism." In Igor Primoratz (ed.), *Terrorism: The Philosophical Issues*. Basingstoke, England: Palgrave: 113–27.
———. 2007. "Civilian Immunity in War: Its Grounds, Scope, and Limits." In I. Primoratz (ed.), *Civilian Immunity in War*. Oxford: Oxford University Press: 21–42.
Sen, A. 1982. "Rights and Agency." *Philosophy and Public Affairs* 11: 3–39.
Simmons, J. 1999. "Justification and Legitimacy." *Ethics* 109: 739-771.
Statman, D. 2006. "Supreme Emergencies Revisited." *Ethics* 117: 58–79.
Rawls, J. 1971. *A Theory of Justice*. Cambridge, MA: Harvard University Press.
——. 1999. *The Law of the People*. Cambridge, MA: Harvard University Press.
Waldron, J. 1993. "A Right to Do Wrong." in Waldron, *Liberal Rights*. Cambridge: Cambridge University Press.
Wallace, J. 2007. "Reasons Relations and Commands." *Ethics* 118: 24–36.
Walzer, M. 1977. *Just and Unjust Wars*. New York: Basic Books.
———. 2006. "Terrorism and Just War." *Philosophia* 34: 1–12.
Watson, G. 2007 "Morality as Equal Accountability." *Ethics* 118: 37–51.

Chapter 16

Agreement as Joint Promise

Hanoch Sheinman

Abstract

This essay proposes a general account of agreements within a largely individualistic framework. According to this account, making an agreement is an essentially joint action, one the parties perform together as one. The action of agreement-making, which can only be performed jointly, can nevertheless be explained in terms of another action, which can also be performed individually, namely promising. Agreement-making on this view is a matter of joint promising. An agreement is more than two promises. Two promises add up to an agreement–i.e. joint promise–just when they are exchanged–or interdepend–in the right way. The interdependence of agreement promises on this view is not a matter of the promises being mutually conditional; indeed, each agreement party promises to do his part of the deal, whatever it happens to be. Instead, the interdependence of agreement promises is a causal-motivational affair. Each party understands that her commitment and that of the other party will stand or fall together, and this understanding is part of what causes and motivates her to make it.

I. INTRODUCTION

When you and I simultaneously open our umbrellas as it starts raining, we open our umbrellas together; when we tango, we tango together *as one*. My general hypothesis is that agreement is like tango: whenever you and I enter into an agreement, we do not simply enter into it together; we enter into it together as one–or *jointly*.

We can also *carry out* an agreement jointly. It is not clear that we have to, however. Arguably, when the agreement requires us to perform otherwise unrelated actions at different places and times (you hand me the goods now; I pay you later), we cannot—or at least do not have to—perform these actions jointly. My hypothesis, then, is not about the carrying out of agreements; it is about the entering into agreements or *agreement-making*. I claim that (the making of) an agreement *is a joint action*[1].

Good, but what is it, exactly, that we do jointly when we enter into an agreement? Well, we jointly make an agreement! This is nonexplanatory, so let me refine the question. What sort of action *that we could perform individually* do we perform jointly when we enter into an agreement? Agreement-making is not something we could perform individually (disjointly): I could not enter into an agreement with you unless you jointly entered into the same agreement with me. Is there something that we do jointly when we make an agreement, which we could also do individually?

According to Margaret Gilbert, agreement parties jointly *decide* to do their respective parts of the agreement.[2] I endorse the most general premise of Gilbert's account, namely that agreement-making is a matter of doing something together as one, or jointly. But I do not endorse her claim that the action in question is deciding.[3] In this paper I will present a different hypothesis, namely that the action in question is *promising*. Here is the basic idea:

Agreement as Joint Promise
A and B enter into an agreement that A is to do X and B is to do Y just when
(i) A promises B to do X.
(ii) B promises A to do Y.
(iii) These promises are exchanged, or interdepend, in some explanatory way, one that would warrant the claim that A and B promise each other together as one or jointly.

This skeletal account has two components. Conditions (i) and (ii) are designed to explain the conjunctive *content* of the agreement in terms of the content of its constitutive promises. Condition (iii) is designed to explain the agreement-making *process* in terms of the process of making the constitutive promises, thereby explaining the *joint* nature of agreement-making.

Conditions (i)–(ii): Each Party Promises to Do Her Part

The joint promise account seeks to explain an action that can only be performed jointly (agreement-making) in terms of an action that can be performed individually as well as jointly (promising). Conditions (i) and (ii) explain the conjunctive content of the agreement by the simple content of its constitutive promises. *It is a key feature of the account on offer that each agreement party promises the other to do her part of (the carrying out of) the agreement, neither more nor less.* This feature has two aspects. First, the constitutive promises are all promises to do something *oneself*. Thus the account makes no use of the notion that A promises B that *they* do X.[4] Nor does it make use of the notion that A promises B *that A is to do X and B is to do Y*. These notions, I suspect, are just as difficult to understand as the agreement we are trying to explain. Second, the constitutive promises are simple or *unconditional*—that is to say relative to the agreement. If the agreement is that A is to do X and B is to do Y, then A (B) commits to do X (Y). Thus, for example, the proposed account makes no use of the notion that A promises B to (do X if B does Y). This explains the intuition that agreements involve relational commitments to do one's part of the deal, or the

> Face Value Principle for Agreements
> When A and B enter into an agreement that A is to do X and B is to do Y, A commits to B to do X and B commits to A to do Y.

Conditions (i) and (ii) provide the simplest explanation of this commonsense principle. After all, individual promises involve relational commitments to do as promised. Presumably, we all believe the

> Face Value Principle for Promises
> When A promises B to do X, A commits to B to do X.

It follows from this second principle that when conditions (i) and (ii) are met, A commits to B to do X and B commits to A to do Y. So each agreement party makes a relational commitment to the other to do his part of the deal. This is just the Face Value Principle for Agreements.

Objection and Reply

But while everyone would probably accept the Face Value Principle for Promises, not everyone would accept the Face Value Principle for Agreements. Consider our agreement that I am to wash the dishes and you are to take out the trash. My account entails that I commit to you to wash the dishes, neither more nor less. If I fail to wash the dishes, I break our agreement *even if you fail to take up the trash*! Surely, so goes the objection, if you do not do your part of the agreement, I cannot be committed to do mine. My account goes wrong in supposing that our agreement commits me to you to do my part of the agreement, neither more nor less. It really commits me to do *less*, namely to do my part of the agreement *if* you do yours. Generally, so goes the suggestion, when A and B enter into an agreement that A is to do X and B is to do Y, A commits to B to (do X if B does Y) and B commits to A to (do Y if A does X).

So there is a fundamental asymmetry between the commitments of promises and agreements: agreement commitments are conditional in a way promissory commitments are not.[5]

But I do not see how the fact that you fail to do your part of the agreement (taking out the trash) can make it okay for me to fail to do mine (washing the dishes). Just because you break the agreement does not mean I can't break it, too! To be sure, since your hands are not clean, your complaint might not be effective. To make the complaint would be to throw a stone in a house of glass. But the sheer fact that making a complaint would fail to be efficacious does not tend to show that there is no complaint to make. And the sheer fact that I have a complaint against you under the agreement doesn't show that you don't have a complaint against me under the same agreement.

Indeed, the suggestion that neither one of us breaks the agreement in this case seems to me to fail to take our agreement seriously. After all, we could enter into a significantly different agreement, namely the agreement that

> I am to wash the dishes if you take out the trash, and you are to take out the trash if I wash the dishes.

Instead, we chose to enter into the agreement that

> I am to wash the dishes and you are to take out the trash.

But from the perspective of this agreement, the case in which I wash the dishes and you take out the trash is clearly preferable to the case in which I fail to wash the dishes and you fail to take out the trash. The first is a case of double success; the second, of double failure. The account on offer explains this; the objection cannot.

Let me try to generalize the problem with the objection. It relies on the view that the relational commitments of an agreement are mutually conditional. This makes it difficult to explain the difference between the case in which A and B choose to enter into an agreement that A is to do X and B is to do Y, and the case in which they choose to enter into the rather different agreement that A is to do (X if B does Y) and B is to do (Y if A does X). Now focus on A's commitments. On my account, the first agreement commits A to do X, and the second agreement commits A to do (X if B does Y). These are obviously different commitments. But on the mutually conditional view, the first agreement commits A to do (X if B does Y), and the second agreement commits A to do [(X if B does Y) if B does (Y if A does X)]. But on reflection, these are not really two different commitments at all. Surely, A breaks the first agreement if and only if B does Y and A fails to do X. She breaks the second agreement if and only if B (does Y if A does X) and A fails to (do X if B does Y). But it seems to me that this conjunction is true if and only if B does Y and A fails to do X.

In the end, the mutually conditional view seems to have this counterintuitive result: it matters not whether our agreement is that (I am to wash the dishes and you are to take out the trash), or rather that (I am to wash the dishes if you take out the trash, and you are to take out the trash if I wash the dishes). Our commitments under these two different-looking agreements are indistinguishable. In each case, each party's commitment is to do her chore if the other does his, a commitment each party breaks if and only if she fails to do her chore and the other does his. Our choice to conditionalize or not to conditionalize our commitments makes no difference to what we are committed to do under an agreement.[6]

According to Agreement as Joint Promise, by contrast, the parties can choose to require one (or each) party to perform some action X if the other performs some other action Y, in which case the commitment of one (or each) will be conditional in a way. But the parties can also choose, alternatively, to require each party to perform some action X or Y, in which case the commitment of each party will be unconditional. Now determining what any given agreement actually requires the parties to do might be a matter of interpretation, and depend on the context as well as the words and deeds of the parties. However, *once it is established that you and I have in fact entered into an agreement that I am to wash the dishes and you are to take out the trash*, my agreement commits me to wash the dishes, period. If I fail to do so, I break the agreement, whether or not you take out the trash. If we both fail to do our chores, we both break the agreement. We both have a complaint under the agreement.

Condition (iii): Agreement Promises Interdepend

The first component of the account (the first two conditions), then, concerns the content of an agreement and its commitments. It translates the composite or conjunctive commitment of an agreement—that A is to do X and B is to do Y—into two simple promissory commitments: A (B) commits to B (A) to do X (Y). The second component of the account (the third condition) begins to explain why these promissory commitments are the commitments *of an agreement*. The most basic idea is that an agreement is an exchange of promises—or *interdependent* promises. The promises of an agreement must interdepend in some explanatory way, one that would warrant the claim that the parties promise each other together as one, or jointly.

An agreement on this view is *more* than promises; it is interdependent promises. If A and B promise each other to do X and Y, respectively, but one or both of their promises does not depend on the other in the right way, they do not enter into an agreement that A is to do X and B is to do Y. To describe the sense in which agreement promises interdepend is to explain what makes them a joint promise. To echo Wittgenstein, interdependence is what's left over if we subtract the fact that each agreement party promises from the fact that they jointly promise each other.

Adequacy Criteria

Some theorists accept that the commitments (or obligations) of an agreement interdepend in some explanatorily important way, but reject the notion that *promissory* commitments or obligations can interdepend in that way. For example, several legal theorists reject the claim that contractual (i.e. legally binding) agreements can be explained as interdependent promises.[7] The complaint seems to have nothing to do with the fact that contractual agreements are legally binding, and everything to do with the fact that they are *agreements*. Arguably, if we could not explain contractual agreements as interdependent contractual promises, we could also not explain noncontractual agreements as interdependent noncontractual promises.

Indeed, skepticism about promissory accounts is not confined to contractual agreements; it extends to agreements generally. The most comprehensive rejection of the notion of agreement as joint promise belongs to Margaret Gilbert. She claims that every account of agreements must meet three criteria of adequacy by explaining how every agreement has the following properties:

> Obligation
> The agreement gives each party an obligation to do her part of the agreement.
>
> Simultaneity
> It gives these obligations simultaneously.
>
> Interdependence
> These obligations interdepend.

Gilbert rejects all promissory accounts of agreements because she thinks that no such account can meet all three criteria of adequacy:

> no promise-exchange, however complex, is capable of simultaneously delivering unconditional, interdependent obligations to the parties. (2006: 220; 2000: 61; 1996: 328)

More to the point, Gilbert claims that no promissory account of agreements can meet criteria (1)–(3) because none can meet criterion (3):

> no pair of promises can meet the interdependence criterion (1996: 221–22; cf. also Mintoff, 2004: 50).

Now Gilbert offers a rather specific definition of the interdependence criterion, which I do not share.[8] So let us assume that no promissory account of agreement can explain how agreement obligations interdepend in her sense. What I wish to take from her critique is the plausible general notion that the obligations of an agreement interdepend in *some* explanatory sense.

For the proponent of Agreement as Joint Promise, the challenge is to spell out condition (iii) in some detail, namely to describe an explanatorily important sense in which two promises interdepend just when they constitute an agreement, which interdependence would warrant the imagery of the parties promising each other together as one, or jointly. Assuming each promise involves a commitment/obligation, meeting this challenge would automatically explain the interdependence—and jointness—of the commitments/obligations of an agreement.

II. TWO ASSUMPTIONS ABOUT JOINT ACTION

An account that explains agreement as joint promising presupposes a working account of joint action. The contours of this account should become clear as we go. Two assumptions of this account are particularly important.

(1) Individualism

The first assumption is *individualism*, understood as the view that joint action consists of interrelated individual actions of personal agents. No appeal is to be made, explicitly or by implication, to a sui generis, irreducibly joint action, agent, or commitment.[9] In this respect, my discussion resembles the one in Bratman (1999: pt. 2).[10]

Let me be more specific about my individualism. I wish to assume that, to each joint intention/action there correspond (at least) two individual intentions/actions. If you and I jointly intend to walk, then you intend to walk and I intend to walk; should one of us stop intending to walk, that would be the end of our joint intention to walk.[11] And if you and I jointly walk, then you walk and I walk; should one of us stop walking, that would be the end of our joint walk. Joint intention/action is *more*—not less—than individual intentions/actions.

To be sure, an account of joint action that abides by my individualist assumption is not going to be useful in every conversational context.[12] But I think it can be useful in the context of explaining agreements. Indeed, to the extent that we think of joint promising as *interdependent* promises, we are already thinking in individualistic terms. That is to say, we are thinking about two individual promising actions that can be said to depend on one another in some interesting sense. More generally, to the extent that we think of joint action as interdependent actions, intentions, or commitments, we are presupposing individual actions, intentions, and commitments that depend on one another. What could possibly interdepend in an irreducibly joint action, intention, or commitment?[13]

(2) Joint Promise as a Special Case of Joint Action

I now wish to assume that those who jointly perform some action do not necessarily *promise* each other anything, and in any event do not necessarily promise each other to do something other than their respective parts of the joint action itself. When you and I jointly move the proverbial sofa neither of us could move by himself, we do not necessarily promise each other to do anything at all. But even if we do, we do not necessarily promise each other to do something other than doing our parts in moving the furniture. In that respect, joint promising is a rather special case of joint action. When parties jointly promise each other that one is to do X and the other is to do Y, the parties *do* in fact promise—and commit or obligate themselves—to do something other than their respective parts of the joint action (promising) itself. That is to say, they promise each other to do X and Y, respectively. Here is another way of putting the point: the promises—and attendant commitments or obligations—of joint promising have absolutely nothing to do with the fact that the parties are performing some action jointly; it has everything to do with the fact that the action they are performing jointly is promising.

As before, the assumption at bar seems useful in the context of explaining agreements. Indeed the notion of agreement-making as joint promising presupposes at least some joint actions that do not involve promises (or promises to do something other than the joint action.) If every joint action involved such promissory commitments, it is just not clear how we could explain the difference between agreement-making and, say, joint furniture-moving.

Synopsis

As stated in the introduction, Agreement as Joint Promise is a skeletal account. What is needed is an elaboration on condition (iii)—an account of the *interdependence* of the constitutive promises of an agreement. I develop such an account by progressively modifying proposals.

Section III examines the natural idea that the interdependence of agreement promises lies in their mutually conditional content. Section IV examines the view that agreement promises are unconditional in content but causally interdependent. The account offered in section V shifts the focus from the causal role of the promises to that of beliefs about them. Section VI presents my considered account (Agreement as Joint Promise), which makes the content of the causally operative belief (bi)conditional in content. That section also extends the account to the case of joint intention to enter an agreement. Section VII examines the objection that Agreement as Joint Promise is too weak because it requires no causal interaction between the parties. Section VIII examines the objection that Agreement as Joint Promise cannot explain agreements that are reached by way of offer and acceptance. I close in Section IX by reconfiguring Gilbert's three criteria of adequacy on accounts of agreement-making and explaining how the proposed account meets them.

III. CONDITIONAL PROMISES

Consider first the simple

> Agreement as Conditional Promises (Version 1)
> A and B enter at t into an agreement that A is to do X and B is to do Y just when, at t
> (1) A promises B to (do X if B does Y).
> (2) B promises A to (do Y if A does X).

The idea here is that, to explain the interdependence of agreement promises, we must make them mutually conditional in content. We have already identified the problem with this account. Given the Face Value Principle for Promises, conditions (1) and (2) imply that A commits to B to do (X if B does Y) and B commits to A to (do Y if A does X). This contradicts the Face Value Principle for Agreements. The simple conditional account implies that each agreement party commits to do *less* than what the agreement itself defines as its part of the deal—and the same as that party would commit to do under a different, mutually conditional agreement.[14]

We can try to fix the problem by changing the condition of the promises. The discussion of shared intention in Velleman (2000: ch. 9 and 242-43) puts me in mind of

> Agreement as Conditional Promises (Version 2)
> A and B enter at t into an agreement that A is to do X and B is to do Y just when, at t
> (1) A promises B to (do X if B promises A to do Y).
> (2) B promises A to (do Y if A promises B to do X).

The basic idea remains the same: we can only explain the interdependence of agreement promises by making these promises mutually conditional in content. But rather than making each party's promise conditional upon the other party's doing her part of the deal, we make it conditional on her *promising* to do her part.

But I think the problem with the first version of the conditional account persists. For again, given the Face Value Principle for Promises, conditions (1) and (2) imply that A and B commit to do *less* than what the agreement defines as their respective parts, in contradiction to the Face Value Principle for Agreements. Like the simpler conditional account, it fails to take the agreement seriously.

Now the condition in the content of the promises under these views is material, but we can also think of accounts in which the condition is causal. To say of events X and Y that X occurs because Y does (or because of Y) is to say that X *causally depends* on Y. I will take the notion of causal dependence as primitive, and use counterfactuals as a proxy; roughly: X wouldn't occur if Y didn't.[15] Bratman's discussion of shared intention (1999: 131) puts me in mind of

> Agreement as Conditional Promises (Version 3)
> A and B enter at t into an agreement that A is to do X and B is to do Y just when at t
> (1) A promises B to (do X because B promises A to do Y).
> (2) B promises A to (do Y because A promises B to do X).

But again, by the Face Value Principle for Promises, the commitments of the agreement are conditional in content, contrary to the Face Value Principle for Agreements. Consider the case in which B does not promise to do his part. Then by condition (1) A is not committed to do X. So A's commitment is less than to do X. But ex hypothesi X is what A is to do under the agreement. On the face of it, the agreement does commit A to B to do X is this case.

The lesson I draw from these attempts is that the interdependence of agreement promises does not lie in their conditional *content*. Agreement promises are simple or unconditional in content, that is to say relative to the content of the agreement. If the agreement is that A is to do X and B is to do Y, then A promises to do X and B promises to do Y. Of course, this hardly means that there is no way in which agreement promises can be conditional in content. On the contrary, it entails the following: When the agreement is that [A is to (do X if B is to do Y) and B is to (do Y if A is to do X)], A promises to (do X if B does Y) and B promises to (do Y if A does X). Hence there is a perfectly good sense in which the parties can choose to conditionalize their commitments. The point is that each agreement party promises to do her part of the deal, *whatever it happens to be.*

All this tends to vindicate conditions (i) and (ii) of the skeletal version of Agreement as Joint Promise. It does nothing to vindicate condition (iii), however. The challenge is to explain how even simple promises can interdepend in such a way that would warrant the image of the parties making these promises together as one or jointly.

IV. CAUSALLY INTERDEPENDENT PROMISES

We can begin to improve matters by narrowing the scope of the causal condition, like so:

> Agreement as Causally Interdependent Promises
> A and B enter at t into an agreement that A is to do X and B is to do Y just when, at t
> (1) (a) A promises B to do X.
> (b) B promises A to do Y.
> (2) (a) Because of (1b), (1a).
> (b) Because of (1a), (1b).

Condition (1) is the sole condition governing the content of the agreement promises and commitments. Notice that this account goes beyond conditions (i) and (ii) of the skeletal account by adding a temporal requirement, namely that the promises be made *simultaneously* whenever the agreement is entered into. You might wonder why I am assuming that the agreement is entered into *at* some point in time. Surely, you might think, an agreement is entered into *over* time. That is surely right. Agreement-making is a process, which takes time. But to count as an agreement, the process must achieve its end. The achievement of the end is a momentary event that takes place at a single point in time. To say that the agreement is entered into at t is to say that the agreement-making process is successfully *completed* at t. Here is another way of putting the point. Promise- and agreement-making are *telic* actions: they have a built-in termination point: the issuing of a promise or agreement.[16] We shall have occasion to return to this point later.

So the present account seems to get the relation between the agreement and the content of its constitutive promises right. But I suspect that its conception of the interdependence of agreement promises—condition (2)—is too strong. To be sure, the basic idea strikes me as exactly right: I think we do want to be able to say that agreement promises interdepend in *some* causal way. But as it stands, the account posits a problematic *causal loop* in which each party's promise both causes and is caused by the other party's promise. This seems to run roughshod over causation's alignment with time's arrow—the fact that the cause precedes the effect. Under condition (1a), A promises at t. Given causation's temporal structure, condition (2a) implies that B promises before t. Yet under condition (1b), B promises *at* t. Since A and B promise each other simultaneously, neither can promise because (i.e. as a result of the fact that) the other does.

Agreement as Causally Interdependent Promises faces another, completely different problem. It explains interdependence in purely causal terms, and this fails to capture the *motivational* aspect of agreement-making. Arguably, when A and B enter into an agreement, B's promise does not simply cause A to promise; it also motivates her to do so. To use a contemporary idiom, we want to be able to say that A *takes* B's promising *as A's reason* to promise. (See, for example, Setiya, 2007; Bratman, 2007.) Presumably, to explain A's motivation we would have to say something about A's *beliefs*. But the account under consideration does not mention belief.

Here is the lesson I wish to draw from this attempt. To say that two promises interdepend in such a way as to warrant the joint promise imagery, we should not require each party to promise because (as a result of the fact that) the other promises at t; instead, we should require each party to promise because (as a result) of her prior belief. Specifically, each agreement party promises at t because of some belief she forms at t – 1 about the other party's promise.

V. THE BELIEF ACCOUNT

Modifying the causal condition (2) in light of these lessons, we can get the

Belief Account
A and B enter at t into an agreement that A is to do X and B is to do Y just when, at t
(1) (a) A promises B to do X.
   (b) B promises A to do Y.
(2) (a) Because of A's belief that (1b), A promises B to do X.
   (b) Because of B's belief that (1a), B promises A to do Y.

Notice that respect for causation's temporal structure requires a tense-sensitive interpretation of condition (2): A believes at t - 1 that B will promise at t.

By focusing on the parties' beliefs, this account begins to explain the motivational aspect of agreement-making. And yet the notion that one's belief causes one's promise is not enough to capture the motivational—or taking-as-one's-reason—aspect of the interdependence we're after. As David Velleman has observed (2000: 2–9), one can perform an action because—i.e. as a result of—one's belief without being aware of this causal fact, as when

Freud sweeps his inkstand on the floor as a result of his belief that this will persuade his sister to buy him a new one. See also Setiya (2007: 33-34). Causally efficacious yet subconscious beliefs move agents without quite motivating them.[17]

We can fix the problem by adding the second-order belief that the agent is acting because (as a result of) of her operative, causally efficacious belief. Hence we need to add condition

(3)(a) A believes (2).
(b) B believes (2).[18]

Objection

This new cognitive requirement raises an interesting psychological worry.[19] As the content condition (1) makes explicit, the constitutive promises are simple or unconditional in content (relative to the agreement). The worry is that, together with the causal condition (2), the cognitive condition (3) effectively *conditionalizes* the promises. To appreciate the worry, suppose that conditions (1a), (2a), and (3a) are met:

(i) A promises B at t to do X.
(ii) Because A believes at t - 1 that B will promise A at t to do Y, A promises B at t to do X.
(iii) A believes (ii).

Put yourself in A's shoes and ask whether your promising here feels any different from what it would feel if you promised at t to (do X *if* B promises A at t to do Y). If these logically different promises are indiscernible from a first-person perspective, the present account is not so much an alternative to Agreement as Conditional Promises (Version 2) as a complicated restatement.

I do not share this worry. In my intuition, these logically different promises are psychologically distinct. Notice that something very much like the distinction at issue is commonly acknowledged with respect to intention.[20] You might correctly believe that your intention to jump in front of the steering wheel and drive off causally depends on your belief that the starter is in functioning condition (roughly, that you wouldn't have that intention if you didn't have that belief). Intuitively, however, this belief remains in the background, and does not affect what you intend to do, which is to drive off. Now if the car does not start, your belief will change, and you will no longer have that intention. But this is phenomenologically different from your intending to drive *if* the starter is in functioning condition, when you suspect that it isn't. I think something similar can be said about promising. You might have the true (second-order) belief that your promising me to do X causally depends on your (first-order) belief that I will do Y. For all that, what you correctly believe you are promising me is to do X.

Matching Cross Promises

If I'm right, an agreement comprises a pair of interdependent promises. Notice however that for every pair of agreement promises there is a pair of matching (exactly similar) *nonagreement* promises, which do not interdepend but cross each other in the dark, as it were. We can refer to them as the agreement's *matching cross promises*. Accounts of agreement should explain why these promises do not amount to an agreement. The Belief Account begins to do so. Consider an easy case.

> *Consecutive Promises*. A to B at t1: "I promise you to do X." B to A at t2: "I promise you to do Y."

Intuitively, A promises B at t1, thereby committing herself to him to do X later, and B promises A at t2, thereby committing himself to her to do Y later. Intuitively, they do not enter into an agreement. And indeed, the case violates condition (1), which requires the parties to promise simultaneously.[21] But matching cross promises can also be made simultaneously. Consider

> *Simultaneous Promises*. Unbeknownst to B, A emails B at t1: "I promise you my car." At the same time, and unbeknownst to A, B emails A: "I promise you $5,000." Both A and B read these messages at t2.

Suppose that promises are completed, and therefore made, when the promisor's intention is successfully communicated to the promisee: when the promisee believes he is being promised. Then A and B promise each other at t2, when they read each other's messages. They simultaneously promise each other, moreover, exactly what they would simultaneously promise each other at t2 if they entered into an agreement at t2: A promises to transfer B the car; B promises to pay A $5,000. So this time, condition (1) is met. Condition (2) remains unmet, however. Take condition (2a). It is only upon reading the e-mail that A learns about B's promise. By this time (t2), however, A has already made her own promise. The belief comes too late to *cause* A to promise. At no point before t2 does A believe that B will promise at t2. Trivially, A would promise at t2 even if she didn't have that belief.

Accepted Offer Agreements

Good. But being able to exclude matching cross promises is not enough; an account of agreements must not leave out genuine agreements. Cases of agreement by offer and acceptance seem to make trouble for the Belief Account, and in fact for any account that explains agreements in terms of promises. Consider

> *Accepted Offer*. A to B at t1: "I offer you my car for $5,000." B to A at t2: "Accepted."

Intuitively, A and B enter at t2 into a sale of car agreement. But none of the conditions of the Belief Account seems to be met. Most basically, condition (1) does not seem to be met. For one thing, it is not clear that anyone is making a promise here. But even if both parties promise, they do not seem to do so *simultaneously*.

I think this objection can be met. Arguably, both parties to accepted offer agreements can be said to promise each other simultaneously. Here then is the basic picture.[22]

When A makes her offer, she doesn't promise anything as yet. However, she makes it the case that, if B promises her to pay $5,000, she promises him the car. (As long as we remember that this does not mean that A promises anything as yet, we can say that A promises-the-car-on-the-condition-that B promises to pay).[23] When B accepts the offer, he promises to pay A $5,000. Therefore, when B accepts, A promises B the car.[24] Hence, at t2, B promises A the car *and* A promises B the money. See Bach (1995) for similar analysis. Later I will consider an objection to this picture. For now, assume that I'm right to claim that the parties in Accepted Offer simultaneously promise each other to do their respective parts of the deal, and so that condition (1) of the Belief Account is met. This does not yet show that the Belief Account can explain the agreement in this case. Indeed, I do not think it can. For it seems to me that condition (2) goes unmet in this case.

Properly understood, condition (2a) implies that A's promise at t2 causally depends on her prior belief that B will promise at t2. Alas, at no point before t2 does A believe that B will promise her at t2! It is only at t2—when B accepts A's offer—that A learns about B's promise. That belief comes too late to cause A to promise at t2.[25]

The Belief Account is too demanding. Often, at least one agreement party does not believe that the other will promise until they both do. That agreement party cannot promise because (as a result) of his belief that the other will. What to do?

An Easy Way Out?

The discussion in Bratman (1999: 154–60) puts me in mind of what might prove to be an easy way out. While we cannot expect each party to believe, before the agreement is concluded, that the other will in fact promise, maybe we can expect each party to believe that the other will *probably* do so. Under "normal communicative conditions," so goes the thought, would-be agreement parties are in a position *reliably to predict* each other's agreement promises. It is this prediction that causes and motivates each party to promise the other. If the parties in Accepted Offer operate under normal communicative conditions, A reliably predicts at t1 that B will accept the offer and so the parties will exchange promises at t2. Apart from that prediction, so goes the thought, A would not offer and eventually promise.

This line of response is too weak to solve the problem with the Belief Account. It is simply not clear that A believes, at any point prior to her promise at t2, that B will probably promise her money. For all we know, when A makes the offer, she reasonably believes that B is much more likely to reject her offer than to accept it. And A might well persist in this belief until she learns about B's highly unlikely acceptance. But clearly, the sheer fact that B's acceptance was highly unlikely does not prevent it from concluding the agreement.[26]

The lesson I draw from the difficulty with the Belief Account is the need to relax the causal condition. We can try to do so by conditionalizing the operative belief.

VI. AGREEMENT AS JOINT PROMISE

Here then is my considered account.

> Agreement as Joint Promise
> A and B enter at t into an agreement that A is to do X and B is to do Y just when, at t
> (1)(a) A promises B to do X.
> (b) B promises A to do Y.
> (2)(a) Because of A's belief that [A promises B to (do X) if and only if B promises A to (do Y)], A promises B to do X.
> (b) Because of B's belief that [A promises B to (do X) if and only if B promises A to (do Y)], B promises A to do Y.
> (3)(a) A believes (2).
> (b) B believes (2).

As before, respect for causation's temporal structure requires a tense-sensitive interpretation of condition (2): A believes at some t – 1 that [A will promise B at t to (do X) iff B will simultaneously promise A to (do Y)].[27] Each party's operative belief is not that the other will, or will probably, promise at t to do his part; it is rather the twofold belief that

(i) I will not promise at t to do my part if he will not, at the same time, promise to do his;
(ii) he will not promise at t to do his part if I will not, at the same time, promise to do mine.

Let me begin by laying out the general thought—or picture—the account is trying to capture. Each agreement party views her promissory commitment as an indispensable part of a package of which the other party's promissory commitment is another indispensable part, and her viewing her commitment in this way is part of what causes and motivates her to make her promissory commitment. Each party takes the fact that the constitutive promises of the agreement will stand or fall together as one of her reasons for promising. From the perspective of each party, the constitutive promises of the agreement and their attendant commitments are essentially reciprocal.[28]

In one way, this account is more complicated than its predecessor: the content of the operative belief is now conditional. But in another way, the account is in fact simpler. For it makes the operative belief of the parties identical in content.

Can this account handle accepted offer agreements? I am not sure. We've already seen how condition (1) can be said to be met in such cases.[29] The more difficult question is whether the new condition (2) can also be said to be met in such agreements. Can the same biconditional operative belief cause the offeror and offeree to promise simultaneously? Here is the general story. As A makes her offer, she understands that, if B accepts it, her offer will transform into two simultaneous promises—her promise to transfer the car and B's promise to pay—and otherwise it won't. A's offer is caused by this twofold understanding of the nature of what she is doing. But A's agreement promise is caused by her offer. Therefore, A's agreement promise is caused by her biconditional understanding. Similarly, as B accepts the offer, he understands that, if his acceptance is completed,[30] it will transform into two simultaneous promises—his promise to pay and A's promise to transfer the car—and otherwise it won't. And B's acceptance is caused by this twofold understanding of the nature of what he is doing. Therefore, A's agreement promise is caused by his biconditional understanding.

Being a causal story, its plausibility depends on our working conception of causation. We have employed counterfactuals as a rough and ready proxy, but this method has its limits. Let me mention the two limits that seem particularly relevant. The first has to do with the transitivity of causation. Someone who holds a counterfactual account of causation might accept that (i) A's agreement promise counterfactually, and therefore causally, depends on her offer (she wouldn't make her promise apart from her offer), and that (ii) A's offer in turn counterfactually, and therefore casually, depends on A's belief that A will make her agreement promise at t if but only if B will (she wouldn't offer apart from her belief), but still reject that (iii) A's agreement promise counterfactually, and therefore causally, depends on that biconditional belief of hers (she wouldn't make her promise apart from her belief). After all, A makes her agreement promise indirectly, through B's acceptance, and counterfactual dependence is intransitive. But I think David Lewis showed a simple way to handle the problem without dispensing with counterfactuals (1986: 167). We simply define causation more broadly in terms of *chains* of counterfactual dependencies (links). We can say that event X causes event Z–in our terminology, that Z occurs because of X–just when there is a chain of counterfactual and causal dependencies (links) leading from X to Z. So understood, causation is transitive. Thus if one endorses (i) and (ii), one should maintain (iii).

Unfortunately, this does not yet vindicate my causal story about Accepted Offer. I still need to explain how A's offer and B's acceptance causally depend on A's and B's biconditional beliefs, respectively. And as long as the account of causal dependence remains counterfactual, familiar counterexamples loom. Focus on my claim that B's acceptance is directly caused by (or causally depends on) his belief that (A will promise at t if and only if B will promise at t). Suppose that, out of the sheer generosity of his heart, B decides at t0 to promise A at t2 to pay her $5,000, so that the offer A makes him at t1 to sell B her car for $5,000 comes as a surprise to B. Nevertheless, B accepts the offer at t2. Surely, so goes the thought, we have an agreement here. But it is not the case that B's promise depends counterfactually on B's biconditional belief–condition (2b) goes unmet. B forms this belief on the basis of A's offer, but B would promise A $5,000 even apart from that offer.

The example fails to show that B's promise is not caused by his biconditional belief, however; it simply illustrates the familiar sense that counterfactual accounts of causation are too demanding. Specifically, explaining causal contribution in terms of counterfactual difference cannot account for causal contribution in so-called overdetermination cases.[31] The basic question is not whether B *would* make a similar promise even apart from his biconditional belief, but whether that belief made at least some casual contribution to the promise he actually made. Arguably, B's belief that his agreement promise will stand or fall together with A's made at least some causal contribution to his acceptance.

Admittedly, an argument for this claim would require an account of causation, which I do not have. But then I am no more wedded to the claim that our overdetermination case features a perfectly good agreement than to the claim that B's overdetermined promise is caused by his biconditional belief. If the best account of causation fails to support the latter claim, so much the worse for the former. That is to say, if the offeree's biconditional belief did not causally contribute to her promise, then I'd say the agreement in the overdetermination case falls outside the central case.[32] Indeed, reproducing the familiar problems of causation is exactly what you would expect from an account that includes a causal condition.

Objection

It will now be objected that my causal story depends on the assumption that the offeror A forms her operative biconditional belief *before* she offers. But arguably, A might only form her biconditional belief *as* she begins offering, too late to cause the offer.

There are two complementary ways of acknowledging the truth in the objection but insisting that the promises of accepted offer agreements interdepend in the way condition (2) requires. The first response emphasizes the fact that, in performing an action such as offering, we perform other, more basic actions as well. Suppose the agreement in Accepted Offer is reached via e-mail. A first *writes* an offer message, then *sends* it to B, and finally *communicates* it to B (leads B to believe that A has made the offer). It is true that the offeror's biconditional belief need not precede every action she performs in offering (or promising). It must still precede at least one such action, however. For example, A need not form her operative belief before writing her offer message, as long as she forms it before she sends the message. But B's acceptance (and therefore A's promise) causally depends on A's sending of the message. So we still get what we want: A's belief causes her promise.

The complementary response reminds us of the simple fact that offering, accepting, and promising are done over time. When we say that A offers, accepts, or promises at t, this is just shorthand for saying that A completes her (telic action of) offering, accepting, or promising at t. It is true that A's operative belief does not necessarily precede her entire offering or promising action, and so cannot cause her to *begin* to offer or promise. It must still cause and motivate her offering and promising action by sustaining it once begun, however.[33] The offeror can kick off the agreement-making process without first acquiring the operative belief, but neither she nor the offeree can continue—let alone complete—that process without that belief's causal-motivational contribution.

Extending the Account

Promises are intentional acts. In the central case, I promise with the intention to promise. The same goes for agreement-making. In the central case of agreement-making we are warranted in saying that the parties *jointly* intend—intend together as one—to enter the agreement. Suppose that the parties enter into an agreement at t. Then I think we should be able to say that they have at t a joint intention-in-action to enter into the agreement. But sometimes we can also say that parties have, at some earlier time t – 1, a prior intention to enter into the agreement later, which intention they may or may not execute. Agreement as Joint Promise suggests

> Joint Intention to Enter Agreement
> A and B jointly intend at t to enter into an agreement that A is to do X and B is to do Y just when, at t
> (1)(a) A intends to promise B to do X.
> (b) B intends to promise A to do Y.
> (2)(a) Because of A's belief that [A promises B to (do X) if and only if B promises A to (do Y)], A intends to promise B to do X.[34]
> (b) Because of B's belief that [A promises B to (do X) if and only if B promises A to (do Y)], B intends to promise A to do Y.
> (3)(a) A believes (2).
> (b) B believes (2).

No doubt Agreement as Joint Promise and Shared Intention to Enter an Agreement presuppose more general accounts of joint action and intention. I leave the extraction of these accounts as an exercise for the reader.[35]

VII. AGREEMENT-MAKING VIA SHARED UNDERSTANDING

Suppose that Agreement as Joint Promise can explain every agreement. It may now be objected that it is not strong enough to demarcate agreements from their matching cross promises. A striking feature of Agreement as Joint Promise is that it explains the claim that "agreement promises interdepend" in causal terms but without positing causation between the promises themselves. Indeed, the only causation goes from each party's belief to that very party's promise. I have steered clear of causation between the promises themselves partly to avoid the specter of causal loops and partly to explain the motivational aspect of agreement making.[36] But according to the present objection, this comes at the unacceptable cost of recognizing promises that do not really amount to an agreement. Consider

> *Tradition.* A and B have a tradition whereby every year on March the fourth A emails B: "I promise you my car," and B replies: "I promise to pay you $X" (the car's market price). Each year, the parties read the messages on March 5. This year is no different, except the market price of A's car is $5,000.

According to the objection I have in mind, the conditions of Agreement as Joint Promise are all met in Tradition, but the parties do not enter into an agreement. I suspect the first claim is correct. Condition (1) of Agreement as Joint Promise is met because on March 5 we have two simple simultaneous promises: A promises B the car; B promises A $5,000. Condition (2) also seems to be met. The parties' tradition is a form of shared agency, namely shared understanding—the parties believe together as one, or jointly. Given that understanding, just before A clicks Send, A believes that on March 5 B will promise her $5,000 and she will promise B the car. So A believes that she will promise B the car if and only if B will promise her $5,000. Since this belief causes A to click Send, and since A's doing so causes her to promise, there is a causal chain leading from A's belief to her promise. We can tell an exactly similar story about B. Condition (3) is also met: given their tradition, A and B are aware of the causal-motivational structure of their promising actions.

There is therefore no escape from assessing the objection's second claim. What prevents the simultaneous promises here from constituting an agreement, so goes the objection, is that no attitude or action of any party causally contributes to any attitude or action *of the other*. To see this, suffice it to show how B's agency makes no causal contribution to A's. Neither A's promise, nor A's intention to promise, nor A's operative belief is caused, directly or indirectly, by B's simultaneous promise, intention to promise, or operative belief. Instead, what plays a causal role in producing A's operative belief is the parties' *tradition* (shared understanding):

In response, I would like to bite the bullet and accept that the promises in Tradition constitute an agreement, after all. Notice that this hardly treats

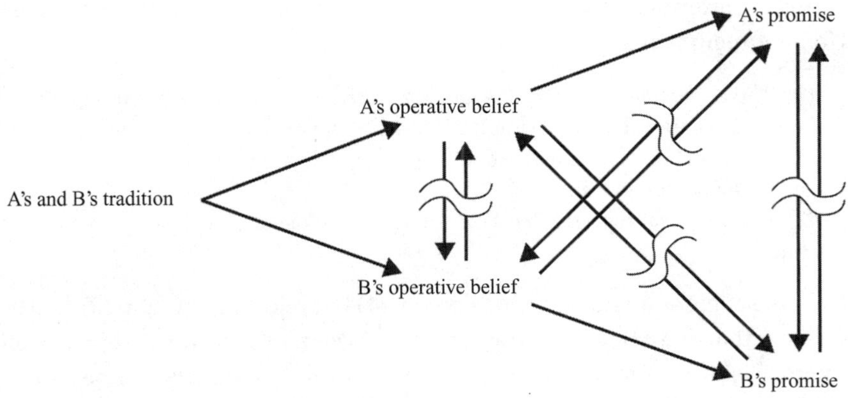

Arrows represent causation (or lack thereof).

Figure 16.1 Tradition

shared understandings as agreements; like promises, agreements are essentially intentional in a way shared understandings are not. The agreement or promises in Tradition are every bit as intentional as in all our previous examples. To be sure, the case is somewhat unusual; in the more common case, the operative belief of at least one party is caused by the other's agency. (In accepted offer agreements, for example, the offeree's operative belief is caused by the offer.) However, when the shared understanding between the parties is robust enough to meet the conditions of Agreement as Joint Promise, I think the image of promises crossing each other in the dark is out of place; the appropriate image is that of parties promising together as one.

VIII. AGENTIAL CONTROL

A final objection questions my explanation of accepted offer agreements. Consider Gilbert's leading example of everyday agreements:

> *Peter and Rita*. Peter to Rita: "Why don't you walk Fido, and I'll groom Tibbles?" After a few minutes Rita replies: "Fine."

Among the promissory proposals Gilbert explicitly rejects is one that looks very much like an application of Agreement as Joint Promise. Under this proposal, Rita and Peter exchange simple promises to walk (groom)—as opposed to conditional promises to walk (groom) *if* the other grooms (walks). This proposal seems on target: to the extent that we understand the agreement here as an agreement that Rita is to walk Fido and Peter is to groom Tibbles, I think we should say that Rita promises Peter to walk Fido, and Peter promises Rita to groom Tibbles. But Gilbert rejects this proposal. Her argument is simple:

> (1) The agreement in Peter and Rita generates Rita's walking obligation and Peter's grooming obligation simultaneously. While Peter speaks first, his statement does not obligate him. He does not get an obligation to groom before she gets an obligation to walk.
> (2) The proposal suggests that Peter promises, and gets his obligation, before Rita.[37]

It should come as no surprise that I accept (1) but reject (2).[38] Claim (2) tacitly assumes that, if we think of the agreement in Peter and Rita as an exchange of simple promises (to walk, to groom), we must think that Peter promises and obligates himself minutes before Rita does. Rita promises when she says fine, but she is the only one promising at that time. This assumption is spurious. More to the point, it is incompatible with the understanding of accepted offer agreements put forward in section V. On this account, Peter's promise-making agency only begins when he makes his statement, which statement is not a promise to do his part of the agreement but an offer to enter into that agreement. The offer makes it the case that, if Rita promises to walk Fido, Peter promises to groom Tibbles. (As long as we remember that this does not mean that Peter promises anything as yet, we can say this: Peter promises-to-groom-on-the-condition-that Rita promises to walk). When Rita accepts the offer, she promises to walk. Therefore, when Rita accepts, Peter promises to groom.[39] It is only when Rita accepts Peter's offer that Peter makes Rita a promise to groom. When Rita accepts Peter's offer, Rita promises Peter to walk Fido, and Peter promises Rita to groom Tibbles.

But just how plausible is this story? After all, Gilbert's assumption that Peter does not promise when Rita speaks appears to be supported by the commonsense

> Control
> What one does (or intends) is up to one.

If Peter promises when Rita accepts his offer, Peter's promise is outside his control; it is in Rita's control, for if she does not accept, he does not promise. (Similarly, if Peter intends to promise when Rita accepts his offer, his intention is outside his control; it is in Rita's control.)

This objection from control equivocates. On a biting interpretation, action (or intention) requires *exclusive* agential control. This interpretation would prevent Peter from promising, but would also make Control unacceptably demanding. Suppose that Peter fires a bullet through a black shoebox, intending to kill whatever animal Rita has placed there (if any). There is a perfectly good sense in which, if Rita placed Tibbles in the box, Peter intentionally kills Tibbles. This is so in spite of the fact that Tibbles's presence in the box was under Rita's control: she could place Fido there instead or leave the box empty. Clearly, Tibbles's death was not in Peter's exclusive control. Rita can make it the case that Peter intentionally kills Tibbles.[40] Since what we do or intend is hostage to contingencies beyond our control—including other peoples' actions and intentions—there need be no mystery about Peter's promising (or intending to promise) upon Rita's acceptance. Peter can promise to groom Tibbles without exclusive control just as he can kill Tibbles without such control. Therefore, Rita can make it the case that Peter promises her.

On the more plausible interpretation of Control, the agent must have *substantial* control over what she does or intends. But Peter has substantial control over his promissory intention and action. After all, he only loses as much agential control over his promise as he voluntarily surrenders to Rita in his offer. True, by accepting the offer, Rita makes it the case that Peter promises her. But without Peter's offer, Rita would have nothing to accept. Peter would not promise *via* Rita if he did not make her an offer first (and refrained from revoking it before she accepted). So when Rita accepts, Peter can hardly disavow his promise by denying substantial agential control.[41]

IX. CONCLUSION

Recall Margaret Gilbert's three criteria of adequacy on theories of agreement: obligation, simultaneity, and interdependence. I do not want to claim—in fact, I do not believe—that Agreement as Joint Promise meets these criteria, as she understands them. I want to close by explaining why I do think Agreement as Joint Promise meets the following three reconfigured criteria.

> (1) Commitment
> An agreement commits each party to the other to do her part of the agreement, whatever it happens to be.[42]

The commitments of an agreement are simple or unconditional, relative to the agreement: they commit each party to do whatever the agreement itself requires her to do, neither more nor less. This does not suggest that agreement commitments are unconditional in every way. The parties are largely free to make one or both of their commitments conditional, in the sense that the relevant party commits to do one action *if* the other party does another action. If the agreement (properly interpreted in context) requires that

> A is to do X and B is to do Y

then the commitments are indeed unconditional in every way: A gets a commitment to do A and B gets a commitment to do Y. But if the agreement (properly interpreted in context) requires that

> A is to do X and B is to do (Y if A does X)

then the commitment of one party is unconditional in every way: A's commitment is to do X, but the commitment of the other party is in one way conditional: B's commitment is to (do Y if A does X). And if the agreement (properly interpreted in context) requires that

> A is to (do X if B does Y) and B is to (do Y if A does X)

then the commitment of each party is conditional in this way: A's commitment is to (do X if B does Y), and B's commitment is to (do Y if A does X).[43] These are immediate consequences of Agreement as Joint Promise.

Agreement as Joint Promise meets this criterion. It claims that each party promises the other to do its part of the deal, whatever it happens to be. Since promises commit the promisor to do what's promised, whatever it happens to be,[44] each party commits to the other to do her part of the agreement, whatever it happens to be.[45]

> (2) Simultaneity
> The parties to an agreement commit themselves simultaneously.

Agreement-making is a telic action: there is a single point in time at which the agreement-making process concludes. This is the point at which each party commits herself and becomes committed to the other. As before, it is important to emphasize that this does not mean that the commitments of an agreement are simultaneous in every way. In particular, the parties are largely free to commit to perform consecutive, nonsimultaneous actions. If the agreement (properly interpreted in context) requires that

> A is to do X at t and B is to do Y at t

then the commitments are indeed simultaneous in every way: A's commitment is to do X at t, and B's commitment is to do Y at t. But if the agreement (properly interpreted in context) requires that

> A is to do X at t and B is to do Y at t + 1

then, in one way, the commitments are non-simultaneous: A's commitment is to do X at t, and B's commitment is to do Y at t + 1 (although they both get these commitments at some t – 1). This just follows from the commitment criterion.

Agreement as Joint Promise meets the simultaneity criterion. When one party initiates the process, he does not make a promise first; at most, he makes an offer, which will issue in a promise if and when accepted. That is when the constitutive commitments of the agreement are made.

The third criterion of adequacy on accounts of agreements should be familiar by now.

> (3) Interdependence
> The constitutive commitments of an agreement interdepend in some explanatory way, one moreover that warrants the claim that the parties commit together as one, or jointly.

The key idea is twofold: (i) an agreement consists of a joint commitment, and (ii) a joint commitment consists of interdependent individual commitments. So understood, there is nothing in this criterion to suggest that agreement commitments are mutually conditional relative to the agreement, either in the internal sense that each party commits to (do her part if the other does his), or in the external sense that, if the other party does his part, each party commits to do hers.

Agreement as Joint Promise meets this criterion. An agreement consists of promissory commitments, and there is a causal-motivational sense in which these commitments can be said to interdepend. Basically, each party's promise is caused by that party's biconditional belief that (she promises just when the other does), and each party is aware of this fact. These causal-motivational and cognitive conditions flesh out an explanatory sense in which agreement commitments interdepend, one moreover that would warrant the joint commitment imagery.

I would like to thank Casey O'Callaghan and David Velleman for very helpful comments on earlier drafts. I would also like to thank Michael Bratman, Josh Brown, Melinda Fagan, Carl Feierabend, Alastair Norcross, and Casey O'Callaghan for very helpful conversations.

NOTES

1. I have nothing to say about agreement in the *cognitive* sense, namely agreement that such-and-such is the case. You and I might happen to agree that Obama's stimulus package was a sound economic policy without doing anything together—in fact, without ever interacting; we simply happen to have the same opinion. This essay concerns agreement as an action, namely the action of making or entering an agreement.

2. See her contribution to this book (Chapter 3). See also Gilbert (2006; ch. 10; 1996; chs. 12, 15; 2000; 27–28, 59–60).

3. It seems to me that, just as I can promise you to do X without deciding to do X, we can jointly enter into an agreement that I'm to do X and you're to do Y without jointly deciding that I'm to do X and you're to do Y. Just imagine that, when we enter into the agreement, neither of us has decided to do his part (although we have jointly decided to enter into the said agreement). It also seems to me that, just as I can decide to do X without promising you to do X, we can jointly decide that I'm to do X and you're to do Y without entering into the agreement that I'm to do X and you're to do Y. Imagine that we've reached a joint understanding that I'm to do X and you're to do Y, but neither has expressed an intention to commit himself to the other to do X or Y (which is different from an intention to commit oneself to the other to do one's part of the *deciding* action itself). It is interesting to note that, on Gilbert's view, every joint action involves joint commitment to do that very action. Thus when we jointly *walk*, each commits to the other to do her part of the *walking*, and if we jointly *move* the proverbial sofa neither one of us could move alone, each commits to the other to do her part of the *moving*. So by the same token, if we jointly *decide* that I'm to wash the dishes today and you're to take out the trash tomorrow, each commits to the other to do her part of the *deciding*. This does not tend to show that each of us commits to the other to *do* X or Y (which is what we do when we enter into the relevant agreement).

4. Cf. Michael Bratman's notion of "I intend that we *J*" (in 1999: pt. 2; 2009: 155–57).

5. Cf. Gilbert (1996: 317): "if one party defaults on his performance obligation, the other ceases to have his original performance obligation." Cf. also Gilbert (2006: 215–219) and Mintoff (2004).

6. Admittedly my objection to the mutually conditional view is inconclusive, for it might be said to depend on my *material* interpretation of the condition in the promises. But we can also give this condition an *indicative* interpretation. And arguably, this interpretation would respect the distinction between the case in which both parties do their parts and the case in which they both fail to do their parts. In the first case, they both keep the agreement; in the second, they neither keep the agreement nor break it.

7. Cf. e.g. Smith (2004: 180-81): "contracts are agreements rather than promises"; Penner (1996: 326): "the notion of *agreement*, rather than *promise*, is the kind of voluntary undertaking in light of which contracts must be understood"; de Moor (1987: 122): "a foundation of the law of contract must radically abandon the notion of promise." Cf. also Black (2004).

8. According to Gilbert, the interdependence criterion is met just when "if one party defaults on his performance obligation, the other ceases to have his original performance obligation" (1996: 317). But first, it is not easy to see how this criterion can be reconciled with Gilbert's first, *obligation* criterion, which says that the obligations of an agreement are "unconditional." Surely, if A's obligation under the agreement is not conditional upon B's subsequent conduct, then A would continue to have it if B defaults. And second, Gilbert's interdependence criterion is incompatible with the considerations I adduced in the previous section in favor of the first component of my own account. I've claimed that if the agreement requires A to do X, then A promises B to do X, just like so. So if promises give obligations, then A's (B's) obligation is to do X (Y), just like so; B's failure to do Y is neither here nor there.

9. Thus I endorse what Gilbert calls "singularism," the view that joint action is to be explained in terms of "individual human person's beliefs, desires, goals, commitments, and so on." Gilbert rejects singularism in favor of the view that joint action is a matter of "joint commitment," which "stands outside" the "singularist conceptual scheme" (2006: 125–26).

10. But as hinted earlier, there is one respect in which I suspect Bratman's account is not individualistic enough: it takes the notion *I intend that we J* as primitive. To me, the only primitive notion in this area is *I intend that I J*. For the same reason, my account makes no use of the notion of irreducible we-intentions. Cf. Searle (2010: ch. 3).

11. Cf. Gilbert's rejection of "personal-intention based" accounts: "there could be a shared intention to do such-and-such though none of the participants personally intends to conform their behavior to the shared intention" (2000: 18).

12. You and I can form a committee whose Charter stipulates that we (as a committee) are to count as walking whenever the President of the United States gives the State of the Union Address. Hence there is a sense in which we jointly walk whenever the President gives the Address, even if neither of us walks. To take a less extreme example, there is a sense in which all representatives jointly vote for a law whenever Congress passes it by simple majority. What these examples show, I think, is that the language of institutional (or group or joint) action can be cheap. The account at work in this essay does not purport to capture the sense in which we can jointly act under the rules of some institution.

13. Compare Gilbert's claim that joint commitment "does not have parts" (2000: 158), and her claim in chapter 3 of this book that "[a] *joint* commitment is not a

composite of two or more personal commitments." (p. 92) What could possibly interdepend in a partless noncomposite commitment?

14. But as I acknowledge in note 6, my objection to the conditional account is inconclusive.

15. See Lewis (1986: ch. 21). Causal dependence implies causation but not the other way around. We will later have to relax the definition of "because of."

16. As Sarah Paul observes, in the case of telic actions, the agent can count as performing the telic action even if the goal of the activity is never successfully achieved (2009: 16–17). Thus A can count as promising B even if he never promised B.

17. In any event, this is not how we think of full-blooded intentional action, and promise-making is an essentially intentional action. At least in the central case, one promises with the intention to do just that. See, for example, Owens (2006: 59–60); see also Anscombe (2000: sec. 47).

18. Notice that this condition requires each party to be aware not only of the causal role that her operative belief plays in her promising, but also of the casual role that the other party's operative belief plays in his promising. (A needs to believe 2b as well as 2a; B needs to believe 2a as well as 2b.) This is needed to exclude Gettier-style counterexamples, where each party promises the other because some bogus tip makes her believe, correctly, that the other will promise her. The promises here do not amount to an agreement, because neither party believes that the *other* will promise because the other believes that one will promise.

19. Cf. the criticism of Bratman's account of joint intention in Velleman (2001).

20. Cf. e.g. Bratman's distinction between conditionally intending that X if p and intending that X on the assumption that p (1999: 154–160). Presumably, the idea is that A intends that X on the assumption that p when the following holds: because A believes that p, A intends that X. (But notice that the statement can also mean something quite different, namely that the following holds: A believes that p, and if p, A intends that X. Here A doesn't intend anything unless his belief is true.)

21. Condition (2) is also violated. It is not true that A promises because she believes B will: at no point before A promises does she have that belief. Trivially, she would promise apart from that belief.

22. I consider a follow-up objection in the essay's penultimate section.

23. Cf. note 20.

24. Alternatively, we can say that when A makes her offer, she makes a conditional promise, namely a promise to (transfer the car *if* B promises to pay $5,000). As before, B's acceptance includes his promise to pay. So when B accepts, A becomes committed under the promise to transfer the car. While A's only promise is made when she makes the offer, it effectively transforms into another promise when B accepts. It is as if A gives a new promise when B accepts.

25. Even if the counterfactual "If A didn't believe at t2 that B promises at t2, A wouldn't promise at t2" were true, it would not be able to track causation because it does not align with time's arrow. In this respect, it is no different from so-called back-tracking counterfactuals. Cf. Lewis (1986: ch. 17). What must be shown is that A promises at t2 because of her *earlier* belief that B *will* promise. The facts of Accepted Offer do not support this claim.

26. Moreover, it seems that perfectly good agreements can be concluded under abnormal communicative conditions. If A sends his offer by airmail during a strike, but B receives and reads the letter anyway, the agreement is concluded, in spite of A's reliable prediction to the contrary.

27. Notice that the biconditional in the content of the operative belief is not counterfactual but material: A believes that her promise to B guarantees B's promise to her, and vice versa. This is consistent with A's belief that [A *would* promise B to (do X) even if B didn't simultaneously promise A to (do Y)].

28. For what is essentially the same picture, see Bach (1995).

29. The essay's penultimate section revisits the issue.

30. Presumably, the acceptance is not completed until it is successfully communicated to the offeror: when the offeror receives and understands it.

31. Here is a familiar *reductio*. One should not be accused of murder unless one made at least some causal contribution to the death. Given the fatal stabs of the others, no Senator made counterfactual difference to Caesar's death. So if making causal contribution requires making counterfactual difference, no Senator should be accused of Caesar's murder. For a recent critical discussion of counterfactual accounts of causation, see Kment (2010).

32. See my discussion of the central case method in chapter 1 of this book.

33. Here I am taking a leaf from Setiya (2007: 57–58).

34. As before, condition (2) requires a tense-sensitive interpretation: A believes at t - 1 that [A will promise B at t to (do X) iff B will simultaneously promise A to (do Y)], and the biconditional in the content of the operative belief is material rather than counterfactual.

35. In a conversation, Michael Bratman has offered a potential counterexample to my working account of joint intention. It is a case of intending to do something together in the "mafia sense." Suppose I intend to go to Naples and to force you to come with me, and you intend to go to Naples and to force *me* to come with you. Arguably, each of us intends to go to Naples because of his belief that he will go there iff the other will. And yet this is hardly a case of joint intention? But this is a problem only if we restrict joint intention to *cooperative* cases. (Bratman himself has been concerned with shared cooperative activity.)

36. See the discussion of Agreement as Causally Interdependent Promises in section IV.

37. Gilbert (1996, esp. 320).

38. See the discussion of the Belief Account in section V.

39. Alternatively, we can say that Peter's offer is a conditional promise, namely a promise to (groom *if* Rita walks). As before, Rita's acceptance includes her promise to walk. So when she accepts, Peter becomes committed, under the promise he has already made, to groom. On this view, Peter's only promise is made when he makes the offer. In effect, however, Rita's acceptance transforms the original promise into another—i.e. unconditional—promise. It is as if Peter gives a new promise when Rita accepts.

40. On a *de re* reading, that is. Rita makes it the case that what Peter intentionally kills is Tibbles, rather than something else (or nothing).

41. Black (2007) proposes to understand agreements as accepted offers. Offers to do what, exactly? We surely do not want to explain an agreement in terms of an offer

to enter an agreement; this would simply presuppose an account of agreements. Perhaps the offer in question is not an offer *to*, but rather an offer *that*. Specifically, we can understand the agreement that (A is to do X and B is to do Y) as an offer that (A is to do X and B is to do Y), plus an acceptance with the same content. But the notion of such a conjunctive offer is no simpler than the notion of the agreement it seeks to explain. After all, it is precisely the conjunctive nature of agreements that calls for an explanation. (An analogous problem seems to me to arise with respect to Bratman's notion of I intend that we *J*.) Cf. note 4 and chapter 1, pp. 28 and 53.

42. I formulate the first criterion in terms of commitment rather than obligation, because the language of obligation often has a moral connotation, and I wish to leave open the possibility that promissory and agreement commitments do not give moral obligations. If you think promises and agreements obligate, feel free to reformulate my commitment criterion in terms of obligation.

43. Hence neither breaks the agreement if neither does anything. Some worry that this would render such an agreement motivationally inert. Cf. e.g. Gilbert (1996: 324–26, 329–30); Black (2004: 77, 81). I do not share the worry. If neither party knows for sure that the other will fail to do his part, the only way each can ensure that she keeps the agreement is to do hers. (And we had better assume that the parties are motivated to keep the agreement; without this assumption it is hard to see how any agreement has motivational force.)

44. This is the Face Value Principle for Promises.

45. Is my commitment criterion compatible with Gilbert's obligation criterion? I cannot be sure, because it does not seem to sit comfortably with her *interdependence* criterion. Consider the agreement that A is to do X at t and B is to do Y at t. In terms of obligation, Agreement as Joint Promise implies that A's obligation is to do X at t. This is neither a conditional obligation to (do X at t if B does Y at t) nor an obligation-to-do-x-at-t-on-the-assumption-that B does Y at t—which is not an obligation at all. So regardless of whether B does Y at t, A has an obligation to (do X at t). But by the same token, Agreement as Joint Promise also implies that B's obligation is to (do Y at t). And this means that, if B fails to do Y at t, B defaults on his obligation under the agreement. But according to Gilbert's interdependence criterion, "if one party defaults on his performance obligation, the other ceases to have his original performance obligation" (1996: 317). In our case, this implies that, if B fails to do Y at t, then at t A has no obligation to do X. But I'm not sure how sensible it is to hold that

(1) regardless of whether B does Y at t, A has an obligation to (do X at t)
AND
(2) since B failed to Y at t, A has no obligation at t to do X.

If B's failure to do Y at t makes it the case that at t A doesn't have an obligation to do X, in what sense did A *ever* have a genuine obligation to do X at t? Since I cannot be sure that my commitment criterion is compatible with Gilbert's interdependence criterion, I cannot be sure that it is compatible with her obligation criterion.

REFERENCES

Anscombe, Elizabeth. 1963/2000. *Intention*. Cambridge, MA: Harvard University Press.

Bach, Kent. 1995. "Terms of Agreement." *Ethics* 105: 604–612.

Black, Oliver. 2004. "Agreements, Undertakings, and Practical Reason." *Legal Theory* 10: 77–95.
———. 2007. "Two Theories of Agreement." *Legal Theory* 12: 1–22.
Bratman, Michael. 1999. *Faces of Intention.* Cambridge: Cambridge University Press.
———. 2007. *Structures of Agency.* New York: Oxford University Press.
———. 2009. "Modest Sociality and the Distinctiveness of Intention." *Philosophical Studies* 144: 149–165.
de Moor, Anne. 1987. "Are Contracts Promises?" In *Oxford Essays in Jurisprudence: Third Series,* ed. J. Eekelaar and J. Bell. Oxford: Oxford University Press.
Gilbert, Margaret. 1996. *Living Together*. Lanham, MD: Rowman and Littlefield.
———. 2000. *Sociality and Responsibility*. Lanham, MD: Rowman and Littlefield.
———. 2006. *A Theory of Political Obligation.* Oxford: Oxford University Press.
———. Forthcoming. "Three Dogmas about Promising."
Kment, Boris. 2010. "Causation: Determination and Difference-Making." Draft. http://www.princeton.edu/~bkment/CausationDeterminationandDifference-Making.pdf
Lewis, David. 1986. *Philosophical Papers II.* Oxford: Oxford University Press.
Mintoff, Joe. 2004. "Is an Agreement an Exchange of Intentions?" *Pacific Philosophical Quarterly* 85: 44–67.
Owens, David. 2006. "A Simple Theory of Promises." *Philosophical Review* 115: 51–77.
Penner, James. 1996. "Voluntary Obligations and the Scope of the Law of Contract." *Legal Theory* 2: 325–57.
Paul, Sarah. 2009. "How We Know What We're Doing." *Philosophers' Imprint* 9: 1–24.
Smith, Stephen. 2004. *Contract Theory*. Oxford: Oxford University Press.
Searle, John. 2010. *Making the Social World.* Oxford: Oxford University Press.
Setiya, Kieran. 2007. *Reason without Rationalism.* Princeton: Princeton University Press.
Velleman, David. 2000. *The Possibility of Practical Reasoning*. Oxford: Oxford University Press.
———. 2001. Review of Michael Bratman (1999). *Philosophical Quarterly* 51: 119–21.

Index

Note: An 'n' following a page number indicates a note.